Palgrave Studies in the History of Economic Thought

Palgrave Studies in the History of Economic Thought publishes contributions by leading scholars, illuminating key events, theories and individuals that have had a lasting impact on the development of modern-day economics. The topics covered include the development of economies, institutions and theories.

The series aims to highlight the academic importance of the history of economic thought, linking it with wider discussions within economics and society more generally. It contains a broad range of titles that illustrate the breath of discussions — from influential economists and schools of thought, through to historical and modern social trends and challenges — within the discipline.

All books in the series undergo a single-blind peer review at both the proposal and manuscript submission stages.

For further information on the series and to submit a proposal for consideration, please contact Wyndham Hacket Pain (Economics Editor) wyndham.hacketpain@palgrave.com.

The series is dedicated to the memory of former editor and distinguished economist Geoff Harcourt.

Jesús Astigarraga • Javier Usoz
Juan Zabalza

The Economic Legacy of José Joaquín de Mora

Spreading Classical Political Economy in the Hispanic World

palgrave
macmillan

Jesús Astigarraga
Department of Applied Economics
University of Zaragoza
Zaragoza, Spain

Javier Usoz
Department of Applied Economics
University of Zaragoza
Zaragoza, Spain

Juan Zabalza
Department of Applied Economic
Analysis
University of Alicante
Alicante, Spain

ISSN 2662-6578 ISSN 2662-6586 (electronic)
Palgrave Studies in the History of Economic Thought
ISBN 978-3-031-49445-1 ISBN 978-3-031-49446-8 (eBook)
https://doi.org/10.1007/978-3-031-49446-8

This Palgrave Macmillan imprint is published by the registered company Springer Nature Switzerland AG.
The registered company address is: Gewerbestrasse 11, 6330 Cham, Switzerland

Paper in this product is recyclable.

To Miguel, Inés and María

Preface

This book is dedicated to the multi-talented Spanish liberal José Joaquín de Mora, one of the most energetic and influential Spanish writers and intellectuals in the first half of the nineteenth century. His activity, which was inspired by a strong political vocation, encompassed at least three clearly defined geographical locations: Spain, where he was born; London, where he had to go into exile and to which he returned decades later; and the emerging Hispanic-American republics of Argentina, Chile, Peru and Bolivia, where he lived and worked as a privileged exile for a decade and on which he left a strong intellectual and political mark.

While Mora's career as an intellectual and reformer has been the subject of much and enduring literature, there was no comprehensive interpretation of the aspect related to political economy and his role as a distinguished disseminator of the ideas of the classical school in Spain and Hispanic America, always against a backdrop of socio-political reform. This book aims to fill that gap. Mora "the economist" has held the authors' attention for some time now, and although previous research has been drawn on to prepare this study, the reconstruction is entirely original. Much of the material used is unpublished and any produced previously has been thoroughly revised and extended.

Research can no longer be carried out in isolation but has to be done as a team in a broad and global academic sense, which entails comparing findings and learning from the active academic community on a daily basis. Over the years we have been fortunate enough to have the opportunity to present the progress made on the research that has eventually become this book at conferences, seminars and other academic meetings. We are more than aware of the debt incurred there and would like to express our gratitude to those who invited us to participate in such occasions, as well as to the numerous and varied universe of scholars, mainly economists and historians, who listened to our interpretations and whose comments, suggestions and criticism contributed to refining them. They all became true allies in improving the final outcome of the research. Throughout this stimulating academic exchange, we have tried to be faithful to the transatlantic spirit that inspired Mora's intellectual and personal journey. The main forums in which we have had the opportunity to discuss this distinguished Spanish liberal include the following: *V Congreso Latino-Americano de Historia Económica* (CLADHE), University of Sao Paulo (Brazil), 2016; *VI Congreso Internacional de la Sociedad Española de Estudios del Siglo XVIII* (SEEXVIII), Madrid (Spain), 2016; *International Conference of the History of Economics Society*, University of Palermo (Italy), 2017; *VIII Congreso Latinoamericano de Historia del Pensamiento Económico* (ALAHPE), University of Montevideo (Uruguay), 2022; *Seminario Ilustración de la Fundación Ortega-Marañón* (FOM), Madrid (Spain), 2023; *Magister y Diplomatura en Historia Económica*, University Adolfo Ibáñez, Santiago de Chile (Chile), 2023; *Maestría en Historia*, Pontifical Catholic University of Peru, Lima (Peru), 2023.

The structure of this book is clear and simple and consists of an introduction and nine chapters. These nine central chapters make up the book's main body and are ordered chronologically according to the most critical stages in Mora's life. They are divided into three sections: (1) "The Making of a Publicist", (2) "Exiles", and (3) "Maturity". The first section contains two chapters that give an account of Mora's youthful years and his early steps as a publicist, first during the *Sexenio Absolutista* (1814–1820, Chap. 2) and then during the Liberal Triennium (1820–1823, Chap. 3). The second section discusses his long years of exile in four chapters: London (1824–1827, Chap. 4), Buenos Aires (1827, Chap. 5), Chile (1828–1832, Chap. 6) and finally Peru and Bolivia; the last chapter also covers his period as a diplomat in London, working for the Confederation formed by these two countries (1833–1843, Chap. 7). The third section covers the last twenty years of his life in Spain in three chapters, dealing with his involvement in the free trade debates (1843–1853, Chap. 8), his ambitious participation in the colossal *Enciclopedia Moderna* (1853–1855, Chap. 9) and his fresh new approach to Hispanic America, which was expressed through the many long articles he published in *La América* and other magazines in Spain in the 1850s and 1860s (Chap. 10). The book closes with a catalogue of press articles and encyclopaedic political economy entries attributable to Mora (1825–1864) and a section covering abbreviations, sources and the bibliography.

The end result has naturally required a great deal of new research in the six countries in which Mora carried out his intellectual and reforming activities. As is clear throughout the book, numerous libraries and archives have been witnesses to our research. Although it is not possible to thank everyone who has helped us in each of these institutions personally, we would like to express our deep gratitude to them collectively but no less intensely for all that. We know that our work would not have been possible without their generous help. However, several university lecturers and researchers who helped us to navigate unfamiliar waters in Peru (Carlos Contreras and especially Claudia Rosas) and Chile (Rafael Sagredo and Manuel Llorca-Jaña) deserve a special mention. Likewise, we would like to thank the *Museo Histórico Nacional* of Santiago de Chile for allowing us to use the portrait of Mora set in its collections.

The authors also wish to highlight the fact that this book has been possible thanks to institutional and financial support received from the University of Zaragoza Interdisciplinary Group of Intellectual and Institutional History (GIIHI; 2020–2022, H26_20D; 2023–2025, H26_23R), the Ministry of Science and Innovation (2021–2024, PID2020-115261RB-100) and the Ministry of Finance Institute of Fiscal Studies (2021–2022). Our gratitude to the latter institution and its staff should be particularly emphasised, since it is thanks to their assistance and financial support that we have been able to publish an anthology of Mora's economics texts, which has recently appeared in one of the Institute's collections. We are also delighted to extend our gratitude to Carolyn Black for her painstaking and exquisite work in translating this book, whose errors can only be attributed to its three authors.

Zaragoza, Spain — Jesús Astigarraga
Zaragoza, Spain — Javier Usoz
Alicante, Spain — Juan Zabalza

Contents

Abbreviations

Archives, Libraries and Publishing Houses

AHN	Archivo Histórico Nacional (Madrid)
AAM	Archivo del Ateneo de Madrid (Madrid)
ARSEM	Archivo Real Sociedad Económica Matritense (Madrid)
BNC	Biblioteca Nacional de Chile (Santiago de Chile)
BNE	Biblioteca Nacional de España (Madrid)
BFBS	British and Foreign Bible Society (London)
BPUCC	Biblioteca Pontificia Universidad Católica de Chile (Santiago de Chile)
CCPB	Catálogo Colectivo de Patrimonio Bibliográfico Español (Spain)
CEPC	Centro de Estudios Políticos y Constitucionales (Madrid)
CSIC	Centro Superior de Investigaciones Científicas (Madrid)
CUP	Cambridge University Press (Cambridge)
EHESS	École des Hautes Études en Sciences Sociales (Paris)
IEF	Instituto de Estudios Fiscales (Madrid)
FCE	Fondo de Cultura Económica (Mexico)
MHN	Museo Histórico Nacional (Santiago de Chile)
OUP	Oxford University Press (Oxford)
PUP	Princeton University Press (Princeton)
RACMP	Real Academia de Ciencias Morales y Políticas (Madrid)
UNMSM	Universidad Nacional Mayor de San Marcos (Lima)
UPV	Universidad del País Vasco (Bilbao)

Press and Books

CBS	*Cartas sobre la educación del bello sexo por una señora americana*, London, 1824
CCL	*Crónica científica y literaria*, Madrid, 1817–1820
CEP	*Catecismo de economía política*, London, 1825
CGM	*Correo general de Madrid*, Madrid, 1821
CLP	*Correo literario y político de Londres*, London, 1826
CPL	*Crónica política y literaria de Buenos Aires*, Buenos Aires, 1827
DLC	*De la libertad del comercio*, Sevilla, 1843
DSC	*Diario de sesiones de las Cortes*, Madrid, 1820–1823
EAP	*El Amigo del País*, Madrid, 1844–1847
EC	*El constitucional, o sea Crónica científica, literaria y política*, Madrid, 1820
ECBA	*El conciliador*, Buenos Aires, 1827
ECO	*El conciliador*, Lima, 1830–1834
ECOBA	*El constitucional*, Buenos Aires, 1827
ECM	*El constitucional. Correo general de Madrid*, Madrid, 1821
EDC	*Eco del comercio*, Madrid, 1832–1848
EDM	*El defensor de los militares denominados constitucionales*, Santiago de Chile, 1830
EDP	*El eco de Padilla*, Madrid, 1821
EE	*El español*, London, 1810–1814
EE	*El español. Diario de las doctrinas y los intereses sociales*, Madrid, 1835–1837, 1845–1848
EEC	*El español constitucional: o Miscelánea de política, ciencias y artes, literatura*, London, 1818–1820, 1824–1825
EEO	*El emigrado observador*, London, 1828–1829
EEP	*El eco del Protectorado*, Lima, 1836–1839
EHM	*El heraldo de Madrid*, Madrid, 1842–1854
EI	*El indicador de los espectáculos y del buen gusto*, Madrid, 1822
EID	*El independiente*, Madrid, 1822
ELC	*El constitucional*, Santiago de Chile, 1828
ELT	*El trompeta*, Santiago de Chile, 1830–1831
EM	*Enciclopedia moderna*, Madrid, 1852–1855
EMC	*El mercurio chileno*, Santiago de Chile, 1828–1829
EMDC	*El mercurio de Chile*, Santiago de Chile, 1822–1823
EPE	*El pensamiento español*, Madrid, 1860–1874

ER	*The Edinburgh Review*, Edinburgh, 1802–1929
ERA	*El repertorio americano*, London, 1826–1827
ET	*El Tribuno*, Madrid, 1822
EVF	*EL Valdiviano federal*, Valdivia, 1827–1844
EZ	*El Zurriago*, Madrid, 1821–1823
GDC	*Guía de comercio y Boletín de fomento. Periódico semanal de intereses materiales*, Madrid, 1843–1851
GE	*Gaceta economista*, Madrid, 1860–1863
IPEP	*Instrucción para el pueblo. Cien tratados sobre los conocimientos más indispensables*, Madrid, 1851
LA	*La América. Crónica Hispano-Americana*, Madrid, 1857–1886
LAD	*La arlequinada diplomática*, Madrid, 1820
LBA	*La biblioteca americana*, London, 1823
LCL	*La clave*, Santiago de Chile, 1827–1829
LME	*La minerva española*, Madrid, 1821
LMF	*La minerve française*, Paris, 1818–1820
LPM	*La periódico-manía*, Madrid, 1820–1821
LT	*La Tercerola*, Madrid, 1822
LV	*La Verdad*, Lima, 1833
MCA	*Miscelánea de comercio, artes y literatura*, Madrid, 1819–1821
MP	*El mercurio peruano*, Lima, 1827–1834
MPF	*Memoria sobre los puertos francos*, Madrid, 1844
MR	*Minerva o el revisor general*, Madrid, 1817–1818
MUC	*Museo universal de ciencias y artes*, London, 1825–1826
OEE	*Ocios de españoles emigrados*, London, 1823–1827
PLC	*El propagador del libre comercio*, Cádiz, 1847–1848
RE	*Revista enciclopédica*, Madrid, 1846–1847
REAM	*Revista española de ambos mundos*, Madrid, 1853–1855
REF	*Revue encyclopédique*, Paris, 1819–1835
REE	*Revista ecléctica española*, Madrid, 1844
REIE	*Revista de España, de Indias y del extranjero*, Madrid, 1845–1848
REM	*Revista económica de Madrid*, Madrid, 1842, 1847
RHA	*Revista Hispano-Americana*, Madrid, 1848
RUA	*Revista universal de la Administración*, Madrid, 1848–1850
VML	*Variedades o Mensajero de Londres*, London, 1823–1825
WN	*The Wealth of Nations*, London, 1776

CHAPTER 1

Introduction

1.1 José Joaquín de Mora: The Forgotten Career of a Communicator *Extraordinaire*[1]

Versatile Spanish writer José Joaquín de Mora (Cadiz, 1783–Madrid, 1864) was one of the country's most prestigious exponents of classical political economy. His long, wide-ranging intellectual and reformist career invokes the traditional profile of an early nineteenth-century Spanish liberal who exercised many varied professions: law, journalism, creative writing, teaching, translation, political consultancy and diplomacy; and distinguished himself in disciplines as diverse as literature —in all its different aspects—, moral philosophy, logic, philosophy, politics and law. Political economy always featured among his interests from his young days and Mora studied the discipline constantly from 1817, when he published his first journal in Madrid, the *Crónica científica y literaria*, until his last pieces of journalism, which were written for the Madrid magazine *La América. Crónica Hispano-Americana* in the early 1860s, towards the end of his life. His long career in the political economy sphere, which spanned almost five decades, merits its own research: he was among the first wave of liberals and one of the first free trade authors in nineteenth-century Spain.

[1] The websites and online information cited in this work were accessed on 23 July 2023.

J. Astigarraga et al., *The Economic Legacy of José Joaquín de Mora*, Palgrave Studies in the History of Economic Thought,
https://doi.org/10.1007/978-3-031-49446-8_1

Mora pursued his interest in political economy wherever he lived, not only in Spain, where he spent his youth and later years, but also in Britain, where he was forced to go into exile because of his liberal convictions. This was followed by Argentina, Chile, Peru and Bolivia, all former Spanish territories and then new republics, where he worked for twelve years, still as an exile albeit in privileged conditions due to his close relationships with leading political figures.

Mainstream historiography tends to neglect the flow of ideas produced outside the central channels of dominant economic traditions and in geographical areas other than the most prestigious and influential academic world. However, both these aspects take centre stage in this book, which deals with the reception, dissemination, adaptation and application of the ideas of classical economics in the Hispanic world, paying particular attention to the still little-known transatlantic flow of these ideas. It focuses on two issues that have not been sufficiently addressed but are moving increasingly to the fore in current academic research. The first is the phenomenon of the spread of economic ideas in all its different aspects, whether academic, intellectual or institutional. The second is this process's importance in the creating of modern economic cultures in the countries discussed in the book. Both questions are addressed here in the light of Mora's far-reaching, militant mission in the field of liberal and free trade economic ideas and reforms. He made his life into a fascinating odyssey in six different countries and became an influential intellectual and reformer in Spain and Hispanic America, influencing the political course taken by the new republics and contributing to the establishing of the classical school there.

However, Mora undertook all this activity not from a standpoint of scientific or analytical innovation but primarily from one of dissemination and application. This was possible because of his great talent for simplifying the analytical and normative complexity of the political economy of his day, in which he was extremely well-versed, in order to convert it into intellectual products that could be understood by educated elites and readers from a range of social backgrounds. His years of teaching at universities and in liberal institutions and especially his vast body of work as a journalist and publiciser in the truest sense of the word meant that he eventually became the most important disseminator and populariser of the economic ideas of classical political economy in the Hispanic world as a whole for several decades. He constantly wrote articles for the press, reviews, textbooks, essays, translations, catechisms and encyclopaedia entries. In short, his ubiquitous and monumental activity as a disseminator of the classical school is a unique prism through which to revisit the school's fortunes in Spain and Hispanic America as a whole.

The study of economic literature for informational purposes is of interest to historians of economic thought in a sense that goes beyond the purely formal or academic reconstruction of the discipline's sources. Although it has been possible to trace a reasonably clear boundary between academic and popular economic literature for many decades, for long periods in history this distinction was less clear-cut. This was especially true before the basis for a more precise definition of the scientific outlines of "economics" and its professional aspect was established at the end of the nineteenth century. At the same time the discipline began to move away from other branches of knowledge to which it had been closely linked, such as moral philosophy, law and politics; prior to this, as noted above, the boundaries between academic and popular economics were extremely blurred and the main economics writers generally accepted that their responsibilities included spreading economic knowledge through catechisms, summaries, popular lessons, press articles and dictionary and encyclopaedia entries. This type of literature normally reached a wider audience than standard textbooks and treatises; moreover, it should not be forgotten, particularly in the context of the historical reconstruction of economic science, that for long periods these intellectual products were a key element in the process that enabled economic ideas to achieve some degree of influence over government policies (Coats 1971, 20; Schumpeter 1955, 435–36).

There is no doubt that the press and encyclopaedic literature, the two fields Mora preferred as a populariser, were fundamental components of this type of popular economics literature. From 1750 to 1820 and even subsequently it was very common for economics writers to contribute articles and economics entries for the press, dictionaries and encyclopaedias, a custom that was shared by some of the major economics writers of the late Enlightenment such as Quesnay, Forbonnais, Morellet and Grivel, many of the classical economists, including McCulloch, Nassau Senior, Malthus, Mill, Say and Sismondi, as well as others who were responsible for the new scientific turn taken by economics from the 1870s onwards —Edgeworth, Menger, Pareto and so forth—. Writing articles and encyclopaedic entries was a means of reinforcing their academic prestige, of fulfilling a vocation for education or of simply contributing to the creation of the "intangible capital" that their countries needed to promote economic development (Augello and Guidi 2001, 298). This active collaboration was a decisive factor in a journal or dictionary becoming a powerful means of spreading economic thought and it should also be recalled that these articles and entries sometimes ended up being compiled into economics texts or teaching handbooks.

It therefore seems necessary to widen the study of political economy sources to include the press or encyclopaedic literature, not only to do justice to some of the main players, of whom Mora was one, but above all to give an adequate account of the time and ideas of the period under study. All the more so since researching literature written to inform and publicise is a highly useful tool for uncovering the differences in "national" character in the ways in which academic economic culture matured and acquired institutional form in different nations.[2] For example, not all countries had high-profile, wide-ranging economic cultures, simply because their "audience" lacked the rate or level of literacy for such publishing operations to be launched successfully. Likewise, there are clear national differences with respect to the schools or currents of economic thought that dominated the theoretical orientation adopted by the press, dictionaries and encyclopaedias. Finally, not all these countries were represented at the great moment in popular economics literature that the appearance of the *Edinburgh Review* in Britain and the *Journal des économistes* in France meant for the press sector and the publication of dictionaries by Coquelin and Guillaumin (1851–1853) in France, Boccardo (1857–1861) in Italy, Palgrave (1894–1899) in the United States and the *Handwörterbuch der Staatswissenschaften* (1890–1894) in Germany in the encyclopaedic literature category. Nor, of course, did they all experience the great "leap" in content quality, particularly at analytical level, which is considered to have taken place in these countries from 1880–1890 onwards. National differences thus seem to stem not only from the quantity of journals or dictionaries with significant economic content, but also from the calibre of the actual content and the sometimes entirely disparate stances on analytical or economic policy that were involved in their production. For example, a late nineteenth-century cross-section would reveal encyclopaedic works dominated by Krausists economists in Spain,

[2] On "national styles" of political economy see Lluch (1980), among others, and on the importance of institutional factors on the development of economic thought see Augello and Guidi (2019, I, 3–19).

Historicists in Germany, liberals with affinities to the classical authors in Italy and the new Marginalist economists in Britain and the United States.

This great diversity was undoubtedly a reflection of far-reaching evolutionary features. There is a significant divide between countries that had journals or dictionaries specialising in political economy —headed by Britain, followed by France, Italy, the United States and Germany— from those that lacked them; but among the latter there is also a substantial difference between those such as Portugal that did not produce any major popular literature and those that did. Spain undoubtedly belongs in the latter group and thus falls in the middle of the ranking: although it still lacked significant specialised journals and dictionaries, between 1825 and 1930 in particular it did produce informative economic literature that was a source for the study of the history of Spanish economic thought and, moreover, of notable interest from the applied economics perspective.[3] As was customary in other countries, this literature was produced by some of the leading economists of each generation such as Álvaro Flórez Estrada, José Canga Argüelles, José Manuel Piernas Hurtado and Mora himself, and was a magnificent reflection of the theoretical and cultural climate of the day and also of the prominence that the different economic and political currents —free traders, protectionists, Krausists and Catholic economists, for example— enjoyed in it.

Given its fullness, geographical diversity and duration Mora's career provides a magnificent vantage point from which to observe both the emergence and configuration of academic and general interest economic literature in Spain —and partially in Hispanic America— during the first sixty years of the nineteenth century, as well as the process by which political economy became consolidated as a mature scientific discipline, together with its gradual but unstoppable institutionalisation. In Spain this process began during the closing decades of the Age of Enlightenment (Astigarraga 2020), finding expression in relatively well-known issues such as the way in which political economy slowly established itself in law and philosophy faculties and other educational bodies from 1807 onwards; the proliferation of institutions devoted, albeit generally not exclusively, to economic matters (economics societies, trade consulates, patriotic societies and the *Ateneo de Madrid*); the publication of the first political economy dictionaries from the 1820s onwards, which were matched thirty years later by the first encyclopaedias with significant economics content, the

[3] There is an initial overview of reality in Iberia as a whole in Astigarraga et al. (2001).

appearance of the first specialised journals in the 1840s and finally, particularly from the 1820s onwards, the mushrooming of handbooks and textbooks for university teaching and for training a new political, commercial and business class.[4]

Not only did Mora witness these processes, he also played a major part in them. Unquestionably a son of the Enlightenment, in his early youth he embraced the economic theories and policies of the classical school, mainly the British and French versions, and remained faithful to them all his life. Although the main core of his economic analysis took shape early on and underwent few alterations in his long career as a journalist, Mora was adept at capturing the changes that were taking place in both the orthodox and heterodox currents of political economy; far from being impermeable to outside events his writings were always open to new ideas, which he incorporated in and adapted to an analytical structure that in essence remained almost intact and was always true to classical liberal principles. Thanks to these changes, which were sometimes almost purely rhetorical or argument-based, he integrated innovations into his analytical and political positions from the 1820s to the 1860s until he had created a complete sequence which ran from Smith and Bentham to McCulloch, James Mill and John Stuart Mill and from Say to Bastiat and Chevalier.

1.2 A Work with an Atlantic and Continental Dimension

There is a second, even more remarkable aspect of Mora's indisputable capacity to adapt. He was undoubtedly an exceptional figure in the almost forgotten transatlantic dissemination of Hispanic economic thought. His life in this field was truly fascinating; after eight years working as a journalist in the Spain of the *Sexenio Absolutista* (1814–1817) and the Liberal Triennium (1820–1823), his activism and liberal convictions forced him into exile in London (1823–1827). This contact with the exhilarating imperial and commercial city conclusively underpinned his Anglophilia and theoretical and normative convictions in favour of liberalism and free trade, which he would also uphold for the rest of his life, albeit with certain nuances. Surrounded as he was by other distinguished Spanish liberals who were also in exile in London (Canga Argüelles, Flórez Estrada, Blanco White, etc.), he became aware of the immense collective feat that the

[4] Vid. Almenar (1996, 2000, 27–32); Martín Rodríguez (1989).

creation of the new Hispanic-American republics represented; on appreciating the enormous importance of their fate for the future of liberalism as a whole, he reinvented himself, always as an exile. Although he had trained as a lawyer in Spain, he soon learned to work as a journalist, writing for publications that he himself had set up and also as a "proletarian of the pen" in the service of specific interests, both business —in London— and political —in Hispanic America—. The new political and economic structures in Spain's former territories required thorough restructuring and this demanded economic and political reforms and far-reaching institutional changes, for which reason the transatlantic flow of Enlightenment and liberal ideas from Europe to these territories had extraordinary repercussions.

Mora's work in this field was absolutely unique and fundamental. He lived in Argentina (1827), Chile (1828–1832), Peru (1832–1834) and Bolivia (1834–1838) for twelve years and worked as a writer and publisher of pro-liberal and free trade political and economic ideas on the countries' foremost journals, such as *Crónica científica y literaria de Buenos Aires*, *El mercurio chileno* and *El eco del Protectorado*. He drafted the 1828 Chilean Constitution; founded educational institutions for both sexes, such as the *Colegio Argentino* and the *Liceo de Chile*, to educate the citizens in republican and liberal principles. He was political advisor to the presidents of Argentina, Chile, Peru and Bolivia, as well as working in the diplomatic field, also at the highest level, first for the Peru-Bolivia Confederation and then for Spain. At the same time, from his prominent position in these countries, he designed a model of economic development for Hispanic America based on classical political economy adapted to the new republics' economic, political and social environments. If this were not enough, in all these countries he produced catechisms, educational handbooks and other writings in the decades that followed his leave from Hispanic America in the late 1830s, usually through "pirate" copies, in which possibly their pupils may have been involved. These works were also published in countries such as Cuba, Colombia, Ecuador, Venezuela, Nicaragua, Brazil and Mexico, where he never lived, in such a way Mora's work achieved a continental dimension. Through all these writings he spread the ideas of natural and international law, Benthamite utilitarianism, the French *Idéologues*' sensualism and the Scottish philosophers' Common Sense.

Equipped with all these weapons and a rationalist and anti-scholastic Baconianism, he was a belligerent opponent of Catholic superstition, religious fanaticism and political absolutism. His youthful aversion to despotism was kindled in the 1820s, first during the lively constitutional period of the Liberal Triennium and shortly afterwards through direct personal contact with British ideas and some of its most distinguished intellectuals. This all came together in a desideratum that interwove the defence of economic liberalism imbibed from the classical economists with their sympathy for constitutional political systems —whether monarchical or republican— based on representative political systems and the recognition of individual rights and the dynamic political action of public opinion. Although he never fully shed an elitist sense of culture and politics inherited from the Enlightenment, from a young age Mora had total faith in freedom of opinion exercised through the press, debating clubs and other enabling institutions in the exemplary British world. He viewed the printing press as the instrument of "mental activity and reform" *par excellence* for spreading the Enlightenment, the "marvellous art that crosses the divides of time and space and distributes the most diverse knowledge equally to all men", while at the same time inspiring public opinion, which it "protects, defends and supplies with weapons" (*Crónica política y literaria*, no. 95, 6/IX/1827).[5] In short, Mora was a key player in the ideological and political modernisation of all the countries in which he lived and in terms of political economy this was mainly reflected in his tireless work of disseminating and adapting the ideas of the classical authors.

Mora's return to Spain in 1843 was not permanent as he returned to London to serve three terms as Spanish Consul during the 1850s (1850–1851; 1853–1854; 1856–1858). On achieving the longed-for reunion with his homeland after twenty years of forced absence he plunged into the lively debates of the day on trade policy and taxation and became an active proponent of free trade, aiming to influence the development of a favourable climate for its introduction into Spanish legislation. Some of his main economics writings date from this period, especially his well-documented and extensive entries, almost in the form of short single-issue treatises, in the *Enciclopedia Moderna* (1851–1855), the first encyclopaedic work in Spain. These entries were largely a summary of all the

[5] Following the quoting guidelines in the Hispanic world for periodical publications, the order used is the title of the publication or its abbreviation, number (no.) or volume (in Roman numerals), day/month/year. Unless otherwise stated, the translation from Spanish to English of Mora's original writings is his own. The Mora's texts orthography has bee modernised.

informative work he had done during the previous three decades. However, he also published vast articles in the Spanish press during the twenty years prior to his death in 1864, which clearly showed attempts to influence Spanish public opinion and to demonstrate the benefits of classical liberalism and free trade and apply them to the two strands of Spanish liberalism with which he was linked, first the moderates and then the progressives. This huge body of work had, moreover, the unique feature of being published in journals that were also aimed at the Hispanic-American public. Even from Spain Mora never ceased to try to influence the fortunes of the new South American republics, which he knew so well and valued so highly.

1.3 The State of Play Summed Up

In common with other studies on Mora, this book has come up against somewhat unusual obstacles. The first is the lack of a complete and detailed account of Mora's life. He left no autobiography and his writings contained only passing references to his life; his personal documents have been lost and his closest contemporaries gave little news of him. Taken together these factors make it extremely difficult to produce a faithful reconstruction of the different phases of the constant movement that characterised his life that culminates in a biography covering them all. The nature of his work, as ideologically coherent as it is physically scattered, mainly produced in formats that are very difficult to access, has also had a huge impact on this question. Such is the case of the articles and other similar brief anonymous, disparate and ephemeral texts that he wrote for a broad readership and with the specific aim of spreading information. This issue, as Antonio Alcalá Galiano, a liberal friend of Mora's openly acknowledged, made academic recognition of the writer and his work very difficult, even in his own time. Alcalá Galiano wrote:

> D. José Joaquín de Mora is one of modern Spain's living and skilful authors, and in spite of that he has not yet produced any important or good work; from whence it arises that he is little esteemed among his countrymen. Not only that, in spite of being so well-read, he is generally regarded as a somewhat trivial man of science. (Trease 1953, 11)

After Mora's death only one other contemporary, Ferrer del Río (1864), wrote an obituary containing relatively full biographical details, which is still virtually the only way to find out about his poorly documented early life. These shortcomings were not fully corrected in subsequent decades, despite a growing awareness among Spanish and Hispanic- American liberal historians that Mora did not write a masterpiece because in reality the whole of his life and written output was a masterpiece. It never ceases to be surprising that the attempts to produce a complete biography of him are so few and far between, or that they ultimately focus on specific stages in his life. Amunátegui (1888) made the first attempt a quarter of a century after his death; its chief virtue is its inclusion of numerous primary sources on Mora, but it was mainly confined to his time in Chile. While it remains the benchmark biographical work on Mora a century and a half later, much subsequent research has shown that it lacks rigour and contains numerous inaccuracies. However, this is not so with two later works by Trease (1953) and Monguió (1967), both of which focused on Mora's literary side and dealt firstly with his long exile and secondly with his time in Peru and Bolivia and then as a diplomat for the two countries in London. Mora's life story is thus characterised by a highly telling asymmetry: just as there is no complete narrative worthy of an intellectual and reformer of his stature, he has never ceased to arouse interest in Hispanism as a whole during the 150 or so years since his death. The most tangible example of this is an excellent recent monograph in which Medina (2022) investigated Mora's life as a whole by reconstructing his deep and enduring veins of Anglophilia. In reality Mora has not been forgotten in any of the countries on which he left his intellectual and reforming stamp and this has produced a bibliography that is normally framed within national boundaries and which there is no need to explore here as attempts have been made to record it in other chapters. Although extensive and wide-ranging, this national profile bibliography is naturally patchy and highlights the fact that more is known about some periods in Mora's life than others. Among the former are his years in London, Argentina and Chile, while the latter include the Liberal Triennium and the last twenty years spent in Spain before his death. In any event, only fragmented glimpses of these different periods are generally available, which, like pieces of a jigsaw, provide merely a blurred and sketchy picture of his life as a whole.

A similar piecemeal image emerges from looking at the literature on Mora from the perspectives of different disciplines. As he was a prolific and thoroughly multidisciplinary author it is not surprising that scholars have studied his texts, ideas and activities from different angles and fields, in many cases obtaining results whose interest goes beyond the subject of study, as the bibliography in this book shows. The main asymmetry in this field is to be found between the enormous interest that Mora's work has aroused among historians of literature, translation and literary criticism vis-à-vis the other fields that he also cultivated, such as education, law, philosophy, moral philosophy, logic, politics and economics. Indeed, the enormous intellectual and reforming interest he took in economics, which for much of his life he acknowledged to be the social science *par excellence*, has not been properly reproduced in the research field, attracting very little interest and then only in specific aspects. While it is possible to find general studies that position Mora and his liberal ideology in the set of economic currents that contributed to the spread of the ideas of classical economics in the Spain of his day,[6] there is no comprehensive analysis of Mora "the economist" along the lines that this book aims to pursue. Although some of the general biographies of Mora have explored this aspect (Trease 1953, 110ff.), the main studies are based on Smith's (1968) pioneering work and focus on specific writings from Mora's long and varied career. Schwartz (1970, 1999) essentially studied *De la libertad de comercio* (1844), analysing its sources and its roots in Mora's other works, especially the *Catecismo de economía política* (1825), while Siegrist de Gentile (1992) did the same with an important manuscript on Spanish "industry and commerce", which was found in Buenos Aires, attributable to Mora and written in the mid-nineteenth century. Both authors re-edited these two major texts.

While Medina's book (2022) focuses on the British roots of Mora's economic thought and its relationship with related branches, especially Benthamite utilitarianism and moral philosophy, another line of research undertaken years ago by the authors of this book analysed specific aspects of his informative writings, focusing in particular on the articles he published in *El mercurio chileno* in 1828–1829 (Astigarraga and Zabalza 2017) and the entries in the *Enciclopedia moderna* from 1851 to 1855 (Astigarraga and Zabalza 2017); they have recently published an anthology of some of the most important entries in this major encyclopaedic collection (Astigarraga et al. 2022). The research aimed to show that these were both ambitious projects to disseminate classical political economy with the purpose of applying it to specific national frameworks and to sketch out the general outlines of economic growth models for

[6] They are mainly to be found in Smith (1957; 1968b), Martín Rodríguez (1989), Almenar (2000) and Lluch and Almenar (2000).

Hispanic-American countries in the 1830s and for mid-century Spain (Zabalza and Astigarraga 2020). These works aimed to distance Mora from a bias which, particularly after Schwartz's studies, had turned him into a secondary author of little merit or interest due to his scant analytical innovation and the notion that he was merely a populariser: unoriginal, repetitive and alien to the idea of scientific progress. The inventory that appears in the Bibliography of this book, as a "Catalogue of Mora's journalistic articles and encyclopaedic entries on political economy and allied Sciences (1825–1864)", clearly shows not only the paucity of our knowledge of Mora "the economist" but also the wrong-headedness and shallowness of these interpretations. In short, as with many of the disciplinary fields that Mora cultivated, the handful of research referred to does absolutely no justice to the global reach of Mora "the economist" and presents only a very patchy picture of him, which this book has attempted to transcend.

The difficulties involved in undertaking a complete reconstruction of Mora's life and intellectual journey have also had a serious impact on the task of identifying the corpus of primary sources for his work as a whole and some of these obstacles have proved insurmountable. Mora published work in all six countries in which he lived —Spain, Britain, Argentina, Chile, Peru and Bolivia— between 1814 and 1864 and he did so in a colossal range of formats: books, translations, treatises, essays, articles, reviews, catechisms, encyclopaedia entries and many other equally diverse intellectual products, whose identification, location and attribution is sometimes extremely challenging. In general, there are fewer difficulties with regard to his books —originals or translations— although the scarcity of reprints of some of them and the remote and uncertain existence of just a few copies mean that these stumbling blocks can never be completely overcome. However, these obstacles only multiply when it comes to identifying, locating and accessing his writings in the press or encyclopaedic collections, which make up a very substantial part of his *oeuvre* as a whole. The not insignificant factor that they were written and published in all the different countries in which Mora lived and worked makes constructing the entire corpus of his work extraordinarily difficult.

Behind this book lies enormous effort, expended in numerous libraries and other archives in the six countries mentioned above,[7] all with the goal of cataloguing as fully as possible Mora's writings on political economy for the first time. The main outcomes of the research appear in the "Catalogue" afore mentioned. However, it is by no means certain that we have been able to identify, recognise and consult the entire body of Mora's writings. There is a further problem, which cannot be described as exactly minor either: attributing the authorship of much of this work to Mora is ambiguous and tremendously tricky. More than a few of the texts published in the press and encyclopaedic collections appeared anonymously or unsigned or even in journals with which Mora may well not have collaborated at all. This is an extremely difficult issue with regard to journals published during the Liberal Triennium, as well as with several others that appeared subsequently in Argentina, Chile, Peru and Bolivia. The criterion adopted here has been to attribute writings to Mora indirectly on the basis of intellectual affinity; content —he used the same magnificent written style in Spanish in all his writings, not only the strictly literary pieces—; intellectual development; the use of similar sources and the position he occupied in the hierarchy of the journal or publication in which the texts in question were published. We have opted to attribute the political economy articles in journals at which he was editor or co-editor or a leading journalist to him. This has made it possible to extend the sources for his writings considerably, as well as the journals with which he collaborated, far beyond the pioneering work carried out in this respect by Amunátegui, Trease and Monguió. The final outcome of our choices will in all likelihood continue to cause debate, and there is nothing to suggest that the future will deliver any additional data that will enable us to move beyond the realm of interpretation.

[7]The list is as follows: Archivo de la Real Sociedad Económica Matritense (Madrid); Archivo del Ateneo de Madrid (Madrid); Archivo Histórico Nacional (Madrid), Biblioteca de la Pontificia Universidad Católica de Chile (Santiago de Chile); Biblioteca de la Pontificia Universidad Católica de Perú (Lima); Biblioteca de la Universidad de Sevilla (Sevilla); Biblioteca del Instituto Nacional de Administración Pública (Madrid); Biblioteca del Instituto Riva-Agüero (Lima), Biblioteca Nacional de Chile (Santiago de Chile); Biblioteca Nacional de España (Madrid); Biblioteca Nacional de la República Argentina (Buenos Aires); Biblioteca Nacional del Perú (Lima); Bibliothèque Nationale de France (Paris); British Library (London); Hemeroteca Municipal de Madrid (Madrid) and Museo Histórico Nacional (Santiago de Chile). It is also undeniable that we have benefitted enormously from sources available on the Internet.

In any event, these difficulties have not prevented the authors from attempting to provide the broadest and most comprehensive view possible of Mora's intellectual journey. We are convinced that political economy was a central and unifying theme in Mora's contributions, not a parallel space, nor circumstantial nor anecdotal. Therefore, the social and moral science conceived by the British classical masters that he so admired may well be deemed the most complete representation of the socio-political attitudes and intellectual spirit of José Joaquín de Mora.

Bibliography

Secondary Sources

Almenar, Salvador. 1996. "Economic Thought in Spanish Periodical Publications of the 18th and 19th Centuries: an Introduction". *History of Economic Ideas* IV-3, 119–47.

Almenar, Salvador. 2000. "El desarrollo del pensamiento económico clásico en España". In *Economía y economistas españoles. Vol. IV. La economía clásica*, edited by Enrique Fuentes, 7–92. Barcelona: Galaxia Gütenberg and Círculo de Lectores.

Amunátegui, Miguel Luis. 1888. *Don José Joaquín de Mora. Apuntes biográficos.* Santiago de Chile: Imprenta Nacional.

Astigarraga, Jesús. 2020. *An Unifying Enlightenment. Institutions of Political Economy in Eighteenth-Century Spain (1700–1808).* Leiden and Boston: Brill Publishers.

Astigarraga, Jesús and Juan Zabalza. 2017. "José Joaquín de Mora y la divulgación de la doctrina económica liberal en Latinoamérica en los inicios del siglo XIX". *Revista de historia industrial* 67, 39–68.

Astigarraga, Jesús, Juan Zabalza and António Almodovar. 2001. "Dictionaries and Encyclopaedias on Political Economy in the Iberian Peninsula (18th, 19th and 20th Centuries)". *Storia del Pensiero Economico* 41, 25–63.

Astigarraga, Jesús, Javier Usoz and Juan Zabalza. 2022. "Estudio preliminar". In *Voces económicas en la 'Enciclopedia Moderna'*, by José Joaquín de Mora, edited by Jesús Astigarraga, Javier Usoz and Juan Zabalza, 11–80. Madrid: IEF.

Augello, Massimo M. and Marco E. L. Guidi, eds. 2001. *The Spread of Political Economy and the Professionalisation of Economists.* London: Routledge.

Augello, Massimo M. and Marco E. L. Guidi, eds. 2019. *Economisti e scienza economica nell'Italia liberale (1848–1922). Una storia istituzionale*, vol. 1. Milano: Franco Angeli.

Coats, Alfred W. 1971. "Editor's Introduction". In *The Classical Economists and Economic Policy*, edited by Alfred W. Coats, 1–32. London: Methuen and Co.

Ferrer del Río, Antonio. 1864. "Necrología. Don José Joaquín de Mora". *La América*, VIII–21 (12/XI/1864), 5–6.

Lluch, Ernest. 1980. "Sobre la historia nacional del pensamiento económico". In *Curso de economía política*, by Antonio Flórez Estrada, edited by Salvador Almenar, vol. I, VII–XXXIII. Madrid: IEF.

Lluch, Ernest and Salvador Almenar. 2000. "Difusión e influencia de los economistas clásicos en España (1776–1870)". In *Economía y economistas españoles. Vol. IV. La economía clásica*, edited by Enrique Fuentes, 93–170. Barcelona: Galaxia Gütenberg and Círculo de Lectores.

Martín Rodríguez, Manuel. 1989. "La institucionalización de los estudios de Economía Política en la universidad española (1784–1857)". In *Elementos de economía política con aplicación particular a España*, by Marqués de Valle Santoro, XI–CCXXXIV. Madrid: IEF.

Medina, Sara. 2022. *José Joaquín de Mora and Britain: Cultural Transfers and Transformations*. Berlin: Peter Lang.

Monguió, Luis. 1967. *Don José Joaquín de Mora y el Perú del ochocientos*. Madrid: Castalia.

Schumpeter, Josep A. 1955. *History of Economic Analysis*. New York: OUP. Spanish translation, *Historia del análisis económico*, Barcelona, Caracas and Mexico, Ariel, 1971.

Schwartz, Pedro. 1970. "*De la libertad del comercio*, por Joaquín de Mora: una defensa del libre-cambio a mediados del siglo XIX". *Anales de economía* 5–8, 189–224.

Schwartz, Pedro. 1999. "Estudio Preliminar". In *De la libertad del comercio*, by José Joaquín de Mora, VIII–XLIX. Madrid: IEF.

Siegrist de Gentile, Nora. 1992. *José Joaquín de Mora y su manuscrito sobre la industria y el comercio de España hacia 1850*. Cádiz: Universidad de Cádiz.

Smith, Robert Sidney. 1957. "La *Riqueza de las Naciones* en España e Hispanoamérica, 1780–1830". *Revista de economía política* VIII–3, 1215–53.

Smith, Robert Sidney. 1968. "El pensamiento económico de José Joaquín de Mora", *Humanitas* IX, 595–607.

Trease, B. David. 1953. *José Joaquín de Mora: A Spaniard Abroad*. PhD. Michigan, University of Michigan.

Zabalza, Juan and Jesús Astigarraga. 2020. "Entre España y Chile. José Joaquín Mora y los proyectos de un diccionario de economía política (1825–1855)". In *El pensamiento económico del reformismo criollo*, edited by José Antonio Piqueras and Johanna von Grafenstein, 435–75. Santa Marta: Editorial Unimagdalena and Instituto Mora.

PART I

The Making of a Publicist

CHAPTER 2

The *Sexenio Absolutista* (1814–1820): The Encounter with Smith and Say

2.1 Preparing the Ground

Mora was barely thirty years old when his career in journalism began during the 1810s. As little is known about his early life,[1] it is not clear how his gradual metamorphosis from a young lover of literature into a more multifaceted figure with a passionate interest in political economy took place. The time and place of his birth were probably not unrelated to this process, however. Mora was born on 10 January 1783, during the last years of Carlos III's reign (1759–1788), when the Bourbon reforms were in full swing; political economy had become part of the language of the country's enlightened elites, as political economy texts and translations had been circulating throughout Spain for forty years. Furthermore, Mora's birthplace, the Andalusian city of Cadiz, was one of mainland Spain's most active centres of economic culture.[2] Its prosperity was closely linked to maritime trade. In 1762 future journalist and high-ranking government

[1] Information about these periods comes from Antonio Alcalá Galiano, Antonio Gil de Zárate and other journalists and politicians that knew Mora in mid-nineteenth-century Madrid. The best sources are Mellado (1842) and Ferrer del Río (1864). The books by Amunátegui (1888) and Monguió (1967) include the references to the contemporary authors cited. The works by Pitollet (1909), Durán (2015, 2018) and Gil Novales (1975, II, 887–88, 2010) are especially useful.

[2] All the details appear in Bustos (2005).

J. Astigarraga et al., *The Economic Legacy of José Joaquín de Mora*, Palgrave Studies in the History of Economic Thought,
https://doi.org/10.1007/978-3-031-49446-8_2

official Mateo Antonio Barberi wrote that the city was a "fair of Europe, in which buying and selling were the only goals" (Bustos 2005, 38). A natural crossroads for the sea routes connecting Europe with the other continents, the Cadiz in which Mora was born looked mainly to the Atlantic for trade. The monopoly on trading with the Indies, which the city held between 1717 and 1765, had made it the most powerful trading enclave in Spain, and it retained this status after the enactment of the free trade decrees (1765, 1778 and 1788) which ended the monopoly and allowed a dozen Spanish ports to trade directly with the Americas. Cadiz was among them and continued to be the frontrunner in the *carrera de Indias*—race to the Indies—: by the late 1780s more than three quarters of exports to America left from there (Bustos 2005, 79). As a result of these liberalising decrees, Mora's childhood years were a period of unprecedented prosperity for Atlantic trade and for Cadiz in particular. Until the Convention War (1793–1795), the city's commercial business, population and age-old façade of a prosperous, cosmopolitan and cultured city, truly unique in Spain, went from strength to strength.

José Joaquín de Mora Sánchez was born into a family of humble social status—his paternal grandfather had been a teacher—and rooted in Andalusia—his mother Micaela Sánchez and his maternal and paternal grandparents came from small villages around Cadiz (Ronda and Chiclana)—,[3] but he grew up in a relatively well-off environment owing to the fact that his maternal grandfather was Mayor of Jerez de la Frontera (Cadiz) and his father, Juan de Mora, had prospered as a lawyer and military prosecutor. According to Ferrer del Río (1864, 5) José Joaquín had an excellent education that included not only the Latin classics but also French and English, essential features of the social surroundings in which he grew up. [4] Eighteenth-century Cadiz lived and breathed trade, witnessing an ever-increasing influx of foreign merchants, particularly from France, such that by the end of the century one out of every two people engaged in wholesale trade was not a native Spaniard and the use of foreign languages was commonplace in the city's everyday life.

[3] AHN, *Consejos*, bundle 13,173.

[4] Mora became fluent in French and English, but he probably acquired them during his sojourns in France and London, in the second and third decades of the nineteenth century, respectively. He will explain in his private correspondence that his education in Cadiz was indebted to a "saintly Jansenist cleric" (Mora to José Hegan, London, 22/I/1855; González 1961, 282–84), in all probability the canon of its cathedral.

There is no indication that Mora was interested in trade, however. After finishing school he moved to Granada to study law at the university. His life underwent a considerable change there, as the city's character was marked by its centuries-old university, which had been founded in 1526. He enrolled at the *Colegio de San Miguel*, one of the most prestigious university colleges, devoted to teaching theology, the arts and law. Here he once again witnessed the effects of the Bourbon reforms, which had a significant impact on the modernisation of the curricula, although, somewhat paradoxically, the impact was more moderate at the three major universities (Salamanca, Valladolid and Alcalá) than in peripheral regional universities such as Granada (Arias de Saavedra 2007). The implementing of the 1776 university reform under which Mora studied was made possible by the fact that a highly dynamic academic sector joined the university teaching staff, ousting the traditionally dominant scholastic theologians of the *Colegio de Santa Cruz de la Fe*.

Although the reform was applied only partially and gradually, it placed the University of Granada at the head of the most innovative establishments of the entire Spanish university system in the closing years of the eighteenth century. In the field of philosophy, not only were advanced mathematics courses created, but Mora also came into contact with certain moderate scientific currents, mainly Catholic (Genovesi, Muschembroeck, Tosca and Verney). The most significant change in the field of law was the merging of the law and canons faculties into a single jurisprudence faculty. Under its aegis, these age-old subjects began to lean towards new approaches to teaching, and this was also the case with roman and canon law, which began to include Heineccio's work and other *regalista* texts. New subjects such as natural law and the law of nations, taught through authors such as Almici, Grotius and Puffendorf, were created, as well as national law, which was in the hands of Spanish jurists Ignacio de Asso and Manuel Rodríguez. However, Mora did not undertake any formal teaching in political economy while in Granada. He completed his degree at the Faculty of Law, with an outstanding grade, in July 1807.[5] From then onwards, Mora's biographers place him in Granada, starting out as a lawyer and philosophy and logic teacher at the university and surrounded by staff and students who were destined to take centre stage in the liberal Spain of the future, such as Francisco Martínez de la Rosa who became prime Minister in 1834. According to Mora's further

[5] AHN, *Consejos*, bundle 13,173.

statements, he was teaching Condillac's *La Logique* (1780) by then—perhaps following Bernardo María de la Calzada's 1784 Spanish translation—and Bentham. It would be further proof in support of the suggestion that texts outside the narrow margins established by officialdom were circulating among Spanish universities at that time. Although Mora certainly put down roots at the university, they did not cause him to abandon either Cadiz or his budding literary interests. As Alcalá Galiano recounts (Amunátegui 1888, 15–17), in 1805 he joined the *Academia del Conde de Casa Rojas* in his home town, which was somewhat ostentatiously called the *Academia de Bellas Letras* and was devoted to rhetoric and poetics.

The outbreak of the War of Independence (1808–1814) soon cut short the legal and teaching two careers on which Mora had embarked in Granada. The Napoleonic army's entry into the north of the peninsula at the beginning of 1808, and the proclamation of Joseph Bonaparte as King of Spain on 6 June, endorsed a month later by the Statute of Bayonne, dramatically divided the people of Spain between the *afrancesados,* who preferred Bonaparte, and the *patriotas*, who supported Ferdinand VII. For six years this conflict, which was international in scope yet civil in nature to the Spanish, created the ideal context for the activating of a revolutionary process that paved the way to independence for the colonies and also took the first steps down the tortuous path by which Spain left the Ancien Régime structures behind and embraced a liberal regime. In 1812 the *Cortes de Cádiz* (1810–1814) decreed the first constitution in the country's history, which established a parliamentary monarchy and to a great extent brought about the materialisation of the plans forged by liberal currents during the late Spanish Enlightenment.

Mora played no part in the intense political activism led by the *doceañista* liberals,[6] with whom he would maintain very close relations in the future, however. He joined the Spanish army organised to fight the French occupiers and, in all likelihood, fought at in the Battle of Bailén in July 1808, which was the Napoleonic army's first defeat. A year later, as a cavalry ensign, he was taken prisoner near Ciudad Real in Castile and was held, quite certainly, in Autun in French Burgundy. His biographers point out that Mora devoted his years of detention to furthering his education, possibly paying special attention to the French *Idéologues.* In 1814 he married his host's daughter, Françoise "Fanny" Delauneux (1791–1887); the

[6] This term refers to the liberal supports of the 1812 Cadiz Constitution.

family was a modest one—her father was an official at the district court—, but she had had a good education and proved to both be learned and practical, playing an important role—unresearched as yet—in Mora's future journalism and educational activities. He probably swore loyalty to Joseph I during this time and, according to Amunátegui (1888, 18), visited London, but it is highly unlikely. There is evidence that family debt landed him in prison in Chalons-sur-Saône in French Burgundy, and that he was released due to financial help from someone with whom he would remain in touch for much of his life: the deeply Anglophile Seville cleric José María Blanco y Crespo, known as José Blanco White. Although he had lived in exile in London since 1810, Mora knew him from his time in Cadiz, where his family owned a business and he had participated in literary gatherings.

In May 1814 Ferdinand VII declared the *Cortes de Cádiz* Constitution and laws "null and void and of no value or effect" (Artola 1973, 43). This marked the beginning of a six-year period of absolute rule known as the *Sexenio Absolutista* (1814–1820), a counter-revolution that entailed a return to the political system of 1808.[7] The old prohibitions on book publishing and the press were reinstated, cultural borders were closed and the *afrancesados* and liberal forces were either banished or driven underground as Ferdinand restored "ministerial despotism", a political system through which he sought to restore the Ancien Régime's estates-based society. The system rested on a feudal and ecclesiastical structure that was chiefly in the hands of the reactionary aristocracy, supported by the power of the Church and the Inquisition. For six long years the legislative activities of Ferdinand's iron-fisted absolutism consisted largely of interrupting and abolishing the reforms put in place by the Cadiz constitutionalism. In this scenario Mora slipped back to Cadiz in 1814, then moved to Madrid, where he obtained an official pardon in 1816; "as retired cavalry second lieutenant", started practising as a lawyer,[8] and began his career as a journalist. He had translated in 1814 Chateaubriand's legitimist work deriding Bonaparte and praising the Bourbons (Chateaubriand 1814), at the dawn of the Congress of Vienna, and this, along with the fact that he had not in taken part in the political struggles before beginning his career, may have

[7] Carr (1968, 128), Fontana (1971, 1979) and Artola (1973, 40–45).

[8] He worked between August 1816 and August 1817 in the office of a private lawyer. The Council of Castile ratified his law degree in December 1818 (AHN, *Consejos*, bundle 13,173).

contributed to his acceptance during the dark years of absolutism. Whatever the case, his intellectual and linguistic background at the age of thirty was unique in the Madrid of the day, and this undoubtedly eased his entry into the capital's carefully guarded cultural circles. With around 200,000 inhabitants, the city was not especially populous, but as the political capital it brought together not only courtiers and the old aristocracy, but also the politicians, journalists, civil servants and professionals who would set the course of Spanish liberalism in the future.[9]

2.2 The *Crónica científica y literaria* (1817–1820)

The first issue of the *Crónica científica y literaria* (CCL, 1817–1820) was published on 1 April 1817. This was Mora's first foray into journalism and appears to have been his main activity and chief source of income during the *Sexenio Absolutista,* although he also translated plays, wrote literary texts and worked as a lawyer. The periodical was a clear example of Mora's ability to make the most of the few remaining openings for civil initiatives in the Madrid of the day, which was almost devoid of cafés and clubs. This was also true of his participation in the debates at the soon to be dissolved *Academia de Literatura*, which were devoted to translating the classics and presenting original literary works (Ferrer del Río 1864), and also in the *Sociedad Económica Matritense.* Although no details of its beginnings remain, the CCL first appeared during a regime of strict censorship; in April 1815 the freedom of printing for books and the press decreed by the *Cortes de Cádiz* in 1812 was abolished. Nevertheless, a few newspapers did exist outside the official press, and the CCL was one of them, appearing a few months before Pedro María Olive's literary gazette *Minerva o el revisor general* (MR, 1817–1818) and more than two and a half years before the *Miscelánea de comercio, artes y literatura* (MCA, 1819–1821), founded in November 1819, in the last months of the absolutist period, by *afrancesado* journalist Francisco Javier de Burgos, following Mora's example (Morán 1996).

It is not easy to assess the huge formative role that the CCL played in the development of Mora's identity as a journalist, particularly his

[9] Historical-semantic analysis shows that expressions such as "partido liberal" and "liberalismo" had been used in Spanish before French or English, even if this did not mean that an articulated and coherent political theory had been adopted (Fernández Sebastián 2012a, 12).

conviction that the profession was both an educational task and a practical and multidisciplinary skill at the service of wide-ranging interests and audiences (Durán 2015, 45). A fortnightly subscription-based publication that was open to external contributions and carried very little Hispanic-American content, the CCL's four-page issues were distributed throughout mainland Spain. Mora was not only editor, but also wrote much of the content,[10] except perhaps during the paper's last months. However, writing was not his only occupation. In late 1819 and early 1820 he undertook a secret diplomatic mission in Italy and in France whose main purpose was quite certainly to visit Livorno to study the operation of its free port.[11]

The CCL's content was largely based on translations from the foreign, mainly French, press. As the "Prospectus" mentioned, the journal aimed to be a sounding board for literary activity in Restoration Europe, which had been revitalised following the Congress of Vienna (1814–1815). Of course, the paper's orientation was greatly conditioned by censorship; obliged to leave "political" issues untouched, it had the multidisciplinary bias typical of all Mora's periodicals. The publication was devoted to "the sciences and literature", with priority given to "agriculture, the rural economy, industry, natural sciences and commerce",[12] and only its acclimatisation to the strict political environment can explain how it survived almost uninterruptedly for three years until the arrival of the new constitutional period.

The CCL was the main vehicle for the spread of scientific and technical innovations in the "almost desert-like" Spain of Ferdinand's absolutism (Ausejo 2000). Great attention was paid to education, placing Mora among the supporters of the Englishmen Andrew Bell and Joseph

[10] Authors from his circle in Madrid collaborated on the journal, among them Manuel Eduardo Gorostiza, who was editor during the last phase and who Mora was to meet again during his exile in London. All unsigned content, which was the vast majority, can be attributed to Mora himself.

[11] Mora admitted so in personal correspondence (Mesa and Gisbert 1965, 16). However, it has also been suggested the nature of these official trips may in fact have been more ambitious. Mora went to Italy to make contact with Capodistria and maybe to recruit members of the Vatican's Swiss Guard to act as royal bodyguards. Then he went to France to ascertain the state of opinion on the establishment of the constitutional regime in 1820, after which he became convinced of the disrepute in which Ferdinand's government was held (Gil Novales 2010, II, 2054). It is also thought that he took advantage of the trip to make connections with liberal sectors and suggest reforms to the government in order to save the regime (Durán 2015, 46).

[12] CCL, "Prospectus" (undated).

Lancaster's educational methods,[13] which he would embrace once and for all during his London and Hispanic-American exiles. At the same time the journal was a mainstay of the literary disputes of the time, taking the side opposing Romanticism (Pitollet 1909). Under the guise of literary neo-classicism, and along with Antonio Alcalá Galiano, Mora was the period's great contradictor of German Hispanist Nicolás Böhl de Faber's Romantic theories. The political connotations of their famous dispute over the scope of Spanish playwright Calderón de la Barca's work were clear: compared with Romanticism, which Böhl de Faber defended as an expression of absolutism and the traditional Catholic thinking then prevailing in Spain, to Mora the classicism ideal was inseparable from the Enlightenment and liberalism, whose principles were called into question by Böhl de Faber's reactionary ideology.[14] The CCL also launched Mora's career as a disseminator of political economy. Ostensibly limiting itself to publishing ideology-free economic information, the journal carried statistics on European population and trade and information on tariffs, prices and commercial geography. It also printed news on consular activities and speeches at the Cadiz, Granada, Cordoba and Madrid economics societies. Although aimed at the educated public and senior government officials, the CCL also carried useful news for "capitalists" in the form of technical instructions; both merchants, to whom various trade guides were recommended, and landowners, as the articles on agriculture dealt with agronomy and related applied arts (chemistry). However, in addition to all this, and in line with the late Spanish Enlightenment, the CCL also used brief anonymous notes, bibliographical information and especially reviews to promote political economy.[15] Mora naturally echoed Ferdinand's reforms in these pieces and also expressed his admiration for Enlightenment reformism, covering the development of *nuevas poblaciones*—new villages—in the Sierra Morena that had been founded by Carlos III in 1767. However, his ideological touchstone was neither Campomanes, Jovellanos nor other late Spanish Enlightenment writers, who were hardly mentioned

[13] Mora even included an extensive summary of Alexandre de Laborde's book, accounting for these pedagogical methods, which were being introduced experimentally in Spain in those years (CCL, no. 176, 4/XII/1818, 5–20; Medina 2022, 63–64).

[14] Just a few years later, at the height of the Liberal Triennium, Mora stated bluntly that liberalism was "on the scale of political opinions what classical taste is on the scale of literary opinions" (*El Constitucional,* no. 526, 16/X/1820, 1).

[15] On the creation during the Spanish Enlightenment of economic reviews as a new popular genre, see Astigarraga et al. (2020).

in the CCL. From its first political economy review in October 1817, the paper referenced Anglo-French classical economics, to which Mora would remain faithful throughout his life.

2.3 Political Economy in the *Crónica científica y literaria*

Mora stressed political economy's recent and foreign origins in the CCL. Although he identified Dugald Stewart—Smith's disciple—as its founder in some passages, this treatment was generally reserved for Smith himself—whose investigations "established political economy in science"—and his "rival" Say. In fact, the CLL represented Mora's first encounter with these two authors, who were the most influential to appear in its pages and were already well known in Spain. *The Wealth of Nations* (WN) had begun circulating there just two years after first appearing in 1776, but the decisive phase in the process occurred during the 1790s, when various versions of Smith's masterwork began to appear at the Court of Madrid. This was the case with both the Marquis of Condorcet's *Compendio*, which was translated by Carlos Martínez de Irujo in 1792 (Condorcet 1792), and the WN, with the publication of José Alonso Ortiz's translation two years later (Smith 1794). His version encompassed almost the entirety of the WN's five books—only one chapter remained untranslated—although it did not escape censorship, particularly with regard to the religious content. Alonso Ortiz added a large set of notes to his version, by means of which he tried to simultaneously qualify and refute Smith, defend Spanish interests from his criticisms and render the translation comprehensible to Spanish readers by adapting it to the country's economic and cultural circumstances. A new, more refined and complete version of this translation was published in 1805–1806, and both were the main means by which Smith's ideas spread throughout the Spanish-speaking world during the nineteenth century. However, as typically occurred in Europe, the WN's influence overlapped almost immediately with that of Say's work. Say's *Traité d'économie politique* (1803) and lesser works such as the *Épitomé* (1814) and *Catéchisme* (1815) enjoyed unusual publishing success in Spain from 1804–1806 onwards. Say dominated Spanish economic thought during the dozen years following the War of Independence,[16] achieving a position of hegemony that Smith never equalled. The WN was usually read only in part and then in a way that was heavily nuanced, although this was less true for analytical than "political" questions. Books Four and Five, which covered the "mercantile system" and public finance, were consulted frequently, but the way in which they were interpreted was somewhat "contaminated" with the legacies of the Spanish Enlightenment tradition.[17]

The CCL clearly reflects the pre-eminence that Say achieved in Spain during the first restoration of the absolutist regime. Like most of his contemporaries, the journal argued that Say had enhanced Smith's legacy by bestowing "order and clarity" on it (CCL, no. 213, 13/IV/1819) and applauded the fact that in 1807 Say's work had been chosen for use by the still scarce political economy chairs in Spain. In line with Say, Mora stressed that political economy was a characteristic component of cultured societies; the discipline, which was concerned with the "art of making riches prosper", studied how wealth "is created, propagated and destroyed" (CCL, no. 68, 21/XI/1817). At the same time, this all confirms the importance of French intervention in classical economics' arrival in Spain, including works by British authors. Most of the economics reviews published in the CCL came from France, quite certainly translated without delay by Mora himself. The most important covered works by Rodríguez Fernández (1817), Ricardo (1819), Destutt de Tracy (1819), Gioia (1819), Menghotti (1819), the Comte d'Hauterive (1820) and Chaptal (1820). He also included two articles devoted to Robert Owen's philanthropic projects, in which the social problems of impoverishment resulting from the industrialisation in England were brought to the fore.[18]

This diversity did not stop Mora from mounting an unwavering defence of the notion that political economy was an experimental science that should flee from "chimerical hypotheses" and base itself on a rigorous and thorough-going examination of the facts about wealth. As he "lived" on

[16] Menudo and O'Kean (2019, 169–92) limit Say's influence in Spain in 1803, situating its boom between 1814 and 1827. His works were translated 23 times; see, likewise, Lluch and Almenar (2000a, 110–15) and Almenar (2000, 21–23, 32–33).

[17] An overall analysis appears in Astigarraga and Zabalza (2021).

[18] The first was a French translation and the second referred to a piece by Owen. Although Mora admitted that his projects had contributed to correcting the low educational and moral condition of the working classes, he considered them generally unrealistic (CCL, no. 105, 31/III/1818, 3–4; no. 175, 1/XII/1818, 3–4).

facts and "many [were needed] to establish any fact as reliable", it is not surprising that Mora believed the discipline to be in its early stages (CCL, no. 234, 25/VI/1819). He understood political economy as a field that was close to statistics: indeed, it was in reality a "statistic in [which] the accuracy of the figures corresponds to the wisdom of the classification" (CCL, no. 304, 25/II/1820). While he criticised "Destutt's obscure abstractions, Ganilh's total errors [and] Sismondi's fictional ideas" (CCL, no. 304, 25/II/1820), he also translated a glowing review of Chaptal's *De l'industrie française* (1819) by French statistician Peuchet, underlining his factual analysis of France's territorial wealth (CCL, no. 308, 10/III/1829). From 1817 onwards, Mora turned the CCL into a pioneering vehicle for disseminating the work of French *Idéologues* such as Condillac and Destutt de Tracy; however, he did not always do so very assertively, precisely because they had little experiential value.[19] The reverse was true of Gioia's *Elementi di filosofía* (1818) which Mora praised highly because it drew general consequences from particular facts (CCL, no. 265, 12/X/1819), and Alexandre de Lanautte, Comte d'Hauterive's *Éléments d'économie politique* (1817) which he presented as being entirely in tune with his view:

> Political economy is essentially a science of facts: the difficulty lies in observing them correctly, facing them, ascribing each of their circumstances its real value, classifying them and drawing from them such logical deductions as will suffice to form a body of theory. (CCL, no. 304, 25/II/1820)

Political economy should not therefore try to produce universal truths, but use "common sense and sound reason" to set out simple and easily applicable principles; hence Mora's praise for Montesquieu's 12-page summary of the science of government (CCL, no. 213, 13/IV/1819). This would all help to combat ideas that were deeply rooted among the common people, such as inevitable intervention in the markets and the rejection of mechanisation.

These criteria all emerged in the CCL's main review, which was devoted to Ricardo's *Principles of Political Economy and Taxation* (1817).[20] Mora consulted the French translation of this work, which was published by

[19] CCL (n. 75, 16/XII/1817). In some cases, with the support of the very young prestigious future economist Ramón de la Sagra.

[20] It was one of the first reviews of this work to be published in Spain; see Almenar (2014).

Francisco Solano Constancio in 1819 with notes by Say (CCL, no. 213, 13/IV/1819). According to Mora, Ricardo was a thinker who was "sometimes too profound", who got tied up "in unintelligible and inapplicable theories" such as the theory of value; unlike Smith, he tried to "penetrate the labyrinth of metaphysical essences that lead nowhere", turning political economy into a sort of "airy science". Mora branded what was termed "the Ricardian vice" thus: Ricardo "attributes such generality to the principles he believes to be right that he regards their outcomes as infallible". The exception was specific applied fields like taxation, banking and exchange rates, in which Ricardo did propose "useful" ideas for government action. In any event, Mora downplayed his results, relying on Say's critical notes on the tendency of wages to match minimum subsistence levels and the desirability of credit.

In Mora's view political economy's complexity was not confined to its principles, but extended to its application. In October 1817 he used his analysis of Rodríguez Fernández's book *Disposiciones seguras para proporcionar abasto y baratura de pan en Madrid* (1816) to maintain that "freed trade is a dogma of the science of government" in line with classical liberalism. Experience dictated that consumer welfare resulted from a competitive system without trading restrictions:

> From the beginning, freedom has been followed by competition, competition by abundance, abundance by low prices, and by a reaction that is no less evident, the obstacles imposed on trade [...] harm reproduction, create scarcity, famine, its daughter, and in the last analysis, hinder state prosperity. (CCL, no. 54, 3/X/1817)

Mora recalled that the trading empires of the ancient world were not underlain by hurdles and restrictions. He thus began his ceaseless struggle against the system of "regulations and prohibitions", which was none other than Smith's "mercantile system". To Mora this "system", of which Colbert was a powerful example, following Menghotti's criticism in *Il Colbertismo* (1819; CCL, no. 278, 26/11/1819), was the fruit of the "barbarism" and "feudal anarchy" which had "prevailed until now", with highly pernicious consequences, because it numbed "traders' enterprising spirit" and "destroyed" wealth.[21] According to Mora this "coercive" system had triumphed because of the popular classes' "opinion", such that

[21] CCL (no. 54, 3/X/1817; n. 289, 4/I/1820).

"all the efforts of the Enlightenment and all the endeavour of a wise and vigorous government" (CCL, no. 54, 3/X/1817) were needed to combat it. It is not therefore surprising that the CCL supported the teaching of political economy and used a wide variety of educational formats, including reviews, summaries, dialogues and dictionaries.

Mora's defence of the "freedom system" was derived from his critique of the "mercantile system", particularly in the applications of political economy, although his defence of free trade was sketched out only briefly in the CCL. The idea that low prices were a consequence of competition and abundance evoked Smith's principles of the "natural order of things" and the "natural value" of grain, which should guide the reform of the agricultural market in Spain (CCL, no. 54, 3/X/1817). In a similar vein, Mora used the CCL to echo Smith, Mirabeau, Serionne, Verri, Sismondi, Ganilh, Destutt and Say's ideas on guilds to oppose a well-known speech by Antonio de Capmany, published in defence of these corporate institutions four decades earlier and detailing the reforms that had been put in place while demanding new ones that would boost the freedom of industry (CCL, no. 70, 28/XI/1817). Say's ideas appeared once again in Mora's defence of mechanisation and, perhaps, of savings banks as an instrument for thrift and saving for all social classes, including the poorest, which would foster capital accumulation.[22] Menghotti's work, which Mora recommended be translated into Spanish, also echoed Smith's ideas on the priority of agriculture in capital allocation and for economic development.[23] Mora defended British agriculture in other pieces, probably following Arthur Young. He sometimes argued that agriculture in England was less well-developed than in Scotland due to the greater availability of elementary education in Scotland (CCL, no. 65, 11/XI/1817), while on other occasions he defended the English institutional and fiscal framework; in contrast to the mainstream Enlightenment Spanish tradition, he supported large estates, since only wealthy landowners could bring about agricultural improvements (CCL, no. 234, 25/VI/1819).

A defender of order, progress and legitimacy, the CCL naturally remained within the confines of Ferdinand's absolutism and provided a space in which to echo official reforms. This was particularly clear with regard to Finance Minister Martín de Garay's 1817 fiscal reform.[24] Given

[22] See CCL (no. 68, 21/XI/1817; no. 194, 5/II/1819).
[23] CCL (no. 278, 26/XI/1819; no. 279, 30/XI/1819).
[24] On this reform, see Fontana (1971, 159–71, 305–11).

the chaos that prevailed in the Treasury during the six-year absolutist period—nine ministers were in charge—, Garay's reform was the most important and was singled out for special praise in the CCL.[25] Partly modelled on the 1813 *Cortes de Cádiz* reform, it established a direct tax which was proportional to each taxpayer's income and replaced the Castilian *rentas provinciales*—taxes on consumption and trade—, their equivalents in Aragon and some minor taxes, with the aim of resolving the desperate situation in the state coffers. Wars, the slowdown in economic growth, the relentless increase in public debt and the loss of American trade—and with it the huge flow of precious metals from the Indies—had all combined to bring the Treasury to the brink of bankruptcy.[26] The situation had been deteriorating since its origins in the 1780s and could clearly not be solved via a set of "administrative" reforms aimed at mitigating "the evils without affecting the structure of the social fabric" (Fontana 1979, 27), as a string of Ferdinand VII's governments had sought to do. In fact, Garay's tax reform only complicated the delicate financial situation further: its implementation created great confusion, strong resistance from the wealthy sectors and, which was even more serious, actually reduced tax revenues. It was repealed in mid-1820 at the beginning of the new constitutional period, without ever having been fully implemented.

In short, the CCL was the main vehicle for the spread of economic culture in the press during the *Sexenio Absolutista*. It compares extremely favourably with the other non-official publications of the day such as Burgos' MCA and Olive's MR.[27] The periodical's unique position may also help to explain Mora's membership of the *Sociedad Económica Matritense*, which he joined in early January 1818,[28] two and a half years after Ferdinand VII had restored in June 1815 Carlos III's economic soci-

[25] See opinions in favour of the "new" Treasury system in the CCL (no. 53, 30/IX/1817; no. 67, 18/XI/1817).

[26] Fontana (1971, 1979, 22–30). At the beginning of the nineteenth century, tax revenue from the colonies represented between 40% and 50% of the Crown's total revenue; Marichal (1999).

[27] During absolutism the MCA only published articles on economic statistics and agronomy. Only after the constitutional restoration did it include articles on political economy by Manuel María Gutiérrez (MCA, no. 43, 7/II/1820; no. 44, 9/II/1829; no. 45, 11/II/1820). For its part, the MR only occasionally provided information on supply policy and reviews dedicated to Saint Aubin (1817) and Tracy (1818).

[28] The information on the *Matritense* in this chapter has been provided by Elisa Martín-Valdepeñas. Mora was also a member of the Granada and Cadiz economic societies.

eties, with relative success—there were 27 by 1827—. However, the societies were subject to tight political control, which was upheld by the uniform, censorious and centralising criteria imposed on them by the *Matritense*. Nevertheless, this was only really true in a formal sense, and Mora encountered sectors of the silent opposition to Ferdinand VII there. In fact, although run by recognised absolutists, the *Matritense* became a stronghold for people who were outside the regime, not of course the leading *afrancesados*, who were quickly expelled, but others who were less committed, as well as future prominent liberals in the constitutional period that lay just around the corner.

During the final period of absolutism, the *Matritense* prioritised charitable and educational activities, as well as others aimed at spreading scientific and technical knowledge, and followed a relatively ideology-free pattern. Nevertheless, it was also one of the main centres for the dissemination of economic knowledge in Spain at the time, as it had been in the last decades of eighteenth century. In 1815 the Society even founded a political economy chair, albeit a very short-lived one. Far more important was its role as a key channel for circulating works by Destutt de Tracy and, above all, Say, throughout Spain. Several of Say's translators were members of the *Matritense*, among them Pascual García and Malaga-born Manuel María Gutiérrez, who held the Consulate of Malaga political economy chair; he also translated Tracy and was a supporter of free trade during those years, corresponding with Say himself (Menudo 2015). Inasmuch as Say was the CCL's flagship economist, it is not unreasonable to think that there may have been some coordination between Mora and the liberal nuclei within the *Matritense*, although his own personal involvement in it was very limited.[29] In fact, a good part of the reviews published in the CLL appeared while Mora was a member of the Society.

2.4 Final Remarks

Like the late Enlightenment writers, and perhaps also in tune with liberal sectors in the *Matritense*, Mora used the language of political economy to address "political" issues and outline a set of reforms that unobtrusively

[29] In 1818 he co-authored a report on de Ramón Valdés' traders' handbook (ARSEM, bundle 262/13).

crossed the boundaries of Ferdinand's absolutism, using an ideological framework established by Smith and the periodical's benchmark economist, Say. Nevertheless, the CLL has been accused of spread "bastard" liberalism, being a mouthpiece for the regime and of "fawning over" Ferdinand VII (Pitollet 1909, 55, 65), as well being as a symbol of Mora's "ambiguous and tortuous" political conduct (Amunátegui 1888, 25) at a time, it should be recalled, when the *afrancesados* and *doceañista* liberals were facing harsh treatment and possible exile (Simal 2012, 65ff.). However, Durán (2018, 180–81) has recently argued, with good reason, that being forced to adapt to the censorship of the day did not entail adopting a similar alignment with absolutism. The CCL was a periodical "of order, but not party", and this alone explains how it endured until the new constitutional period dawned, when Mora himself was forced to issue a blunt reminder that the journal's survival "was nothing other than a perpetual struggle with the severity of censorship and the malignity of informers" (*El Constitucional*, no. 363, 6/V/1820, 1). In this sense, Mora's adherence to classical orthodox liberalism gives credibility to his hypothetical links with the underground opposition to absolutism, which included his probable attendance at "meetings of patriots" in Madrid (Gil Novales 2010, II, 2054) but probably did not go as far as the civil resistance organised around Masonic lodges (Carr 1968, 134). All this better explains Mora's emergence among liberal currents, after which, following a series of conspiracies and statements in favour of re-establishing the constitutional regime fuelled by "a mixture of military discontent, frustrated ambition and liberal principles" (Carr 1968, 132) *General* Rafael de Riego triumphantly decreed the Constitution of Cadiz on 1 January 1820, ushering in the Liberal Triennium (1820–1823). In fact, when Mora returned from his diplomatic trip to Europe at the end of 1819, he found that his country was once more operating under a constitutional system (Mellado 1842, V, 543b).

Bibliography

Translations and Reeditions

Chateaubriand, François-René de. 1814. *De Buonaparte y de los Borbones, por F. A. de Chateaubriand. Traducido al castellano por José Joaquín de Mora.* Cadiz: Imprenta de R. Howe.

Primary Sources

Condorcet, Jean-Antoine-Nicolas de Caritat, Marquis of. 1792 *Compendio de la obra inglesa intitulada Riqueza de las naciones, hecho por el Marqués de Condorcet, y traducido al castellano, con varias adiciones del original por don Carlos Martínez de Irujo*. Madrid: Imprenta Real.

Mellado, Francisco de Paula. 1842. "Mora, José Joaquín". In *Diccionario universal de historia y geografía*, vol. V, 543–44. Madrid: Establecimiento Tipográfico.

Smith, Adam. 1794. *Investigación de la causa y la riqueza de las naciones. Obra escrita en inglés por Adam Smith, doctor en leyes*. Valladolid: Viuda e hijos de Santander.

Secondary Sources

Almenar, Salvador. 2014. "The Reception and Dissemination of David Ricardo's Ideas in Spain". In *The Reception of David Ricardo in Continental Europe and Japan*, edited by Gilbert Faccarello y Masashi Izumo, 152–77. London and New York: Routledge.

Amunátegui, Miguel Luis. 1888. *Don José Joaquín de Mora. Apuntes biográficos*. Santiago de Chile: Imprenta Nacional.

Arias de Saavedra, Inmaculada. 2007. "La Universidad de Granada en la época moderna: estudio y estado de la cuestión". In *Universidades hispánicas: modelos territoriales en la Edad Moderna*, edited by Luis Enrique Rodríguez San Pedro, 237–68. Salamanca: Universidad de Salamanca.

Artola, Miguel. 1973. *La burguesía revolucionaria (1808–1869*). Madrid: Alianza.

Astigarraga, Jesús and Juan Zabalza, eds. 2021. *Adam Smith and 'The Wealth of Nations' in Spain. A History of Reception, Dissemination, Adaptation and Application, 1778–1840*. London and New York: Routledge.

Astigarraga, Jesús, Javier Usoz and Juan Zabalza. 2020. "Entre la economía, la política y la opinión pública: el nacimiento de las reseñas económicas en España (1737–1805)". *Revista de estudios políticos* 190, 259–88.

Ausejo, Elena. 2000. "L'émergence de la science dans la fureur absolutiste: la Crónica Científica y Literaria (1817–1820)". Sciences et Techniques en Perspective 4–2, 207–20.

Bustos, Manuel. 2005. *Cádiz en el sistema atlántico. La ciudad, sus comerciantes y la actividad mercantil, 1650–1830*. Madrid: Sílex.

Carr, Raymond. 1968. *España, 1808–1939*. Barcelona: Ariel.

Durán López, Fernando. 2015. *Versiones de un exilio. Los traductores españoles de la Casa Ackermann (Londres, 1823–1830)*. Madrid: Escolar y Mayo.

Durán López, Fernando. 2018. "José Joaquín de Mora contra el romanticismo en la *Crónica científica y literaria* (1817–^#-1820)". In *José Joaquín de Mora o la inconstancia. Periodismo, política y literatura*, edited by Salvador García and Alberto Romero, 179–225. Madrid: Visor.

Fernández Sebastián, Javier. 2012a. "Introducción. En busca de los primeros liberalismos iberoamericanos". In *La aurora de la libertad. Los primeros liberalismos en el mundo iberoamericano*, edited by Javier Fernández Sebastián, 9–35. Madrid: Marcial Pons.

Ferrer del Río, Antonio. 1864. "Necrología. Don José Joaquín de Mora". *La América*, VIII–21 (12/XI/1864), 5–6.

Fontana, Josep. 1971. *La quiebra de la monarquía absoluta, 1814–1820.* Barcelona: Ariel.

Fontana, Josep. 1979. *La crisis del Antiguo Régimen, 1808–1833.* Barcelona: Crítica.

Gil Novales, Alberto. 1975. *Las sociedades patrióticas (1820–1823).* Madrid: Tecnos.

Gil Novales, Alberto. 2010. "Mora, José Joaquín de". In *Diccionario biográfico de España (1808–1833). De los orígenes del liberalismo a la reacción absolutista*, edited by Alberto Gil Novales, vol. II, 2054–57. Madrid: Fundación Mapfre.

González, Carlos. 1961. *Francisco de Paula González Vigil: el precursor, el justo, el maestro.* Lima: Escuela de artes gráficas del Politécnico Nacional Superior José Pardo.

Lluch, Ernest and Salvador Almenar. 2000a. "Difusión e influencia de los economistas clásicos en España (1776–1870)". In *Economía y economistas españoles. Vol. IV. La economía clásica*, edited by Enrique Fuentes, 93–170. Barcelona: Galaxia Gütenberg and Círculo de Lectores.

Marichal, Carlos. 1999. *La bancarrota del Virreinato. Nueva España y las finanzas del imperio español, 1760–1810.* México: FCE.

Medina, Sara. 2022. *José Joaquín de Mora and Britain: Cultural Transfers and Transformations.* Berlin: Peter Lang.

Menudo, José Manuel. 2015. "Correspondencia y economía política en España (1809–1831). La relación epistolar con Jeremy Bentham y Jean-Baptiste Say". *Cuadernos de Ilustración y Romanticismo* 21, 109–20.

Menudo, José Manuel and José María O'Kean. 2019. "Ediciones, reimpresiones y traducciones en español del *Tratado de economía política* de Jean-Baptiste Say". *Revista de historia económica* 37–1, 169–92.

Mesa, José de and Teresa Gisbert. 1965. *José Joaquín de Mora secretario del Mariscal Andrés de Santa Cruz.* La Paz: Academia Nacional de Ciencias de Bolivia.

Monguió, Luis. 1967. *Don José Joaquín de Mora y el Perú del ochocientos.* Madrid: Castalia.

Morán Ortí, Manuel. 1996. *La "Miscelánea" de Javier de Burgos: la prensa en el debate ideológico del Trienio Liberal*. Madrid: Universidad Europea and CEES Ediciones.

Pitollet, Camille. 1909. *La querelle caldéronienne de Johann Nikolas Böhl von Faber et José Joaquín de Mora, réconstituée d'après les documents originaux*. Paris: Félix Alcan.

Simal, Juan Luis. 2012. *Emigrados. España y el exilio internacional, 1814–1843*. Madrid: CEPC.

CHAPTER 3

The Liberal Triennium (1820–1823): Bentham and Radical Liberalism

3.1 A New Institutional and Cultural Framework

In stark contrast to the dreary absolutist period, the almost four years of a constitutional regime, during the Liberal Triennium (1/I/1820–1/X/1823), involved a revitalisation of the political and cultural environment that was both turbulent and tenacious. In March 1820 Cadiz Constitution was restored and accepted by Ferdinand VII, and the *veinteañistas*, also known as "exalted" liberals, took advantage of the new freedoms of assembly, association and the press to create an institutional framework that was more conducive to the spread of knowledge.[1] In 1820 Parliament activated the 1813 *Cortes de Cádiz* decree to breathe new life into the economics societies, but along different lines: the *Matritense*'s central and censorious role was suppressed in favour of a more decentralised model that turned these institutions into agencies for spreading technical and economic knowledge, as well as advising provincial councils and municipalities on educational activities and supporting agriculture.

Even more significant was the creation of new cultural and educational organisations such as the *Ateneo de Madrid*, which was founded in May 1820. This "patriotic and literary" institution brought together Madrid's leading intellectuals and was established with the aim of encouraging

[1] On the politicisation of public space during the Triennium, see, among others, Gil Novales (1980, 76–81) and Rújula and Chust (2020, 42–46).

J. Astigarraga et al., *The Economic Legacy of José Joaquín de Mora*, Palgrave Studies in the History of Economic Thought,
https://doi.org/10.1007/978-3-031-49446-8_3

public education and debate, drawing on the legacy of the Enlightenment. Its founding charter declared that "without public enlightenment there is no true freedom: the constitutional system's consolidation and advancement and the faithful upholding of the new institutions depend first and foremost on this". However, the clearest symbols of the new political climate ushered in by the Spanish revolution of 1820 were the patriotic societies. In the European context as a whole, these were exceptional examples of liberal ideology's penetration of society (Gil Novales 1975) and were possible largely because of the way that this ideology acted as a cohesive force between elites and ordinary people as a result of the acceptance of the egalitarian notion of citizenship. Although they were created along the lines of Enlightenment economics societies, the new institution had grassroots bases, democratic aspirations and a political attitude that was lacking in those. Around 275 were created throughout Spain, and they became the cornerstones for the scrutiny of parliamentary life, the political education of the citizenry, the shaping of public opinion and the spread of constitutional political culture in all major Spanish cities. Lively and dynamic, these spaces embraced Freemasons, the *Carbonari* and other foreign liberal political exiles that were attracted by the reverberations of the Spanish constitutional revolution. The pervasive feeling of excitement increased following the 1822 law, which was far less restrictive than that of 1820, in marked contrast with the mood behind the *Ateneo* doors. Although originally a patriotic society, the *Ateneo* soon became a closed elitist institution, which was controlled by liberal parliamentary elites to encourage education, political debate and literary pursuits. The institution founded ten chairs in disciplines that had been rejected under absolutism, including natural law, ideology and political economy, and attracted around five hundred students (Gil Novales 1986; Labra 1878, 26–37). The political economy initiative was a further symbol of the firm liberal commitment to consolidating the discipline's place in formal education. Caballero's 1807 education plan, which had been aborted by the War of Independence, was recovered, soon to be followed by a new state education plan (1821). Economics and statistics teaching in university law and philosophy faculties began to flourish as a result of these actions, and several previous attempts to establish chairs in the disciplines in economics societies (Madrid and Seville) and trade consulates were revived (Barcelona and Malaga; Martín Rodríguez 1989).

A further aspect that illustrates the elation in the public sphere during the Liberal Triennium was the increase in publishing initiatives. *La*

Periodicomanía (LPM, 1820–1821), one of the newspapers with the largest readership, referred to this as follows: "The Constitution has left us jobless; it is essential to find another trade: none seems better to us than that of writer" (LPM, no. 1, 5). This was reflected in the revival of an Enlightenment tradition, which was the translating of texts. Some were by authors that had been well-known in the closing decades of the eighteenth century but were still unpublished in Spain (Verri, Schmid d'Avenstein, Montesquieu, d'Holbach and Condorcet), while others were new censorship-free versions of works by previously translated writers (Filangieri, Beccaria and Mably) and the latest wave of authors (Tracy, Sismondi and Bentham).

The most prominent symbol of the new desire to inform was the press. To a great extent there was a rekindling of events that took place during the War of Independence, when newspapers and journals had become overtaken the Church and political powers as powerful creators of public opinion. Although no specialised economics press emerged, political and cultural publications assiduously carried information on political economy, a field that was by no means marginal although still lacking rigorous study. Freedom of the press laws in March 1820 and February 1822 led to an extraordinary boom in newspapers and journals, with hundreds of titles bearing witness to this *periódico-manía*,[2] which was even more intense in the provinces than Madrid: although the capital enjoyed the largest print runs, it only accounted for a third of new ventures. The press faithfully reflected the hotbed of political activity fuelled by Riego's uprising, as a result of which the sector shifted away from political power, focussing instead on the ideological pluralism inherited from the Enlightenment and Cadiz constitutionalism and establishing a new relationship with its readership, essentially relying on subscriptions and direct sales.[3] The emergence of political factions was a crucial factor.[4] Absolutist and *afrancesados* groups, who had distrusted the 1812 Constitution for being too radical, lingered on during the Liberal Triennium; at the same time, a split in the liberal front between the "moderate" *doceañistas* and the "radical"

[2] The term *periódico-manía* refers to the widespread interest in publishing journals According to Gil Novales (1975, II, 983–1047) there were 689 titles. After a painstaking "expurgation", Fuentes (1994, 167–68) cut this down to 345. On the press during the Liberal Triennium, see also Larriba (2020).

[3] Estimated daily newspaper sales in Madrid fluctuated between 1500 and 10,000 (Fuentes 1994).

[4] See Zavala (1971, 45–55), Gil Novales (1980) and Rújula and Chust (2020).

veinteañistas, began to take hold, with the latter tending to gain power at the expense of the former (Gil Novales 1975, II, 985). The press's impact was also magnified by the spread of reading groups, patriotic societies— under whose auspices some 31 newspapers were founded— and "talk clubs", where reading together was a popular activity.

3.2 Mora during the First Stage of the Liberal Triennium

Mora wasted no time in making the most of the new opportunities for participating in public life opened up by the Spanish revolution of 1820. Free from the constraints of having taken part in the *Cortes de Cádiz* alongside the *doceañista* liberals, and with an indisputable leading role as an opinion-former, he rubbed shoulders with the senior politicians, parliamentarians and journalists with whom he would later share his exile in London. His rapid immersion in public life is clear from his translations of Bentham (1820) and d'Holbach (1823), among others, and his participation in various patriotic societies, in particular the *Café de Malta o Amigos de la Constitución* (Gil Novales 1975, I, 94–102) and the *Ateneo de Madrid*, of which he was a founder and teacher; it was here that he presented his translation of Bentham and taught natural law (Gil Novales 1986; Ruiz Salvador 1971, 26–27). However, along with the other cultural mediators of the day, his main watchtower was the press. Since the headings and articles were usually published anonymously, it is not easy to find out which journalistic undertakings Mora was involved in. Gil Novales (2010, II, 2054) is the main guide to this.

Between 1820 and 1823 Mora immersed himself fully in journalism in Madrid, playing a major role in the radical transformation of the press: eighteen newspapers were founded in the three weeks after Ferdinand VII swore to uphold the Cadiz Constitution in March 1820 (Larriba 2020, 190–91), one of them, *El Constitucional* (1820), published by Mora. He soon began publishing *La Minerva Nacional* (1820) and *La Arlequina diplomática* (1820) and edited *El Eco de Padilla* (1821); he wrote for *La Antorcha española* (1821), *El Independiente* (1822), *El Patriota español* (1822), *El Tribuno* (1822) and *El Indicador* (1822–1823), as well as collaborating on *El redactor español*, according to the journalist Mesonero

Romanos.[5] As his contemporaries noted, the intensity of this activity reflects Mora's heightened sense of political opportunity and his excellent skills as a journalist, but also the brief lives of most of the titles.

The longest-lived newspaper was *El Constitucional, o sea Crónica científica, literaria y política* (EC, 1820), which was in fact a continuation of the CCL.[6] Although it had become a daily instead of a biweekly, the same numerical sequence and format were used. Nonetheless, the addition of "political" to the title was a far from trivial change and emphasised "constitutional" commitment. In fact, the EC was the best representation of the politicisation of the few unofficial newspapers to emerge from Ferdinand's absolutism. It was a digest containing theoretical articles on political issues and events, reports from the *Cortes* —which were soon removed to prevent "reader fatigue"— and national and international news, and was more open to the Hispanic-American world than the CCL had ever been. However, as an enemy of the *afrancesado* and moderate centrist newspapers such as Javier de Burgos' MCA, which had also a newly acquired "political" orientation, the EC grew more radical in its support for "exalted" liberal ideas, in line with the ups and downs in Mora's own life. In June 1820 he was sanctioned for using allegedly insulting words against Madrid City Council, and at the end of the same year he was involved in the uproar —almost a riot— surrounding the *Café de Malta* cause and was imprisoned for almost two months (Gil Novales 1975, I, 591–595), which is why the newspaper ceased publication on 31 December 1820. Mora then joined the staff of *El Constitucional. Correo general de Madrid* (ECM, 1821), which he edited from March to June 1821; broadly similar to the EC, the ECM positioned itself at the end of the spectrum of radical titles, declaring its aim to be "focussing public opinion on its true interests".[7]

The EC's international outlook was made crystal clear in one of its first reviews, which discussed Madame de Stäel's *De l'esprit des traductions* (1816). Mora's later pieces clearly demonstrated his membership of the European liberal intellectual network, together with the Spaniards who

[5] All these newspapers have been consulted except for *El patriota español*, *La antorcha española* and *El redactor español*, the whereabouts of which are unknown.

[6] Also collaborating with Mora were literary and diplomatic figures like Agustín de Letamendi and the Mexican Manuel Eduardo de Gorostiza —who signed the paper's introduction and may have been editor for the first two months— and also perhaps Félix Mejía.

[7] In the meantime, Mora participated in the publishing of *La arlequina diplomática* (LAD, 1820), a short-lived satire of the training and selection of diplomats and statesmen.

were in exile in London during the *Sexenio Absolutista* and with whom he already had connections. The EC was a striking departure from the CCL. Its pages were filled with authors such as Constant, Dumont, Filangieri, Tracy, Bentham and Say, from whom personal letters were published. It was thus light years away from the narrow confines of the CCL, and closer to the landmark *El Español* (EE, 1810–1814), the Anglophile monthly founded in London in 1810 by Mora's friend Blanco White, whose EE pseudonym was *Juan sin Tierra*. The paper focussed on respect for constitutional culture—the British Constitution, not the Spanish—, the rights of man, anti-slavery, the independence of the Spanish colonies and free trade with them.[8] In short, when he arrived in London Mora did not have to wait long to become part of a great transnational intellectual and militant movement aimed at replacing the old despotic and arbitrary regimes with new constitutional representative governments.

Although it had a variety of sources, Bentham was the EC's leading light. In fact, his work had appeared in the CCL, albeit very sporadically —a piece on establishing criminal colonies, for example (CCL, no. 198, 19/II/1819)—; Blanco White's EE had also published his writings on a more frequent basis some years earlier.[9] The fact that Tracy's sensualism and Bentham's utilitarianism began to feature regularly in Spanish universities during the years of the Liberal Triennium is not simply anecdotal (Garrorena 1974, 510). According to the publisher Mellado (1842, V, 543b), thanks to the CCL Mora had embarked on a "close relationship" with the "learned" Bentham, who he also described as "my teacher". However, this relationship is more likely to have taken shape before. When the newspaper first appeared, Mora had already established personal relationships with two restless Benthamite advocates, John Bowring in 1819 and Edward Blanquiere a year later, who were both deeply committed to

[8] Other prominent exiles collaborated on the EE, such as Martínez de la Rosa and Flórez Estrada.

[9] EE (no. VI, 30/IX/1810; no. 46, III/IV/1814.) Utilitarian principles found an echo in the periodical not only through Bentham, but also through the lengthy summaries published in 1813 and 1814 of the work of William Paley, who adapted the utilitarian approach to the treatment of theology. While in exile in London years later, Mora himself began to translate Paley's *Natural Theology* (1802), which finally was published by a clergyman: Joaquín Lorenzo Villanueva (Llorens 1968, 160–61). We may speculate that the publisher may have, for appearance's sake, reassigned the translation to a man of more respectable religious views (Trease 1953, 30). However, Mora later that Paley's work was published, did not stand up to comparison with those by moralists Locke, Stewart and Grocio, among others (*El mercurio chileno*, no. 14, 15/5/1829).

the Spanish Revolution of 1820. It was through them, in the late summer of 1820, that Mora began his correspondence with Bentham,[10] who had a "very favourable opinion" of Mora and chose him as a prime vehicle for influencing Spain (Conway 1989, 116, 180) and triggered the growing interest in Britain which would culminate in his exile in London. Indeed, Mora played a decisive role in the fact that Bentham became "one of the holy men of liberalism" in Madrid, where he was named honorary associate of the *Sociedad Patriotica de Amigos de Cruz de Malta* (Gil Novales 1975, I, 101) and also helped to fund the EC.[11] This all came about when Bentham's constitutional and legal principles were beginning to spread rapidly in Spain via translations, following Blanco White's example. Although the new versions published by the nucleus of university law teachers Ramón de Salas and Toribio Núñez in Salamanca at the beginning of the Liberal Triennium (1820–1821) played a major role in this process,[12] it was Mora that was most active in spreading throughout Spain the numerous writings in which Bentham raised his criticisms of the Cadiz Constitution, defended the freedom of the colonies and, more generally, tried to influence the fortunes of both Spanish and Portuguese constitutionalism (Bentham 2012). It should not be forgotten that Mora himself addressed the Spanish *Cortes* in 1820 to convey Bentham's offer to draw up a code that was worthy of the "century's luminaries".[13] Nonetheless, his reading of Bentham's extensive work was selective, only sometimes consistent and conditioned by the demands of the Spanish context.

Mora's many educational and translating activities reflected his affinity with Bentham. He taught a natural law course at the *Ateneo* in which he gave an account of Burlamaqui with "corrections taken from Bentham's works" (EC, no. 593, 22/XII/1820), describing Bentham as "the newest and most original writer of all those who have dealt with legislative matters", building "the whole edifice of positive laws on those two cornerstones (pain and pleasure)" (Mora 1821, 19). In the same year he translated the pamphlet *Consejos que dirige a las Cortes y al pueblo español*

[10] Other distinguished Spanish liberals, as Agustín Argüelles, Antonio Alcalá Galiano or Toribio Núñez, were among Bentham's correspondents. About four dozen letters he exchanged with Mora between 1820 and 1823 are known (see Conway 1989, 1994). Full details of the relationship between the two, including Bentham's dispatch to Mora of many of his writings, can be found in Medina (2022, 70–87).

[11] Schwartz (1976, 48–49), Schwartz and Rodríguez (1983) and Menudo (2015).

[12] Schwartz (1976, 42–47) and Robledo (2014, 204ff., 241ff.).

[13] *Diario de sesiones de las Cortes* (DSC), 24/X/1820.

(Bentham 1820),[14] which enjoyed a remarkable circulation: it was not only read at the *Café de Malta* and the *Ateneo* but also brought in the *Cortes* in August 1820. The purpose of the pamphlet, which was finally fulfilled, was to stopping the *Plan de Cámaras* which aimed to change the 1812 Constitution to establish an unelected second chamber of aristocrats, as moderate liberals intended.[15] According to Bentham himself, that year Mora started translating *On the Liberty of the Press, and Public Discussion* (1820; Bentham 2012), in which the author criticised the restrictions on the freedom of the press and freedom of assembly put in place by the *Cortes* in 1820, but the work was left unfinished due to Mora's imprisonment in December (Bentham 1821, 9; 2012). During final stage of the Liberal Triennium, Mora, was also translating Bentham's anticolonialist pamphlet *Rid Yourselves of Ultramarina* (1821),[16] but was again prevented from completing it by the fall of the liberal regime (Schwartz and Rodríguez 1983, 60).

Mora meanwhile transformed the EC into a mouthpiece for Bentham and utilitarianism, publishing reviews of Étienne Dumont's French translations of his treatises on legislation, the main way for the coming to Spain of this work before Toribio Núñez's Spanish version was spread across the country (EC, no. 498, 18/IX/1820; no. 570, 29/XI/1820). He also published a letter written by Bentham in which he tried to influence the Spanish *Cortes*' legislative activity (EC, no. 510, 30/IX/1820). In another piece Bentham was presented to readers as a defender of patriotic societies, an EC "collaborator" and the writer who "most worthily upholds the glory, which he was able to acquire in the most important science, the legacy of Blackstone and Hume" (EC, no. 498, 18/IX/1820). Mora

[14] The original was *Letter to the Spanish Nation on a Then Proposed House of Lords* (1820; Bentham 2012) and came into Mora's hands through Blanquiere. Bentham's writing rebutted the view in favour of the setting up such a second chamber by a very influential authority among Spanish liberals: Lord Holland.

[15] In defence of the single-chamber system, Bentham's pamphlet warned that the British constitutional system was a good example of the ills produced by "the coalition of the few who command against the many who obey" (Bentham 1820, 9) and, by no means, a good model for Spain. Bentham preferred the Cadiz Constitution to the British constitution, but he considered the former "a mixture of arsenic and sugar" and was highly critical of the treatment of the colonies and the *Cortes*' weakness vis-à-vis the power of the executive (Fernández Sarasola 2012, 15–17). Mora's translation was reviewed in the EC (no. 467, 18/VIII/1820).

[16] Bentham sent Mora his pamphlet in 1822. By then, Mora had already made clear to him his support for the independence of the Spanish colonies (Conway 1994, 126, 153).

reaffirmed the usefulness of his treatises as guides to the legislative codes that the Spanish *Cortes* were beginning to devise in favour of publicity in the courts and written codes, among other issues. Inspired by Bentham he stated that Spain should construct a complete body of laws in which "nothing but reason and the greatest happiness of the greatest number would prevail" (EC, no. 525, 15/X/1820). Bentham's influence had been discernible from the early days of the Liberal Triennium and came about because of the need to find a liberal philosophy that would serve as a foundation for the new political situation and furnish an alternative to the legacy of the late Enlightenment. Based on the dichotomy between the historical —or "gothic"— and the *iusrationalist* constitution, this was accompanied by the arrival in Spain of the constitutionalism that emerged from the French Revolution (Fernández Sarasola 2015). In contrast to both, Bentham's empirical route facilitated the construction of a practical utilitarianism-based liberalism and its embodiment in a positive legal system that would be capable of combatting the abstract approaches of rationalist idealism, to which the Cadiz Constitution was no stranger (Garrorena 1974, 416ff.).

The EC also continued to spread Tracy's *Idéologues*. These had emerged in the CCL as further recurring guides to founding constitutional principles, although their importance waned when Mora began a long-lasting attachment to the philosophy of the Scottish school of Common Sense, which was based at the University of Edinburgh and was far removed from the sensualism characterising the *Idéologues*. His chosen vehicle was the "*Historia compendiosa de las ciencias metafísicas, morales y políticas*", which was probably an allusion to the *Elements of Philosophy* (1792–1827, 3 vols.) by Hutcheson and Smith's disciple Dugald Stewart; Mora was familiar with the French translation and advised translating it into Spanish in order to improve the poor quality of Spanish philosophy faculties (EC, no. 575, 4/XII/1820). At the same time, in other issues that underlined his debt to Enlightenment culture, Mora published a review of the translation of Condorcet's *Esquisse d'un tableau historique de l'esprit humaine* (1795; EC, no. 435, 17/VII/1820) and a review of the Spanish translations of works by d'Holbach and Saint Lambert,[17] recommending the latter's *Principes des moeurs chez toutes les nations* (1798) for teaching purposes and praising its popularising value. D'Holbach's work —the 1812 Spanish

[17] EC (no. 435, 17/VII/1820). It was written by Manuel Díaz Moreno, secretary of the *Cinco Gremios de Madrid*.

translation of *La morale universelle* (1776), which was reprinted in 1821—was more important, given that Mora translated his *Essai sur les préjuges* (1770) towards the end of the Liberal Triennium.

The EC showed more interest in economics than the CCL and the first article on the subject—"*Subió el pan y murmuró el pueblo*"— reinforced the idea that the discipline was still in its tyro stages. Proof of this was the social discontent created by the rise in the price of bread, which was in reality due to ordinary concerns: "to reason it is not necessary to have read Say, Smith or Genovesi, and simple reasoning is enough to lessen the terrors that the rise in bread prices inspire, when it is the inevitable course of cause and effect" (EC, no. 408, 20/VI/1820). Not unsurprisingly, therefore, the EC made the boundaries between political economy, statistics and political arithmetic very plain,[18] and repeated information on the economics chairs founded during the Liberal Triennium.

A further note, enlighteningly headed "*Del influjo de las ideas liberales en la economía política*", emphasised that representative democracy and the constitutional system were the best framework for developing the ideas of classically rooted political economy, on the basis of individual interest and a pared-down state that did not hinder the exercise of that interest:

> if establishing a constitutional regime such as ours does not raise economic theory to the highest possible degree of perfection, we will have to grasp the harsh reality of forever circling around partial improvements and paltry results. (EC, no. 541, 31/X/1820)

Mora presented the purported "minimum state" in the United States of America as a model, expressing a preference for local government and fewer civil servants, only those "absolutely necessary to preserve order"; following Smith, he treated them as "unproductive wage earners" (EC, no. 541, 31/X/1820).

The EC acted as a powerful sounding board for the liberal reforms triggered by the constitutional *Cortes.* They were hampered by the delicate situation at the Treasury, as well as by the scant monetary and fiscal reforms undertaken,[19] which were largely the consequence of the instable political

[18] EC (no. 534, 24/X/1820). The author of the original text was Gonzalo de Luna.

[19] On these reforms see Moral (1975); on the presence of Smithian liberalism in the Liberal Triennium *Cortes*, see Zabalza (2022).

climate: there were four different governments in barely four years. This was due to a number of factors, mainly fragmentation among the liberal sectors and the extreme division of powers between the legislative —the *Cortes*— and the executive, which was a result of the fact that so many powers were in the hands of the monarch: the Cadiz Constitution's main flaw, according to Varela (1996). Even so, the EC reverberated with acrimonious parliamentary discussions about the policy of borrowing using disentailed church property, a fruitless attempt to balance the books and address the enormous public debt, which only increased even more during those years (Fontana 1979, 32–33). Although the budgets were approved in parliament for the first time during the Liberal Triennium and had liberal tendencies thanks to Finance Minister José Canga Argüelles, poor foresight forced the *Cortes* to pass an extraordinary budget in December 1822 (Beltrán 1977, 181–89).

The reviews in Mora's journal covered numerous Spanish works. Some were devoted to landmark late Enlightenment publications —a clear example is *Pan y toros* (c.1797), a seditious pamphlet attributed to León de Arroyal which criticised "decrepit and superstitious" Spain—, but most were by-products of activity in the *Cortes.* In the economic sphere the *Cortes* rounded off and expanded on Cadiz parliamentary decisions, abolishing seigneuries and entailed estates, carrying out expropriations, reducing tithes and redistributing common land and wastelands. In a review of the anonymous *Discurso sobre señoríos territoriales* (Madrid, 1820) the EC opposed seigneuries and endorsed parliamentary legislation on them (EC, no. 421, 4/VII/1820). A further review dedicated to Juan Laviano's *Memoria sobre la renta del tabaco* (Madrid, 1820) advocated abolishing the state-run tobacconists and supported the freedom to plant tobacco, as well as the liberalisation of associated land and its free distribution (EC, no. 483, 3/IX/1820). José Vasconi's commentary on the *Memoria sobre el sistema de contribuciones* (Madrid, 1820) recalled previous attempts to introduce direct taxation (1813 and 1817), arguing that this was essential if the Spanish Treasury were to balance its books (EC, no. 525, 25/IX/1820). The commentary on the *Memoria sobre el empréstito solicitado por el Ministro de Hacienda* (1820) ratified its anonymous author's opinion about public debt; in view of the lack of revenue from America, it proposed activating paper money and adapting state expenditure to revenue, and there were further echoes of the distrust of civil servants and the example of the United States government (EC, no. 467, 18/VIII/1820). The EC review of the *Memoria sobre los males que sufre el comercio español*

(Cadiz, 1820), the work of a group of Cadiz merchants, was incomplete but echoed the work's proposal for lower taxes on internal and American trade and establishing a 15% maximum tariff in the face of protectionism (EC, no. 602, 31/XII/1820). Gonzalo de Luna's commentary on the unique version of the WN published in 1819–1820 took a less mainstream line; despite its proximity to the "mercantile system", the EC praised the work for having applied Smith's principles to Spanish reality (EC, no. 544, 3/XI/1820). These reviews clearly showed the EC's affiliation with liberal-leaning reforms with a theoretical background of classical economics.

The EC also carried reviews of foreign works by authors such as Chaptal and Say. The most noteworthy was devoted to Say's *Lettres à M. Malthus* (1820) and included his criticisms of Sismondi and Malthus in defence of Say's law (EC, no. 507, 28/IX/1820; no. 521, 11/X/1820). Mora began his hallmark defence of free trade there, for the very reason that on 5 October 1820 the *Cortes* approved a prohibitionist tariff.[20] The *Cortes* ignored the opinion of future Finance Minister Canga Argüelles, who expressly quoted Smith in support of less harsh customs legislation, and instead followed the more rigid criteria adopted by the 1816 *Junta Especial de Aranceles.* Although the legislation ostensibly set moderate duties — maximum *ad valorem* rates of 30% for imports and 10% for exports— and included numerous technical improvements, it was in fact more prohibitionist than protectionist. The decision came on top of a decree banning grain imports that had been passed two months earlier. Both measures aimed to make the interests of agricultural regions —Castile, Extremadura and Andalusia— compatible with those of manufacturing regions — Catalonia—. Nevertheless, Mora immediately placed his publication at the service of stances opposing strict and absolute prohibitionism, following the views expressed in the *Cortes* by influential parliamentarians such as Flórez Estrada, the Conde de Toreno, Vadillo and Martínez de la Rosa.[21] He thus became part of the first generation in Spain to defend free trade; Flórez Estrada, Pebrer and Vadillo were already prominent leaders and their viewpoints reached a wider audience as Say's influence spread. In November 1821 the EC printed a brief note to the effect that the prohibitive system both harmed national manufacturing and encouraged smuggling, and it also carried a long review of an anonymous work that set out

[20] On this issue, see Comín (2000a, 639).

[21] See the DSC 1820, especially 19 and 31/IX, 24/X and 6/XI.

a more systematic critique of the high tariff regime. The trade war against England showed that the "mercantile system" was not only contrary to the principle of comparative advantage, but also stifled international trade as a whole, which harmed the working classes above all. England should therefore waive its Navigation Acts and high levels of customs protection, which would result in a multilateral lowering of tariffs. Domestic industry that needed high tariffs to survive should shift its capital to other sectors so as not to encourage smuggling. These arguments were all based on the defence of free trade, with Say as the only author cited, and also included criticisms of the prohibitions put in place by the *Cortes* in November 1820 to boost the Catalan textile industry, in line with the *Barcelona Junta de Comercio*'s traditional protectionist interests.[22] In short, it was necessary to "establish trade on its natural basis, which is each country's freedom to mutually exchange the products and articles of its particular industry" (EC, no. 564, 23/XI/1820).

In addition to its preference for free trade the EC prioritised agriculture as a sector for the use of capital. Improving agriculture required government action, dividing up large holdings and spreading agronomic innovations.[23] The paper therefore sought a strategy to develop agriculture and free trade following Spain's most distinguished liberal economists of the day such as Canga Argüelles and Flórez Estrada,[24] who put forward the most refined analysis. However, there is no trace of this strategy in the *Correo general de Madrid* (CGM, 1821), the short-lived journal that replaced the EC and kept Mora busy in May and June 1821 —however, it carried several articles opposing the slave trade—.[25]

A year prior to these events, when the EC's circulation was at its peak, Mora had founded *La minerva española* (LME). The significance of this new initiative lay not in its life span, which was also brief—four booklets, between May and July 1820—, but its potential readership —its

[22] EC (no. 564, 23/XI/1820; no. 565, 24/XI/1820; no. 569, 28/XI/1820). On the dominance of "industrial prohibitionism" in Catalonia, which *maître à penser* was Jaumeandreu (1816, 1836), see Lluch (1973, 211ff.).

[23] EC (no. 551, 10/XI/1820; no. 554, 13/XI/1820; no. 564, 23/XI/1820).

[24] Almenar (1976, 2000b, 380–83); Lluch and Almenar (2000, 104ff.). This agriculturalist approach, rooted in the late Spanish Enlightenment, conditioned the identity of early Spanish liberalism, including that inspired by Smith (Astigarraga et al. 2022b, 121–37).

[25] The CGM is relatively unimportant from this study's perspective of. A faithful mouthpiece for parliamentary discussions on issues such as tobacco taxation and land tax, it carried reviews of works by Mariano Amadori and Canga Argüelles.

moralising perspective was aimed at Spanish rulers— and its format, which was a departure from the tried and tested EC and CGM format. The LME was organised around short essays, which the other two papers did not carry and that aimed to "bolster public spirit on the path of the new institutions".[26] While not doubting the usefulness of "everyday papers", Mora felt that these "fleeting and light publications" could not be the setting for a "sustained and erudite discussion [...] indispensable when issues that embrace all that is most precious and sacred in society are raised".[27]

The LME was modelled on *La minerve française* (LMF, 1818–1820) and many of its articles in were taken from the latter's nine volumes, including the half dozen with economic content, which Mora adapted to circumstances in Spain. The LME continued to publicise Bentham's work and paid closer attention to Britain, while at the same time anticipating Mora's proposal for a work on "unlimited free trade" following parliament's approval of the 1820 tariff measures. Two articles dealt with the subject, both opposing the "yoke of English economic power", which was based on prohibitive laws with which Britain had "declared war on mankind", creating a monopoly that concentrated wealth in the hands of a few.[28] While one article proposed drafting a free trade agreement,[29] the other outlined a set of economic regulations for a constitutional regime. In addition to rejecting prohibitive laws and monopolies, the regulations were to tackle the clergy's privileges, the unequal distribution of wealth, the opaqueness of state finances, the complex structure of state revenue and excessive public spending that required too many government bureaucrats.[30] It was the last issue that defined Mora's position on state borrowing: borrowing had to be at moderate levels in a constitutional system, as it answered to the inalienable moral principles of certainty, prudence and trust.[31] The LME also provided Mora with his struggle against slavery.[32] This was linked to a rejection of the Spanish colonial system and part of

[26] "Prospecto a La Minerva Española" (LME, 1821, 1/IV/1820).

[27] "Prospecto..." (LME, 1821, 1/IV/1820).

[28] "Sobre las causas del estado actual de Inglaterra" (LME, 1821, 132–45); "Bases de un sistema económico de un pueblo libre y representado" (LME, 1821, 158–73).

[29] "Economía política. Proyecto de un tratado de comercio" (LME, 1821, 26–44).

[30] "Bases de un sistema económico..." (LME, 1821, 158–73).

[31] "Del crédito público" (LME, 1821, 249–60).

[32] "Del tráfico y de la esclavitud de los negros y de los blancos" (LME, 1821, 341–66). It was a review of Henri Gregoire's well-known book: *De la traite et de l'esclavage des noirs et des blancs* (1815).

the incipient process of the creation of the new Hispanic-American republics, and which he would later reinforce in exile in London. At the same time, Mora never rigorously analysed the reasons for the old colonies' independence but he did put forward his main explanation in the LME: the Spanish colonial system was not only "an outrage against nature",[33] but was "absurd and unjust" and should therefore "collapse beneath its own weight, and has in fact done so" (LME, 1821, 21). Mora's stance here appears close to Blanco White's, who he deemed a pioneer in the defence of the emancipation of the Americas.

3.3 Mora during the Second Stage of the Liberal Triennium

As previously noted, the fortunes of the press were affected by the split in the liberal front between moderate and radical sectors as the Liberal Triennium unfolded. The division was partly tactical but also reflected deep differences over the scope of the Constitution, as well as differing views of the historical narrative due to the radicals' tendency to make use of the "liberal" heroes of bygone days (Fernández Sebastián 2012b, 276–82). In the air since April 1820, the Royal Guard's failed absolutist uprising in July 1822 tipped the balance in favour of the radicals, who transformed many patriotic societies into political *juntas*; almost in parallel with the *Cortes*, these demanded that the monarch's powers be reduced, political freedom broadened and liberal institutions put in place without delay.[34] From that moment on the conservative press ceded its primacy to the more radical sector, especially in Madrid (Fuentes 1994, 169–79). The latter, meanwhile, reflected the internal divisions among the Freemasons and other secret societies, which witnessed the creation of the *Confederación de los comuneros o hijos de Padilla* as a radical political movement, akin to the Italian *Carbonari* although, unlike them, they were not republicans. The *Confederación* imitated popular, satirical and scathing political vocabulary, had a grassroots base —in their egalitarian sense, they somehow resembled the Jacobin clubs and the French *sans-culottes* (Zavala 1971, 67–92)— and their own mouthpieces such as *La Tercerola* (LT, 1822) or *El Zurriago* (EZ, 1821–1823). Mora played no part in these, but he was involved in three similar if rather less radical newspapers: *El eco de Padilla*

[33] LME (1821, 355).

[34] See Zavala (1971, 45–55) and Gil Novales (1980, 56ff.).

(EDP, 1821), *El independiente* (EID, 1822) and *El indicador de los espectáculos y del buen gusto* (EI, 1822). Although this meant distancing himself from Bentham's cautious reformism, which opposed revolution and social upheaval, Mora nevertheless continued to invoke his principles.

Despite its short-lived existence, the EDP did contribute to the ideological shaping of the radical currents.[35] During the first two months its defining feature was theoretical articles defending the constitutional regime and representative system, in which Mora cited Mably, Montesquieu and the contractualist principles of natural law, albeit once again tinged by Bentham's utilitarianism. The paper's radical approach was clear from both its condemnation of tyranny, which led it to delve into the anti-despot roots of old Spanish constitutions, and its economic content. Its pages bristled with harsh criticism of the nobility and the Church for their ownership of huge swathes of land, as well as state monopolies and high taxes. However, its most important contribution was a series of four issues in which Mora laid out a theoretical basis for his free trade doctrine for the first time, beyond the antecedents in the EC and LME.[36] His aim was to continue to influence the tariff debate in the *Cortes*, and he relied on José Manuel de Vadillo, a free trade parliamentarian who was also from Cadiz, to insist that "*laissez faire* [...] is true political economy and the only basis for trade legislation". Mora's defence of the fusing of economic and political freedoms seemed to be aimed at the radical factions: the former —free trade included— were one more component of the system of political liberties, "which we have brought to such a high degree of perfection" and should therefore be raised to the same level. Moreover, since the main beneficiaries of free trade would be consumers, or most of the population, reforming the tariff system was doubly justified (EDP, no. 97, 5/XI/1821).

Mora's pro-free trade contributions included a short piece by Vadillo (1821).[37] He showed that tariffs achieved none of their objectives: they

[35] The paper's name recalled the old Castilian warrior Juan Padilla. It included a range of articles to guide government action, for example, a "*Bosquejo de las cualidades que debe tener un ministro de Hacienda*"; EDP (no. 13, 13/VIII/1821).

[36] EDP (no. 31, 1/IX/1821; no. 38, 7/IX/1821; no. 45, 14/IX/1821; no. 50, 19/IX/1821).

[37] However, by the time he wrote his articles, John Bowring had probably already published Bentham's pamphlet "*Observations on the Restrictive and Prohibitory Commercial System*" (1821), which contained a harsh diatribe against Spain's 1820 Tariff.

did not increase tax revenue since they restricted economic activity; they did not prevent the outflow of precious metals, which were always hoarded by industrial countries, and finally, far from boosting "infant industry", they encouraged smuggling and discouraged private producers. In short, in contrast to the "gothic economists", Mora supported "almost unrestricted freedom in foreign trade", the only framework to respect the natural order of the destination of capital, along with self-interest, which was in itself sufficient to "spur men on". Together with reduced tariff rates, stimulating the economy also required cutting public spending, in line with the principles of classical orthodoxy (EDP, no. 96, 4/IX/1821). However, at the same time as the EDP defended these ideas, for the first time it introduced a topic that would frequently appear in Mora's future writings and which contradicted these principles: the creation of a free port in Spain, specifically in Cadiz.[38]

In late 1821, after five months of activity, the EDP underwent certain changes, which resulted in the creation of EID and *El Tribuno* (ET, 1822) among other titles. The EID was the only publication to carry information about economics,[39] and while it continued its pro-free trade propaganda (EID, no. 55, 24/II/1822) the economic content essentially referenced just two names: Bentham and Constant. Bentham's name now appeared in connection with the drafting of the 1822 Penal Code, whose articles and lengthy parliamentary discussions took up a good part of the EID's content. It was not by chance, then, that the paper published a review of Volume I of the *Cartas de Jeremías Bentham, al señor Conde de Toreno sobre el proyecto de Código Penal presentado a las Cortes* (1821), which praised his acerbic and detailed critique of the Code.[40] However, it was actually Constant that was responsible for the paper's longest and most noteworthy review: an analysis of *De la liberté des anciens comparée à celle*

[38] EDP (no. 195, 13/XI/1821). The suggestion tacitly invoked the example of Livorno, which Mora had visited.

[39] The ET barely went beyond the confines of reports from the *Cortes* and parliamentary debates and lacked relevant economic content.

[40] EID (no. 48, 17/II/1822). The pamphlet contained only three of Bentham's six letters (2012). In view of the large number of shortcomings Mora found, Bentham offered to draft an entirely new Code (Bentham 2012). In additional writings he criticised the laws passed during the Liberal Triennium on the limiting of press freedom and the possible suppression of patriotic societies (Bentham 1821, 10).

des modernes (1819).[41] The EID endorsed Constant's theories: not only was there a real gap between the freedom of "ancient" and "modern" peoples, but the latter were superior, and this was identified with the emergence of more civilised peoples on the basis of private property ownership, sturdy trade and industrial structures.

Mora's contribution to the radical press included the EI as well as the EDP and EID. His association with the EI began in September 1822 after the failed July absolutist uprising, when the EI ceased to focus on arts and entertainment and took on a strong political slant, going on to become the unofficial mouthpiece of the *Sociedad Landaburiana* a month later.[42] The periodical featured a range of information on political economy and an initial note advised imitating England in applying the principle of freedom of work, the main source of the country's wealth. Montesquieu's idea that land "is not cultivated because of its fertility, but because of its freedom" was cited as a "compendium" of political economy (EI, no. 153, 7/X/1822). A subsequent note defended the official wasteland redistribution policy because "the sharing out of property is as favourable to population increase as its accumulation in a few hands is disastrous", referencing Malthus' "famous sophisms" on the tendency to overpopulation (EI, no. 200, 20 /XI/1822). The paper also published three reviews of works by Pecchio, Owen and Filangieri.[43] The second, previously reviewed in CCL, was the most significant in terms of its departure from the classical orthodoxy that Mora cultivated. Although never actually finished, the review detailed and praised Owen's cooperative manufacturing experiences in Scotland, which were linked to the origins of "utopian" socialism, perhaps with the aim of serving as an inspiration for the strong democratic grassroots sectors that supported the radical press.

This connection with more extreme liberal currents may explain why Mora accepted an anonymous commission to translate a work with roots in the radical French Enlightenment: d'Holbach's *Essai sur les préjuges* (1770; d'Holbach 1823).[44] It is no coincidence that Mora's version was published at the end of the Liberal Triennium, when he was an opinion

[41] EID (no. 63, 4/III/1822; no. 64, 5/III/1822; no. 67, 8/III/1822; no. 69, 10/III/1822).

[42] EI (no. 199, 19/XI/1822). The *Sociedad* paid a tribute to Mamerto Landáburu, a soldier who was assassinated by his own troops in Madrid in July 1822.

[43] See EI (no. 118, 8/IX/1822; no. 131, 15/XI/1822; no. 160, 11/X/1822).

[44] A summary of his translation was included in Mora's 1840 translation of d'Holbach's *La morale universelle* (d'Holbach 1840).

leader among these passionate currents. His translation was relatively faithful to the original and heavily annotated. D'Holbach believed that society's ills stemmed from ignorance, error and prejudice. His remedy was to establish truth through a philosophical and critical spirit, which should embrace religion, moral and politics. The "ultimate error" was one that was enshrined in religious ideas. With its fanaticism and control over education, the clergy created harmful opinions and social customs, and this could only be prevented by bringing religious institutions under the control of political authority. Corruption and ignorance also stemmed from "false politics", however; the nobility, bound to their privileges, and military governments, anxious for new conquests, were also responsible for the fact that existing institutions were "old" and "feudal" (d'Holbach 1823, 98). This was clear from the economic privileges and exemptions, which aborted "any idea of justice" (d'Holbach 1823, 110). It was therefore a question of creating new institutions and legal codes that were adapted to modern needs. Among these was the desirability of fostering the creation of a "middle class", which was distinguished from the "grandees" and the *tiers-état* by being "one that loves good order and occupies a middle ground between the extremes" (d'Holbach 1823, 44). Always protective of social order, Mora openly expressed his distrust of "the dregs of society" and the "imbecilic rabble", to which he attributed "harmful revolutions". In short, d'Holbach's text was presented as an antidote against ecclesiastical and political authority, fanaticism and superstition, in the conviction that "truth must sooner or later triumph over error". As well as education Mora relied on universal tolerance and freedom of thought and expression, and his translation was thus perfectly in line with his newspapers' propaganda supporting the exercise of these rights within the framework of a representative and constitutional system, essential elements for the spread of good ideas. To defend these rights, Mora did not hesitate to copy lengthy extracts from Bentham's *On the Liberty of the Press* (EDP, no. 83, 22/X/1821; n. 84, 23/X/1821), which he himself had attempted to translate.

3.4 Final Remarks

Mora's career as a journalist during the Liberal Triennium conveys the image of a ubiquitous and tireless professional who unquestionably played a leading role in the press of his times. He showed an extraordinary ability to adapt to the turbulent circumstances in which he lived, subsisting on the margins of Ferdinand's absolutism, although without being part of it, and then participating in the most radical factions of Liberal Triennium liberalism a few short years later. The overall impression could be that of an opportunist, as some have claimed. However, it is important to remember that, unlike many of his contemporaries, who were quick to place themselves at the service of absolutist power when it was restored in 1823, Mora immediately went into exile, from where he played a major part in Hispanic liberalism in the second quarter of the nineteenth century. His interest in political economy, which was manifest in most of the journalistic ventures in which he was involved, means that clear lines of continuity can be traced in his work during this period and in later years. He was a staunch supporter of the principles of classical economics —including free trade— and although he took a broad approach which encompassed a wide range of authors to these principles, what especially stands out during the Liberal Triennium is the pervasiveness of Bentham, who with Smith and Say completes the triad of core authors in Mora's life prior to his exile. Bentham's work played an essential role in the turbulent years of the Liberal Triennium because Mora saw it as a useful guide for establishing the constitutional principles that *veinteañista* liberalism was struggling to breathe life into. Although his relationship with Bentham likely cooled after 1823, the Liberal Triennium marked the height of Mora's Benthamism.[45] Nevertheless, it should be emphasised that his reading of the English philosopher was somewhat selective —his greatest disagreement was his sympathy with natural law, repudiated by Bentham— and, indeed, perhaps influenced by Dumont, a moderate Benthamite, Mora did not allow himself to be carried away by Bentham's political radicalism, well embodied in his democratic theory. This was difficult to fit in with the elitist conception of political participation that Mora championed for much of his life. In any case, like all good journalists, Mora was capable of tailoring the way in which he expressed the ideas of classical economics to the ever-changing environment in which he moved, adapting them to the range of audiences at whom his tireless work as a journalist was aimed, whether they were the literary and political elites or the radical currents during the last part of the Liberal Triennium. His unwavering adherence to the latter represented an exceptional period of radicalism in his life and

[45] This may have been due to Mora's deep disappointment at Bentham's harsh, haughty and aloof personal character after their private meeting in London, as he recounts during his stay in Buenos Aires in the *Crónica política y literaria* (no. 72, 8/VIII/1827).

sealed his immediate fate. The arrival in Spain of the Hundred Thousand Sons of Saint Louis in April 1823 to fulfil the terms of the Holy Alliance brought about the second restoration of absolutism, again under Ferdinand VII, which was known as the Ominous Decade (1823–1833). While the new absolutist power was busy decimating the Liberal Triennium's economic legislation, including the 1820 Tariff—a new one, also highly prohibitionist, was decreed in 1825—, newspapers were closed down, censorship was reinstated and the implacable demolition of the major expressions of the liberalism of the previous years, including the patriotic societies and the *Ateneo* began, Mora was embarking on what would be a very long period in exile.

Bibliography

Books[46]

Mora, José Joaquín de. 1821. *Discurso inaugural que pronunció en el Ateneo español D. José Joaquín de Mora, uno de sus socios, al abrir un curso de Derecho Natural, el día 7 de marzo de 1821*. Madrid: Imprenta del censor. Reed. 1843. Sevilla; Establecimiento tipográfica.

Translations and Reeditions

Bentham, Jeremy. 1820. *Consejos que dirige a las Cortes y al pueblo español Jeremías Bentham: traducidos del inglés por José Joaquín de Mora*. Madrid: Repullés.

Holbach, Paul-Henri-Thirty d'. 1823. *Ensayo de las preocupaciones, escrito en francés por el barón de Holbach, y traducido con correcciones y adiciones por José Joaquín de Mora*. Madrid: Imprenta de don José del Collado.

Holbach, Paul-Henri-Thirty d'. 1840. *La moral universal o los deberes del hombre, fundados en su naturaleza por el Barón de Holbach. Aumentada con el interesante discurso que publicó este célebre escritor sobre el origen y estado de las preocupaciones. Traducido por el literato D. J. J. de Mora*. Madrid: Oficinas del establecimiento central.

[46] On the prolix reprints of the *Catecismos*, *Cursos* and other works of Mora in the Hispanic world, see Roldán (2003), Macintyre (2018) and Medina (2022).

Primary Sources

Bentham, Jeremy. 1821. *Cartas de Jeremías Bentham, al señor Conde de Toreno, sobre el proyecto de Código penal presentado a las Cortes.* Madrid: Imprenta de Diego García Campoy.

Bentham, Jeremy. 2012. *On the Liberty of the Press, and Public Discussion, and other Legal and Political Writings for Spain and Portugal.* In *The Collected Works of Jeremy Bentham*, edited by Catherine Pease-Watkin and Phillip Schofield. Oxford: Oxford Clarendon Press.

Jaumeandreu, Eudaldo. 1816. *Rudimentos de economía política.* Barcelona: Oficina de D. Antonio Brusí.

Jaumeandreu, Eudaldo. 1836. *Curso elemental de economía política con aplicación a la legislación económica de España*, 2 vols. Barcelona: Imprenta de Gaspar.

Labra, Rafael María de. 1878. *El Ateneo de Madrid.* Madrid: Imprenta de Aurelio J. Alaria.

Mellado, Francisco de Paula. 1842. "Mora, José Joaquín". In *Diccionario universal de historia y geografía*, vol. V, 543–44. Madrid: Establecimiento Tipográfico.

Vadillo, José Manuel. 1821. *Discurso sobre los medios de fomentar la industria española y contener o reprimir el contrabando.* Madrid: Imprenta de la Calle de Greda.

Secondary Sources

Almenar, Salvador. 1976. "Agrarismo y librecambio en la crisis del Antiguo Régimen". *Información Comercial Española* 517, 58–81.

Almenar, Salvador. 2000b. "Flórez Estrada y la economía política clásica". In *Economía y economistas españoles. Vol. IV. La economía clásica*, edited by Enrique Fuentes, 369–411. Barcelona: Galaxia Gütenberg and Círculo de Lectores.

Astigarraga, Jesús, José Manuel Menudo and Javier Usoz. 2022b. "Nuancing Adam Smith. *The Wealth of Nations'* Reception and Influences in Spain, 1800–1820". In *Adam Smith and 'The Wealth of Nations' in Spain*, edited by Jesús Astigarraga and Juan Zabalza, 121–37. New York and London: Routledge.

Beltrán, Miguel. 1977. *Ideologías y gasto público en España (1814–1860).* Madrid: IEF and Ministerio de Hacienda.

Comín, Francisco. 2000a. "Los economistas clásicos y los políticos liberales ante los problemas de la economía española". In *Economía y economistas españoles. Vol. IV. La economía clásica*, edited by Enrique Fuentes, 621–703. Barcelona: Galaxia Gütenberg and Círculo de Lectores.

Conway, Stephen, ed. 1989. *The Collected Works of Jeremy Bentham. The Correspondence of Jeremy Bentham, Vol. 9.* Oxford: OUP.

Conway, Stephen, ed. 1994. *The Collected Works of Jeremy Bentham. The Correspondence of Jeremy Bentham, Vol. 10.* Oxford: OUP.

Fernández Sarasola, Ignacio. 2012. "La Constitución de Cádiz en Inglaterra". *Historia Constitucional* 13, 1–21.

Fernández Sarasola, Ignacio. 2015. "Constitution Projects during the Spanish Enlightenment". In *The Spanish Enlightenment Revisited*, edited by Jesús Astigarraga, 129–47. Oxford: Voltaire Foundation.

Fernández Sebastián, Javier. 2012b. "Liberalismo en España (1810–1850). La construcción de un concepto y la forja de una identidad política". In *La aurora de la libertad. Los primeros liberalismos en el mundo iberoamericano*, edited by Javier Fernández Sebastián, 236–301. Madrid: Marcial Pons.

Fontana, Josep. 1979. *La crisis del Antiguo Régimen, 1808–1833*. Barcelona: Crítica.

Fuentes, Juan Francisco. 1994. "Estructura de la prensa española en el Trienio Liberal: difusión y tendencias". *Trienio* 24, 165–96.

Garrorena, Ángel. 1974. *El Ateneo de Madrid y la teoría de la monarquía liberal, 1836–1847*. Madrid: IEF.

Gil Novales, Alberto. 1975. *Las sociedades patrióticas (1820–1823)*. Madrid: Tecnos.

Gil Novales, Alberto. 1980. *El Trienio Liberal*, Madrid: Siglo XXI, edited by Ramón Arnabat. Zaragoza, Prensas de la Universidad, 2020.

Gil Novales, Alberto. 1986. *El primer Ateneo de Madrid, 1820–1823*. Madrid: Ateneo.

Gil Novales, Alberto. 2010. "Mora, José Joaquín de". In *Diccionario biográfico de España (1808–1833). De los orígenes del liberalismo a la reacción absolutista*, edited by Alberto Gil Novales, vol. II, 2054–57. Madrid: Fundación Mapfre.

Larriba, Elisabel. 2020. "La prensa". In *El Triernio Liberal (1820–1823). Una mirada política*, edited by Pedro Rújula and Ivana Frasquet, 187–211. Granada: Comares.

Llorens, Vicente. 1968. *Liberales y románticos. Una emigración española en Inglaterra, 1823–1834*. Madrid: Castalia.

Lluch, Ernest. 1973. *El pensament econòmic a Catalunya (1760–1840)*. Barcelona: Edicions 62.

Lluch, Ernest and Salvador Almenar. 2000. "Difusión e influencia de los economistas clásicos en España (1776–1870)". In *Economía y economistas españoles. Vol. IV. La economía clásica*, edited by Enrique Fuentes, 93–170. Barcelona: Galaxia Gütenberg and Círculo de Lectores.

Martín Rodríguez, Manuel. 1989. "La institucionalización de los estudios de Economía Política en la universidad española (1784–1857)". In *Elementos de economía política con aplicación particular a España,* by Marqués de Valle Santoro, XI–CCXXXIV. Madrid: IEF.

Medina, Sara. 2022. *José Joaquín de Mora and Britain: Cultural Transfers and Transformations*. Berlin: Peter Lang.

Menudo, José Manuel. 2015. "Correspondencia y economía política en España (1809–1831). La relación epistolar con Jeremy Bentham y Jean-Baptiste Say". *Cuadernos de Ilustración y Romanticismo* 21, 109–20.

Moral Ruiz, Joaquín del. 1975. *Hacienda y sociedad en el Trienio Constitucional (1820–1823)*. Madrid: IEF.

Robledo, Ricardo. 2014. *La universidad española, de Ramón de Salas a la guerra civil*. Salamanca: Junta de Castilla y León.

Ruiz Salvador, Antonio. 1971. *El Ateneo científico, literario y artístico de Madrid*. Londres: Tamesis Books.

Rújula, Pedro and Manuel Chust. 2020. *El Trienio Liberal en la monarquía hispánica*. Madrid: Catarata.

Schwartz, Pedro. 1976. "La influencia de Jeremías Bentham en España". *Información Comercial Española* 517, 37–57.

Schwartz, Pedro and Carlos Rodríguez. 1983. "Cartas españolas de Jeremías Bentham". *Moneda y Crédito* 165, 59–88.

Trease, B. David. 1953. *José Joaquín de Mora: A Spaniard Abroad*. PhD. Michigan, University of Michigan.

Varela, Joaquín. 1996. "La Monarquía imposible: la Constitución de Cádiz durante el Trienio". *Anuario de Historia del Derecho Español* 66, 653–88.

Zabalza, Juan. 2022. "Adam Smith in the Economic Debates during the Liberal Triennium (1820–1823): the Second Liberal Exile and Hispanic America". In *Adam Smith and 'The Wealth of Nations' in Spain*, edited by Jesús Astigarraga and Juan Zabalza, 205–21. New York and London: Routledge.

Zavala, Iris M. 1971. *Masones, comuneros y carbonarios*. Madrid: Siglo XXI.

PART II

Exiles

CHAPTER 4

London (1824–1827): The Approach to British Classical Political Economy

4.1 Introduction: L.ondon and "Little Constitutional Spain"

In late 1823 and throughout 1824 Britain and France became the main destinations for exiled Spanish liberals.[1] Aided by the similarity between the languages and the lower travel costs the Spanish diaspora in France was more numerous and was essentially made up of soldiers and the humbler classes, who were always under the watchful eye of the French government for fear that the new arrivals would become a focal point for revolutionary tendencies. Although facilitated by the authorities' laxity and national emigration legislation (Simal 2012, 195–96, 199), the exodus to England was less numerous —only about 1000 families settled in London (*El emigrado observador*, EEO, 1828–1829; no. 3, IX/1828, 99)— but it brought together important professionals, politicians and journalists, of whom Mora was one. This predominantly intellectual group of exiles, who had arrived in London via Gibraltar or France, settled in the Euston area of north-east London, especially in Somers Town, a humble neighbourhood and former refuge for French exiles, which, according to Alcalá Galiano, in a few short months became "little constitutional Spain", the meeting

[1] The overall framework for this chapter is to be found in the works by Llorens (1968), Roldán (2003), Muñoz and García (2011), Simal (2012) and Durán (2015). On the influence of early Spanish liberalism on Hispanic-American countries, see Breña (2011).

J. Astigarraga et al., *The Economic Legacy of José Joaquín de Mora*, Palgrave Studies in the History of Economic Thought, https://doi.org/10.1007/978-3-031-49446-8_4

point of the "the liberal party nucleus" common to all towns and cities (Llorens 1968, 24, 46). During the approximately four years that Mora lived in London he was surrounded by men such as Blanco White, a resident of the city since 1810, and other liberals, some of them habitual exiles who were also fleeing from absolutism and with whom he had had contact during the Liberal Triennium. They included Agustín Argüelles and Antonio Alcalá Galiano, two of the best speakers in the *Cortes*, writers José Luis and Jaime Villanueva, and, finally, José Canga Argüelles and Álvaro Flórez Estrada, who produced three key works of Spanish economic liberalism during their exile in London: the former wrote *Elementos de la ciencia de la Hacienda Pública* (1825) and the *Diccionario de Hacienda* (1826–1827) and the latter the *Curso de economía política* (1828). These books were merely a sample of the intensive cultural activity engaged in by the group of exiles, who were responsible for a great many texts, translations and periodicals. While Spain once again sank into political repression and censorship —all newspapers were banned in January 1824— and the exiles in France were producing works on languages, religion, legislation and government, Mora and his circle took an interest in education and politics. London thus became the hub of Hispanic liberalism between 1823 and 1830, the year in which many London exiles moved to Paris, attracted by the July Revolution (Llorens 1968, 23). Argüelles himself rightly stated that "English printing is conducive to Spanish freedom" (*El español constitucional*, EEC, 1818–1820, 1824–1825; III, no. 21, V/1820, 400).

Their encounter with London's imperial and commercial splendour —the city had 1,500,000 inhabitants at the time— engendered a natural fascination among the emigrants, who came from all corners of Spain. In his absorbing *Cartas sobre Inglaterra* Blanco White described the London of business, activity and other pursuits as the head of the "richest, happiest, and most civilised nation in History" (*Variedades o Mensajero de Londres*, VML, 1823–1825; I, no. 1, I/1823, 15). "Everything is big here, and all drawn on an immense scale" (*Ocios de españoles emigrados*, OEE, 1823–1827; III, no. XIII, April 1825) enthused the anonymous author of the deeply Anglophile *Cartas de un emigrado español* in 1825. Mora also contributed to this undoubtedly idealised idea of London as a huge and vibrant city and the cradle of Britain's greatness (Medina 2022, 42–47). However, beyond the mighty city itself, the British system of political, civil and religious freedoms captured the émigrés' collective imagination and equipped them with new arguments in their bitter struggle against Ferdinand VII's corrupt regime. While they all became Anglophiles to some extent, the process was uneven, partly due to the fact that the London exile resulted in the separating of Spanish liberalism into its moderate and radical factions; collaboration between the two was more theoretical than real, even though they shared the same material deprivations. The impoverished Spanish colony managed to scrape a living through manual labour or modest government aid, as well as funds from the philanthropic actions of the relief boards promoted by the Whigs and radical sectors; these had been set up on the initiative of John Bowring, the Hispanist and active Benthamite, among others, and were supported by both Bentham himself and Ricardo (Simal 2012, 206). The more fortunate survived thanks to the book business and writing or teaching Spanish, including at university level —Alcalá Galiano and Pablo Mendíbil both held newly founded chairs in Spanish at University College and King's College—. However, these hardships did not prevent them from leaving a deep mark on the history of Hispanism. Before the *Ateneo español* was founded for Spanish émigrés' children in 1829, by which time Mora had emigrated to Hispanic America, their meeting places included the house belonging to Whig politician Henry Vassall-Fox, Lord Holland. Friend of Jovellanos and a great London host of moderate and radical Spanish liberals from 1823 onwards, his influence in the defence of the British political tradition vis-à-vis historical constitutionalism went back to the *Cortes de Cádiz* and continued during the 1820s through Blanco White and Alcalá Galiano. Other social hubs included the two main symbols of Spanish culture in London, Marcelino Calero's *Imprenta española*, a printing company, and Vicente Salvá's Spanish and Classical Library, as well as the *Repository of Arts*, the printing company and lithograph school owned by London-based publisher from Saxony Rudolph Ackermann, whose soirées brought together Spanish émigrés, Hispanic-American diplomats and British intellectuals. The cultural ecosystem frequented by Mora must have been defined by Regent Street, Goswell Street and the Strand, where the three establishments were located, and to describe his routes around London is to a large extent to explain the close ties that bound him to Ackermann.

4.2 Mora and the Ackermann Factory

After two and a half decades devoted to typography, publishing and the book and art trade, by the 1820s Ackermann had become one of London's most influential and shrewd cultural entrepreneurs. A self-made man, he was among the first to spot the commercial opportunities opened up by the independence of the Hispanic-American republics for the dissemination of Spanish-language cultural products. The milieu in which he moved was particularly conducive to this, as Hispanic-American journalists had begun to produce journals in the service of a nascent linguistic, scientific and cultural Americanism, the most noteworthy example of which was the short-lived *La biblioteca americana* (LBA, 1823). Published by a "Society of Americans", it was the work of Blanco White cohort, Caracas-born Andrés Bello, and was followed by *El repertorio americano* (ERA, 1826–1827).[2] Britain was the first country to recognise the new republics in 1825 and they had become a lucrative market for loans, capital investment and the export of manufactured goods. The new political conditions, the free circulation of books and the increased press freedom provided an excellent framework for the sale of informative and educational texts on all kinds of subjects; aimed at audiences with little education, including women, they could lay the foundations for the budding educational reforms and help to build a civil and liberal order in accordance with the new republican institutions (Roldán 2003, 31–33). Ackermann saw education and the circulation of knowledge through print culture as two formidable tools for the new republics' development, although his interests were not strictly political but business-related. On this basis he produced a catalogue of 26 catechisms and 80 books and magazines in Spanish between 1823 and 1830, and while his agenda does not seem particularly well-defined, his publications covered a wide range of subjects, although religious books were deliberately thin on the ground (Roldán 2003, 53, 243–54). Ackermann's commercial success extended to Hispanic-American countries and during the 1820s his publications accounted for 72% of Spanish-language texts that were exported to these countries (Roldán 2003, 24); he also managed to make his books into a kind of antidote to the French texts which dominated the market, as he intended. Many of his publishing cycles continued for much of the nineteenth century, albeit usually through fraudulent printing.

[2] Both were published with Juan García del Río's collaboration.

However, Ackermann's commercial success can only be explained through a combination of other factors. Firstly, many Hispanic-American diplomats living in London soon recognised the usefulness of his entrepreneurial approach for their nations' development. Future Hispanic-American presidents and statesmen such as Bernardino Rivadavia, Borja Mignoni, José Cecilio del Valle and Vicente Rocafuerte, as well as journalists and writers such as Andrés Bello, contributed to the expansion of Ackermann's business market, on the basis of a criterion that was not commercial gain but ideological action for their countries' benefit. To this end they proposed publishing certain books, sponsored them financially and, as Mora would do on his journey through Hispanic America, helped to distribute them via their diplomatic bags or the bible shipments sent by the British and Foreign Bible Society (BFBS), with which some of them collaborated (Roldán 2003, 110).[3] In doing so they provided strong support to the network of bookshops owned by Ackermann himself in Hispanic America —his own son managed the shop in Mexico; also had commercial agents in Buenos Aires, Colombia, Chile, Peru and Guatemala—. The most important of these diplomats was the Guatemalan Rocafuerte; well-known to Spanish liberals because of his role as Hispanic-American representative at the *Cortes de Cádiz*, this future president of Guatemala used his post as chargé d'affaires at the Mexican Embassy in London to influence Ackermann and the group of Spanish émigrés, and was the second key player in Ackermann's success. Ackermann was not their only publisher, but he was the most important: without his company, Calero's printing house and help from the bookseller Salvá, their printed output would have been meagre to say the least. Ackermann recruited Blanco White, Pablo Mendíbil, José de Urcullu and José Luis de Villanueva among others to put together his publishing products, but only three worked exclusively for him. Mora was crucial to his project; financial support was naturally one of the reasons for the close ties that developed between the two men from 1824 onwards, and certainly the main one. The handsome salary of thirteen pounds a month that Ackermann paid Mora (Roldán 2003, 63) must have been enough to support his "large family" and make a living from his pen alone in London, without help from the limited government aid for exiles (Mellado 1842, 543).

[3] Mora praised the Society's efficient book distribution system in *El mercurio chileno* (no. 11, 1/2/1829).

Nevertheless, this is only part of the story. Mora's immersion in the Ackermann factory ran parallel to his growing admiration for England and everything English and his discovery of the opportunities opened up by the Hispanic-American world, as yet conceived of without any particular interest in specific nations. Although the region had attracted his attention during the Liberal Triennium —as various articles in the EC and LME reflect— in London Mora's rhetoric acquired an intense Hispanic-Americanist flavour for the first time (Asensio 2011). This was immensely significant in the literary sphere: he strongly advocated the production of indigenous American literature in London, guided by a sort of "literary Americanism", still with no defined national borders. To this end he revisited old ideals with roots in the Enlightenment: he believed that political science was closely linked with advances in good taste, a mighty weapon in the service of education and civilisation, which should emerge in a free, well-governed country in which reason prevailed. Spain itself was a good example of this: intellectual and literary perfection, whose spirit had to be acquired if good taste were to be cultivated, was personified in authors to whom despotism was entirely alien such as Jovellanos, Blanco White and Quintana (Monguió 1967, 34–37), "beacons of good taste" to whom he referred repeatedly throughout his life.

Nonetheless, Mora's keen survival instinct must have warned him that making the most of the opportunities in the Hispanic-American world required a hasty shift from the *veinteañista* liberal radicalism inherited from the Liberal Triennium to moderate *doceañista* liberalism, the terrain occupied by Ackermann and the Hispanic-American diplomats who were pulling their influential strings from London and who he needed as allies. Durán (2015, 18, 23–24, 43, 52–53) give an excellent account of the decisive role played by Blanco White here. Not only did he put Mora in touch with Ackermann, but he was also crucial in his speedy ideological acclimatisation to London: in short, he was the guide that helped Mora to cover the path that he had been treading since 1810 more quickly.[4] Blanco White had been an expatriate in London since this year and was a pioneer in the presentation of Britain as a model for the Hispanic world. Repudiating the *doceañistas* and the French and Cadiz constitutions, he embraced moderate British liberalism, respecting its hallmarks of bicameralism, the balance of powers, individual rights and religious tolerance. These principles filled the pages of his first London newspaper, EE, and were revisited in the VML, Ackermann's first Hispanic venture. In the latter, which Blanco White deepened his criticism of the Spanish colonial system, which had prolonged the "civil infancy" of Hispanic-American nations through oppression (VML, no. XI, 1/1825, 2), embracing their independence and seeking to steer them away from their traditional French orbit towards the British. His relationship with Ackermann was not easy, however. Blanco White's unwillingness to tolerate Ackermann's overseeing of the VML led to its closure and Mora then became the "go-to" person in Ackermann's overall project. He was easier to deal with than Blanco White and no other exile showed the pragmatism and versatility necessary to adapt to Ackermann's ambitious range of commissions or to learn how to create cultural hybrids that fused elements of Spanish, British and American culture, and therefore to operate in a transnational framework whose hubs were London, Hispanic America and Spain, the latter open to its own European dimension (Tully 2011). He achieved all this, moreover, with enviable efficiency: not only was Mora one of the London diaspora's most prolific authors —as attested to in the OEE (IV, no. XX, XI/1825)—, but he was also the key figure in the structuring of Ackermann's enterprise. In him Ackermann found someone who was capable of writing and translating rapidly for the Spanish-American

[4] Blanco White held a favourable opinion about Mora: "he writes with great ease and very well […] I believe him to be the most skilful of all the Spaniards who have taken up refuge here" (Trease 1953, 15). On their side, Mora never hid his intellectual devotion to Blanco White, whom he considered a master of journalism and good taste. Proof of this esteem is the fact that in 1844, he reprinted Blanco White's *Cartas sobre Inglaterra* from Spain (Blanco-White 1844), which he expanded with four additional letters (no. VII–X), substantially taken from *Lettres sur l'Anglaterre* (Paris, 1825) by Auguste–Louis de Staël–Holstein. His glowing comments on Blanco White can be found in, for example, the *Crónica política y literaria* (no. 90, 31/VIII/1827) and *El mercurio chileno* (no. 2, 1/V/1828) —similar praise was heaped on Ackermann's publications as a whole; see *El mercurio chileno* (no. 11, 1/II/1829), for example—. Despite all this, their personal relationship was never good, apparently due, as mentioned, to a debt from Mora's youth that was never settled.

audience, and it is no accident that the peak of his company's production in 1827 coincided with Mora's tireless work for him (Roldán 2003, 28–29).

Meanwhile, Mora's Anglophilia was taking shape. Already present in embryonic form during the Liberal Triennium, both in his newspapers—the EC and especially LME— and his alignment with Bentham, it now formed part of his innermost convictions. Although it was less marked in him than in Blanco White, as Mora was not a supporter of parliamentary monarchy, he began to see Britain as a model of political stability, good customs, individual freedoms and economic development, which could help to regenerate Spain and build the new Hispanic-American republicanism. Those years also saw the beginnings of a move towards Protestantism, which he would finally embrace some thirty years later, and he accepted religious tolerance under Blanco White and Villanueva's influence. By means of a somewhat meandering process, he also consigned his old dispute with Böhl de Faber to the past and moved closer to romanticism, which he no longer associated with political reactionism, by intertwining it with liberalism. To this mix he added a certain detachment from the Spanish cultural and intellectual spheres and began to project his ideas onto the Hispanic-American republics, having abandoned all hope of regenerating the "sad wasteland" into which absolutism had turned his homeland.

Mora collaborated with Ackermann for almost the entire four years of his London exile, producing five catechisms and some 15 titles for his catalogue, in some cases under Rocafuerte and also perhaps Rivadavia's patronage.[5] He edited the almanac *No me olvides* (1824–1829), which was based on Frederic Shoberl's *Forget-Me-Not* (1822–1846) and wrote and translated various books on poetry, literature, travel and history into

[5] Mora's closeness to Ackermann also increased his chances of contributing to the British press. This was common among the Spanish émigrés, who, among other journals, wrote for *The Athenaeum*, the *Quarterly Review*, the Tory Party's mouthpiece, and the *Westminster Review*, the organ of Bentham's radicals, which was edited by John Bowring. Mora sent frequent reviews to the *Revue Encyclopédique* (REF, 1819–1835) and poems and genre articles to *The European Review* (Llorens 1968, 342ff.). Outside Ackermann's orbit he was also able to produce a translation of Fénelon (1825). This was a brief informative summary of the philosophers of the Ancient World, which Mora used to express ideas of his own time, for example, sensualism as the origin of knowledge or self-love as the motive for human behaviour. Mora viewed Fénelon as a pioneer in the struggle against despotism, based on tolerance and virtue; see *El mercurio chileno* (no. 12, 15/IV/1829). Anyway, Mora's literary activity in London was really intense. In 1826, he even drafted a collection of poems inspired by William Blake's illustrations, which were published in the work.

Spanish, increasingly adhering to the traditional system of adapting the works to the features of the target culture (Durán 2015). Some were deeply political, such as the Spanish versions of works by Francisco Saverio Clavijero —on Rocafuerte's advice— and William Davis Robinson on the history of Mexico and its path to independence (Clavijero 1826; Robinson 1824). The fact that Ackermann also commissioned him to write works for women underlines their importance in his publishing plan. In 1824 he brought out *Cartas sobre la educación del bello sexo* (CBS; Mora 1824a) anonymously, complementing this with another text on women's physical education in the same year (Mora 1824b). It is not clear exactly who inspired the CBS, whether it was Mora himself with his wife Fanny Delauneux, a tenacious women's educator who followed their guidelines to the letter, or Rivadavia, as the work reflected his creation of a charitable society named the *Sociedad de Beneficencia* in the province of Buenos Aires in 1823 (Mora 1824a, IX).[6] The CBS were essentially a treatise on moral education for women, highlighting the advantages of the British model over the French and suggesting a series of notable reforms in female education, including abolishing corporal punishment, respecting religious tolerance and broadening traditional training in household management to include useful disciplines such as botany and astronomy. However, the CBS also had a strongly marked political meaning; as Macintyre has outlined, they were intended to demonstrate the potential modernising role of women in the "formation of strong republican societies" and "nation-building purpose":[7] as the text states, without women "political reforms can produce only imperfect fruits" (Mora 1824a, 203). Interwoven once again with an all-embracing eulogy to all things British, its adaptation to the Hispanic-American world, in which it enjoyed enormous success,[8] called for a means of developing proper education for women in rural environments. The CBS thus opened up a recurring theme in Mora's writings: the priority of agriculture, the desirability of women's participation in rural industry and, in short, the advantages of the countryside over the city, which encouraged a virtuous and healthy life, dominated by the

[6] The appendix contained the founding documents of this official institution, perhaps so that it could be emulated; it was reminiscent of the *Juntas de Damas* created by Spanish economic societies.

[7] All the details are in Macintyre (2010, 39–44, 114–17, 182–83).

[8] The book was reprinted in the nineteenth century in countries such as Argentina, Cuba, Venezuela, Mexico, Chile, Nicaragua and Brazil.

"moderation of desires" and far removed from the "factitious idols of fashion and opinion" (Mora 1824a, 194, 197).

A fruitful series of writings on economics emerged in the framework of Mora's collaboration with Ackermann, chiefly the *Catecismo de economía política* (CEP, 1825) and a number of articles that were included in the two publications which Mora devised for him: the *Museo universal de ciencias y artes* (MUC, 1825–1826) and the *Correo literario y político de Londres* (CLP, 1826). These works all contained a vision that renewed prior intellectual sources, based on the principles of classical political economy and aimed at Hispanic-American elites. Mora's reading and use of Say, more than Bentham, led to his receptiveness to economists such as Mill —a close friend of Blanco White's— and McCulloch, with both of whom he had personal contact during his years in London (Mora 1843).

4.3 Mora and Ackermann's Catechisms: The *Catecismo de economía política* (1825)

The CEP was part of the collection of 26 catechisms published by Ackermann between 1824 and 1828 (Mora 1825). Organised on a question-and-answer basis, these texts are excellent examples of Ackermann's modus operandi: they were brief, cheap and had large print runs of 4000 copies; they were also clearly commercially oriented, with several overseas promoters —including Rocafuerte— and producing them involved a great deal of work in the background on the part of the Spanish exiles (Durán 2015, 81). They were originally based on the success of the catechisms written by Irving, Mavor and especially William Pinnock in Britain (Roldán 2003, 139), but Ackerman's collection also drew on original catechisms or others with different sources. The more mainstream works were based on Pinnock, and their divergences have already been pointed out: Mavor's were adaptations aimed at the broad Hispanic-American audiences and therefore included information about America as well as generally being secular; explicit references to Protestantism were omitted, probably because of Rocafuerte's support for religious tolerance (Roldán 2003, 84–97). Moreover, they were designed with educational purposes in mind as a quick and cheap way of spreading useful knowledge among a population with poor literacy levels such as that in Hispanic America. They were also a useful a vehicle for transmitting the virtues of the British model, as Mora did in his *Catecismo de geografía* (1824): while he described the Spanish as "workshy", he praised the industriousness of the English, intertwining this with the "wisdom of their institutions, the freedom enjoyed by their citizens, religious tolerance, the great stimuli which encourage all useful and profitable enterprises, and the protection afforded by the government to application, merit and industry" (Pinnock 1824, 23, 26).[9]

Ackermann's catechisms functioned not only as school texts but also as self-instruction handbooks for adults and even for professional audiences. The fact that civic and political "patriotic" catechisms, which were clearly differentiated from religious ones,[10] proliferated in Hispanic America in the 1820s may have encouraged Ackermann to promote this publishing format (Roldán 2003, 142). According to Durán (2015, 81–82), this could also have been inspired by Blanco White, Rocafuerte or Mora himself, who witnessed their spread during the turbulent Liberal Triennium and, as he explained in the MUC (I, no. 4, IV/1825, 216–17), was an unconditional supporter of Ackermann's aims. What is certain is that they were unquestionably successful and made up the most profitable segment of his many entrepreneurial initiatives. Ackermann's use of Hispanic-American diplomats to distribute the catechisms in their own countries was a contributory factor, as was their usefulness in the Bell-Lancaster "monitorial" educational system —known as "mutual" in Hispanic America— which was then being introduced. These manageable catechisms meant that the work of teachers could be reduced, as the pupils switched between master and learner roles in the reading and oral repetition of the texts. Mora had expressed his approval of these educational methods in the CCL, seeing in them an admirable demonstration of the advantages of the division of labour (MUC, I, no. 4, IV/1825, 217), and it is not surprising that he used them in his future education projects in Hispanic America. His was not an isolated case, however; Ackermann's catechisms were used in "mutual" education in Argentina, Bolivia, Venezuela and Colombia, either introduced by Lancaster himself or due to the personal involvement of authorities at the highest level such as Rivadavia.[11] This is all proof of the importance attached to catechisms as

[9] Mora expressed similar ideas in the MUC; see I, no. 5/VII/1825, 285, for example.

[10] The heading made it clear that Ackermann's catechisms were not devoted to religious subjects and were used "in all educated and Catholic countries in Europe".

[11] Not without opposition from reactionary sectors, as occurred in Buenos Aires, according to Mora in the *Crónica política y literaria* (no. 18, 19/IV/1827).

instruments of the legitimisation of a new republican citizenship based on egalitarian criteria. Their future proliferation was due to fraudulent editions of all kinds, and they became the most widespread and enduring of Ackermann's texts, with a notable presence not only in Hispanic America, but also in Spain and France for much of the nineteenth century.

Mora was one of the most prolific authors of Ackermann's catechism collection. He is credited with writing those on Latin grammar, Spanish grammar, geography and chemistry, as well as political economy. A general overview suggests that the latter formed part of a wider collection of five catechisms, one of which was not produced by Ackermann, all distinguished by the fact that they had been designed for specific professional audiences and thus to fulfil wider social functions than simply to educate. This is clearly reflected in José Urcullu's *Catecismo de aritmética comercial* (1825), whose content was akin to that of merchants' handbooks. It was adapted to the Mexican publishing market and was very straightforward, going no further than the rule of three and interest rate calculation, which may have contributed to its widespread use and helps to explain its extraordinary success.[12]

Two other dictionaries dealt with agricultural subjects. The *Catecismo de industria rural y doméstica* (1824) was aimed at rural workers of different types;[13] published anonymously and highly practical, the text aimed to show the usefulness of Britain and France's experiences of domestic and scattered rural industry, including machinery, for the Hispanic-American countryside. The benefits for public and private wealth were underlined: there would be work all year round for families, including women and children, better quality food and greater self-sufficiency, and possibly new branches of trade. The text was very similar to the *Catecismo de agricultura* attributed to Esteban Pastor (1825). Its chief aims was to demonstrate that Britain's exemplary agricultural prosperity was due to its having adopted the principles of the "new agronomy" —crop rotation, using a variety of fertilisers and creating artificial pastureland—[14] as well as tools and equipment —the seed drill and threshing machine— and to underscore the social utility of practical experiences and the importance of

[12] The appendix contained the equivalences of weights, measures and coins in Mexico. It was republished throughout the nineteenth century in Spanish and occasionally in English; in Paris, in numerous editions until 1878, and also in Santiago (1846), Bogota (1861) and Mexico, where the corrected and extended 42nd edition was published in 1887.

[13] It was reissued in Paris in 1825.

[14] John Sinclair is expressly cited.

promoting rural industry.[15] Its usefulness for Hispanic America, where development was driven by agriculture, was patent in the appendix. Revisiting the principles set out in the 1824 CBS, agriculture was presented as the "cornerstone of public wealth and the welfare of the people" and the most honourable productive activity (Pastor 1825, 1, 85), and the reforms that had made English agriculture exemplary were outlined. The government must respect the freedom of farmers —including the right to enclose land—, reduce taxes, restrict communal services, undertake public works and boost the spread of crop-growing, creating new landowners. Particularly significant was the praise for the Board of Agriculture and British Agricultural Societies as vital bodies for producing statistics, promoting agricultural colleges, distributing seeds and agricultural equipment and awarding prizes (Pastor 1825, 4, 87–88). Pastor, however, distanced himself from "good modern economists" —a tacit allusion to classical authors— by advocating protectionist tariffs that would help to maintain "a constant preference in favour of one's own fruits" and subsidies for agricultural exports (Pastor 1825, 89). The *Catecismo* therefore contained a precise programme of agrarian reforms for the new republics and it was an enormous success; the first edition of 4000 copies quickly sold out. Its audience was none other than "the legislator, the statesman", to whom Pastor appealed not to view agriculture "with contempt [...] however petty it may seem to them" (Pastor 1825, 100).[16]

Policy makers were also the target audience for public finance and political economy handbooks. The first of these, Canga Argüelles' *Cartilla de Hacienda* (1825), which was published by Llorens and not Ackermann (1968, 174), noted its close similarity to the catechisms, a sign of the fine line separating text production among the Spanish exiles. The *Cartilla* was apparently supposed to be published by itself but in the end Canga included it in the *Elementos de la ciencia de la Hacienda Pública* (1825) as an appendix. He produced the work in March 1825, commissioned by Rocafuerte and with a very specific aim: given the "scarcity" of "true knowledge of political economy" in Hispanic America, Rocafuerte requested a book with "the most exact principles of political economy applied to the management of public finance", which was also eminently

[15] Reference was made to the future *Catecismo de industria rural* on this question. Published anonymously, it could also have been written by Pastor.

[16] In addition to two editions in London in 1824 and 1825, it was reissued, albeit corrected and extended, in Cordova (1836 and 1839) and Madrid (1839).

practical: "It is not enough to study Smith, Say, Ricardo and Storch in the abstract; it is necessary to apply the principles of this modern science to political business, to the liberal arrangement of trade, to the distribution of taxes and the usefulness of loans". Underlying the assignment was the strategic importance of public finance in the fate of the new republics, and to this end Canga Argüelles reworked a text he had drafted during his detention for political reasons in Spain in 1814. Although he mentioned Verri and Necker's ideas to locate public finance within the wider discipline of political economy, the content corresponded faithfully to the need for liberal public finance "devoid of feudal elements" (Comín 2000b, 430–32). The *Cartilla*, for its part, consisted of a summary of this broader work; structured around questions and answers, it was denser and more complex than Ackermann's catechisms, which may explain why it was called a "*cartilla*", or primer, rather than a "catechism".[17] Influenced by Smith, Say and Mill, it was organised according to the usual sequence of wealth production, distribution and consumption, but this was broken up by the introduction of a Chapter on the stumbling blocks placed in the path of wealth advancement by "opinion" and "laws", which evoked Jovellanos and Cabarrús (Canga 1825, 360–62). Nevertheless, the *Cartilla* laid out the fundamental principles of classical public finance: balanced budgets, a rolled-back state, low public spending and a combination of direct and indirect taxes, all in the service of a gradual and pragmatic reform strategy. Book V of the WN covered the functions of the state, but with a certain tolerance towards the use of protective tariffs for "some fledgling industries" (Canga 1825, 363, 372).

Mora's CEP may also have been a response to the concerns of Hispanic-American elites about the lack of a succinct book in this field. In an article published in 1826 in the REF, Mora stated that he had used Mill and Ricardo's treatises as intellectual sources for the CEP (Llorens 1968, 172). Although the book does contain traces of Mill and various themes that Ricardo specifically examined, it cannot be said to be a summary of Mill's *Elements of Political Economy* (1821), and even less so, of Ricardo's *Principles of Political Economy* (1817) since Mora objected to the latter's abstract methodological assumptions. The CEP rather brought together the general principles of classical economics, insofar as elements of this

[17] However, in the edition of the *Elementos* produced in Madrid in 1833, the *Cartilla* had disappeared and all the work's "*Nociones preliminares*" appeared under the question-and-answer system (Canga 1833, 11–77).

tradition are identifiable without specific affiliations to any particular author, in a somewhat disorganised —or rather, organised to suit Mora's purposes— account of ideas from Smith, Say, Mill and perhaps some notions from Ricardo. Nevertheless, Mora's identification of political economy with "four main objects" —production, distribution, exchange and consumption— matches Mill's *Elements* perfectly.[18] Although this structure is less overt in the later stages of the work, its Chapters cover each of the four categories: production (Chap. II), distribution (Chap. III), exchanges (Chaps. V–X) and consumption (Chaps. XII–XXXIII). However, this structure is also broadly similar to that of Say's *Traité*, which Mora is known to have read in Spain and which he continued to use in his economic articles in London,[19] and so the best way of characterising the CEP's intellectual sources would therefore be to describe them as a conflation of Mill and Say.[20] Thus, Mora follows Say in using the term "subdivision" and analyses its benefits in some detail (Mora 1825, 7–8; Say 1821, 42–52). Say's shadow also seems to fall on the CEP with regard to the theory of value, when it states that the first element that influences the "value of products" is the "possibility and ease of adapting them to meet a need, and the second, scarcity" (Mora 1825, 10–11; Say 1821, 1–5).[21] At the same time, Mill also features in other passages in Mora's writing. Chapter IV of the *Elements*, "Consumption", is undoubtedly the source for the CEP's Chapters XII to XXIII, on matters such as the distinction between productive and unproductive consumption, the balance

[18] There is a Spanish translation of the *Elements* from around this time, produced in Buenos Aires in 1823. Two later translations were published in Paris (1827) and Madrid (1831). Mill was a keen sympathiser with the American cause. A friend of Bentham's, he corresponded with Del Valle and Rivadavia.

[19] The production-distribution-consumption structure of wealth also characterises McCulloch's *Principles* (McCulloch 1825), although there is nothing to show that Mora used it when writing the CEP.

[20] Historians have pointed to Mill's adopting of Say's law from his early work *Commerce Defended* (1807), and the two economists are known to have had a close personal and intellectual relationship (Baumol 1977, 154–56; Hollander 2005, 219–22). Thus, for example, an analysis of the contents of Mill's Chapters on production reveals barely any mention of the benefits of the division of labour.

[21] Schwartz (1999, XXX) holds that Mora employs a labour theory of value based on Mill. However, there are passages in the CEP that state that the "value of products that can be used as objects of exchange" depends on "1. The product-demand ratio. 2. The cost of production" (Mora 1825, 30). Nevertheless, the cost of production is made up of the "labour employed in producing" (Mora 1825, 30).

between annual production and consumption in Britain, and the description of the effects of different taxes on "public wealth" (Mill 1821, 178–226; Mora 1825, 53–80). However, it should also be noted that the first traces of McCulloch's influence on Mora are to be found in the CEP, especially the article entitled "Taxation" that was published in the *Supplement to the Encyclopaedia Britannica*, which Mora used for his chapters on tax-related issues (Mora 1825, 53–80).

However, Mora was not especially interested in the theory of value, but rather in practical questions directly related to economic activity and its effects on prosperity. This explains why many of the themes that characterise his later writings emerge in the CEP, naturally presented in an unquestionable manner that left no room for objection. The text thus contained a comprehensive set of chapters devoted to the classical principles of public finance, defending limits on public spending, the number of civil servants and public borrowing. At the same time Chapter XXIV outlined a succinct set of individual economic freedoms that were appropriate for creating a framework of order, certainty and respect for private property, which would facilitate wealth creation: freedom of production, with no monopolies, exclusive privileges or guilds; free circulation and trade, with no internal customs barriers and with moderate duties on foreign trade and the construction of public works, and, finally, consumer freedom (Mora 1825, 83–86). Somewhat paradoxically, however, Mora was a supporter of free ports, citing the positive example of Livorno (Mora 1825, 69–71).

Chapters VI and XI of his writings in particular raise the question of the beneficial economic effects of international trade, a crucial recurrent theme in his work. To this end, Mora used the example of the exchange of flour from the United States and cocoa from Caracas, which Schwartz (1999, XXXI) considers to be a reference to the theory of comparative advantage as theoretically underpinning free trade —although he went on to state that Mora was unable to grasp its complexity—. However, while it is true that Mora's treatment of the theory was inconsistent, this is much more likely to have been a deliberate simplification that was imposed on him by the CEP's readers, for whom the theoretical depths of economic science were probably best left unplumbed (Mora 1825, 36–38). Mora must have been familiar with them, however, and certainly dealt competently with Smith and Ricardo. His support for free trade continued in Chapter XI of the CEP, in which he discussed the "legislative measures which influence the exchange of commodities", namely, "1. Restrictions.

2. Prohibitions. 3. Prizes", which Schwartz attributes to Bentham's influence (Mora 1825, 47–53; Schwartz 1999, XXX–XXXI). He was well aware of the importance of the monetary aspect in the new republics, which were beset by cash shortages, and was thus in favour of adopting paper currency —fiduciary money— while also warning against its dangers. In Mora's view these did not apply when paper currency was backed by metals, which would come about if banking competition were guaranteed "by multiplying the number of private establishments or banks that were authorised to issue it" (Mora 1825, 42–43). Still on the topic of the new republics' financial woes, he states that "the consequences of not giving due preference to agriculture [...] if capital is invested in industrial and commercial enterprises" would lead to an inability to guarantee "competition with products from other countries, in which circumstances favourable to industry are present" (Mora 1825, 12–14). This was an overt message to the economic elites in Hispanic America to integrate their economies with the international division of labour, chiefly the British economy, although, as previously noted, Mora shared his support for this development strategy with the early Spanish free traders. In fact, the CEP was clearly geared towards the new republics. From a stance that was the polar opposite of absolutism, Mora argued that the correct application of political economy required three principles that were related to them: political representation through parliament, guaranteed individual rights and freedom of the press, as where the latter prevailed "it is almost impossible for economic and administrative abuses to remain hidden" (Mora 1825, 82–83). At the same time, he continued his propaganda in favour of religious tolerance, since it attracted industrious workers and facilitated trade and capital accumulation (Mora 1825, 26).

The CEP ended with an interesting appendix titled "On the Teaching of Political Economy" (Mora 1825, 87–102), in which Mora expressed his deep convictions regarding political economy as the most important of the sciences of government and legislation, in terms of its practical usefulness at both national and individual level and its potential capacity to promote prosperity in republican contexts. However, there were also references to "abuses" arising from the distorting of economic principles via "metaphysical and obscure language" —a veiled reference to Ricardian abstractions— and "blind trust" in the universality of economic laws. Revisiting ideas previously put forward in the CCL, Mora argued that the basis of political economy was the study of facts (Mora 1825, 90). He also argued that its universal theoretical principles should be reduced, to differentiate them from the complexities that arose when it came to their application. A good example of this was the conclusions, erroneous in his opinion, drawn by Malthus and his "sect" in their theory of population, which were invalid for a context such as that of Hispanic America where there was such a manifest imbalance between population and agriculture (Mora 1825, 97). He therefore believed that entirely disparate effects were generated in function of national or local circumstances; hence applying the same laws to both contexts entailed accepting different assertions and economic policy recommendations (Mora 1825, 86–100). This was of course a rhetorical strategy to gain the interpretative leeway required to apply the principles of classical economics to the new institutional and economic environment of the Hispanic-American republics. However, it did confirm the methodological choice that Mora made in Spain, which now continued in London, as well as its success. Ackermann produced three editions of the CEP between 1825 and 1828 and a "pirate" edition also appeared in Seville in 1827 under the title *Lecciones de economía política* and attributed to José Herrera Dávila and Antonio Alvear. There were two major differences with the original: firstly, Mora's appendix was elevated to the status of an introduction to the text (Herrera and Alvear 1827, 3–26), which implied that it could serve as a methodological guide to the science of political economy as a whole, and secondly, Chapter XXIV on the framework of political and civil liberties —including religious tolerance— which required a correct application of political economy, both unacceptable to Ferdinand VII's absolutism, was omitted.

4.4 Mora's Journals

The two journals that Mora produced for Ackermann, the MUC and the CLL, are among the seven periodicals published by Spanish exiles between 1824 and 1830.[22] This abundance can be explained not only by their authors' intellectual stature, but also by the scope of the Hispanic-American market at which they were aimed, as well as by the split between moderate and radical liberals, with their profoundly divergent readings of

[22] See Ruiz Acosta (2016) for journals produced by the exiles; for those produced by Mora, see Llorens (1968, 325–35), Durán (2015, 72–80) and Durán-Muñoz (2016, 66–73).

the validity of the *Constitución de Cádiz.*[23] The most striking proof of their differences is to be found in EEC and the OEE.

The first was the radical wing's flagship publication. It enjoyed two phases of activity, 1818–1820 and 1824–1825, always under the management of Pedro Pascasio Fernández Sardino,[24] a doctor and journalist with a spotless track record as a radical liberal; Mora must have known him well, as they moved in the same circles during the Liberal Triennium. The EEC had essentially political ends (Varela 2016, 330–33) and during its second phase of activity the three sections —politics, sciences and arts and a mixed bag of essentially literary items— not only exuded forceful anti-absolutism and anti-Papacy, but also, as the "Prospecto" warned, kept a sharp eye on accountability vis-à-vis the recent revolution in Spain, resulting in the merciless censure of political opponents. Akin to the *comuneros*, the ECC was implacable in its criticism of the *doceañistas*, who it accused of hiding under the guise of liberals in order to provoke "an atrocious war on those who really were" (EEC, no. XXXVII, V/1825, 350) and to sidestep the laws "in the name of absolutism" (EEC, no. XXXIV, XII/1824, 128–29). According to the EEC the examples of revolutionary France and Cadiz were suitable for neither Spain's constitutional future nor the new Hispanic-American republics; adopting a clearly pro-American attitude, the journal observed the republics with hope, out of respect for their recent independence processes. However, there was little room for political economy in its vast political analyses. Although it had the talent —and perhaps the financial support— of Flórez Estrada, the most important economist among the London exiles,[25] the EEC's paltry contributions to the field seem to have been penned by Spanish free trader Pablo Pebrer.

The counterpoint to the EEC's political radicalism was the OEE, the journal that best represented the exiles in London. It was written by José Canga Argüelles and brothers Joaquín Lorenzo and Jaime Villanueva —following his death in 1824, the latter was replaced by

[23] Also the object of a notable controversy among British elites, the Constitution was translated into English in 1813, 1820 and 1823 (Fernández Sarasola 2012).

[24] Manuel María Acevedo and María del Carmen de Silva, Fernández Sardino's wife, also contributed to the publication. On the intellectual career of this proto-republican, known as the "Spanish Robespierre" and with six newspapers behind him before the ECC, see González Hermoso (2018).

[25] Flórez Estrada published there his well-known *Representation*, one of the liberal émigrés' most biting texts against Ferdinand VII (Flórez Estrada 1819; EEC, I, no. 1, 26–51; no. 2, 65–92). With a similar anti-absolutist sense, presumably, Mora wrote a biography of Ferdinand VII (Mora 1824c).

Pablo Mendíbil— and carried broader content than the ECC, dealing with "selected observations on Spanish literary, economic and political history" to attract the attention of émigrés and Britons with an interest in Spanish affairs. However, from the fourth issue onwards, which appeared in July 1824, it began to cover Hispanic-American topics due to intervention from Rocafuerte, who contributed to its financial support in exchange for overseeing the content and underwrote 200 copies of each issue on behalf of the Mexican Embassy (Llorens 1968, 309–10). Circulation consequently rose to 1000 copies per issue and the journal become the most enduring of the London exiles' publications. The fact that Canga Argüelles was exclusively responsible for its political content explains the fact that coverage of economic issues was broader than the EEC's. It respected the journal's overall orientation to the letter; in keeping with the purpose of early Spanish liberalism, which was heartily repudiated by *comunero* radicalism, Canga explored means of reconciling modern constitutionalism and Spanish historical-legal constitutionalism: his own historicism led him to advocate an Anglophile political system that would purge the radical tendencies persisting in the *Constitución de Cádiz* and redirecting Spanish liberalism towards moderantism (Fernández Sarasola 2012, 8ff.; Varela 2016, 333–35).

In a similar vein Canga's contributions on economics sought to reconcile the late Enlightenment principles in which he had been educated with the ideology of classical economics. His contributions began with a lengthy and apologetic historical digression aimed at persuading readers that economic science had been cultivated in Spain early on, when "in other nations it was viewed with indifference" (OEE, I, IV/1824, 13). This discourse effectively aligned Canga with Campomanes, Cabarrús and other eighteenth-century Spanish economists, who were repeatedly cited in the journal. The OEE's framework for economics content was provided by this question, Hispanic-Americanism, Anglophilia and defence of the British economic model, especially the reforms initiated by William Huskisson. The approach to the first issue was the most original; Canga's assiduous reports on Colombia, Chile, Buenos Aires and Mexico's economic and especially fiscal situations were dominated by his characteristic statistical vision and peppered with suggestions for reform. They invoked the principles of classical economics in terms of the shaping of the institutional framework (free initiative, property rights, competition law, etc.) and its implications for public finances (budgetary balance, limits on the size of the civil service, consolidation of public borrowing, etc.). This was especially evident with regard to Mexico, for which the journal presented a comprehensive plan for public finance reform. It is therefore reasonable to assume that under Rocafuerte's influence Canga's articles were actually an application to Mexican circumstances of the principles set out in the *Cartilla* and *Elementos*, which were reviewed in the OEE (III, no. XIV, V/1825, 472). However, at the same time, this strong Hispanic-American stamp was also being projected onto Spain: its "anarchy" was no longer to be found in the old colonies, but in the country itself, and since its woes stemmed from the lack of a "wise, vigorous and far-sighted government", that is, a constitutional government capable of correctly applying the principles mentioned, these republics were raised to the level of being models for Spain.[26]

While the EEC and the OEE evaded Ackermann's control, Mora's two journals, the MUC and the CLL, were the fruit of the two men's collaboration. The former appeared from July 1824 to October 1826 and was devised with a clear informative vocation to complement Blanco White's VML. It aimed to circulate empirical science and technology —especially English technology— in Hispanic America as the bedrock of material progress and well-being, thus evoking the CCL in some sense. The publication's star field was the mechanical arts, especially those that used steam power, and their utilitarian applications. The MUC also carried interesting articles on economics, built around the *filo rosso* of introducing Hispanic-American readers to the British capitalist economic model, its ingredients, the adapting of its principles to the new republics' economies and their ultimate economic and commercial integration with the British economy. According to Mora, "the attraction between England and the new states in South America is one of the most unique features of our times [...] and the relationships arising from it can have only beneficial consequences for both parties" (MUC, 1825–1826, I, 128). Moreover, as Mora himself points out, his journal aimed not only to reveal the sources of financial prosperity, but also "to serve as a school for those in a position to influence the fate of other peoples" (MUC, 1825–1826, I, 79). In other words, although the journal was aimed at a general readership, he especially aimed

[26] This dimension is less evident in a later monthly published by Canga Argüelles himself when Mora was no longer in London: EEO. He used it to make a radical political shift in defence of Ferdinand VII, the only liberal exile disaffection, according to Llorens (1968, 334–38), which enabled him to return to Spain in 1829.

to stimulate reforms by exerting intellectual influence on economic and political leaders in Hispanic America, which explains why the CEP's didactic and even academic and somewhat authoritarian tone gave way to a more persuasive writing style that was more open to debate and intellectual skirmish in the MUC.

British capitalism was thus both the model and the linchpin for the MUC's articles, and viewed from both theoretical and applied perspectives Mora's approach can be said to have penetrated the doctrinal depths and debates that this new economic system had generated in England. In the 1820s, however, there was no consensus among economists about the emerging industrial capitalism's unlimited possibilities for growth and prosperity. Mora was no stranger to these uncertainties and pointed out that the "advance of the arts and industry tends to multiply products so excessively that it is to be feared that disposing of them all will be impossible" (MUC, 1825–1826, I, 91). Certain authors who were not exactly minor figures were already pointing to the phenomenon of overproduction, which was generally ignored in conventional classical economics. Mora referred to two of these writers, Malthus and Sismondi, in his article "Political Economy" in order to contrast their pessimistic forecasts with the prosperous reality of English society. He opposed Sismondi's adherence to the orthodox mainstream in favour of Say's law —the law of markets—, according to which the free market guaranteed that all supply would be consumed and so overproduction crises could not arise in a capitalist economy. Most of the article was in fact a transcription of a long extract from Say that aimed to demonstrate that this type of crisis was impossible and concluded that the English experience and the current state of industry there gave credence to this doctrine, as "overall prosperity increases as the means of production are simplified and made cheaper" (MUC, 1825–1826, I, 93). Moreover, this industrial efficiency, which, according to the "doctrine of Messrs Ricardo and Say", permits an ever-increasing consumption of products, also generates beneficial "moral effects", since "the perfection of the means of production awakens competition, sharpens ingenuity, requires the cultivating of the sciences and thus spreads civilisation in general" (MUC, 1825–1826, I, 93). This naturally closed the circle: morals and economics would underpin each other if they were based on the right principles.

Mora used the MUC to echo another theoretical aspect that was highly controversial among classical economists: mechanisation. In his *Essay on Profits* (1815) Ricardo had attributed low grain prices to the use of agricultural machinery. However, in the third edition of his *Principles* he introduced a Chapter —"On Machinery"— that highlighted machinery's "injurious effects" on workers (Freni-Salvadori 2019). While he did not actually employ Ricardo's theories, Mora did allude to an unnamed French economist who opposed the introduction of machinery (MUC, 1825–1826, I, 389–99). However, as he had done in the CEP (Mora 1825, 32–36), in the end he accepted the classical economists' canonical and hegemonic position, faithfully following the arguments in Chapter VII of Say's *Traité*: machinery generated price reductions, profits and capital accumulation and, with all this, economic prosperity. As in his CEP, the famous example of the printing press in the *Traité* was a case in point (Say 1821, 34–41; MUC, 1825–1826, II, 44).[27]

However, the aspect of the British capitalist system that Mora was attempting to defend was not simply ideological. His overall aim was to forestall the growing doubts as to the system's viability in the Americas, and when he was writing the British economy had been hard hit by the Panic of 1825. The most likely cause of the crisis was the fear of inflation from previous monetary expansion, which led to the contraction of the monetary base after the Bank of England sold Exchequer bills. This was aggravated by fact that the Bank not only failed to act as lender of last resort, but also raised interest rates, with the result that there was a massive withdrawal of bank deposits and subsequent bankruptcies. The financial crisis spilled over into the real economy, causing a marked slowdown in economic activity (Gayer et al. 1953, 17). This situation was far from trivial to Mora, as it caused the prices of the new Hispanic-American republics' bonds that had been issued on the London market to halve. It was therefore useful to give a detailed account of this crisis in the financial and real economies; the fact that it had already attracted the Spanish exiles' attention is clear from various works by Flórez Estrada and Pebrer, who published a pamphlet that Mora reviewed in the MUC. Pebrer's analysis of the 1825 crisis was reasonably in line with contemporary historiographical interpretations and also furnished empirical data on the development of English manufacturing. Mora poured all this information into his

[27] McCulloch mentions the case raised by Ricardo in the *Principles*, which he describes as improbable, arguing, like Mora, that machinery is not detrimental but beneficial to workers because it helps to reduce prices (McCulloch 1825, 186–92). However, although Mora may have been aware of these arguments, he probably relied mainly on Say with regard to this question.

journal, aiming to show that the financial crisis was less serious than was supposed and that British capitalism was of course out of danger; hence, "the friends of liberty need not be alarmed" (Pebrer 1826; MUC, 1825–1826, II, 161–64).

However, if the British capitalist model were to be transferred to the economically underdeveloped Hispanic-American republics, it would need to be properly adapted. The most feasible way forward was to adopt a free trade agrarian development model, which Mora had advocated during the Liberal Triennium and had also evoked in the CEP and which now reappeared as a means of capitalist modernisation for the new republics. Free trade was one of the most common themes in Mora's economics writings; his initial interest during the Liberal Triennium achieved its maximum expression in the numerous lengthy articles he wrote in Hispanic America and, especially, Spain during the 1840s and 1850s. However, in the 1820s it was both complex and controversial to argue from England for the reduction of tariffs on products that were imported —and exported— by the new republics. Apart from the fact that during the eighteenth and early nineteenth centuries England had prospered by implementing protectionist policies, the British economy's high productivity levels were a threat to the new republics' emerging manufacturing sectors. On the other hand, Mora therefore made a special effort to persuade his readers of the benefits of free trade, mainly its positive effects on economic prosperity.

In short, as "an essential element in the organisation of civilised societies", political economy was called upon to play a central role in the construction of the new republics, to the point at which, were its principles not correctly applied, "they would drift about, driven by the random interplay of circumstances, rising at times to a fictitious prosperity yet continually moving towards complete bankruptcy" (MUC, 1825–1826, II, 43). Although Mora had spent enough time in London to have a working knowledge of English economics literature, he still stuck to the economic orthodoxy he had learned in Spain. Say remained "of all the writers on economics [...], the most accomplished" (MUC, 1825–1826, II, 43).

The complex density of the MUC's contents may have been a brake on its initial popularity among Hispanic-American audiences, and so from April 1826 onwards Mora began to fill the journal with lighter articles such as literary pieces and moral tales, to the detriment of scientific content. This shift brought the MUC's profile closer to that of Mora's second periodical, the CLP, which ran from January to October 1826. Publication began following the closure of Blanco White's VML as a result of his disagreements with Ackermann, and perhaps for this reason there were many formal similarities between the two, such as their frequent use of illustrative plates. However, in terms of content, Mora shunned "profound theories" and "that admirable mixture of erudition and good taste which distinguishes Blanco White's writings" (CLP, 1826, 1–2). In short, Mora respected Ackermann's criterion of creating a lightweight journal that would spread "useful, pleasant and interesting knowledge" and "literary taste" in the new republics, yet without venturing into the murky waters of "opinion". In fact, the CLP covered a very wide spectrum and discussed topics that ranged from literature, geography, history and politics to fashion and gardening, but it had no overtly economics content. Such subjects were filtered in via three reviews, the first of which discussed the progress of political science (CLP, 1826, 357–61), while the second commented on the *Letters on England* (1825) by Madame de Staël's son, Auguste Louis Baron Staël-Holstein (CLP, 1826, 70–75, 110–16, 201–209, 305–12). Devoted to describing the English political system and its positive consequences for economic prosperity, the sharp contrast drawn between this system and France accentuated the book's pro-English feel: "England has long been serving as a politics and legislation school for continental Europe" (CLP, 70). The third review referred to the *Cartas de un americano sobre la ventaja de los gobiernos republicanos federativos*, published by Rocafuerte in 1826. Mora unequivocally defended the book's central argument: of the six republics created from the break-up of the Spanish empire, only two had adopted the federal system, despite the fact that it was more efficient than a centralised system, as the example of the United States also showed (CLP, 352–56). Mora thus aligned himself with majority opinion among Hispanic-American diplomats in London — Rocafuerte wrote tacitly on behalf of the federal First Mexican Republic— as well as with Canga's authority as set out in the OEE. At the same time, other CLP contents laid bare the Hispanic-American agenda. The journal included four lengthy biographies of heroes from these countries and a history of Guatemala by José Cecilio del Valle. To sum up, like the MUC, the CLP was the forum in which Ackermann's commercial interests met Mora's intellectual concerns, embodied in his unwavering desire to present Britain as the pinnacle of civilisation and a worthy role model for Hispanic America. It is not unreasonable to surmise that the panegyric of capitalism and free trade with which Mora fuelled his London publications was to Ackermann's taste. Both were committed to the institutional and national development of the new republics, and this may perhaps have been one of the values that Ackermann most appreciated in Mora.

4.5 Final Remarks

Mora's profile as an intellectual at the service of disseminating information and ideas matured considerably during his years of exile in London. Llorens (1968, 344) defined him as the "true journalist of liberal emigration", while according to Amunátegui (1888, 82), he contributed a style that was hitherto unknown in Hispanic-American journalism. This was wholly possible due to the time he spent at the Ackermann factory, where he learned to work as a "proletarian of the literary republic", as he put it, so efficient and pragmatic that he would sacrifice his ideological positions to satisfy his employer's business interests if need be. His unquestionable ability to work in a transnational context, to write in different styles (poetry, narrative, history, etc.) and formats (books, articles, catechisms, etc.), as well as his elegant intermingling of pages of dense content with others that were more entertaining and superficial are excellent examples of his maturity as a craftsman. However, his time in London represented more than that. The fact of being embedded in the heart of the hotbed of political exiles that the city had become speeded up both the process of his Anglicisation and the invention of a space of culture and freedom for independent Hispanic America in which to implement his liberal ideology, something that was denied him in Spain.

Political economy was a prominent feature of this space. Of all the writers who worked for Ackermann, Mora was undoubtedly the leading exponent of the discipline, which was barely touched on in other comparable journalistic ventures such as those of Blanco White and Andrés Bello. His time in London was decisive in this aspect too. His belief in the Enlightenment ideals of material progress, faith in reason, education, the advances in civil liberty and the spread of knowledge, although present in earlier stages, were nickel-plated in Ackermann's London thanks to his rapprochement with the principles of British classical economics, with some of whose figures he had personal relationships. The idea of an anti-revolutionary conservative social order —liberal in Spanish terminology— which he would adapt to the new scenarios in which he lived, also took shape in those years. Mora would never again repeat his Liberal Triennium flirtations with *comunero* radicalism, but neither would he really shake off a certain social paternalism and intellectual elitism, which was very typical of the Enlightenment and combined a rejection of absolutism and clericalism with a certain sense of detachment towards the working classes. Given his well-honed competence it was not surprising that several Hispanic-American leaders tried to obtain his services once he had found his niche within moderate liberalism. José Cecilio del Valle, an influential Guatemalan deputy, tried to do so in 1826 (Durán 2015, 54), but the only invitation that Mora accepted was one from President Rivadavia to move to Buenos Aires a year later. As he announced in his farewell to the CLP, he was placing himself at the service of "the triumph of republican principles over tyranny, fanaticism, treason and ignorance", although behind this ideological sophistry lay the desire to become something more than a proletarian of the pen selling his labour on a piecework basis to an entrepreneur.

Bibliography

Books[28]

Mora, José Joaquín de. 1824a. *Cartas sobre la educación del bello sexo por una señora americana.* London: R. Ackermann.

Mora, José Joaquín de. 1824b. *Gimnástica del bello sexo, o Ensayos sobre la educación física de las jóvenes.* London: R. Ackermann.

Mora, José Joaquín de. 1824c. *Mémoires historiques sur Ferdinand VII, roi des Espagnes, et sur les événemens de son règne. Par Don****, avocat près des tribunaux espagnols. Traduits en anglais sur le manuscrit espagnol, par Michael J. Quin, et en français par M. G. H****.* Paris: Librarie Universelle de P. Mongie aîné.

Mora, José Joaquín de. 1825. *Catecismo de economía política.* London: R. Ackermann.

Mora, José Joaquín de. 1843. *De la libertad de comercio, por José Joaquín de Mora.* Sevilla: Establecimiento tipográfico, Imprenta de Carlos Rubio y compañía.

Translations and Reeditions

Blanco-White, José. 1844. *Cartas sobre Inglaterra dirigidas a don Alberto Lista, por don José Blanco-White y continuadas por don José Joaquín de Mora.* Santiago de Chile: Imprenta del Siglo.

[28] On the prolix reprints of the *Catecismos*, *Cursos* and other works of Mora in the Hispanic world, see Roldán (2003), Macintyre (2018) and Medina (2022).

Clavijero, Javier. 1826. *Historia antigua de México, sacada de los mejores historiadores españoles y de los manuscritos y de las pinturas antiguas de los indios*, 2 vols. London. R. Ackermann.

Fénelon, François. 1825. *Compendio de las vidas de los filósofos antiguos, escrito en francés por Fenelon, y traducido al castellano por J. J. de Mora*. Paris: Librería de Cormon y Blanc.

Pinnock, William. 1824. *Catecismo de geografía, o Introducción al conocimiento del mundo y de sus habitantes*. London: R. Ackermann.

Robinson, William Davis. 1824. *Memorias de la revolución de Méjico y de la expedición del General D. Francisco Javier Mina: a que se han agregado algunas observaciones sobre la comunicación proyectada entre los dos océanos, Pacífico y Atlántico, escritas en inglés por William Davis Robinson; y traducidas por José Joaquín de Mora*. London: R. Ackerman.

Primary Sources

Canga Argüelles, José. 1825. *Elementos de la ciencia de la Hacienda Pública*. London: Macintosh.

Flórez Estrada, Álvaro. 1819. *Representation to H. C. M. Ferdinand VII, King of Spain, in defence of the Courts*. London.

Herrera Dávila, José and Antonio Alvear. 1827. *Lecciones de economía política*. Sevilla: Imprenta de Mariano Caro.

McCulloch, John Ramsay. 1825. *The Principles of Political Economy, with a Sketch of the Rise and Progress of the Science*. Edinburgh and London: Adam and Charles Black-Longman, Brown, Green and Longmans.

Mill, James. 1821. *Elements of Political Economy*, London: Baldwin, Cradock and Joy.

Pastor, Esteban. 1825. *Catecismo de agricultura*. London: Ackermann.

Pebrer, Pablo. 1826. *Five Questions on the Actual Mercantile Distress*. London: Effingham Wilson.

Say, Jean Baptiste. 1821. *Tratado de economía política o exposición sencilla del modo con que se forman, se distribuyen y se consumen las riquezas*. Madrid: Fermín Villalpando.

Secondary Sources

Amunátegui, Miguel Luis. 1888. *Don José Joaquín de Mora. Apuntes biográficos*. Santiago de Chile: Imprenta Nacional.

Asensio, María Pilar. 2011. "Mora en Londres: aportaciones al Hispanoamericanismo". In *Londres y el liberalismo hispánico*, edited by Daniel Muñoz y Alonso García, 111–24. Madrid and Frankfurt am Main: Iberoamericana and Verbuet.

Baumol, William J. 1977. "Say's (at least) Eight Laws, or What Say, and James Mill May Really Have Meant". *Economica* 174: 145–61.

Breña, Roberto. 2011. "El primer liberalismo español y su proyección hispano-americana". In *Liberalismo y poder. Latinoamérica en el siglo XIX*, edited by Iván Jaksic and Eduardo Posada, 63–88. Santiago de Chile: FCE.

Comín, Francisco. 2000b. "Canga Argüelles: un planteamiento realista de la Hacienda liberal". In *Economía y economistas españoles. Vol. IV. La economía clásica*, edited by Enrique Fuentes, 413–39. Barcelona: Galaxia Gütenberg and Círculo de Lectores.

Durán López, Fernando. 2015. *Versiones de un exilio. Los traductores españoles de la Casa Ackermann (Londres, 1823–1830)*. Madrid: Escolar y Mayo.

Durán, Fernando and Daniel Muñoz. 2016. "Periódicos españoles en Londres: prensa 'en' y 'desde' el exilio". In *La prensa hispánica en el exilio de Londres (1810–1850)*, edited by María José Ruiz Acosta, 45–77. Salamanca: Comunicación social.

Fernández Sarasola, Ignacio. 2012. "La Constitución de Cádiz en Inglaterra". *Historia Constitucional* 13, 1–21.

Gayer, Arthur D., Rostow, W. W. and Schwartz, Anna Jacobsin. 1953. *The Growth and Fluctuation of the British Economy, 1790–1850*, 2 vols. Oxford: Clarendon Press.

González Hermoso, Alfredo. 2018. "Fernández Sardino y María del Carmen Silva: periodismo y exaltación". *Cuadernos de Ilustración y Romanticismo* 24, 669–700.

Hollander, Samuel. 2005. *Jean-Baptiste Say and the Classical Canon in Economics.* Abingdon-New York: Routledge.

Llorens, Vicente. 1968. *Liberales y románticos. Una emigración española en Inglaterra, 1823–1834.* Madrid: Castalia.

Macintyre, Iona. 2010. *Woman and Print Culture in Post-Independence Buenos Aires.* London: Tamesis.

Medina, Sara. 2022. *José Joaquín de Mora and Britain: Cultural Transfers and Transformations.* Berlin: Peter Lang.

Monguió, Luis. 1967. *Don José Joaquín de Mora y el Perú del ochocientos.* Madrid: Castalia.

Muñoz Sempere, Daniel y Alonso García, Alonso, eds. 2011. *Londres y el liberalismo hispánico.* Madrid and Frankfurt am Main: Iberoamericana and Vervuert.

Roldán, Eugenia. 2003. *The British Book Trade and Spanish American Independence. Education and Knowledge Transmission in Transcontinental Perspective.* Aldershot: Ashgate.

Ruiz Acosta, María José, ed. 2016. *La prensa hispánica en el exilio de Londres (1810–1850).* Salamanca: Comunicación social.

Schwartz, Pedro. 1999. "Estudio Preliminar". In *De la libertad del comercio*, by José Joaquín de Mora, VIII–XLIX. Madrid: IEF.

Simal, Juan Luis. 2012. *Emigrados. España y el exilio internacional, 1814–1843*. Madrid: CEPC.

Trease, B. David. 1953. *José Joaquín de Mora: A Spaniard Abroad*. PhD. Michigan, University of Michigan.

Tully, Carol. 2011. "Ackermann, Mora and the Transnational Context: Cultural Transfer in the Old World and the New World". In *Londres y el liberalismo hispánico*, edited by Daniel Muñoz and Alonso García, 153–64. Madrid and Frankfurt am Main: Iberoamericana and Verbuet.

Varela, Joaquín. 2016. "La prensa liberal española en Londres y París ante la Constitución de Cádiz, 1824–1830". *Cuadernos de Ilustración y romanticismo* 22, 329–38.

CHAPTER 5

In Rivadavia's Buenos Aires (1827): Coming Down in the Reformist Practice

5.1 Introduction

Hispanic America was not a popular destination for liberal Spanish exiles. The long and costly journey was full of hardships, the inhabitants of the new republics had serious misgivings about the Spanish after the years of military conflict and during the Liberal Triennium there had been a series of disputes between overseas representatives and Spaniards from the peninsula over the American territories' constitutional status: none of this created an appealing environment for political émigrés (Simal 2012, 235–36). Mora's move from London to the Republic of Argentina at the end of 1826 should therefore be interpreted as a relatively exceptional occurrence. His main reason for going there was the excellent offer he received from Rivadavia: paid passages for the entire family—he had two children by then—and a handsome salary of 2,000 pesos, in exchange for "entering public service" and "upholding the principles of his government by means of the press".[1] To Mora this was a sign of the prestige he had acquired in the Hispanic-American world through his publications and open support for the independence of Spain's old territories.[2] Ferdinand

[1] Mora to Rivadavia, Santiago de Chile, 7/IV/1828; Piccirilli (1960, III, 405–407).

[2] This is a reference to Spain's American territories, since the concept of empire was never enshrined in the law of the time (Portillo 2006, 17–19), although, as recent historiography has shown, it could well be referred to as a colonial empire (Fradera 2005).

J. Astigarraga et al., *The Economic Legacy of José Joaquín de Mora*, Palgrave Studies in the History of Economic Thought,
https://doi.org/10.1007/978-3-031-49446-8_5

VII's absolutism was still firmly entrenched in Spain and Mora's transatlantic voyage, with stopovers in Paris and Montevideo, was the start of a fifteen-year period of exile spent working for the new republics in Argentina (1827), Chile (1828–1831), Peru (1831–1834) and Bolivia (1834–1838), just as he served the two latter countries as a diplomat in London (1838–1843).

Pinpointing the moment at which Mora joined the Hispanic-American cause is not easy. His absence from the Spain of the Cortes of Cadiz when he was deported to France meant that he was prevented from witnessing the events surrounding the thorny issue of the colonies during those years. However, it is worth noting that positions supporting their emancipation were almost non-existent during the first phase of Spanish liberalism, which was embodied in the 1812 Constitution, and were also in the minority later on until Spain officially recognised the new Hispanic-American nations in 1836. The Constitution of Cadiz, which was drawn up with little representation from the American colonies, effectively established a single, indivisible sovereign state that included the European and American territories; this of course ran quite contrary to aspirations for independence, which in almost all cases, especially in Central America and part of Peru, had previously only involved demands for more autonomy. It is more than likely that Mora's support for the new countries began to take shape during the Liberal Triennium when his criticism of the anachronistic Spanish colonial system became harsher and his rapprochement with Bentham led him to undertake the unfinished translation of the anti-colonialist work *Rid Yourselves of Ultramarina* (1821). However, it was his formative experiences in London that finally brought about a shift in his sympathies towards open support for the new nations. The intellectual milieu in which he moved and which guaranteed his livelihood undoubtedly contributed to this: his close relationship with Blanco White—as stated Mora, the "first European writer to take up his pen in defence of American emancipation" (CPL, no. 39, 16/VI/1827)—, Bentham, Mill and McCulloch, also supporters of independence, and his connection with Hispanic-American diplomats and Ackermann, whose publishing company was involved in defending the interests of the new republics, especially when they were recognised by Great Britain in 1825. As a result of these influences Mora's relationship with Hispanic-American countries could be described as "British-style".

The socio-political reality that Mora encountered on his arrival in Buenos Aires in February 1827 was certainly still suffering the aftermath of the convulsions caused by the recent independence of Spanish territories in America. The most decisive steps in that direction had first been taken during the 1820s and their direct origins lay in reactions to the dynastic crisis engulfing the Spanish Bourbons, who were being held captive in Bayonne by Napoleon. He had crowned his brother Joseph King of Spain, a move that was rejected by the majority of the population of all social classes in both Spain and in America and gave rise to three interrelated and truly unique phenomena in what was known as the "Age of Revolutions". The first was a peninsular war of independence; the second, in the terminology of the day, was a liberal "revolution" challenging the Ancien Régime, and the third, from an institutional-political perspective, was the innovative and arguably spontaneous creation of *Juntas*, bodies that would represent the deposed dynasty until it recovered its lost position and thus fill the power vacuum. These three processes created a breeding ground in which the American independence movements blossomed; related to the diverse family of pre-1840s "liberalisms", they were described by Fernández Sebastián (2012a, 14–15) as being in their "formative Atlantic phase", still "universalising" before being confined "within the borders of each state resulting from independence".

In fact, the American revolt against Napoleon's invasion of the Iberian Peninsula was predominantly seen by the elites in the different regions as an opportunity, while fighting against an illegitimate monarch, to achieve greater political and administrative independence from Spain, to which they were initially loyal for the most part. However, inasmuch as these expectations were not fulfilled, mainly because Ferdinand VII restored absolutist power, but also due to immobility and lack of decisiveness in Spanish liberal sectors, the *Juntas* and the Creole-society that dominated socio-political framework that they represented became more radical and drifted towards pro-independence positions. This was especially true in the south, although the territories of New Spain, Central America and part of present-day Peru remained loyal to Spain for longer (Guerra 1992, 48). A complex series of factional wars were triggered from this period onwards, and while it is not feasible to give a full account of them here, it is important to point out that although each had its own specific characteristics, they all influenced one another, and that the individuals that stood out were the great figures of independence, Simón Bolívar and José de San Martín.

Hispanic America, in which Mora lived and worked for twelve years, was one of the areas into which French Enlightenment ideology had most penetrated and which had therefore been most open to far-reaching socio-political transformations (Guerra 1992, 48). It was no accident that it was these areas, especially Argentina and Chile, which manifested themselves as insurgent from the outset. Argentina had been the Viceroyalty of Río de la Plata since 1776 and on 25 May 1810 it became the United Provinces of Río de la Plata, declaring independence from Spain on 9 July 1816 and becoming the Republic of Argentina on 24 December 1826. Chile officially declared independence on 12 February 1817 after a tempestuous journey that had begun in 1810 as well. Mora also worked in Peru and Bolivia, whose historical journey took place during the same period and had many shared elements: with the decisive intervention of the *Expedición Libertadora del Perú* under the command of Argentinian General José de San Martín, Peru declared independence on 28 July 1821 and Bolivia did the same on 6 August 1825 via the *Asamblea General de Diputados de las Provincias del Alto Perú*, first calling itself the State of Upper Peru, then the Republic of Bolivar and finally the Republic of Bolivia on 3 October of the same year.

When Mora arrived in Buenos Aires in February 1827, the new republic-building process was at its height. Europe had turned towards monarchical—or even absolutist—regimes and the republics were emerging as authentic constitutional laboratories in which new political concepts bloomed and old ones acquired new meanings (Fernández Sebastián 2009, 25ff.). Mora played his part in this enterprise with an awareness that it was an immense collective undertaking, a kind of radically new and liberating utopia: Spain's former territories had "suddenly shifted from slavery to independence" and he wished to contribute to shaping their "new civil, political and economic existence". In keeping with this ambitious challenge, Mora's profile became more solid and mature during his years in Hispanic America. Taking on a more important role than he had had in London, for the first time he was a political insider, working in for authorities at the highest level: Rivadavia in Buenos Aires, Pinto in Chile, Gamarra in Peru and Santa Cruz in Bolivia. He pushed his talent for ubiquity and his capacity for work to the limit and took on responsibilities far beyond his routine devotion to the press, including teaching, political consultancy and diplomacy.

5.2 A New Political Context

In one of his first articles for the *Crónica política y literaria de Buenos Aires* (CPL, 1827), which had the expressive title "*De la moderación política*" (CPL, no. 2, 6/III/1827), Mora attempted to persuade the Buenos Aires elites of the advisability of establishing a regime of "moderate and just" liberty, evoking the civic republicanism of ancient civilisations in which "freedom's excesses" had been ring-fenced by virtue. The article reflected the diversity of republican models that would appear in the CPL; however, they were based on a duality of negative experiences—the French Revolution—and positive ones—the American Revolution and British parliamentarianism under Cromwell—. In fact, the "moderate and just" freedom that Mora called for was none other than the freedom that had inspired Rivadavia's set of reforms and which marked the intellectual and political climate he encountered when he arrived in Buenos Aires. From 1821 to 1824, while he was a minister in the Province of Buenos Aires government led by Martín Rodríguez and supported by the *Partido del orden*, Rivadavia had set in motion a series of modernising changes aimed at addressing the permanent governability crisis, which was manifestly reflected in the "political anarchy" of 1820 (Ternavasio 1998, 2002, 54–73). Meanwhile, with the aim of leaving the colonial legacy behind, its two most representative institutions, the Cabildo and the Trade Consulate of Buenos Aires, were abolished; a representative system via direct suffrage was established whose symbol was the *Sala de Representantes* and a range of laws on freedom of education, property, trade and printing, which had been sanctioned in 1811, were decreed, as well as a *regalista*-inspired re-founding of the status of the Church.[3] These innovative reforms were known as the "*feliz experiencia*" and were also intended to breathe new life into cultural practices and political consciousness. In the 1820s several new institutions were created in Buenos Aires—among them the *Sociedad Literaria* (1821) and the *Universidad de Buenos Aires* (1821)—which emerged as new social spheres that created an interim space between political power and society. At the same time, this climate gave rise to an embryo of public opinion that departed from the "official" version, transcending the Rivadavia elites in Río de la Plata (González 2003, 671) to nurture the new "republican-enlightened" citizenship and sustain the

[3] The term "*regalista*" refers to the policy deeply rooted in the Hispanic world to make political power prevail over ecclesiastical power.

infant representative, liberal political regime. Around this time the term "liberal" began to take on a more specific political meaning under the influence of Rivadavia's political acts; bogged down by ambiguity, the failure of a single political party to support it and its significance as a simple expression of the negation of despotism and Spain's past (Wasserman 2012), during the 1820s the concept of "liberal" began to be equated to a set of individual rights imbued more by the freedom of Benjamin Constant's "moderns" than by the prevailing semantics of collective patriotism (Entin 2014, 57). Yet, as in so many other countries that were witnessing similar profound changes, Rivadavia's reforms were actually a kind of "enlightened" or even "neo-Bourbon" reformism (Myers 2003), in that, as in the late Spanish Enlightenment, they were initiated from the top and by policy-makers who had to fulfil their obligations as rulers while at the same time working towards the creation of a public space that was designed to exercise its autonomy (Goldman 2000, 19).

When Martín Rodríguez's government fell in 1824 Rivadavia became an active diplomatic agent in Europe for sixteen months. He became acquainted with Destutt de Tracy in Paris and then met Bentham and Mill during a longer sojourn in London. Under Tracy's influence he recruited Neapolitan liberal Pedro de Angelis for his cause before leaving Paris for Buenos Aires in 1826 (Quinziano 2013, 258–59), followed in London by Mora, who he met in the circles surrounding Ackermann's hub-like *Repository of Arts*. Rivadavia's recruitment of these two intellectuals was undoubtedly related to the delicate situation he was facing in his second stage in politics, this time as president of the Provincial Government of Buenos Aires. This situation was mainly the result of tensions between *unitarios* and *federales*, which were inherent to the creation of the Argentine Nation and meant that the constitutional debate during those years was in essence more about the form of government—monarchy/republic, unitary/federal—than about the scope of individual rights or the division of powers (Goldman 2009). The provinces' rejection of the 1826 unitary, republican Constitution of the Argentine Nation, which was endorsed by Rivadavia's supporters, triggered the adopting of constitutional charters aimed at establishing provincial autonomy and pushed political factions to identify with either the unitary party, which advocated a republic based on popular sovereignty, or with the federal party, which favoured a confederation of sovereign provinces (Chiaramonte 2004; Verdo 2006). Rivadavia resigned in July 1827 at the height of one war at home and another with Brazil, prompting Mora to abandon Buenos Aires in December 1827, only ten months after he arrived.

Central to Rivadavia's political legacy was his promoting of the spread of learning, to which the remarkable economic expansion of the 1820s contributed, bringing Buenos Aires into the international economy as a leather supplier for the overseas market. As Gallo says (2002, 2004), it was after meeting Tracy and Bentham that Rivadavia began to sketch out plans for his government. Although there are signs that his personal relationship with Bentham cooled after 1825, Rivadavia must have continued to give credence to the reforms and policies that Bentham and British utilitarianism and the French *Idéologues* put forward. Their stamp is visible in some of the key reforms of his term in office, whether ecclesiastical, political or educational: the structure of the *Cámara de Representantes* and the *Universidad de Buenos Aires* may have been the fruit of Bentham's influence.

Rivadavia created Chairs in Agriculture, Ideology and Political Economy at the Universidad de Buenos Aires. The latter represented the first attempt to teach the discipline formally in Argentina (Acevedo 1949), as well as a kind of culmination of the lengthy process begun thirty years earlier by Manuel Belgrano and José Hipólito Vieytes to spread European economic ideas in Buenos Aires circles. The Chair in Political Economy was founded in 1823 and in the same year Rivadavia commissioned Santiago Wilde to translate James Mill's *Elements* (1821), the first version in the entire Spanish-speaking world, with the aim of promoting the teaching of the discipline. The Chair was also intended to boost the "application of the theory of this science to the corresponding practice in such new countries". Two preparatory courses were designed to this end; the first was theoretical and based on Mill, while the second was applied and covered domestic and commercial economics, as well as statistics and public finance, for which it was suggested that a textbook summarising this applied vision of Mill's book and also including notions of the history of political economy should be written. The Chair was re-established in 1826 and incorporated into Jurisprudence studies, thus losing its obligation to adhere to Mill and opening up a space for Say's *Traité*. It was headed by Fernández Agüero, who held the Chair in Ideology from 1821 to 1827 and wrote a textbook based on Tracy, which was partially published in 1824 and 1829 with help from Rivadavia's government (Di Pasquale 2011). If the fact that Bentham was covered in Civil Law studies is added to this mix, what emerges is a faithful picture of the anti-scholastic and modernising atmosphere that Rivadavia breathed into university teaching in Río de la Plata and which Mora encountered on his arrival there.

5.3 Mora in the Service of Rivadavia

No sooner had Mora arrived in Buenos Aires than he returned to the intense activity that he had carried out in London. He produced a third edition of the *Catecismo de geografía descriptiva* (1824), correcting the errors and omissions in the English editions, and edited two journals with Angelis, *El conciliador* (ECBA, 1827) and the afore mentioned CPL.[4] However, Mora must have been the main editor of both, as Angelis had no previous experience in journalism and could not write in Spanish. In fact, as would happen in Chile with the *El mercurio chileno*, the ECBA and CPL bristled with Mora's characteristic intellectual hallmarks: they were pro-American, pro-Bacon, sensualist, rationalist, liberal and utilitarian, akin to the British Common Sense school—in the CPL he spread its principles through the work of Dugald Stewart—and opposed to superstition, political absolutism and religious fanaticism, to the point of presenting Spain as a pernicious example of clericalism and excessive church power (CPL, no. 25, 5/V/1827). Both were tremendously high-brow and featured Stewart, Condillac, Tracy, Constant, Bentham, Smith, Mill and other distinguished authors from the European enlightened and liberal tradition.

Of the two journals, only the CPL covered economic issues. The ECBA ceased publication chiefly because of the poor relationship between its two editors (Trease 1953, 76). Just a single issue was published (May 1827), which included only the first instalment of an essay on the political history of the Provinces of Río de la Plata from the Buenos Aires liberal and unitary perspective of the revolutionary phase that began with the creation of the first *Junta* in 1810 in order to provide a contrast with the dark period under the Cabildo; in fact, it was a paean to the new political framework that emerged after independence. The issue also contained three long reviews of works on the Constitution of Bolivia, the Congress of Panama and the first issue of a London journal, Bello's *Repositorio Americano* (ECBA, May 1827, 65–82), in which Mora—who was undoubtedly the author—highlighted the importance of popularising the arts and sciences

[4] He has also been credited with editing the 147 issues of the periodical *El constitucional* (ECOBA, 1827), but Monguió rules this out on the basis that the CPL and ECOBA criticised one another harshly, and he particularly points out that ECOBA directly accused "a mercenary pen"—almost certainly Mora—of being an enemy of the new republic, as well as having plagiarised several British journals and *El Mensajero de Londres* (Monguió 1965, 305–306).

and encouraged the promotion of a new "indigenous" literature to raise Hispanic America to the level of enlightened nations. Mora stressed the notion that the advance of political science went hand in hand with the advance of good taste. He underlined the importance of the press, the theatre and the use of reason in literature to achieve this, since every free regime relied on the rule of reason and literature was an emblematic institution of every free regime (Monguió 1965, 326).

The CPL sought to raise the level of debate in the public sphere by imitating European cultural journals, while at the same time attempting to create and sustain "purely American" politics (CPL, no. 3, 8/III/1827). It became a tool for the legitimisation of Rivadavia's liberal economic and political reform project, almost an official mouthpiece of his government—it was initially published by the state printing press—. The first issue came out on 3 March 1827 in the aftermath of the publishing wave brought about by the 1821 Press Law. Firmly in the political milieu, it was published during the last four months of Rivadavia's project, coinciding with serious trade problems, as well as the civil war and the war with Brazil. Originally appearing three times a week, from issue 49 onwards there was an issue every day except Sundays; the project was financed from the public purse, with a little help from advertising and subscriptions; in the context in which it was founded, only the state could guarantee its acceptance by society and survival. The content did not generally run to over four pages, with all issues keeping to roughly the same structure (De Rosa 2019, 254–56). There was a range of permanent sections covering national and foreign news (Hispanic-American and European) and a section headed "*La Crónica*", which carried articles on economic issues and utilitarian philosophy.

By far the most important aspect of the CPL and ECBA was the educational purpose. Both papers echoed Mora's enlightened and optimistic view of progress and the perfectibility of mankind and institutions, as well as education's central role in this, especially in a hitherto untouched scenario such as Hispanic America. The ECBA stated unequivocally that "despotism is founded on ignorance" and therefore recommended that the Buenos Aires elites should organise elementary schools rather than academies, "which presuppose a more advanced civilisation than ours" (ECOBA, 18/V/1827, 17). The new world of political freedom, cultural progress and material wellbeing that Mora yearned for was at odds with the continuing deep-rootedness of scholastic teaching; in an attempt to combat this, Mora resumed the teaching work he had done at the

Universidad de Granada and the *Ateneo de Madrid*, founding the *Colegio Argentino*, a short-lived private girls' school in 1827 with his wife Fanny and Angelis' Swiss wife Melanie Dayet (CPL, no. 62, 26/VII/1827).[5] He and De Angelis also put together a plan for the *Ateneo Argentino*, a boys' secondary school; Angelis finally founded this in June 1828 when Mora was in Chile, but it was also a short-lived project. Both schools spoke to the need for a thorough-going overhaul of education that would bring about changes in social mores and Mora's enormous literary output throughout his time in Hispanic America contributed to this. His works included poetry, novels and plays, translations and essays on literary criticism, and with them he aimed to instil good taste and mould manners in the new civic morality exuded by the hopeful spirit of republicanism.

Mora's educational and literary activities were just one more component of a more complex system designed to promote the spread of knowledge. In keeping with the cultural mould shaped by Rivadavia, Mora aimed to use the CPL to show the Buenos Aires elites that learning was indispensable for strengthening and enhancing the political freedoms that had been won.[6] Not without a certain utopian element, he argued that the new representative and free governments should not restrict the flow of learning to a few elites, for "enlightening the people is the true way of teaching them to seek out their real interests" (CPL, no. 2, 6/III/1827). His eulogies on the benefits of printing and news of improvements in typographic techniques are no surprise; he also acted on Burke's recommendation to create annual record books, raising to the level of state policy the founding of reading groups, libraries, museums and organisations that would encourage the arrival in Hispanic America of books, these tools of "civilisation" and "virtue". These elements were all part of the cultural battle waged by the *Rivadavianos* against powerful enemies; the CPL carried accounts of the opposition to using Ackermann's much-praised catechisms mounted by religious sectors, who Mora branded as "ignorant, fanatical and superstitious" (CPL, no. 18, 19/IV/1827). The journal effectively mixed his longing for the British model of society with the effervescence of 1820s Buenos Aires, in which the *Sociedad Literaria* and

[5] Mora and Fanny reproduced this experience in Chile and far more information is available about this than about the *Colegio Argentino*; see. Chap. 6.

[6] The Chilean *El mercurio chileno* (10/3/1829) explicitly stated "if enlightened ideas need freedom to grow and spread, freedom in turn needs enlightened ideas to be preserved and secured on solid foundations".

the University were the great torch-bearers. The press, another of the major symbols of Rivadavia's policy (Quinziano 2013, 260–61), was recognised as the most powerful tool for spreading knowledge and dissolving excessive cultural elitism. Mora devoted three CPL articles to defending the "public" or "association" spirit,[7] presenting them as vigorous weapons for cohesion between public and private interests that sought, as he stated in one passage, to iron out the most obvious dangers of commercial society such as the alienation resulting from increased division of labour. Above all, however, at the heart of these articles lay the yearning for the British social model and the *Rivadavianos*' attempts to open up new public spaces that would breathe oxygen into the Buenos Aires political imagination. In a highly expressive passage Mora underscored the importance of the persuasive instruments used by the British Tory party, as opposed to those of the Spanish *Apostólicos*: reason, religious tolerance and the promotion of merit (CPL, no. 9, 22/III/1927). The desire to stimulate the emergence of public opinion also underlay this strategy of revitalising culture and knowledge. Although Mora and Angelis were Rivadavia's mouthpieces and their papers sought to explain and defend his reforms, they also helped to sow the seed of the notion of public opinion as the "highest court" and "reason", an opinion which in their words arose from the "clash of views" and the "habit of discussion", and was designed to create a well-educated and capable public to counteract the iniquity of political power (CPL, no. 26, 8/V/1827).

The CPL had a profoundly multidisciplinary slant. While it was full of literary, scientific and everyday news, it was oriented towards the problems arising from Rivadavia's unitary policy. Mora did not hesitate to abandon the federalist ideas that he had defended in London, to show that he was unequivocally pro-unitary: "federalism is lethal for emerging states" (CPL, no. 42, 23/VI/1827). His numerous reports on the Republic of the United States hit a wall on this issue; despite praising its economic and cultural achievements—including the prolific expansion of the press—Mora felt that it was not possible to "transfer" the decentralised North American experience to Argentina. The numerous articles on economics took the unitary principle as a starting point and were worthy original products, of which Mora was undoubtedly the author.[8] They should be scrutinised in light of the path he first took in London regarding the

[7] CPL (no. 12, 29/III/1827; no. 20, 21/IV/1827; no. 43, 26/IV/1827).

[8] The contents of articles published in the Chilean *El mercurio chileno* are a perfect match.

emerging Hispanic-American republics' need for institutional reforms that broke with the colonial past and guaranteed their economic survival. The limited spread of economic culture there meant that they could not be introduced into the international flow of ideas by "one economist to another", but instead this process had to be mediated by the political and cultural elites. In fact, given the context in which they were created—high rates of illiteracy, linguistic diversity and the absence of a "literary market"—, Mora's journals essentially circulated among these elites, and policy makers were a component of their target readership. The dichotomy between "science" and "art" inherent in political economy (Shumpeter 1955, 534 ff.), which Mora took from James Mill, enabled him to underline the irrelevance of these close political players, as the cost-benefit analysis of reform was "a matter of government policy and not of political economy" (CPL, no. 103, 17/X/1827). However, there is no denying that the CPL also aimed to nurture an orientation that applied to circumstances in Río de la Plata in the university political economy courses. With these criteria in mind Mora's articles for the CPL had a threefold aim: to spread the principles of classical political economy; to develop an economic growth model for the Republic of Argentina and the other republics as a whole, and of course to provide a theoretical underpinning for the policies and reforms of Rivadavia's project.

5.4 The *Crónica* and Classical Political Economy

Mora's first objective was partially achieved with an article entitled "*Revista sumaria de los progresos de la economía política*" (CPL, no. 56, 19/VII/1827). It presented this science as key knowledge for achieving welfare and social progress, thus preventing "mankind's long childhood" from going on for ever. It covered the entire history of economics as a discipline and highlighted the watershed represented by "the immortal Englishman Adam Smith", who "laid the foundations of true political economy" by showing "that labour is the universal agent of wealth creation". Mora sought to convince educated readers of the analytical defeat of the "mercantile system", aiming to uproot the belief that gold and silver were the "sole origin of public and private wealth" and that international trade was a zero-sum activity, as the new "science of production" had become widespread in all countries thanks to the works of Say, Sismondi, McCulloch, Malthus, Ricardo, Mill, Gioja, Storch and many others. These authors all appeared one way or another throughout Mora's work during his stay in Hispanic America, whether he criticised or accepted their theories. Furthermore, the CPL carried accurate and glowing reports of other writings that Mora had brought from London such as the new French editions of Say's *Traité* (CPL, no. 14, 3/IV/1827) and Flórez Estrada's *Reflexiones* (CPL, no. 21, 26/IV/1827), which discussed the theory that the British trade crisis was due to the emancipation of the American colonies (1827; the English edition was from 1826).

In Buenos Aires, however, Mora's economic thought began to turn towards the ideas of McCulloch, "one of the men who had most driven economic theory forward". He discussed this in the article "*Sobre las opiniones de Mr. McCulloch*" (CPL, no. 61, 26/VII/1827). As previously mentioned, Mora knew McCulloch personally in London and must have been impressed by his work—in fact, he cited it in the CEP—and given his commitment to an experimental form of economic science that was far removed from Ricardo's abstract constructions, McCulloch's methodology, which constructed economic theories "with the help of positive data and current facts", probably appealed to him. The figure of McCulloch enabled Mora to emphasise that political economy was the "social science par excellence", whose positive consequences spilled over into customs, good taste and justice; in short, into society as a whole. In any event, Mora's core article aimed to "do our readers a service by giving them some idea" of his economic principles and to prepare the ground for a model of economic development for Río de la Plata—and for the Hispanic-American republics in general—which proposed a set of reforms and economic policies that were clearly rooted in liberalism and free trade. Indeed, these two purposes are interwoven in Mora's account of McCulloch's economic ideas, which he credits with having "pushed back the boundaries of science" in the fields of the theory of money and credit and the theory of trade, while at the same time helping to guarantee private property; abolish obstacles to industry and foster it by means of moderate taxation; denounce monopolies, and of course promote free trade. McCulloch—"one of science's brightest lights"—thus became the intellectual corner stone on which Mora built his economic development model for the new republics, a point that he raises at the end of the article when stating that McCulloch "must have a more direct influence on our fates, and therefore has a stronger claim on our thoughts" (CPL, no. 61, 26/VII/1827).

Bentham's prestige among the *Rivadavianos* left a profound mark on the CPL. It carried brief descriptions of many of Bentham's works, which were written by Mora and laid out in four articles. Mora aimed to make up for the lack of a "complete collection of his works and lack of translations, except Dumont's into French".[9] The articles included commentaries on works on parliamentarianism and government in general—the *Plan of Parliamentary Reform* (1817) and *Fragments on Government* (1776)—; on crime—*The Panopticon Writings* (1790)—and on legal issues—the first and second *Letter to Lord Pelham* (1802) and *Scotch Reform* (1806)—. A more prominent position was afforded to *An Introduction to the Principles of Morals and Jurisprudence Actions* (1789), which Mora described as a "fundamental work", and *A Table of the Springs of Action* (1817), a "masterpiece of logic, analysis and reasoning", which analysed the consequences of applying the principle of utility to legislation and jurisprudence (CPL, no. 72, 8/VIII/1827). Perhaps rather oddly, he was less precise when citing *Defence of Usury* (1787), Bentham's main work on political economy, referring to it as "Defense of the Economy" and then barely commenting on it—which suggests that he may not in fact have read it (CPL, no. 74, 10/VIII/1827)—. Mora also reviewed the anti-colonial *Rid Yourselves of Ultramarina* (1821).

5.5 The *Crónica* and the Construction of an Economic Model for Río de la Plata

Some of the components of Mora's economic development model are outlined in the CPL, but it still lacks cohesion. This was undoubtedly the articles' secondary purpose, although the fact that publication of the CPL was suddenly interrupted on 6 October 1827 meant that the final version of the model had to be postponed until Mora's sojourn in Chile. Nevertheless, he still had time to sketch out the three central elements: free trade, the distribution of the tax burden and the importance of promoting agriculture.

Mora returned to the topic of free trade. However, as in the London MUC, he again failed to provide any theoretical basis for it in the CPL, nor did he ever mention Smith or Ricardo's theories of international trade, although there are echoes of them in expressions such as the "balance which the products of the land and industry tend to take among different countries in the world", and also in an extract from Section XVI of Mill's *Elements* which is included in the periodical (CPL, no. 103, 17/IX/1827;

[9] Mora omits to mention here that Toribio Núñez and Ramón de Salas' Spanish translations had been published by then.

Mill 1821, 159–60).[10] However, he undoubtedly gave some thought to the international division of labour, and this is clear from his insistence—following the pattern adopted in the MUC—on the need for the new nations, particularly the Republic of Argentina, to "encourage our agriculture, which is undeniably the most plentiful, safest and most moral branch of public wealth" (CPL, no. 103, 10/III/1827).[11] When the expansion of leather exports was at its height, Mora was confident of the potential of the South American market—with the exception of Brazil—as a destination for Argentinian agricultural surpluses (CPL, no. 103, 17/X/1817). Furthermore, evoking the theory of the stages of economic development, he felt that "before being manufacturers, it is necessary to be farmers", so that in a context like the Argentine Republic agriculture should be the preferred destination of capital should Mill's free use requirement be met (CPL, no. 100, 13/IX/1827).

On this basis, the "infant industry" argument as theoretical support for protectionism, a favourite among "old-school economists" and prevalent in Buenos Aires circles, vanishes. Mora did not even bother to refute it in the CPL, confining himself instead to spelling out the practical consequences of protectionism and free trade. While recognising the importance to the public purse of collecting "import duties", he stressed the instability of this type of revenue, which depended on numerous factors beyond government control; the high collection costs—administration, public officials and warehouses, the negative impact on consumers and, along the Smith's lines, the dire consequences for morals and crime—(CPL, no. 97, 10/IX/1827).[12] In contrast, free trade promoted economic prosperity and, among other aspects, favoured population increases without causing money shortages, according to Torrens.[13] Underlying Mora's entire rationale is complete confidence in the power of self-interest to transform material conditions by means of increased needs, for which the practical model was the British economy and British capitalism. In this

[10] The CPL itself contains statements such as: the "issue at hand is more appropriate for a treatise than for a newspaper" (CPL, no. 103, 17/IX/1827).

[11] The CPL encouraged the regular teaching of agriculture and agronomic techniques in a number of articles (no. 60, 27/VI/1827; no. 62, 27/VII/1827). Mora cited John Sinclair in defence of agriculture's economic sway in British history.

[12] To show that industry is a "spontaneous plant" that does not grow under privilege, Mora cited the example of Catalonia during the Liberal Triennium, in which the cotton mills did not flourish under prohibitionist trade measures (CPL, no. 100, 13/IX/1827).

[13] Mora is probably referring to *An Essay on the External Corn Trade* (1815).

respect, it is not surprising that the CPL repeatedly mentions the recent tariff reduction policy promoted in Britain by William Huskisson, who Mora presented as a "disciple" of Smith (CPL, no. 57, 20/VII/1827; no. 97, 10/IX/1827).[14]

Mora's free trade proposal entailed abolishing customs tariffs on imports—even unilaterally—and creating a single free port in Buenos Aires, since the possibility of "extending free port legislation to an entire nation" was still wholly utopian. The free port of Livorno in Tuscany appeared again as an exemplary trading enclave with these characteristics (CPL, no. 103, 17/IX/1827). However, abolishing customs tariffs required parallel reflection on how to finance the republic, and the need to replace these tariffs with "more secure and more productive" forms of revenue. Mora spelled out Smith's four principles of taxation to show that customs duties were inconsistent with them, drawing on sources as wide-ranging as Uztáriz and Turgot to show that increasing tax rates slowed consumption and thus tax revenue. He also outlined some elements of his theory of taxation, which he developed in detail during his years in Chile. He already seemed to be thinking of the ability-to-pay principle and replacing customs revenue with a direct tax imposed essentially on agriculture as the country's main source of wealth (CPL, no. 104, 18/IX/1827). Underlying his reflections on these issues was his rejection of the practices of the "mercantile system". Customs duties were not only unnecessary barriers to economic growth, but also flashpoints of "oppression, arbitrariness and despotism". Moreover, as he repeatedly explained, these harmful practices were likely to turn the "spirit of trade" into a "spirit of monopoly", sacrificing general interests to benefit producers and exploiting a greed for collecting taxes that was deeply harmful to consumers.

5.6 The *Crónica* and *Rivadaviano* Reformism

Many of Mora's economics articles endeavoured to support the liberal reformism of Rivadavia, who he "defended hotly, without excusing compromises". He was required to broach theoretical topics relating to monetary and financial policy, chief among which was undoubtedly the financing of the new republic, especially in view of the serious budgetary problems caused by the war.

[14] Mora uses information reported by Canga Argüelles in the London OEE.

The protagonist in the monetary sphere was the successor to the *Banco de las Provincias Unidas del Río de la Plata*, the *Banco Nacional*, which was created by Rivadavia in 1826 as part of the nation-building process. The bank had the two-fold aim of concentrating the granting of credit and being a tool for "political unity", that is, political centralisation; its capital consisted of funds from the Buenos Aires Province *Banco de Descuentos*, which was founded in 1822 thanks to a loan from Baring Brothers & Co and private shareholders. Its main functions were those of a deposit bank that gave loans and also could also issue currency, over which it theoretically had a monopoly. In December 1826, shortly before Mora arrived in Buenos Aires, a law was passed requiring the bank to lend the government—its main shareholder—unlimited cash to finance the war with Brazil. In order to restore the bank's credit and its shareholders' confidence a treasury finance commission was set up which produced several proposals, some of them clearly contrary to government interests, such as "the fullest sacrifice of the government's rights to the bank's interests" and the "gradual and total extinction of paper money" (CPL, no. 74, 10/VIII/1827). Mora took it upon himself to refute these two suggestions in a series of articles in the CPL—"*Casa de moneda*", "*Bosquejo histórico de un banco nacional*" (1 and 2), "*Bancos*", "*De los bancos particulares de Escocia*" and "*Crédito público*"—.

The first issue was eminently political. Mora showed his loyalty to Rivadavia in this regard by defending the government's point of view, although it was somewhat implausible from an analytical perspective. While acknowledging with Say the dangers "to which this alliance between the bank and public finances may lead"—he cited Say's notes to Storch's *Cours d'économie politique* (1823; CPL, no. 71, 7/VIII/1827)—, in line with both Sismondi and Say he relied on customary practice in European countries for banking to continue to supply the government with credit; the example of similar practices at the prestigious Bank of England could not be more illuminating in this respect. Where the second proposal is concerned, Mora attempted to refute the belief that there was a paper money surplus in the Republic of Argentina by following the maxim that a country's specific circumstances, in this case the financial backwardness of former Spanish colonies vis-à-vis England, totally conditioned any analysis of the monetary situation. He also raised a further matter that was directly related to paper money: the question of its convertibility and the necessary proportionality between the *Banco Nacional*'s issue of paper money to meet the state's financial needs and its metal reserves.[15] Mora declared himself first and foremost in favour of the issuance of paper money, supporting this stance with a passage from Chapter XXVII of the French version of Storch's *Cours d'économie politique* (Storch 1823). In fact, the "project" supported the cancelling of government credit on the basis of the bullionist argument that "the only effective way of guaranteeing the value of notes issued by any bank is that they should be convertible into precious metals". However, he believed that lack of capital was the chief "obstacle holding back the impetus of agriculture and gainful enterprises" in the Republic of Argentina, and that this justified issuing paper money (CPL, no. 69, 4/VIII/1827), arguing that public borrowing was preferable to windfall taxes, since the latter directly harmed capital accumulation. However, as presumably befitted a republican regime, this credit had to be used properly, that is, to finance spending that would stimulate demographic and economic growth and thus enhance repayment conditions (CPL, no. 99, 12/IX/1827). Moreover, following McCulloch, he estimated the level of interest rates, a key variable in determining whether a country had a paper money surplus, to be quite low in the Republic of Argentina, which indicated a shortage instead. Mora again evoked the principle set out in the Appendix to the CEP that economic laws could not be universally applied. This was crucial for understanding how the monetary theory that he shared with McCulloch and from which different economic policy requirements were drawn depending on the national context could be adapted to Hispanic America (CPL, no. 81, 20/VIII/1827).

Another issue with some political importance which Mora discussed in several articles was the refuting of one of the corollaries of the Malthusian theory of population and its arithmetical and geometrical rules, which directly affected the Rivadavia government policy: the idea that the steady population increase in the United States was due to "procreation".[16] On the basis of information from European and American newspapers and specialist studies of the censuses of various states in North America, Mora believed that he had "assembled the most positive evidence" to show that the population growth in the United States was due to the influx of "immigrants". Mora had already refuted Malthus' theory and its pessimism over

[15] In spite of this, Mora, who used data from the *Registro Nacional*, estimated that the *Banco Nacional* had maintained proportionality (CPL, no. 71, 7/VIII/1827).

[16] He had already transcribed paragraphs from a colonisation project in the Republic of Argentina for the MUC (1825–1826, I, 257–62).

the problem of population in the development of capitalism in similar terms in the MUC, and he now attempted to convey his critical stance to the CPL's enlightened readers. However, his ultimate aim was to provide theoretical backing for the policy of Rivadavia's government, which was committed to creating agricultural colonies in the frontier territories to be peopled by immigrants from Europe: a political strategy for the territorial consolidation of the new republic. He therefore recommended changing the emigration laws when the war was over and evoked American regulations, undoubtedly aiming to inspire action in this respect (CPL, no. 30, 17/V/1827). He also repeated Malthus' advice to found the new colonies on the basis of small landowners, since the accumulation of power over territory only created a privileged class with tendencies to power abuse, idleness and corruption (CPL, no. 99, 11/IX/1827).

5.7 Final Remarks

Although Mora's economics articles for the CPL still fell within the ideological and conceptual boundaries that were established during his time in London, it is possible to catch the first glimpses of the germ of a suitable economic development model for the Hispanic-American republics, which grew to fruition during his years in Chile. In this respect, it is clear that Mora was more than just a journalist who legitimised the discourses of power. His goal was the shaping of a critical and educated public opinion, capable of drawing a line under the colonial period for good and Americanising the roots of European liberal and enlightened thought. To a great extent this is what he aimed to do in the CPL through skilful use of the conceptual framework of classical economics in the service of an agricultural development strategy and the construction of the new Argentinian nation-state, and this explains why he placed greater emphasis on institutional aspects—monetary, fiscal and customs systems—than on any detailed determining of the scope of individual rights. However, Mora was prevented from developing these thoughts into a consistent theory at the time by the sudden end of Rivadavia's presidency on 7 July 1827. Indeed, both Mora and Angelis were deprived of their salaries as a result, and on 6 October the publication of the CPL came to an end, just seven months after it had begun, amidst the hostile climate created by the promotion of an implacable adversary of Rivadavia's Unitarian party—Manuel Dorrego—to the position of governor of Buenos Aires Province. Nevertheless, the differing fortunes of Mora and Angelis speak volumes about the former's ultimate motivation. With their relationship marred by insurmountable disagreements, which were also related to the creation of the *Colegio Argentino*, Angelis shifted with the same conviction from Rivadavia's unitary, liberal project to Manuel de Rosas' federal, authoritarian enterprise, becoming one of its foremost spokespersons. Meanwhile, a new phase of Mora's seemingly endless exile began when he moved to Santiago de Chile under President Pinto's regime.

Bibliography

Primary Sources

Mill, James. 1821. *Elements of Political Economy*, London: Baldwin, Cradock and Joy.

Storch, Heinrich Friedrich von. 1823. *Cours d'économie politique*. Paris: J. P. Aillaud.

Secondary Sources

Acevedo, Carlos Alberto. 1949. "La enseñanza de la ciencia de las finanzas en la Universidad de Buenos Aires desde su fundación hasta 1830". *Revista del Instituto de Historia del Derecho* 2, 11–46.

Chiaramonte José Carlos. 2004. *Nación y Estado en Iberoamérica. El lenguaje político en tiempos de las independencias.* Buenos Aires: Editorial Sudamericana.

De Rosa, Nicolás Andrés. 2019. "La *Crónica política y literaria de Buenos Aires* (1827). Una aproximación de Mora y De Angelis en sus años rivadavianos". In *Prensa y política en Iberoamérica*, edited by Fabián Herrero and Alejandra Pasino, 249–75. Buenos Aires: Universidad de Buenos Aires.

Di Pasquale, Mariano. 2011. "La recepción de la *Idéologie* en la Universidad de Buenos Aires". *Prismas. Revista de historia intelectual* 11, 63–86.

Entin, Gabriel. 2014. "Libertad: Argentina/Río de la Plata". In *Diccionario político y social del mundo iberoamericano*, edited by Javier Fernández, vol. II, 49–68. Madrid: UPV-CEPC.

Fernández Sebastián, Javier, ed. 2009. *Diccionario político y social del mundo iberoamericano. La era de las revoluciones, 1750–1850.* Madrid: Sociedad Española de Conmemoraciones Culturales and CEPC.

Fernández Sebastián, Javier. 2012a. "Introducción. En busca de los primeros liberalismos iberoamericanos". In *La aurora de la libertad. Los primeros liberalis-*

mos en el mundo iberoamericano, edited by Javier Fernández Sebastián, 9–35. Madrid: Marcial Pons.

Fradera, Josep Maria. 2005. *Colonias para después de un imperio.* Barcelona: Bellaterra.

Gallo, Klaus. 2002. "Jeremy Bentham y la 'feliz experiencia'. Presencia del utilitarismo en Buenos Aires (1821–1824)". *Prismas. Revista de historia intelectual* 6, 79–96.

Gallo, Klaus. 2004. "En búsqueda de la 'República ilustrada'. La introducción del utilitarismo y la *Idéologie* en el Río de la Plata a fines de la primera década revolucionaria". In *Revolución, política e ideas en el Río de la Plata durante la década de 1810*, edited by Fabián Herreo, 85–100. Buenos Aires: Ediciones Cooperativas.

Goldman, Noemí. 2000. "Libertad de imprenta, opinión pública y debate constitucional en el Río de la Plata (1810–1827)". *Prismas. Revista de historia intelectual* 4, 9–20.

Goldman, Noemí. 2009. "Constitución: Argentina-Río de la Plata". In *Diccionario político y social del mundo iberoamericano. La era de las revoluciones, 1750–1850*, edited by Javier Fernández, 325–37. Madrid: Sociedad Española de Conmemoraciones Culturales and CEPC.

González Bernaldo de Quirós, Pilar. 2003. "Sociabilidad y opinión pública en Buenos Aires (1821–1852)". *Historia contemporánea* 27, 663–94.

Guerra, François-Xavier. 1992. *Modernidad e independencias. Ensayos sobre las revoluciones hispánicas.* Madrid: Mapfre.

Monguió, Luis. 1965. "José Joaquín de Mora en Buenos Aires en 1827". *Revista hispánica moderna* 31, 303–28.

Myers, Jorge. 2003. "La paradoja de la opinión. El discurso político *rivadaviano* y sus dos polos: el 'gobierno de las luces' y la 'opinión pública'". In *La vida política en la Argentina del siglo XIX: amas, votos y voces*, edited by Hilda Sábato and Alberto Lettieri, 75–96. Buenos Aires: FCE.

Piccirilli, Ricardo. 1960. *Rivadavia y su tiempo*, 3 vols. Buenos Aires: Editorial Peuser.

Portillo, José María. 2006. *Crisis atlántica. Autonomía e independencia en la crisis de la monarquía hispánica.* Madrid: Marcial Pons.

Quinziano, Francisco. 2013. "Prensa periódica y campo cultural en el Río de la Plata. Pedro de Angelis, 'escritor oficial'". *Anales* 25, 253–81.

Simal, Juan Luis. 2012. *Emigrados. España y el exilio internacional, 1814–1843.* Madrid: CEPC.

Ternavasio, Marcela. 1998. "Las reformas *rivadavianas* en Buenos Aires y el Congreso General Constituyente". In *Revolución, república, confederación (1806–1852)*, edited by Noemí Goldman, 161–97. Buenos Aires: Sudamericana.

Ternavasio, Marcela. 2002. *La revolución del voto. Política y elecciones en Buenos Aires, 1810–1852.* Buenos Aires: Siglo XXI.

Trease, B. David. 1953. *José Joaquín de Mora: A Spaniard Abroad.* PhD. Michigan, University of Michigan.

Verdo, Geneviève. 2006. *L'independece argentine entre cités et nation (1808–1821).* Paris: Publications de la Sorbonne.

Wasserman, Fabio. 2012. "Entre la moral y la política. Las transformaciones conceptuales de 'liberal' en el Río de la Plata, 1750–1850". In *La aurora de la libertad. Los primeros liberalismos en el mundo iberoamericano*, edited by Javier Fernández, 37–73. Madrid: Marcial Pons.

CHAPTER 6

Chile (1828–1832): An Economic Development Model for the Hispanic-American Republics

6.1 Introduction

Mora arrived in Santiago de Chile to work in the service of President Pinto on 10 February 1828, after a journey across the Andes that took over a month.[1] The conditions of his relocation had been agreed beforehand with Miguel Riesco, a Chilean former member of the *Cortes de Cádiz* and Chilean Consul in Buenos Aires (Iglesias 2017) and included housing, a salary similar to that in Buenos Aires—2000 *pesos* a year—, the opportunity to begin practising law immediately and a government position, which resulted in his appointment as a senior official in the Ministry of State. Mora was already known to both the liberal party, which welcomed him, and the Chilean elites before his arrival. In 1827 *La clave* (LCL, 1827–1829; no. 26–27, 2–12/XI/1827) had reproduced one of his pro-free trade articles from the CPL[2]; moreover, his literary pieces and catechisms were already circulating there as Chile was a routine destination for Ackermann's Spanish-language works. However, Mora was not the first intellectual liberal Hispanic exile to arrive in Chile. Under the aegis of London-based Chilean diplomat Mariano Egaña, who was in charge of

[1] He had become familiar with the ups and downs of Chilean politics in Buenos Aires; see, for example, the CPL (no. 55, 18/VII/1827).

[2] Mora may also have been behind a series of articles on state borrowing in the same journal; see LCL (no. 85, 19/II/1829; no. 86, 5/III/1829; no. 92, 4/IV/1829).

J. Astigarraga et al., *The Economic Legacy of José Joaquín de Mora*, Palgrave Studies in the History of Economic Thought, https://doi.org/10.1007/978-3-031-49446-8_6

recruiting professionals for Chile there (Iglesias 2017), two men who would later work with Mora had left London for Santiago in 1825 to work as teachers: physician-surgeon José Passamán and mathematician Andrés Gorbea, who were followed in July 1829 by Andrés Bello, an old acquaintance from London. All this helped Mora to immerse himself speedily in Santiago life. His impressive range of activities led to the Chilean parliament rapidly granting him citizenship "by special grace" in 1829 as a reward for "uncommon merits" (Amunátegui 1888, 178–79).

This is not the place to review the spread of liberalism in Chile, but it should be noted that the political atmosphere in the country was a good breeding ground for Mora's reformist, liberal ideas. After independence in 1818 Chilean nation-building was driven by an elite with a republican ideology that rejected the Spanish colonial heritage.[3] This indigenous tradition, which was embodied by Manuel de Salas, Juan Egaña and Camilo Henríquez, did not, however, escape the influence of enlightened Spanish and European thought. Nonetheless, the idea of freedom rooted in pro-independence republicanism took on a different political dimension during the 1820s when the old "patriot/realist" dichotomy was replaced by "liberal/conservative" (Fernández Sebastián 2009, 758ff.). When Ramón Freire's government came to power in 1823, replacing Bernardo O'Higgins, political initiative passed into the hands of the *Pipiolos*, who, according to their conservative opponents, or *Pelucones*, constituted a compact group underlain with liberalism. On 25 February 1828 after the failure of the federalist attempt and President Freire's abdication the *Pipiolos* led by Pinto—together with the former federalists and their allies—achieved the majority in the legislative House with a political project opposed to that of the *Pelucones*, who supported traditionalism and authoritarianism and tended to accept guidance from the Catholic Church. The liberals' arrival in power coincided with Mora's appointment as government adviser.

6.2 Mora in the Service of Pinto

Mora's first service of note for Pinto was the drafting of a new Constitution. Approved on 6 August 1828, it replaced Juan Egaña's 1823 Constitution, the first in Chilean history, which had barely been in force for a year. In

[3] On the onerous economic legacy from the colonial period, see Llorca-Jaña and Martínez-Barraza (2023) for a comprehensive overview."

contrast to the latter's conservative basis, the 1828 document represented the culmination of the process by which a liberal political identity had grown to maturity in Chile during the 1820s (Fernández Sebastián 2009, 360, 760–61; 2014, V, 112–14). For the first time the Constitution enshrined the Republic as a form of government—specifically a "popular representative Republic"—based on a bicameral system; a property-based electoral system; the division of powers; a healthy balance between central and local power that still retained a unitary sense, provincial assemblies created as a concession to the federalists and the recognition of individual liberties, both natural, as in the previous Constitution, and civil.[4] In contrast to the 1823 document, a sort of "civic aristocracy" imbued with "national morality" (*Constitución* 1823, Tit. xxii; Stuven 2012, 192–93), Mora's version opened with a chapter devoted to individual rights (*Constitución* 1828, Chap. iii), which recognised as "inalienable and inviolable" rights "liberty, security, property ownership, the right to petition and to publish one's opinions"; it also ratified the abolition of slavery, established equality before the law, the absence of privileged classes—including in the taxation field—and abolished primogeniture and entailments (*Constitución* 1828, Arts. cxxv, cxxvi).

The discussions over the draft constitution were not free of controversy, which Mora made no attempt to avoid. *El constitucional* (ELC, 1828) railed in tremendous detail against core points in the draft over five dense issues published throughout June and July 1828, although without actually managing to change its final focus.[5] At the same time, an anonymous *Memoria*, attributed to Juan Egaña, was published, which defended not only the legal and economic benefits of entailments, but also Congress's lack of competence to legislate on them (Anonymous 1828). Mora's meticulous and detailed response was an excellent reflection of what was at stake. In 1818 O'Higgins had attempted and failed to abolish entailments and this objective was therefore included in Article 121 of the draft constitution. Mora's *Respuesta a la Memoria* extended the scope of his analysis beyond the serious problem of entailed land: he stated clearly that

[4] However, Iglesias (2017) argues that Mora's position vis-à-vis the political system was unclear during his time in Chile, referring that, in spite of his support for the republic, he was not entirely opposed to a constitutional monarchy in which the citizens elected the ruling dynasty.

[5] Although occasionally attributed to Mora, the ELC's format and sources suggest otherwise; its content also positions the paper on the front line of opposition to Mora's constitutional principles.

the Constitution's ultimate purpose was to sweep away the "decrepit legislation" in which "the abuses of feudalism and whims of absolute power were recast" (Mora 1828, 5). Flagging quotations from the anonymous *Memoria* as spurious, wrong or decontextualised, he used his habitual sources of Tracy, Bentham, Montesquieu, Storch, Heineccio, Lauderdale and Smith, adding expressive paragraphs from Jovellanos' *Informe de Ley Agraria* (1795), to emphasise the utilitarian and economic underpinning of the entailment problem: "we have reached a time when the principle of utility is the only crucible of human institutions" (Mora 1828, 21). In his opinion, there was no doubt that abolishing entailments would benefit society since it would lead to a drop in land prices, improved harvests, a population increase and greater equality. The backdrop to the *Memoria* was a perfect reflection of the displeasure that the Constitution aroused among privileged groups, and so Mora viewed it as a legitimate opportunity to refresh political dynamics in Chile. Rather than the traditional estates, representation in the new chambers should begin to centre on the commercial classes, who were the cornerstones of the entire constitutional edifice, since, according to political economy, labour and production were the sources of national prosperity:

> in modern constitutions it is not the armed forces, nor the clergy, nor the nobility who should call the shots, but those who create, those who promote, those who perpetuate the sources of general wealth: in a word, producers. (*El mercurio chileno*, EMC, 1828–1829; no. 6, 1/IX/1828, 283)

While Mora appealed to the example set by the diverse representation in the two chambers of the British parliament, he was actually more inspired by the rise in Restoration France of the "productive" classes, "wealthy farmers, hard-working capitalists, busy bankers and skilled manufacturers" (EMC, no. 7, 1/IX/1828, 281–83). They had the additional advantage of being educated in economic science—at least in its practice—and were therefore more capable of applying their know-how in a constitutional framework such as that in 1828, which sidestepped the previous Constitution's rigid, centralised economic directives.[6] Mora's political economy articles in the EMC can thus be viewed as a development of the

[6] The 1823 Constitution revolved around a *Dirección de Economía Nacional* (Tit. xvii) and a powerful national Treasury (Tit. xxi), while that of 1828 shared the functions of "promoting Enlightenment, agriculture, industry and foreign and domestic trade" between the two parliamentary chambers (Art. 46) and the provincial and municipal councils (Chap. 10; Art. 119.4).

limited principles established in the 1828 "liberal" Constitution—as it is known in Chilean history—while at the same time as a key piece in the political struggle that broke out in its wake.

Education was a particularly revealing battlefield. Once in Chile, Mora, who had been appointed official advisor in this area,[7] saw no reason to interrupt his campaigning on the importance of education in shaping republican citizens: together with a welfare policy organised around poor-houses, education was the essential pillar of "modern societies" (EMC, no. 2, 1/V/1828, 84). His first step was to reproduce his innovative Buenos Aires girls' school in Santiago; founded in May 1828 with support and partial financing from Pinto's government and with around fifty pupils, it was personally managed by Fanny—the LCL (no. 65, 1/IV/1828) called it "*Señora* Mora's school"—. The *Liceo de Chile* opened a few months later, in January 1829, with almost a hundred students, under Pinto's protection and Mora's management (Stuardo 1950). Designed as a secondary school for the Chilean elites, the *Liceo* reflected Mora's educational principles: a universal, standardised education in this preparatory stage of schooling, which preceded the professional training undertaken in special schools, although this was also open to private schools to avoid the risks of a state monopoly—such as indoctrination—and to be able to benefit from competition: "education is an industry and like all others it prospers with rivalry and spreads with competition" (Stuardo 1950; EMC, no. 1, 1/IV/1828, 32–42).

The *Liceo* was a good reflection of Mora's modernising zeal and the difficulties of bringing this to fruition in a context such as Chile. The main problems came from conservative sectors, who immediately viewed the school as the alter ego of the *Instituto Nacional de Chile* (1813), the new republic's main symbol of education, which was underlain by conservatism. To these were added financial woes—the *Liceo* had initial funds and the government and parliament granted state financing for sixty-two scholarships—and the lack of suitable teaching staff. Mora made unsuccessful attempts to recruit teachers in Europe and Buenos Aires but finally he and Andrés Gorbea took over the teaching of humanities and sciences, and Antonio Portés, formerly a teacher in Sorèze (France), took over philosophy in March 1829. There was also a shortage of books (EMC, no. 11, 1/II/1829, 522ff.). Mora was disturbed by the low quality of the translations available in Hispanic America—the work of "hacks" and

[7] According to Mora, Pinto's aim, which he did not achieve, was to make him "Head of state education" (Mora to Florencio Varela, Santiago, 15/II/1828; Rodríguez 1924, 36).

"hungry copyists"—as well as by the scarcity of foreign texts arriving in Chile, which were eventually limited to those Ackermann sent from London which Mora used in his classes in support of the Lancasterian system (Stuardo 1950, 6). His solution was to propose setting up a company of entrepreneurs devoted to importing and reprinting foreign books, particularly those that would spread useful knowledge:

> The veneration [...] with which we regard the immortal works of Montesquieu, Filangieri, Constant and Bentham is undoubtedly great; in spite of this, we would prefer [...] those of others more humble in their aims, but infinitely more useful in their application. (Stuardo 1950, 6; EMC, no. 11, 1/II/1829, 527)[8]

The book shortage was a fundamental problem given the *Liceo*'s modern curriculum. Latin was passed over as a teaching medium and the methodology included practical sessions, which functioned as a seedbed for orators and public figures as they did at English universities (Stuardo 1950, 22). The curriculum was widely broadcast in the EMC and LCL,[9] and the humanities, Mora's responsibility, included a semester devoted to political economy, using a select group of authors: Smith, Say, Sismondi, Storch and Jovellanos; however, inspired by his attachment to Britain and influenced by his experience in Argentina, he respected the "order" established in James Mill's *Elements* (1821).[10] Mora had more ambitious plans, however. The *Liceo* provided two branches of professional training, military and business; the latter was based on subjects normally taught in schools of commerce—accounting, commercial geography and bookkeeping—but Mora actually intended to transform it into a pioneering legal education centre. By April 1829 he had designed a three-year curriculum, the *Curso nacional de derechos.* Its lofty list of sources reflected Mora's intellectual maturity and included political economy, which would be

[8] Mora once again recalls the efficiency of BFBS in this context (EMC, no. 11, 1/II/1829, 502–11).

[9] Mora's writings were regularly divided up in order to achieve greater social impact. The BPUCC and the BNC keep printed copies in pamphlet form of his inaugural lecture for the *Liceo*, his exams, his public speaking course and several EMC articles, which were circulated independently (Mora 1830a).

[10] The *Instituto Nacional*, which pioneered the teaching of political economy in Chile, managed to set up a course in this discipline after re-opening in 1819, but based on Say's works (Will 1964, 17).

taught following Mill and "other economists who wrote before and after". As there was no textbook that covered the entire course, in August 1829 he launched a public subscription drive to fund a seven-volume work called *Curso de Derechos del Liceo de Chile*,[11] based on the theories of Bentham, Comte, De Lolme and Campomanes among others (Stuardo 1950, 61–65). Significantly, the work was "applicable to all the new republics in America"—indeed, that was its subtitle—; once again it included a volume on political economy, now associated with constitutional law—Mill was again the chosen author, complemented by Smith, Say, Ricardo, Jovellanos, Storch and McCulloch—, but there was heightened attention to commercial law, as "trade is the soul of society today".

As noted, the *Liceo*'s backbone was built around legal education, in line with the enormous importance that Mora had attributed to legal reforms since his youth and now ascribed to the Chilean legal system. Once again, his model was Britain, whose experience inspired him to advocate improving the law-making process to embrace transparency, publicity and the simplifying of abstruse principles, as well as to promote the institution of juries, the benefits of which he had first commended in Buenos Aires and which he felt should be universalised in the new republics. Mora aspired to use the *Liceo* to educate "orators, economists, good public men",[12] in short, a new Chilean civil service that would demolish the "gothic remains of a decayed edifice" and raise the foundations of the young republic. His plan began with the philosophical foundations of law, for which his students took a course in "legal logic" or "philosophy of law", disciplines that Mora fostered throughout his entire life. The *Curso de Derechos del Liceo de Chile* (1830a),[13] the first volume of the seven he intended to publish, guided the teaching of natural law and the law of nations, maintaining the distinction between the two that Heineccio introduced in the *Elementa juris naturae et gentium* (1737). This was used in the sphere of the new

[11] It was structured as follows: Vol. 1. Natural law and the law of nations; 2. Roman law; 3 and 4. Civil and criminal law; 5. Commercial law; 6. Canon law, 7. Political economy and constitutional law.

[12] Mora to Florencia Varela, 11/V/1828; Rodríguez (1924, 48).

[13] A second edition with corrections and additions by Ramón Brisefio was published in 1841.

American republics, especially after Juan Egaña introduced it into Chile in 1812 and 1813 for teaching purposes at the *Instituto Nacional*.[14]

In the *Curso*,[15] Mora gave forceful expression to the notion that there was an urgent need for a complete overhaul of the "decrepit legislative system", which was made up of disparate parts in accordance with the ideology of despotic monarchies and alien to the new republics' needs, which were based on the "unlimited exercise of freedom". Since this could not feasibly be achieved in a radical manner, Mora settled on a new way of teaching law that would provide "indirect means of correcting errors and filling in the gaps in law", through a "sound philosophy" that was consistent with the "representative order". Ultimately, he claimed to draw on Cicero's teachings on the one hand and his observation of conduct in the "French and English courts" on the other. His pragmatic approach to teaching forced him to "accept the vulgar distribution into natural law and the law of nations, Roman law, national civil law and canon law, instead of first teaching the eternal foundations of all legislation and then the various divergences of positive law in a single theoretical body" (Mora 1849, "*Discurso preliminar*"). In fact, when he referred to "the eternal foundations of all legislation", he was essentially referring to "natural law", considering the "law of nations" or "international law" a specific branch of the former, although it had a "positive" manifestation in the form of treaties and laws; legislation which, however, the textbook would not cover as he always remained in the sphere of principles. Mora's multidisciplinary vision of the legal profession was part of the same rejuvenating concept and he felt that its study should include "fine classical literature, the regulator of good taste", "political economy, an essential element of the art of governance", and the "natural sciences, which allow so much scope for the imagination". With all this, he pointed out, "jurists will not be noted for the vulgarity of their knowledge" (Mora 1849, "*Discurso preliminar*").

Mora proposed a conception of the course in natural law that seemed to share the theory of Common Sense, although no specific sources were

[14] On Heineccio' influence in the fledgling American republics, see Pérez Godoy (2017), according to whom Mora "readapted [Heineccio'] theory of Roman law for use by students" in his work *Curso de Derecho romano extractada de la famosa obra de Heinecio* (Cochabamba, Tipografía de Gutiérrez, 1865; Pérez Godoy 2017, 544). The work became part of the *Curso de Derechos*, the continuation of which was thwarted.

[15] The "*Discurso preliminar*" is dated 1 April 1830 and the same date appears in the 1849 edition used in this study. It should be recalled that Mora had taught natural law at the *Ateneo de Madrid* during the Liberal Triennium.

cited. As opposed to "moralism" which rooted natural law in "conscience" and distanced it from the "outside world", "between these two extremes", Mora believed that it had to be "reduced to a science of observation, like chemistry", such that "all difficulty consists in linking the facts ascertained, so that a principle which deserves the name of law may result from their universality" (Mora 1849, XVII). Legislation therefore had to be evaluated in terms of "principles and results", an idea which, although intuited by Roman jurists, coincided "to a great extent with Bentham's principle of utility" with respect to the study of law, although he commented that the latter "applies it to positive laws and, consequently, from this point of view, it does not fit in with the present course" (Mora 1849, xvii). The reference to "results" was a distinctive and largely original feature of Mora's work. He emphasised it when basing "the obligation to observe natural laws" on "the visible effects that result from the infringing of natural obligations", such infringements being "reduced well-being", "pain" and "death" (Mora 1849, 36). On the other hand, as regards received influences, Mora emphasised the defence of the principles of liberty, equality and property when dealing with "civil society" in accordance with Locke's theory, as he noted. Other express references in the field of natural rights, specifically regarding the interpretation of universal laws in accordance with circumstances, were Grotius and Cicero. With regard to the "law of nations" or "international law", Mora specified that the terrain in which he moved was that of "Grotius, Heinetius, Puffendorf and Vattel", although he separated the constitutional law component of these sources in accordance with the specialisation process that modern law was undergoing, as was also the case in the "sciences" and "factory work", where "one of the least uncertain maxims of political economy is proved, namely, that professions are divided as consumption increases" (Mora 1849, 41). For this reason, Mora intended to deal specifically with "purely constitutional principles" in the "last volume" of the *Cursos*, although this failed to materialise (Mora 1849, 42).

Ideology was a further innovative component of the *Liceo* curriculum. As previously noted, Mora had shown interest in the French *Idéologues*, especially Destutt de Tracy, in Spain before his exile to London. However, it was not until his sojourn in Chile that he had the opportunity to promote ideology as a subject for study. He saw a powerful anti-scholastic antidote in Condillac's sensualist followers, whose views had roots in the late Spanish Enlightenment in which authors such as Bernardo María de la Calzada and Valentín de Foronda had spread Condillac's principles of epistemology and logic to some extent. However, Mora seemed to be more in tune with the interpretation of Tracy's work that surfaced in Spain during the Liberal Triennium; although it began to lose influence in France from about 1815, it was translated into Spanish in its entirety from 1820 onwards. In the *Idéologues* Mora found the key to almost completely illuminating a new philosophy in the radical principles that inspired them: all ideas—simple and complex—and the faculties of human knowledge—memory, judgment, perception and will—derived from sensations, and so these constituted the basis for all the sciences and even theology itself. At the same time, because there were no innate ideas, education was an essential factor for promoting human development, a notion that took on more than a little importance in a context such as the new republics, in which it was necessary to train good citizens if the obligations of self-government were to be adequately fulfilled. However, and as was also the case among the Hispanic-American elites among which Mora moved, many other *Idéologues* principles, as well as interest in education, must have helped to keep his sympathy for them alive: trust in democracy, the perfectibility of mankind, the separation of church and state, and interest in human progress from the perspective of respect for economic and scientific laws. During his stay in Buenos Aires the omnipresence of Tracy's ideas in the circles that surrounded Rivadavia and fuelled his reforms, together with the creating of a Chair in Ideology at the *Universidad de Buenos Aires*, quite certainly strengthened Mora's interest in introducing the discipline into his plans for the *Liceo de Chile*. In fact, his curriculum provided for teaching based on "Destutt de Tracy's treatise, while instructing pupils in the main opinions of Plato, Aristotle, Descartes, Malebranche and the School of Scotland at the same time". To respect this criterion, Mora probably added a separate appendix to the *Curso de Derechos del Liceo* with the title of *Elementos elementales de Ideología*, which in reality was an 1826 Spanish translation of Tracy's work broken up into eighteen lessons.[16] However, other sources state that the chosen author was in fact the Frenchman Pierre Laromiguière, a disciple of Tracy—albeit not very a faithful one—who Portés had used in his philosophy classes (EMC, no.

[16] Destutt de Tracy (1826). The translation had the advantage of presenting a faithful version of the *Eléments d'Idéologie* together with a set of notes by the translator in which he corrected the "inaccuracies" and "flippancies" in the French original. At the same time, Mora repeatedly referred very positively to Condillac's "analytical method", which was also taught on the philosophy course (EMC, no. 13, 1/IV/1829, 582–93).

12, 1/III/1829, 581ff.). In all likelihood neither political economy nor ideology was ever taught at the *Liceo*; although Mora always considered it a suitable component for fuelling the revival of philosophy, he undoubtedly lost interest in it—this was already noticeable in the 1840s—shifting instead towards Scottish Common Sense, which was less inflexible and radical and on which he wrote a famous textbook that was published during his time in Peru.

The first issue of the EMC[17] appeared on 1 April 1828 before the *Liceo* was founded. A monthly paper, it was launched on Pinto's mandate and although subscription-based its survival depended on the political power, which guaranteed the purchase of 250 copies per month for 1500 pesos. Pinto left the paper in the hands of two trusted editors: Mora, who was responsible for the articles on literature, law, politics and economics, and Pasamán, who covered medicine, charity and hygiene.[18] Pinto aimed not only to emulate a scientific-literary publication similar to those in Britain, of which he declared himself an admirer, but also to "dispose public opinion, by means of theories, to the institutions that are being readied".[19] Even though the EMC reached only small circles—yet the most influential—, Mora still considered the press the most powerful tool for spreading knowledge and dissolving an elitist sense of culture:

> In educated nations the impossibility of making all classes of citizens partake of the springs of knowledge in massive classical works has suggested the idea of publishing the ideas most appropriate to the demands of the moment and the daily advances made by the Enlightenment in short newspapers, popularizing by this convenient and simple means the progressive work of reason, which, without such help, would be the exclusive privilege of a small number of enthusiasts. (EMC, no. 1, 1/IV/1828, 3–4)

However, Mora's presence in Pinto's administration was essential to ensure that the EMC guaranteed the public dissemination of reforms to which he was no stranger. His correspondence reveals a close relationship with Finance Minister Francisco Ruiz-Tagle, to whom he was also an

[17] There is a recent re-edition: *El mercurio chileno* (2009).

[18] The botany articles were the work of Italian naturalist Carlos Bertero (Amunátegui 1888, 108–109).

[19] Mora to Florencio Varela, Santiago 11/V/1828; Rodríguez (1924, 49).

advisor, so much so that in 1829 he participated, probably as secretary, in a government commission to analyse the banking issue.[20]

The EMC's semi-official nature was plain from its economics articles. Notable in terms of length, content and positioning in each issue—they were usually the first that readers came to—they marked the paper's overall identity,[21] which was in line with Mora's awareness that the new republics' survival depended on their economic success and that it was therefore necessary to broaden the social base of those who engaged with the discipline:

> Most of the issues of this journal [EMC] have been devoted to the study of political economy. Our purpose has been less to illustrate its principles than to increase its popularity. We are intrinsically convinced that its aid is absolutely necessary to govern state revenues successfully and we believe that when it has made such rapid progress and its application has been so sustained in all the educated nations of our times, any [state] that aimed to found its stock exchange system on bases other than those provided by its theories would be condemned to shameful inferiority. (EMC, no. 16, 15/VII/1829, 725)

It is probably no accident that the new journal's name evoked Camilo Enriquez's *El mercurio de Chile* (EMDC, 1822–1823), the main populariser of classical economics in Chile before Mora's arrival (Will 1964, 8). In spite of its short life—only sixteen issues were published—, the EMC enjoyed enormous intellectual stature. Its sources included the most distinguished authors of European enlightened and liberal culture, ranging from Montesquieu, Bentham and Filangieri to Smith, Say and McCulloch among others, and, as was always the case with Mora, its criteria were up-to-the-minute: in 1829 it carried a brief review of James Mill's *Analysis of the Phenomena of the Human Mind* (1829), which was published in the same year (EMC, no. 16, 15/VII/1829, 768). Mora's economic agenda, with a Hispanic-American backdrop and initiated in London and Buenos Aires, finally took shape in the EMC. It was structured around a theory of growth with a complementary conceptual framework that could be split into three major areas: monetary theory, public finance theory and international trade theory. Mora extracted a series of principles from each of

[20] Mora to Florencio Varela, Santiago, 15 /VII/1828; Rodríguez (1924, 59).

[21] See a summary of these articles in Will (1964, 10–15) and in more detail in Astigarraga and Zabalza (2017).

these that provided the basis for a consistent reform and policy programme that was Chile-specific but which he understood to somehow fit into the economic, institutional and political circumstances of all the Hispanic-American republics (Zabalza and Astigarraga 2020).

6.3 *El Mercurio Chileno*: Economic Growth Theory

Historical accounts of the of the Republic of Chile's economic situation during the 1820s diverge. Some economic historians emphasise the way in which the period laid the foundations for the economic dynamism of the 1830s, while other authors point to the monetary problems and budget deficits that persisted after President O'Higgins was deposed in 1823. However, whatever the economic conditions in the 1820s, it is indisputable that Chile's economy relied on agriculture, livestock and mining—in 1828 around half the active population was employed in these sectors—. However, the growth of manufacturing—which amounted to little over a quarter of workers—was held back due to high customs duties, monetary contraction and the budget deficit.[22] It therefore seems reasonable that intellectuals such as Mora were interested in economic issues would pay particular attention to economic growth and the public policy spheres that directly influenced it: public finances and monetary and trade policies.

The theory of growth that Mora outlined in his EMC articles adhered to the following theoretical structure: a country's economic prosperity is firstly associated with capital accumulation, which requires a considerable level of "ordinary product", that is, a high profit rate on capital that enables the profits from savings to be accumulated in the form of capital, since otherwise "capital cannot be raised, and without capital it is impossible to satisfy labour, the source of all wealth, decently" (EMC, no. 3, 1/VI/1828, 115). High profit rates derive from the application of labour to productive activities (EMC, no. 4, 1/VII/1828, 155). The central importance of the productivity of labour together with the role of savings and

[22] GDP per capita hardly changed during the 1820s (from 122,724 to 124,281 *pesos* between 1820 and 1828), following an undoubtedly poor start to the decade. To this must be added the decline in productivity from the beginning of the Republic until 1820, when it became relative stable until 1828 (Braun-Llona et al. 1998, 23, 36). Although not comprehensive, see Salazar (2009) on Chile's economic history and Riveros and Ferraro (1985) from a monetary perspective; on protectionism, see also Villalobos and Sagredo (1987). An optimistic view about the performance of the Chilean national economy and institutional change in Llorca-Jaña and Navarrete-Montalvo (2017).

capital accumulation reveals Mora's debt to Smith's economic growth model; however, Mora's use of profit rates suggests that his inspiration came from McCulloch's authoritative interpretation of it.

The second determining factor was the division of labour, particularly its international dimension, again following the structure of the Smith-McCulloch growth model. However, much of Mora's rhetoric about the positive consequences of the division of labour comes from the *Cours d'Économie Politique* (1823), written by Russian economist and optimist follower of Say, Henrich Storch, who was well known in Spain in the first half of the nineteenth century (Almenar 2000a). Although Mora also used Say's *Traité*, he usually cited it via the *Cours* (Storch 1823).

However, Mora was not inclined to long theoretical discussions and instead focused his efforts on pinning down the origins of the specific advantage of a nation, in this case Chile, based on *Le Commerce au dix-neuvième siècle* (1825). The work, which was reviewed in two articles in the EMC, was written by Moreau de Jonnès, an official in the French Ministry of Trade statistics service, who Mora deemed the moderniser of the tradition of Petty and Davenant's Political Arithmetic (EMC, no. 15, 15/VI/1829, 677–84; no. 16, 15/VII/1829, 757–61). Under its influence he came to believe it necessary to compile quantitative information by means of an institutional framework coordinated by two central statistical and accounting offices which, in his view, should be modelled on efficient institutions in England—the Board of Trade and the parliamentary commissions—and, to a lesser extent, the Duchy of Tuscany (EMC, no. 16, 15/VII/1829, 727). The offices would be responsible for collecting statistical data in five areas: geography and physics; population; police and justice; agricultural wealth, and trade wealth. Revisiting ideas in the CEP, Mora felt that these data were essential for the development of theoretical economics and political decision-making.

However, before these factual investigations were underway, Mora ventured to speculate on the type of industry that is "most suited to our circumstances". This was to be established by taking as the main criteria "the nature of the products, the ease of the work and the advantages of trading" (EMC, no. 4, 1/VII/1828, 150). It seems clear that Mora was trying to pinpoint a product for which Chile could provide lower production costs and therefore lower prices in international markets; that is to say, an absolute advantage. If the stipulation that the condition for this division of labour was freedom of trade were added to the mix, the Smith-McCulloch economic growth model re-emerged to its full extent. Furthermore, like

Smith, Mora maintained that capital accumulated in Chile, which should come from trade and whose ultimate condition was freedom of trade, should be used for agriculture in the first instance, since, respecting the "natural tendency of things", this sector of production guaranteed higher profitability than industry, used less capital and its producers had less incentive to leave their country than merchants or manufacturers, thus guaranteeing the growth of the indigenous population.[23] In Chile's case the fact that its population was "purely agricultural by custom and interest" and the productive advantage derived from factors such as climate, the amount of land, the abundance of minerals, agricultural resources and geographical position for trade were also added. Its trade model was therefore geared to exporting national agricultural products—Mora occasionally mentioned wheat, oil, wine, cured meat, nuts and of course copper and precious metals—and importing manufactured goods. Despite the omnipresence of foreign trade in the Pacific ports, which should "be exclusively ours", Mora counted on consolidating markets for Chilean agricultural surpluses—he suggested creating storage ports of deposit, like those in France, around Chile's coasts—and on this trade generating the capital accumulation needed to finance imports and stimulate the gradual birth of domestic industry. However, he stressed that the country's comparative advantage would be undermined if it were not accompanied by a series of legal requirements and an agricultural land structure that was appropriate for accumulating capital (EMC, no. 15, 15/VI/1829).[24]

Far from settling for the economic argument in favour of Chile's agricultural specialisation, Mora bolstered his power of persuasion with moral considerations. As he had in the CBS and CEP, he argued that agricultural activity was morally superior to manufacturing, among other reasons

[23] This reading of the WN prevailed during the Spanish Enlightenment (Astigarraga and Zabalza 2022). However, some passages in the EMC suggest that Mora had in mind a notion of economic development by stages, such that industry required a level of economic maturity and prior capital accumulation. The agricultural and commercial stages of course correspond to the last two stages of Smith's development theory. In any event, to Mora, capital was best used to foster agricultural improvements. In addition to recommending formal agricultural education, he turned his attention to British agriculture, which he considered superior to French due to questions such as land enclosure, man-made meadows, machinery, irrigation and numerous agronomic innovations (EMC, no. 15, 15/6/1829, 680, 698).

[24] Mora seems to have favoured the benefits of small farms, or he at least understood that the accumulation of land into a few hands should run parallel to that of industry and commerce (EMC, no. 15, 15/6/1829, 682); but without capital the "immense" dimensions of Chilean agriculture were "condemned to barrenness".

because it was more conducive to "the preservation of good morals [and]. ... good health", and with reference to Chile "it would be painful if the interests of this precious majority [of the population] were sacrificed to the impracticable chimeras of the promoters of industry, repressing the beneficial force that is accelerating the development of our rural treasures" (EMC, no. 6, 1/IX/1828, 266). As usual, this rationale was met with enthusiasm when it was realised that reason and morality embraced one other in the pursuit of a single aim. This was a common rhetorical trick in Mora's writings and he used it repeatedly in the EMC to enhance the persuasive capacity of the economic arguments on which his reformist project was based.

Spanish liberal economists Flórez Estrada and Canga Argüelles, who, as previously noted, were among Mora's fellow exiles in London and were in the vanguard of a minority that favoured a pro-agriculture and free trade development strategy, do not feature among the intellectual sources cited in his EMC articles.[25] Although not materialising in policy until the 1840s, they had notable intellectual influence in the minority circle of liberal economists. It is not difficult to position Mora's thought in this reformist sphere, partly because of his political affinity with the group—moreover, with roots in his native Cadiz—and partly because of his interest in economic issues, and it is not surprising that it was projected onto his reformist proposals for Chile, a nation which, in his own words, "is split into two great portions: agriculture and trade; they march in time with one another and live in close harmony" (EMC, no. 9, 1/XII/1828, 393). In fact, as already noted, the discourse that finally came together in the EMC had its basis in the British classical economists and their French followers, who had also influenced the pro-agriculture Spanish liberals (Almenar 2000a). The EMC was therefore an indisputable prop for establishing classical economics in Chile within a Spanish Enlightenment discourse dominated by the idea of *fomento*—promotion—, once a small group of Chileans, many of them like Henríquez trained in Argentina, began to spread and apply the classical doctrines of the Spanish Enlightenment during the 1820s (Will 1964, 4–10; Edwards 2018, 372–76).

Finally, it is worth noting Mora's concern over a phenomenon that seemed self-evident to contemporary economists and which affected the "opulent, manufacturing and powerful" nations, whose advanced state of

[25] On the other hand, Campomanes, Jovellanos and other late Spanish Enlightenment authors were referred to positively in the EMC.

capital accumulation did not protect them from "horrible ills" such as the "harsh scourge of excessive population, devastating poverty and ruinous taxation to relieve it" (EMC, no. 6, 1/IX/1828, 266). This is of course a veiled reference to the stationary state and the social consequences of capital accumulation in industry, such as pauperism. In keeping with his theory of growth, Mora understood that access to an advanced state of capital accumulation did not guarantee a country's prosperity if the "profits" from capital were not high. If the notion that the condition of the working class and all classes as a whole was "much happier in the progressive state of society—that is, when it is advancing along the road of acquisitions—than when it has reached the end" (EMC, no. 6, 1/IX/1828, 265) is added to this, is it is not difficult to conclude that this was a situation in which profit rates stagnated. Mora explicitly attributed the origin of this concept to Smith but, despite his numerous mentions of it in the WN, it was really more akin to McCulloch's approach (EMC, no. 6, 1/IX/1828, 265; McCulloch 1825, 105–107). There is less evidence regarding the factors that inclined profit rates to stagnate; that is, whether this was due to specific mechanisms such as diminishing returns in agriculture, rising wages or the gradual drying up of investment opportunities. Whatever the determining factor, the important question for Mora was whether "modern French writers' endless lamentations on the penury, the backwardness, the dependence in which the poor live in that country" could be "applied to us [Chile]". Without further explanation, Mora stated that the "liquid profits produced in our Republic by capital and labour exceed by much more than half what the same resources produce in the United States, where profits are 80 to 50 in relation to England" (EMC, no. 4, 1/VII/1828, 168).[26] However, the new republics' prosperity needed a series of institutional requirements to be met and the implementing of specific economic policies, which were a by-product of this growth theory.

In fact, like the classical economists, especially Smith and McCulloch, Mora presented a set of interrelated economic variables in functional dependence, thus leaving his mark on what is understood by economic theory. However, again following the guidelines set out by these two authors, according to his criteria, economic development demanded a series of institutional requirements, beginning with an adequate legal

[26] The effects of the 1826 crisis had already become evident in France and England. Mora's concern with state stagnation and its link to low wages seems to be based on McCulloch (EMC, no. 3, 1/VI/1828, 115).

framework. This could be none other than Bentham's utilitarian principles, which held that society's aim was "the greatest happiness of the greatest number". To attain this a series of individual rights had to be recognised that would ensure that citizens had the "free and legitimate use" of their faculties (EMC, no. 2, 1/V/1828, 53–54), amongst which Mora mentions freedom, security and the "sacred" right to property ownership.[27] These principles measured the "rightness or wrongness" of human institutions, such that Mora referred to them time and again, especially in his analysis of the tax, trade and customs systems. He also added a tax system capable of financing the structure and functions of the liberal state, a banking system that would guarantee the necessary liquidity for economic activity—or rather an adequate supply of capital—and finally free foreign trade, which, in agreement with Smith, Mora deemed to be limited by the scope of the market. These issues will be examined in the following sections.

6.4 *El Mercurio Chileno*: Monetary Theory

According to historiography the monetary problem affecting the Hispanic-American republics in their early days was rooted in the subordination of the imperial Treasury and monetary policy to the financial and trade interests of the Spanish crown (De Haro 2013). In the case of the Republic of Chile, there seems to be a striking consensus over the tremendous scarcity of currency and the weakness of the financial structure from 1823 to 1830 (Hurtado 1984, 45–46; Riveros and Ferraro 1985; Salazar 2009). The oft-repeated mention in the EMC of the need to provide the national economy with "cash", that is, increase the money supply, comes as no surprise. Mora not only grasped the problem, but deemed it so important that his rhetoric acquired a certain mercantilist air. One contributing factor was his denomination of money as a "preferred product", a term originating with the French neo-mercantilist economist Charles Ganilh, who criticised Smith's monetary theories despite accepting his notion of the close link between the prosperity of European industry and the discovery of the American mines (EMC, no. 14, 15/V/1829, 665ff.; Ganilh 1815,

[27] As he had in the CEP Mora argued that religious tolerance created a more favourable institutional framework for trade. Underlying his view was the idea, which he acquired in London, that Protestantism was more rational than Catholicism, which was mired in fanaticism and superstition.

386–409). Mora was aware of the confusion that could be caused among EMC readers by the central role of money in economic development, which could lead to the mercantilist idea of considering cash to be wealth, and so he repeatedly explained that:

> far from being supporters of the mercantile system [...], far from wishing that the future plans of Chile's Treasury were based on the puerile desire to accumulate the symbols of value in preference to real value, we are thoroughly convinced of the sad consequences that would inevitably follow such erroneous conduct. (EMC, no. 4, 1/VII/1828, 157)

A detailed analysis of the monetary passages in the EMC shows that Mora not only took into account the deposit function of money, as mercantilists did, but also its functions as a means of payment and in the circulating of goods, such that, along the lines of the classical economists and Smith in particular (O'Brien 1989, 199), cash played a central role in his theory of growth. In his view money resembled any other asset and as such was subject to the law of supply and demand; hence, the "interest on money rises when its consumers, who are needy speculators, ask for more money than is available from capitalists". According to Mora this was the case in Chile, where interest rates rose above 24% as a result of the money shortage, which stemmed from the fact that the Republic was at an economic stage in which "money fertilizes all sources of production" and had not yet reached a higher one in which these "supply all the money necessary for circulation by themselves" (EMC, no. 4, 1/VII/1828, 155). In other words, the scarcity of accumulated capital in relation to demand for it in Chile prevented entrepreneurs from using it in their productive activities. Mora was undoubtedly thinking of the negative consequences of the high interest rate on profit rates, since he seems to consider it a fundamental component of production costs. On this point he followed McCulloch to the letter in assuming that a contraction in the money supply was passed on to activity levels (O'Brien 1970, 153–59).

On the other hand, keeping faith with Smith, Mora believed that the solution to this problem lay in promoting discount and circulation banks, that is, those "that lend not cash but a symbol that represents it, which acquires all its value from the confidence inspired by the bank". These banking institutions could therefore supply capital and credit to productive activities through the issuance of "paper" that could be converted into gold or silver (EMC, no. 4, 1/VII/1828, 159; Giacomin 2007). Following the tradition that began with Cantillon, continued with Smith and peaked with various classical economists, Mora thus identified paper money as a key factor in growth, accompanied by a growing role for "discount and circulation banks", which today would be commercial banks.[28] However, fully aware of the fear that the use of paper money as a means of payment had aroused in different spheres, Mora frequently stressed the dangers that could arise from what he called "credit abuse", that is, when the money supply exceeded "the needs of consumption and production". In so doing he, of course, echoed the problems arising from depreciation in the value of currency as a consequence of a relatively abundant supply, which was in turn the result of unchecked issuance of paper money and came not only from the financial system itself, but largely from loans to governments. This was undoubtedly a veiled reference to what became known as the Bullionist Controversy in the field of monetary theory. One of the most serious concerns of economists during the first thirty years of the nineteenth century was the issue of paper money's convertibility into precious metals in the aftermath of rumours that French troops had set foot on British soil in 1797. The ensuing banking panic resulted in a massive demand among English depositors for their bank notes to be converted to gold, to the point that the Bank of England decided to temporarily suspend convertibility. The crisis also triggered an intellectual controversy regarding, among other questions, the convertibility of paper money into gold. Known as the Bullionist Controversy, two basic points of view emerged from it: on the one hand, authors like Boyd, Wheatley, Thornton and Ricardo adopted what was known as the bullionist position, insisting on the restoration of convertibility to avoid excessive issuance that would inevitably create inflation; on the other, supporters of non-convertibility such as Smith, Torrens and John Stuart Mill advocated pegging the issuance of paper money to the volume of trade.[29] The debate was, of course, more complex than this, but from 1812 onwards it essentially focussed on the restoration of convertibility.

It is difficult to situate Mora's monetary approach within the terms of this debate on the basis of his EMC articles. His citing of Smith and Say

[28] Mora's model seems to have been the Bank of England, whose operations he described in minute detail. Information on the operating of European banks (France, Genoa, etc.) can be found in Vol. IV of Storch's *Cours*.

[29] It is an oversimplification to include Smith among supporters of non-convertibility; in reality, his real bills doctrine, as his point of view on the issue was known, could lead to interpretations that were either favourable or otherwise to convertibility.

on monetary issues and Thornton's *An Enquiry into the Nature and Effects of the Paper Credit of Great Britain* (1802), from which he references Chapter IV, which is critical of Smith, suggests that he must have had deeper and broader knowledge of the Bullionist Controversy than his articles imply; as Mora himself pointed out on several occasions, this was partly because he felt that such discussions were too complex and abstract and therefore of limited use for the EMC. In any event, he seemed fairly unconcerned about paper money surpluses, stating that "the greater the amount of paper issued, the greater the benefit to the public and the greater the profit for entrepreneurs" (EMC, no. 4, 1/VII/1828, 160). If his belief in the existence of a natural cap to the issuance of money, which was set by "the amount of credit the bank enjoys in public opinion" and which obliged financial institutions to self-regulate the paper money they issued is added to this, it would be possible to conclude that Mora was not a supporter of currency convertibility. However, at the same time, he also expressed the opposite point of view when he suggested that the viability of banks and mercantile activity "consists in the general certainty that paper can be converted into gold at any time [... such that] it is not licit [...] to increase the issuance to an unlimited supply"; and consequently "there is no need to think of setting up banks if the public is not willing to restrain its urge to own bits of metal" (EMC, no. 4, 1/VII/1828, 160–61). This ambiguity is likely to have stemmed from Mora's doubts about the structure of the Chilean financial system. He seemed to be in favour of a bank monopoly over issuance when he stated that "[public] finances cannot be regularized or restored to their former vigour without a solid and respectable establishment that facilitates their operations and simplifies their mechanism", such that through an "open account with the Treasury" it could "save the government from the yoke imposed on it by speculators" (EMC, no. 4, 1/VII/1828, 167). The article on the "*Banco Nacional*" continued along these lines; Mora seems to have been especially involved in this project, as he was appointed secretary and endorsed it via public subscription in the EMC (EMC, no. 7, 1/X/1828, 327–31). In this case, as is generally accepted today, convertibility was a requisite for maintaining monetary stability and thus avoiding inflationary processes. However, in an article entitled "*De los bancos de descuento y circulación*" Mora adopted a more ambiguous stance and although he mentioned that the bank would come into being sooner or later because of the "rule of needs", he also pointed out that the solution to the cash shortage problem was "discount and circulation banks" (EMC, no. 4, 1/VII/1828, 159,

167), in which case competition among banks meant it that was unnecessary to impose convertibility in order to guarantee monetary stability, as modern economic theory shows.

It is probably this uncertainty about how the Chilean financial system should be structured that led Mora to dispense with the convertibility argument to show that credit "abuse", the most visible and worrying issue in the debate, was unlikely to occur in an emerging nation like Chile. However, given that he was such an extraordinary populariser, there is always the possibility that it occurred to him to use more accessible, less technical and, let it be said, more rhetorical arguments to persuade an educated but non-specialist audience such as EMC readers. Mora used two such arguments in particular. The first was historical-political and emphasised that "credit abuse" was less likely in republics founded on the principles of freedom and justice and in which law and equality before the law prevailed than it was in absolutist states, as shown by the disparate experiences of England, France and Prussia on the one hand and Spain and Russia on the other, the latter being countries in which public finances were in a wretched state, as:

> the Catholic Monarchs and autocrats, who are entirely convinced that they are the masters of lives and estates by divine right [...], have not had the least scruple about sacrificing the well-being of the peoples who groan under their yoke to the disarray of their estates and the extravagance of their courts. The extravagance of the measures advised by economists in Madrid and St. Petersburg can be compared only with the stupidity of the public men who have sanctioned them with their signatures. (EMC, no. 4, 1/VII/1828, 166)[30]

The second argument was intellectual. According to Mora, the "continuous advances in economic science" and its dissemination contributed to the simplification of state administration, reducing dependence on credit and speculators (EMC, no. 4, 1/VII/1828, 167).

Concern over money shortages seems to have been a common pattern in the initial stage of the independence of Hispanic-American republics. This set in motion a series of theoretical and political monetary disputes in which the influence of texts from the late Enlightenment and early liberalism in Spain is noticeable, especially with regard to Peru and the *Ensayo*

[30] In fact, Smith or Ricardo's criticism of mercantilist finance lay behind this idea.

económico sobre el sistema de la moneda-papel (1796) by José Alonso Ortiz, author of the Spanish translation of the WN that Mora used in the EMC and the basis for the *Banco Auxiliar de Papel Moneda* (De Haro 2013). After a thorough account of the advantages and disadvantages of paper money, Ortiz, a faithful follower of Smith and his monetary theory, expressed his confidence that this financial instrument would not trigger inflationary processes as long as there was a limit to banknote issuance that would guarantee confidence in paper money and was pegged to the volume of trade (Alonso 1796). Mora shared these ideas, as well as the scant attention paid to the convertibility issue, for the reasons explained above. However, there seems to have been no intellectual link between the two authors and Mora, whose analysis was less refined than Alonso Ortiz's, left no evidence of one in the EMC either. Nonetheless, they also shared approaches to public debt analysis, which was closely linked to monetary analysis.

6.5 *El Mercurio Chileno*: Public Finance

It is clear from Mora's EMC articles that building the Chilean Republic's institutions required a public finance system capable of funding the new institutional framework and contributing to socio-economic progress. This requirement was also justified because after years of political instability—a period marked by conflicts, financial woes and unbalanced budgets known as the "war economy"—the Chilean tax office urgently needed a thorough overhaul.[31] Mora dealt with two issues in depth in the EMC: the structure of the tax system and public debt.

Mora spared no effort in emphasising the different between the tax system in the American republics with respect to the absolute monarchies in Europe, especially Spain, which was perverted by "frivolous" expenses and a "tyrannical" Treasury, contrary to the general interest (EMC, no. 2, 1/V/1828, 54). In his opinion, the wastefulness that typified them was unlikely to be reproduced in the American republics, where, thanks to the "responsibility of government agents, all danger of pointless expenses and bad administration is kept away" (EMC, no. 3, 1/VI/1828, 103). This is so because, following Bentham, in a republican framework it is a matter of

[31] However, the period was more productive in terms of ideas and attempts to rationalise public accounts by ministers such as Nolasco-Mena and Benavente; there is an overview of the evolution of Chilean public finances in the period in Sagredo (1997).

achieving "the greatest happiness of the greatest number" and therefore of "meeting the public's needs while at the same time promoting the prosperity of the individuals that make it up", such that "public finances are nothing but the necessary nourishing of common requirements" (EMC, no. 2, 1/V/1828, 53–54). Consequently, in this framework "individuals are forced to bear general tax burdens" and not only to maintain current expenditure "but to contribute, by means of useful enterprises, to improving social conditions" (EMC, no. 2, 1/V/1828, 62). Where these issues are concerned, it is not difficult to recognise the functions that Smith attributed to public finances in Book V of the WN, such as the administration of justice, public order, national defence, the promotion of specific infrastructures, education, the legal safeguarding of contracts and property rights, all of which demanded "a system of finance and a fixed revenue plan in the Treasury" (EMC, no. 2, 1/V/1828, 54, 62). Nevertheless, while Mora was not a proponent of "political stoicism" he was concerned about the state's excessive unwieldiness and a certain ambiguity surrounding productivity levels in the civil service.

The core issue in designing a tax system was to "specify the classes, professions and branches" on which the tax burden should fall (EMC, no. 2, 1/V/1828, 62), that is, how it should be distributed. The core dilemma lay in the choice between direct taxation—levied on "production and property"—and indirect taxation—levied on "trade and consumption"—. This was a major dichotomy for the classical economists (Dome 2004) and most of them, such as Bentham, Smith, Say and McCulloch in his later writings, opted for indirect taxation; James Mill adopted a position halfway between the two, and the exception was Ricardo, who defended direct taxation on the basis that indirect taxes, especially those levied on trade, such as customs duties, had a negative effect on growth; his alternative was an income tax that would ultimately affect profits (O'Brien 1989, 340). The work by McCulloch that Mora read also advocated direct taxation on incomes and profits (Dome 2004).[32] In spite of continually citing Smith, Say and Sismondi, Mora was unequivocally in favour of direct taxes on surpluses, whether income from land or profits:

[32] This is a reference to the *Principles* (1825) and the article "V. Remarks on the Financial Situation of Great Britain" "(McCulloch 1827). McCulloch would later change his attitude to direct taxation (Dome 2004).

> The legislation views the entire stock of productive goods as a single homogeneous whole; it calculates the annual profit which issues from it; the new wealth which it creates and puts into circulation, and from this capital, which is to pay for production expenses and producers' profits, it deducts a part, which it awards to the Exchequer and which forms the nation's real wealth. (EMC, no. 3, 1/VI/1828, 113)

He introduced this debate by presenting a faithful account of Smith's famous four maxims of taxation—equality, certainty, convenience and economy—and Sismondi's precepts. From this he deduced, somewhat confusingly, three principles that should govern all tax systems: minimal contact between the tax office and taxpayers, eliminating the coercion of tax collectors and thus revenue, which is highly characteristic of Smith (O'Brien 1989, 337); observing "the natural development of useful work", such that lowest tax was levied on activities that were most in need of a boost while the best-established would be the most highly taxed (EMC, no. 2, 1/V/1828, 56), and finally what he called "freedom properly understood in all the wellsprings of production" (EMC, no. 2, 1/V/1828, 60), that is, subordinating the tax structure to the laissez-faire principle and thus reducing taxes on the trading of goods and especially import duties to a minimum, all issues that were common to the classical economists.

Mora used the last two principles, which can be reduced to what modern public finance calls the principle of tax efficiency—that is, the consequences of taxation on growth—to infer the convenience of direct taxation. This was levied on "production and capital", while indirect taxation was levied on "consumption and circulation" and therefore basically affected the classes with lower purchasing power on one hand and customs tariffs on the other; consequently, it had a negative impact on profit rates, savings rates and capital accumulation. This reasoning clearly respected the sequence of Mora's theory of development and he underpinned it by adding a comprehensive assessment of the advantages and disadvantages of direct and indirect taxation: the latter's apparent benefits—invisibility, equal distribution and appropriate proportion to taxpayers' wealth (let us not forget that Mora compared it with tithes and the old taxes imposed by absolute monarchies)—were "illusory", since, according to Sismondi, a massive, coercive inspection structure was required. On the other hand, direct taxation had many advantages: popularity, certainty—according to Mora, property and production were less transient issues than consumption—, fraud was more difficult and it was fairer, since it conformed to what today would be called the ability to pay principle.

Mora's favourable position vis-à-vis direct taxation was not unrelated to attempts to incorporate it into the tax system prior to Pinto's government. Diego José Benavente, a minister, had suggested it in 1823, together with a reorganisation of indirect taxes and the moderating of customs duties, also on the basis of liberal principles (Sagredo 1997, 305–307). Like Benavente and his successor Ventura Blanco, who drafted a bill on state borrowing in December 1828, Mora nevertheless believed that tax revenue was insufficient to finance the building of the Chilean republic and underpin its economic prosperity (Sagredo 1997, 312).[33] In the same vein, he argued that "no government can pull itself out of sad mediocrity with its ordinary resources" and asked rhetorically: "what would become of Great Britain today without the powerful assistance of borrowing?" (EMC, no. 1, 1/IV/1828, 15); recourse to public debt was therefore unavoidable. This was the basis of Mora's determination to spread what he called the "theory of state borrowing", throughout Hispanic-American countries, and he used the EMC as a space in which to gather together echoes of the debate raised by the question in Argentina and Chile, which he deemed central to his reformist project (EMC, no. 4, 1/VII/1828, 159). He made no secret of his enthusiasm for the issuing of public bonds and, more specifically, for the system of repayment by means of "regular and successive" instalments, which reduced the capital borrowed and cushioned the burden of debt, and which he considered one of financial science's great innovations. However, if it were to be successful "three vital conditions" of public borrowing had to be fulfilled: "national representation", that is, the guarantee provided by republican legislation on the country's debt, transparency of information and prompt interest payments (EMC, no. 1, 1/IV/1828, 20). It has been established that Mora lifted both the details of financial instruments and the jargon from two monographs on public debt by Hennet (1816, 24–79) and Dufresne Saint-Leon (1824), senior officials in the French Treasury.

On this issue Mora was clearly guided more by practical considerations than by the classical economists' theoretical insights. The continuous growth of the debt burden in Europe and Britain at the beginning of the

[33] There is a review of public finance in the new Hispanic-American republics in Marichal and Carmagnani (2006); on the introduction of direct taxation in the new republics, see Pinto (2012).

nineteenth century is known to have contributed to their negative opinions on the issue; Smith and above all Hume had anticipated this, pointing out the mercantilist roots of the state's gradual slide into debt. New arguments followed such as the capital consumption caused by indebtedness—that is, the crowding-out effect, meaning that excessive state activity pushes out private investment—and the burden on future generations that debt represented (O'Brien 1989, 361; Tsoulfidis 2007).[34] Of course, both the problem and the classical economists' critical position were well known in liberal political circles in the Hispanic-American republics. In fact, just a month after the EMC's first issue came out *El valdiviano federal* (EVF, 1827–1844) began a lengthy critique of ideas supporting state borrowing lasting over seven issues and five months.[35] This must have forced Mora to hone his persuasive skills in order to provide a coherent explanation of his point of view. Despite including statistical examples from the English Treasury and others from Hennet's monograph, his argument rested more on warning of the limitations imposed on theory by political practice, as he did repeatedly in the EMC.[36] Mora thus unabashedly entered the field of politics by appealing to the new republics' basic needs. In his view credit was the crucial factor that "can consummate the great work of [their] independence" (EMC, no. 1, 1/IV/1828, 25), as it was the means to promote "the great cause of the general good" through state investment in social capital to create the conditions for domestic and foreign trade. At this point Mora again returned to the theoretical backbone of his entire career as a spreader of economic ideas: free trade as a catalyst for growth and therefore the Smithian "limitation" imposed by market scope.

Finally, it is worth mentioning the popularity of state borrowing in Spanish liberal circles in the early nineteenth century, especially in the second part of the *Ensayo* by Alonso Ortiz, who was highly influential in

[34] There were exceptions, however, such as Mill's lukewarm criticism and Malthus' positive attitude towards debt, within limits (O'Brien 1989).

[35] The author must have been the journals' editor José Miguel Infante, a stalwart supporter of the federation vis-à-vis unitary governments: see EVF (no. 15, 29/V/1829; no. 16, 9/VI/1829; no. 17, 13/VI/1829; no. 18, 27/VI/1829; no. 19, 2/VIII/1829; no. 20, 30/VIII/1829; no. 21, 23/IX/1829).

[36] The exception is his determination to refute the disparaging arguments against public debt put forward by Sismondi, who he accused of belonging to the "sect of the timorous" (EMC, no. 1, 1/IV/1828, 7), and those springing from civic republicanism via Mably. On the other hand, he occasionally relied on Colquhoun to confirm that a "debt is real wealth for the country" (EMC, no. 1, 1/IV/1828, 7, 11–12).

Peruvian monetary policy. He was in favour of public borrowing and like Mora attached great importance to confidence and the constitutional link with public opinion in the functioning of a financial system.

6.6 *El Mercurio Chileno*: Free Trade

Free trade was a central theme in the EMC articles. As previously noted, Mora must have come into contact with Spanish free trade circles—Flórez Estrada, Vadillo, Pebrer and so forth—during the Liberal Triennium and his London exile. However, for the first time, the EMC carried not only an organised interpretation of their positions on free trade, whose origins Mora situated in Quesnay and Physiocracy, but also abundant evidence on their international trade theory, its authorities and application to Chilean circumstances. His position enriched a debate on the question of customs tariffs that began in 1827 and was dominated by Pedro Félix de Vicuña's protectionist views. Mora of course took the opposite stance, arguing that "laissez faire" should be the "motto of our economic legislation". Meanwhile, according to the CEP, the principles of "total" freedom to produce and trade should be introduced into the domestic market. The free trade rhetoric of the EMC articles was based on an elementary theory of international trade. However, like Smith, it closely linked economic growth and free trade and was thus distinctly classical despite its unique features. Mora's work naturally made no mention either now or later of Ricardo's sophisticated comparative cost theory. He was instead inspired by Smith's theory of absolute advantage—as well as that of McCulloch and other classical economists—which he considered sufficient to defend his free trade position without resorting to Ricardian complexities. Elements of this theory were easily identifiable in the EMC; as previously pointed out, the origin of trade thus lay in the varying "absolute" cost structure in different countries, which was due to differences in the production levels of certain goods and manifested itself in lower prices for goods in which there was an advantage, which could be exported in a free trade context (EMC, no. 6, 1/IX/1828, 249). All these classic features of Smith and McCulloch's approach to international trade, which were Mora's main sources, were clear in the EMC. As noted previously, in Chile's case natural conditions, geography and the structure of land ownership were suitable for agricultural specialisation, much to Mora's satisfaction.[37] In contrast with Europe, however, he believed that the embryonic state of Chilean industry disqualified it as an engine for growth, and that this state of affairs would continue as long as the enormous disparity between a low population and vast untapped natural resources continued, a situation that had already been addressed in Europe. Little space in the EMC was devoted to industry or the potential mechanisation of production. Moreover, there was barely a trace of the late Enlightenment agrarianism-industrialism debate, beyond confirmation that wealth produced by industry and trade was less stable and more temporary than agricultural wealth due to the volatility of fashion and taste and the vagaries of trade wars. Like Flórez Estrada in the *Examen Imparcial* (1811), Mora seems to have accepted the theory of the four stages of economic development developed by Smith among others, and especially the possibility of agricultural economic development through free trade should an absolute advantage exist (Almenar 2000b, 35).

These theoretical principles informed an economic policy agenda based on a substantial reduction of import duties on foreign goods, which "enrich the public coffers at the expense of imports and exports". Behind these positions lay the fundamental desire to reform the prohibitionist customs regulations issued in 1822 by Minister of Finance Rodríguez Aldea (Sagredo 1989). Mora understood that customs duties were not only a source of revenue, but also an instrument for economic development, and he focused his persuasive efforts on demonstrating that protection for foreign goods should be reduced to a minimum. His main argument was that "the imprudent raising of import duties" means a decrease "at the same time and all at once [in] domestic consumption [...] and the general aggregate of public welfare" (EMC, no. 16, 15/VII/1829, 761). This approach coherently placed the import duty debate in the broader field of economic development theory insofar as it analysed the impact on profit rates and therefore on economic growth. Adopting this position on the unilateral dismantling of customs duties, which was typical of other Spanish free traders such as Flórez Estrada, obliged Mora to come

[37] Mora saw copper's export potential, although he estimated that its mining required considerable capital application (EMC, no. 6, 1/IX/1828, 263–64). It should be recalled that the great technical innovation that multiplied copper production—reverberatory furnaces for smelting that used sulphide ores—was introduced around 1831 when Mora had left Chile (Folchi 2001, 153–57). In contrast, he estimated that gold and silver mining had little future, probably because of the uncertainty at the time about the lifespan of precious metal reserves.

up with an arsenal of persuasive tactics to enrich the central theoretical argument based on the theory of absolute advantage. Thus, citing Vattel and more frequently Grotius, Mora framed free trade in the "primitive law of nations", concluding that this law did not admit restrictions. To this he added a utilitarian analysis of customs duties, concluding that they reduced social welfare and, as if that were not enough, he went on to highlight "ideas that are not so much the preserve of science as of common sense", which he borrowed from classical economists. To begin with he rejected the "infant" industry notion as a justification for highly restrictive customs policies which condemned consumers to paying high prices without guaranteeing positive results in the long run (EMC, no. 9, 1/XII/1828, 427–32) and argued that if any branch of national industry required customs protection, "mild duties" should be imposed. At the same time, he undoubtedly drew on McCulloch to dismantle the mercantilist myth by disproving the positive relationship between customs duties and increased government revenue (EMC, no. 5, 1/VIII/1828, 199–200)[38]; in his view high import duties lowered tax revenue by reducing the consumption of taxed products. Furthermore, he agreed with Smith that high import duties encouraged smuggling, thus multiplying the reduction in revenue, not to mention the cost of the administrative structure required to collect them (EMC, no. 5, 1/VIII/1828, 205–207; Smith 1776 [1976b], 897–933).[39] However, as with other issues addressed in the EMC, Mora's relationship with President Pinto, and the resulting opportunity to influence economic policy, suggest that during this period he adopted a less doctrinaire free trade policy than in later writings and was thus in line with a certain view of pragmatism towards customs duties that prevailed among Chilean elites at the time (Sagredo 1989). In fact, in the EMC he was open to supporting import duties on agricultural products and keeping tariffs on industrial goods active, "as a necessary and transitory evil", but softening them for imports.

In the same vein, certain institutions that Mora suggested to facilitate foreign trade were not taken from the heart of his growth theory but were instead the results of practical experiences, some of which he himself had

[38] Mora was again following McCulloch here, specifically his articles in the ER (McCulloch 1827; for example, ER, "V. Remarks on the Financial Situation of Great Britain", XLVI, 390–414).

[39] On customs arrangements in Chile during the 1820s, see Will (1964, 6ff.) and Sagredo (2001). Mora seems to have had leanings towards the French customs system, which he described in great detail in the EMC (no. 10, 1/I/1829, 466–70).

witnessed. This was the case of free ports, which Mora valued highly as a trading instrument but to which classical economists paid little attention. His position seems to have come about from his 1819–1820 visit to the port of Livorno (Ramos 2000), to which he attributed part of the economic prosperity of the Duchy of Tuscany. However, the link between such institutions and the trade policy pursued by mercantilist states forced him to make an extra persuasive effort[40]; once again, theoretical arguments carried little weight, as Mora simply pointed out that free ports attracted population, capital and new industries and encouraged merchants and sailors to settle there, thus boosting the demand for agricultural products and put forward no further reasons for the institution's positive economic consequences (EMC, no. 9, 1/XII/1828, 394–400). He used practical experience as a way of presenting the advantages of free ports as a stimulus to trade, drawing on sources that were certainly unusual for a classical economist such as the *Essai sur les ports francs* by Ferrier, who eulogised the creation of three free ports in France—Bayonne, Dunkirk and Marseilles—on Colbert's initiative (Ferrier 1803, 32–34; EMC, no. 9, 1/XII/1828, 400–403). Mora believed that the motives prompting Colbert, Louis XIV's finance minister, to undertake such a project—a low population and shortage of circulating capital—were echoed in Chile. It was thus practical experience and its positive results for trade and eventually growth that inspired Mora's proposal to found free ports in Valparaíso, Coquimbo and Talcahuano. This amounted to a further expression of his pragmatism, which enabled him to reconcile different intellectual sources and policy proposals with the essence of his economic thought while retaining its genuinely classical nature. This eclecticism earned him a reputation as a superficial thinker; however, as Smith (1968) stressed, Mora wrote in simple terms about complex issues that he understood in depth.

6.7 Final Remarks

Mora's articles for the EMC had an enormous influence on his later work, especially the free trade writings published in Spain during the 1840s and 1850s which culminated in the entries in the *Enciclopedia Moderna* (1851–1855). In Chile, however, his influence was more limited owing to the turbulent political context, in spite of the fact that his intangible assets included numerous instances of influence on legislative action during

[40] On free ports in the sixteenth and seventeenth centuries, see Loromer (1987, 19–26).

those years—on issues such as press regulation, the banking question and the introduction of juries—. His fate was closely linked to Pinto's, whose resignation in November 1829 was followed by the victory of Diego Portales, leader of the *Pelucones*, in April 1830 at the height of a civil war. The conservatives, Mora's sworn enemies, stepped up their opposition to his leadership in education and culture and the EMC was closed in July 1829, then in May 1830 an assault against the *Liceo de Chile* began involving two conservative-controlled schools, the *Instituto Nacional* and the recently created *Colegio de Santiago* (1829). After several failed attempts at reform the *Instituto* was clearly in decline, but the *Colegio* was founded as an alternative to the *Liceo* and with the same modernising spirit, recruiting much of its teaching staff from France,[41] but the appointment of Andrés Bello as headmaster in 1830 sparked a bitter and well-documented controversy with the *Liceo* (De Ávila 1982, 112–97). Although it took a literary guise, the dispute was actually a continuation of the political rivalry between Mora and Bello, two brilliant and well-matched brains, during their exile in London. They operated in opposite trenches: each headed a college associated with a different political party and their interests—and salaries—were bound up with their victory or otherwise of their supporters. However, Portales' accountability to Mora and the *Liceo* was unflinching (Stuardo 1950, 105–140), not only in terms of the harsh personal attacks he received from the conservative press—"fugitive parvenu", "disgusting pamphleteer", "infernal viper that Chile harboured in its bosom"—, but also with regard to the fate of the *Liceo*. Part of its curriculum was suspended and public funding was withdrawn and given to the *Instituto Nacional*—the *Colegio de Santiago* closed in 1831—and Mora was dismissed as headmaster in September 1830.

Subsequent events are also well-known. Far from giving in, Mora began writing for *El defensor de los militares denominados constitucionales* (EDM, 1830), a short-lived newspaper published in July 1830 by a number of army officers who Portales had stripped of their rank for opposing him in the civil war, in which he published articles that were highly critical of the new government. He used *El trompeta* (ELT, 1830–1831), a new journal

[41] The *Colegio de Santiago* taught political economy, splitting into a historical part "until its advances in the works of Quesnay, Montesquieu, Condillac, etc.", and an analytical part, based on Smith and especially Say. Following Bello's arriving, the courses were absorbed into "Legislation Science", which was based on Bentham and also covered authors such as Filangieri, Montesquieu and Constant (De Ávila 1982, 62, 92, 96–99).

which appeared in December 1830 as a continuation of the EDM, to launch even more pointed attacks on the government's violent and arbitrary acts, aiming them personally at Portales. After the EDM closed in February 1831, Mora and other editors and contributors were arrested; after spending a few days in prison, he was summarily deported to Peru.

The liberal utopia that Mora embodied reached a dead end when the 1833 Constitution was approved. Enacted by Mariano Egaña, another of Mora's opponents, it meant a return to an oligarchic approach to politics, with more authoritarianism and state orders than individual freedom (Fernández Sebastián 2009, 352–63, 756 ff.; Stuven 2000, 29–53; 2012, 198). It was not until the 1840s that the climate of détente towards liberalism that Portales had buried was recovered thanks to several of Mora and Bello's followers, above all, José Victorino Lastarria.[42] Short-lived though it may have been, Mora's experiment ran extremely deep from this perspective, as it was the first challenge of the premise, deeply rooted in Chilean history (Stuven 2000), that the concepts of republicanism—freedom from arbitrary government—and liberalism—the pre-eminence of individual rights—were interchangeable. The economics articles in the EMC laid bare the fact that the two concepts represented different alternatives for the future. In the face of the prolonged success of a profoundly authoritarian political system—the 1833 Constitution was in force until 1924—, these articles interpreted the 1828 Constitution in an unambiguously liberal sense and sought to shift political leadership from the classes of the Ancien Régime to the actors of commercial society. Two fundamental strands underpinned this: recognition of the scientific nature of political economy and an attempt to persuade educated Chileans and Hispanic-American elites as a whole of the importance of applying it correctly in building the Republic and, as Mora intentionally intended, encouraging the timid awakening of a public sphere dedicated to economic issues, which had begun in the Chilean press during the 1820s with the controversies over foreign trade, entailed estates and state borrowing. The fact that, despite his recourse to minor authors or even those opposed to classical liberalism, and also in spite of his pragmatism, Mora constructed

[42] As a belated recognition of Mora's time in Chile, Lastarria, as Dean of the Humanities Faculty, appointed him honorary member of the Faculty in 1861. On their relationship, see Subercaseaux (1981, 21–33). Mora's moving letter of thanks to his old disciple ("we're all Chileans at heart in this house"), dated Madrid 8/II/1861, can be found in the MHN (3-41836).

the framework of his economic thought on the principles of classical economics has been discussed in some detail. In contrast to the small group of authors who had begun to spread classical economics in Chile—among them Henríquez and Vicuña—, he was a pioneer in keeping the faith with these principles—including free trade—thus anticipating the work of liberal economist Jean Gustave Courcelle-Seneuil as an educator and political adviser to Chile's republican institutions three decades later.

Bibliography

Books[43]

Mora, José Joaquín de. 1825. *Catecismo de economía política*. London: R. Ackermann.

Mora, José Joaquín de. 1828. *Respuesta a la Memoria sobre los mayorazgos de Chile publicada en Santiago el 9 de junio de 1828*. Santiago de Chile: Imprenta de Rengifo.

Mora, José Joaquín de. 1830a. *Curso de derechos del Liceo de Chile, por José Joaquín de Mora, director de aquel establecimiento. Tomo único. Derecho penal y Derecho de gentes*. Santiago de Chile: Imprenta republicana.

Mora, José Joaquín de. 1849. *Lecciones elementales de Ideología*. In *Curso de derechos del Liceo de Chile por Don José Joaquín de Mora, director de aquel establecimiento. Tomo único. Derecho natural y derecho de gentes*, 1–60. La Paz de Ayacucho: Imprenta del Pueblo.

Primary Sources

Alonso Ortiz, José. 1796. *Ensayo sobre el sistema de la moneda-papel y sobre el crédito público*. Madrid: Imprenta Real.

Anonymous. 1828. *Memoria sobre los mayorazgos de Chile dedicada al público por algunos sucesores inmediatos*. Santiago de Chile: R. Rengifo.

Constitución política del Estado de Chile. 1823. Santiago: Imprenta Nacional.

Constitución política de la República de Chile. 1828. Santiago: Imprenta de R. Rengifo.

Destutt de Tracy, Antoine-Louis-Claude. 1826. *Elementos de Ideología por Destutt-de-Tracy, incluidos en diez y ocho lecciones, e ilustrados con notas críticas, por el Catedrático D. Mariano S.* Paris: Casa de Masson e hijo.

[43] On the prolix reprints of the *Catecismos*, *Cursos* and other works of Mora in the Hispanic world, see Roldán (2003), Macintyre (2018) and Medina (2022).

Dufresne Saint-Leon, Louis-Cesar-Alexandre. 1824. *Étude du crédit public et des dettes publiques.* Paris: G. de Bossange.

El mercurio chileno. 2009. Edited by Gabriel Cid. Santiago de Chile: Centro de investigaciones Diego Barros Arana.

Ferrier, François-Louis-Auguste. 1803. *Essai sur les ports francs.* Bayonne: Chez Fauvet.

Flórez Estrada. Álvaro. 1811. *Examen imparcial de las disensiones de la América con la España, de los medios de su reconciliación y de la prosperidad de todas las naciones.* Cádiz: Imprenta Manuel Ximena de Carreño.

Ganilh, Charles. 1815. *La théorie de l'économie politique.* Paris: Deterville.

Hennet, Albert-Jospeh-Ulpien. 1816. *Théorie du crédit public.* Paris: Testu et C.

McCulloch, John Ramsay. 1825. *The Principles of Political Economy, with a Sketch of the Rise and Progress of the Science.* Edinburgh and London: Adam and Charles Black-Longman, Brown, Green and Longmans.

Mill, James. 1821. *Elements of Political Economy*, London: Baldwin, Cradock and Joy.

Smith, Adam. 1776 [1976b]. *An Inquiry into the Nature and Causes of the Wealth of Nations*, edited by Roy H. Campbell, Andrew S. Skinner and William B. Todd. Oxford: OUP.

Storch, Heinrich Friedrich von. 1823. *Cours d'économie politique.* Paris: J. P. Aillaud.

Secondary Sources

Almenar, Salvador. 2000a. "El desarrollo del pensamiento económico clásico en España". In *Economía y economistas españoles. Vol. IV. La economía clásica*, edited by Enrique Fuentes, 7–92. Barcelona: Galaxia Gütenberg and Círculo de Lectores.

Almenar, Salvador. 2000b. "Flórez Estrada y la economía política clásica". In *Economía y economistas españoles. Vol. IV. La economía clásica*, edited by Enrique Fuentes, 369–411. Barcelona: Galaxia Gütenberg and Círculo de Lectores.

Amunátegui, Miguel Luis. 1888. *Don José Joaquín de Mora. Apuntes biográficos.* Santiago de Chile: Imprenta Nacional.

Astigarraga, Jesús and Juan Zabalza. 2017. "José Joaquín de Mora y la divulgación de la doctrina económica liberal en Latinoamérica en los inicios del siglo XIX". *Revista de historia industrial* 67, 39–68.

Astigarraga, Jesús and Juan Zabalza, eds. 2022. *Adam Smith and 'The Wealth of Nations' in Spain. A History of Reception, Dissemination, Adaptation and Application, 1778–1840.* London and New York: Routledge.

Braun-Llona, Juan, et al. 1998. "Economía Chilena 1810–1995. Estadísticas Históricas". WP no. 187. Pontificia Universidad Católica de Chile. Instituto de Economía.

De Ávila Martel, Alamiro. 1982. *Mora y Bello en Chile*. Santiago: Universidad de Chile.

De Haro, Dionisio. 2013. "Papel para un Perú independiente: el pensamiento económico español y la creación del Banco Auxiliar de Papel Moneda". *Revista Complutense de Historia de América* 39, 203–27.

Dome, Takuo. 2004. *The Political Economy of Public Finance in Britain (1767–1873)*. London and New York: Routledge.

Edwards, José. 2018. "Historia del pensamiento económico en Chile, 1790–1970". In *Historia política de Chile, 1810–2010. Tomo III. Problemas económicos*, edited by Claudio Robles, 369–95. Santiago de Chile: FCE.

Fernández Sebastián, Javier, ed. 2009. *Diccionario político y social del mundo iberoamericano. La era de las revoluciones, 1750–1850*. Madrid: Sociedad Española de Conmemoraciones Culturales and CEPC.

Fernández Sebastián, Javier, ed. 2014. *Diccionario político y social del mundo iberoamericano*, 10 vols. Madrid: UPV-CEPC.

Folchi, Mauricio. 2001. "La insustentabilidad de la industria del cobre en Chile: los hornos y los bosques durante el siglo XIX". *Revista Mapocho* 49, 149–75.

Giacomin, Alberto. 2007. "Paper-Money: A Reassessment of Adam Smith's Views". In *Money and Markets: A Doctrinal Approach*, edited by Alberto Giacomin and Maria Cristina Marcuzzo, 181–89. London and New York: Routledge.

Hurtado, Celso. 1984. "La economía chilena entre 1830 y 1930: sus limitaciones y sus herencias". *Colección de Estudios CIEPLAN* 12, 37–60.

Iglesias, Graciela. 2017. "José Joaquín de Mora in Chile: From Neo-Europe to the *Beocia Americana*". *Bulletin of Latin America Research* 36–2, 326–39.

Llorca-Jaña, Manuel and Juan José Martínez (Eds.) (2023). "Historia económica colonial de Chile". Santiago de Chile: Fondo de Cultura Económica.

Llorca-Jaña, Manuel and Juan Navarrete-Montalvo (2017). "The Chilean Economy during the 1810–1830s and its Entry into the World Economy". *Bulletin of Latin American Research* 36(3), 354–369.

Loromer, David G. 1987. *Merchants and Reform in Livorno, 1814–1868*. Berkeley: University of California Press.

Marichal, Carlos and Marcello Carmagnani. 2006. "Mexico: From colonial regime to liberal financial order, 1750–1912". In *Transferring Wealth and Power from the Old to the New World: Monetary and Fiscal Institutions in the 17th Century through the 19th Centuries*, edited by Michael D. Bordo and Roberto Cortes-Conde, 284–326. New York: CUP.

McCulloch, John Ramsay (1827), "V. remarks on the Financial Situation of Great Britain". *The Edinburg Review* XLVI(XCII), 390–414.

O'Brien, Denis Patrick. 1970. *J. R. McCulloch, A Study in Classical Economics*. New York: Routledge.

O'Brien, Denis Patrick. 1989. *Los economistas clásicos*. Madrid: Alianza.

Pérez Godoy, Fernando. 2017. "Johannes Heineccius y la historia trasatlántica del *Ius Gentium*". *Revista chilena de Derecho* 44–2, 539–72.

Pinto, José Joaquín. 2012. "Los orígenes del impuesto directo y progresivo en América Latina". *Historia y Sociedad* 23, 53–77.

Ramos, Carlos. 2000. "La cultura jurídica en la época de la Confederación Peruano-Boliviana". *Revista de estudios históricos-jurídicos* 22, 267–97.

Riveros, Luis and Rodrigo Ferraro. 1985. "La historia económica del siglo XIX a la luz de la evolución de los precios". *Estudios de economía* 12–1, 50–78.

Rodríguez, Gregorio. 1924. "Cartas autógrafas de Don José Joaquín de Mora a Don Florencia Varela". *Revista chilena de historia y geografía* 54, 35–66.

Sagredo, Rafael. 1989. "Pragmatismo proteccionista en los orígenes de la República". *Historia* 24, 267–86.

Sagredo, Rafael. 1997. "Chile 1823–1831. El desafío de la administración y organización de la Hacienda Pública". *Historia* 30, 287–312.

Salazar, Gabriel. 2009. *Mercaderes, empresarios y capitalistas. Chile, Siglo XIX*. Santiago: Editorial sudamericana.

Smith, Robert Sidney. 1968. "El pensamiento económico de José Joaquín de Mora", *Humanitas* IX, 595–607.

Stuardo, Carlos. 1950. *El Liceo de Chile. Antecedentes para su historia, 1828–1831*. Santiago de Chile: Imprenta universitaria.

Stuven, Ana María. 2012. "De la autonomía a la república: el debate constitucional en Chile, 1808–1833". In *El laboratorio constitucional iberoamericano: 1807/1808–1830*, edited by Antonio Annino y Marcela Ternavasio, 179–202. Madrid and Frankfurt am Main: Iberoamericana and Verbuet, 179–202.

Stuven, Ana María. 2000. *La seducción de un orden: las elites y la construcción de Chile en las polémicas culturales y políticas del siglo XIX*. Santiago: Universidad Católica.

Subercaseaux, Bernardo. 1981. *Cultura y sociedad liberal en el Siglo XIX. Lastarria, ideología y literature*. Santiago: Aconcagua.

Tsoulfidis, Lefteris. 2007. "Classical Economists and Public Debt". *International Review of Economics* 54, 1–12.

Villalobos, Sergio and Rafael *Sagredo*. 1987. *El proteccionismo económico en Chile. Siglo XIX*. Santiago de Chile: Instituto Blas Cañas.

Will, Robert M. 1964. "The Introduction of Classical Economics into Chile". *Hispanic American Historical Review* 44–1, 1–21.

Zabalza, Juan and Jesús Astigarraga. 2020. "Entre España y Chile. José Joaquín Mora y los proyectos de un diccionario de economía política (1825–1855)". In *El pensamiento económico del reformismo criollo*, edited by José Antonio Piqueras and Johanna von Grafenstein, 435–75. Santa Marta: Editorial Unimagdalena and Instituto Mora.

CHAPTER 7

In Peru and Bolivia (1834–1843): From Lawyer to Free Trade Apostle

7.1 Introduction

Mora was already well known in both Peru and Bolivia before he arrived at the port of Callao on 13 March 1831 at the age of forty-eight. As Lima, because was one of the Ackermann Company's main distribution hubs, his works were available to the Peruvian public in the city's bookshops. The *Catecismo de Geografía*, which was published in London in 1824 and included a concise history of Peru, was reprinted in Cuzco in 1826, while periodicals such as the *Mercurio Peruano*, *La Miscelánea* and *El Fénix de Lima* had already published many of his poems, fables and writings on literature and education (Monguió 1967, 31). It is not surprising, therefore, that the Lima press announced his arrival enthusiastically, highlighting his intellectual prowess, his commitment to promoting liberal institutions and the hardships he had suffered after Pinto's resignation. In fact, the *Mercurio Peruano* (MP, 1827–1834) reproduced an article from the Chilean ELT containing an account of the *Liceo de Chile* students' protest at the school's closure and stating that "there will be no liberal government that does not welcome Mr. Mora with open arms" (MP, 15/III/1831). For his part, Mora had shown remarkable knowledge of the Peru and Bolivia political and literary worlds and related issues since his time in Buenos Aires.

J. Astigarraga et al., *The Economic Legacy of José Joaquín de Mora*, Palgrave Studies in the History of Economic Thought,
https://doi.org/10.1007/978-3-031-49446-8_7

True to form, Mora did not put his name, with some exception, to a single article during his time in Peru. Monguió's (1967) landmark work revealed his authorship of many poems and political articles that were published in the Lima press, circumscribing subsequent research in the literary, educational and political fields; however, his failure to identify any political economy contributions led to the belief that the discipline was no longer one of Mora's main concerns. This chapter will show the opposite: that Mora wrote more pieces on political economy than any other topic while in Peru, that his activity as a populariser of the discipline was unceasing and that he attempted to influence the Peruvian government's economic policy through his numerous publications.

Current historiography on Mora's sojourn in Peru thus limits his activities to three spheres: the theatre and literature, education and politics. The theatre scene in Lima was going through a lean patch when he arrived because the economic crisis was emptying venues, and consequently his humorous-educational comedy *El marido ambicioso* was only performed twice. More successful were the theatre readings of the thirty-eight poems he published in Lima, many of which were clear expressions of his most personal convictions: the prevalence of reason and its harmony with faith; utilitarianism and scientism; the horrors of Ferdinand VII's absolutist regime; his affinity with Scottish Common Sense philosophy and his Anglophile literary tastes. Mora also used his unquestionable talent as a poet to spread free trade ideas.[1]

On the educational front, true to his belief that liberal institutions could only flourish through education, Mora devised a project to open a school, which was announced in the Lima press in autumn 1831. Unlike the *Liceo de Chile*, the planned *Ateneo del Perú* would take day pupils and would teach natural and public law, history, geography and chronology, literature, pure mathematics, French and political economy. However, despite his efforts to publicise the school, too few pupils enrolled and Mora decided to teach courses in natural and public law and Roman law privately instead (Monguió 1967, 122–25) as well as teaching at the Lima Military College. The courses created a bitter controversy in the Lima press, with Mora's detractors accusing him of materialism and atheism. However, although its content was more likely to attract this kind of criticism, the *Cursos de lógica y ética según la Escuela de Edimburgo*, which was published in Lima in late 1832, was well received.

[1] This is clear from the poem-fable "*El banquete de los filósofos*", which was published in *La Miscelánea* on 13 June 1833 (Monguió 1967, 56–57). Mora wrote: "[...] *Y los economistas/ Extienden sus conquistas/Destacando los tiros más crueles/Contra los aranceles*".

7.2 Mora and Common Sense

The *Cursos* were the main expression of the philosophical side that Mora developed not only in Peru but throughout his life, as he taught philosophy and published articles and reviews in the press on the subject, as well as producing two books that were mainly for teaching purposes: not only the *Cursos* but also the *Tratado de la evidencia* (1846). The latter was published in Lima in 1846 but was probably written around the time of the *Cursos* between 1831 and 1834 (Medina 2022, 102). Mora's philosophical side can be interpreted not so much as an independent part of him but as another component, or even as the effect of his political and economic conceptions. Indeed, these two works show that, in step with his study of political economy, Mora had moved beyond the influence of Condillac and Tracy's sensualism towards Common Sense. As previously noted, he had already shown signs of sympathy with this school of thought—especially the work of Dugald Stewart—in the CCL and EC, the Spanish newspapers of his youth, and also in the Buenos Aires CCP, although, after his exile in London, his support undoubtedly deepened. Mora called this doctrine the "Edinburgh School", referring more specifically to the philosophers of the Scottish School of Common Sense and it aligned perfectly with his classical economic thought in terms of origin and content. [2] In fact, this Scottish Enlightenment school, of which Thomas Reid, James Beattle, James Oswald and George Campbell were prominent members, also included Adam Smith and his successor to the Edinburgh Chair of Moral Philosophy, philosopher and teacher Dugald Stewart, who Mora met in London through Blanco White and on whose works he based the *Cursos*. The *Tratado* was in fact an annotated translation of Campbell's *The Philosophy of Rhetoric* (1776) to which several translations of other writings ascribed to the Common Sense school were added as well as an original text by Mora himself. All this is evidence of the profound interweaving of philosophy, politics and economics permeating Mora's work and which he would bring to fruition years later by popularising John Stuart Mill's writings.

To the type of enlightened economist that Mora was, as well as to the figures he was inspired by, prioritising an interest in the material

[2] Nevertheless, Tracy and above all Condillac were still present in Mora's ideas, as shown especially in Lesson 25 of his *Curso de lógica* (Mora 1832, 41–42). On Mora and Common Sense see Medina (2022, 98–105).

improvement of individuals and societies entailed firstly reason and logic-methodology and secondly, and more fundamentally, a moral or ethical perception; in other words, a certain ideology. Mora therefore opted for Scottish Common Sense because this philosophical doctrine formed part of the bedrock of his economic thought, constituting an apt compromise between materialism at one extreme and idealism at the other. Furthermore, as Mora himself pointed out, the school's roots were deep, broad and tolerant: "In it are recast Bacon's innovative spirit, Locke's depth, Condillac's clearest discoveries and all are infused with a gentle style, a modesty of documents, a tolerance of opinions, which are rarely found in scientific discussions" (Mora 1832, "*Discurso preliminar*").

In fact, the Common Sense school enabled Mora to base his economic discourse on an ideology and a methodology which, in his opinion, had incorporated scientific progress and surpassed abstruse and syllogistic scholastic thought without falling prey to Hume's scepticism and relativism (Medina 2022, 99); an ideology and a methodology which, like the laws of political economy, advocated simple and useful explanations that resulted from combining observation and the use of logical reason as a way to access knowledge. Moreover, both were very well suited to Mora's needs in terms of teaching, a matter of great importance in his project to spread British liberal ideas in Peru and throughout the new American republics, in which central stage was occupied by a privileged Creole sector whose desire for liberation had been—and would ultimately be—more influenced by the French Enlightenment.[3]

The *Cursos* and the *Tratado* certainly did not aim to contribute original elements to Common Sense philosophy but rather to provide the Hispanic world with an adapted summary of the theory for teaching purposes—in principle Mora's teaching at the Lima Military College in 1833, although they were also used as textbooks in Peru and Bolivia during the 1830s, not without some opposition[4] (Monguió 1967, 145–46)—and to provide a high level of information in a space in which this philosophy was practically unknown. Mora designed the logic course as a complement to law

[3] On Mora's role in the introducing of Scottish philosophy into Hispanic America see Macintyre (2018) and Ibarz and León (2009).

[4] Macintyre (2018, 14) refers to the opposition to the *Cursos* by Juan Ignacio de Gorriti, an Argentinian priest and educator who fought for independence in upper Peru, criticising author's error in departing from pure logic, to go into the question of how humans form ideas, something that Gorriti might have deemed contrary to religious moral order. On the opposition to the Mora's law teachings, see Anonymous (1838).

studies, while the ethics or moral course was aimed at the citizens of the new republics as a whole, particularly the young elites who were to govern them. The *Cursos*' purpose was therefore not to delve into philosophical debate but to act as an introductory course that would put a distance between the students and "all the scholastic artefacts and all the enigmas that have been amassed on Philosophy courses", in accordance with D'Alambert's idea that "the true principles from which every science must begin [...] are the simple facts, which can be neither explained nor questioned" (Mora 1832, unpaginated). Where the scientific spirit was concerned, Mora recalled that morality needed science and quoted Bacon to that effect. As for the motives that drove him, his words in the "*Advertencia*" to the *Curso de ética* are highly revealing:

> If we are interested in the perfection of the inventions that enhance physical life, the doctrines that influence the improvement of institutions, all the branches that contribute to the promotion of wealth, and if for these reasons we devote ourselves so eagerly to mechanics, chemistry, legislation and political economy, how much more precious should the well-being which results from the right use of the moral faculties be to us, and how much more earnestly should we apply ourselves to the doctrines by whose means alone it is given to us to attain it! The ease, the pleasures, the agreeable sensations produced by the advancement of the arts and the physical and political sciences cannot be compared with the inseparable delight of moral perfection.

In keeping with its title, the *Cursos* had two parts, the first devoted to logic, whose object was "truth", and the second to ethics, whose aim was "moral goodness", although Mora added numerous paratexts that insisted on the deep link between the two; in short, between truth and will.

The part dealing with logic especially aimed to present the various means and tools for accessing knowledge, in which it was essential to know how the analytical, rational mind operated as well as its properties, limits and possible errors; care was taken not to enter into metaphysical questions, which would exceed the *Cursos*' educational brief. In this part Mora relied above all on Stewart's *Outlines of Moral Philosophy* (1793) and *Elements of the Philosophy of the Human Mind* (1792) in addition to works by Reid, Bacon, Locke, Hume, Hartley, Tracy and Jouffroy. His course in logic, meanwhile, benefited from information obtained from treatises on medicine and education and if the quotations from Aristotle, Descartes and Condillac are added it is clear that his adaptation of the doctrine of Common Sense incorporated many diverse influences, indicating a vision that was a far cry from fanaticism and had moderate leanings (Medina 2022, 101).

The same applies to the course on ethics, which were understood as fact-based and therefore founded on experience and observation. In this sense, it was a conception that was informed by the scientific spirit, in which truth pursued by logic was linked to moral perfection. Mora followed the structure of the second part of Stewart's *Outlines*, incorporating ideas from *Principles of Moral Philosophy*, a work by Paley, with whom Mora was very familiar, from Smith's *The Theory of Moral Sentiments* (1759) and from his teacher Hutcheson. He also made frequent references to Hume, especially in Lesson Eighteen.

The *Tratado* was sponsored by Peruvian politician José Chipoco River and was initially a translation of part of Campbell's *The Philosophy of Rhetoric* (1776), specifically Chapters 5 and 6 of Book I. Mora set out the content in eleven lessons, although, as he noted, the fourth was based on the ideas of Jouffroy, a follower of Common Sense who had translated Stewart's *Outlines* into French. He also included the Spanish translations of five texts by Jouffroy, Stewart and John Abercrombie, all "distinguished philosophers of the Edinburgh School" in the book, making it clear in accordance with his overall philosophical intention that the purpose of these contributions was to serve as a "commentary" on the *Tratado*, as they "contain the capital doctrines of the school of Scotland" (Campbell 1846, 41). The translator "very especially" recommended the first of the texts chosen, which was by Jouffroy, because it contained "sound protection against a certain type of materialism" (Campbell 1846, 41). The *Tratado* also included a text by Mora titled "*Manual de lógica práctica, o principios sacados de las principales obras de la Escuela de Edimburgo y aplicables a la conducta del entendimiento*", setting out the doctrine's basic tenets on logic in twenty-four sections with the aim of making the translated texts easier to understand.

To Mora the philosophy of knowledge in the earlier works constituted the basis on which scientific progress rested, among which were the moral sciences and political economy. That was the underlying thrust of his summary of Scottish Common Sense, with its inseparable strands of logic and ethics and focus on the perception of facts and the way the human mind operates. Political economy was consequently the fruit of a method that was not one of prosaic materialism, oblivious to morality and ethical ends, but neither was it extreme idealism that overlooked real-world facts and material needs. In fact, without expounding on the specific content of Common Sense here,[5] some aspects should be highlighted that inform the interweaving of philosophy and economics, so characteristic of the intellectual tradition to which Mora adhered, in which, as frequently noted, Bentham's utilitarianism played a leading role.[6] Both Mora's *Cursos* and his annotations to the texts he translated in 1846 therefore included references and examples that expressly alluded to political economy, as did discussions on perception and the constructing and specifying of definitions of concepts, especially new ones, and the classifying of phenomena and facts.

One of these premises appears in the *Cursos* when the subject of "perception", one of the "mental operations of understanding", is raised. Mora (1832, 9) expressly alluded to Smith in stressing the importance of the complementary action of the senses of sight and touch in order to gain a correct impression of reality. Furthermore, when dealing with the problems that mistaken, incomplete or confused conceptualisation can cause, Mora gave the example of political economy, expressly following Malthus when he stated:

> This is a common flaw in the political and moral sciences, either when they are in their infancy or their doctrines have undergone a great revolution. We have a recent instance of this truth in the nomenclature of political economy, whose normal terms, and even the very ones used by the celebrated Adam Smith, have occasioned the fiercest disputes. (Mora 1832, 26)

Mora again alluded to Malthus when, in one of Stewart's translated texts in which the latter referred to the confusion of terminology characterising the "scholastic brouhaha", he introduced a lengthy footnote to make it clear that this confusion was applicable "to the present state of human knowledge", referring in this respect to "an excellent little work by Malthus titled *Definitions in Political Economy*" (1827). Mora quoted verbatim Malthus' observation in this work that it "is still more difficult, in

[5] There is an up-to-date conceptual framework in Bradford's work (2018).

[6] Mora cited Bentham in the *Cursos* when dealing with the distinction between "mental association" and "moral association", the former being capable of becoming "a universal principle to which we submit all our knowledge". Thus, it is that Bentham, in establishing the principle of utility as the basis of legal doctrines, believes that he has discovered in it a "sure method of appreciating the rightness of laws" (Mora 1832, 33).

the sciences of morals and politics, to use terms which may not be understood differently by different persons, according to their different habits and opinions", as was the case with the words "virtue, morality, equity, charity", to which Malthus then added "liberty, civil liberty, political liberty, national sovereignty and constitutional government" which are "frequently understood in a different sense by different persons", ending by stating the following:

> In political economy, however much one may wish to approximate its nomenclature to that of the mathematical sciences, we see nothing but incessant doubts as to the meaning of the terms wealth, value, production, wages, demand and all the others that make up the science's indispensable language. In spite of the care with which they have endeavoured to methodise their technical terms, were not the French economists obviously mistaken when they spoke of the wealth of a nation, or at least, did they not make great mistakes by taking that word in a sense different from the one used in society? Say has made the same mistake with the word utility, basing himself on the principle that what has no value is not useful; Ricardo, by saying that expanding foreign trade does not immediately increase values, whereby it is seen that he uses the word value in a different sense from the one that we all give it; McCulloch by giving a definition of wealth which may either include or exclude non-material pleasures, we do not know; Torrens, confusing net product with capital, etc. (Campbell 1846, 63–64)

Mora added to this idea by stating that "there is scarcely a word used in the moral and political sciences to which observations analogous to these cannot be applied. This is very a serious hindrance and can only be avoided by means of clear and authoritative definitions" (Campbell 1846, 63–64). Moreover, he deemed this especially significant in the case of political economy, largely because "the words used have been taken out of common usage and cannot but retain the associations of their origin", as is the case with "the words wealth, public interests, liberty, etcetera", which "we have been forced to remove from society and which have been incorporated into the science, without yet having an exclusively scientific meaning" (Campbell 1846, 63–64).

Mora no doubt had a special interest in warning his Peruvian students that political economy terminology was confusing. He considered the issue "one of the concerns most opposed to the right exercise of the operations of the spirit", which consisted of "accepting abstract ideas and freely using the words that represent them, without first making an inventory of their constituent parts" (Campbell 1846, 98–99). At stake was political economy's very progress as a science, as "its most positive steps forward have been due to the care taken to purify abstract ideas and their respective symbols of all heterogeneous ingredients", a merit he attributed largely to Adam Smith, whose "great innovation" in the science of public wealth "consists principally in the proper definition of the terms used in it". As cases of the "abuse of words" in political economy, Mora then referred to the examples of "balance of trade", which "every economist explains in his own way", with very contradictory results, and "public wealth". With regard to the meaning of this term, Mora noted that "some find it in the rapid increase in population", and "others in the high price of agricultural products", such that what counts to the latter is "the activity of circulation", while what matters to the former is "the abundance of circulating capital", from which he concluded that "such a notable divergence can only be the effect of the incorrectness of abstract ideas".

The classification of phenomena also affected political economy's rigour (Campbell 1846, 106–107). Having pointed out the error of "placing together two ideas that do not match"—"political representation" and "civil mandate" were linked under "the noun mandate", for example—, Mora decried the "opposite effect", which consisted of "separating the species that should be included in it from a classification", pointing out that "to this class belongs the false idea of money held by economists in the last century, sometimes considering it a general sign of wealth, sometimes a universal means of exchange". This gave rise to "mistaken theories" until "science perfected by observation" discovered that "money is a product and consequently follows in its creation, circulation and consumption the same laws as all the products of mankind's labour".[7] According to Mora this discovery, which was "insignificant in the eyes of common people", had led to "immense results in practice" and in line with his unwavering pro-free trade stance had succeeded in making "the barbarous restrictions with which governments wanted to fix metal wealth to the ground in defiance of men's propensities and needs" give way. Mora had no doubt that this progress was made possible by "observing" and "studying" the facts, hence "the need to expand the field of our observations and to collect as many positive data as possible when we have to rationalise about practical matters" (Campbell 1846, 107). The reciprocal significance of political economy and the philosophy of knowledge would

[7] Mora (1846a, 107). He was criticising Ganilh's monetary ideas in this passage.

become apparent years later when Mora summarised and recommended the Spanish translation of John Stuart Mill's *A System of Logic* (1843) in Spain. This all serves to underscore the notion that, especially from a teaching perspective, Common Sense was still the essential path between French-rooted sensualism and the prevailing ontologism in Germany, which was personified in Hegel, and for this reason Mora continued to recommend the works of Stewart, Abercrombie, Campbell and Smith's *Theory of Moral Sentiments* in later years, thus retaining the connection with works in this philosophical current that was forged during his years in Peru.

This may go some way to explaining the prolonged success of the *Cursos*. Mora intended them to be used as a textbook in schools in Peru and Bolivia, but although this never actually happened it did not prevent them from being widely distributed in Hispanic America. The *Cursos* were reprinted in La Paz (1834, 1844, 1846), Sucre (1840) and Bogotá (1840);[8] moreover, the part on logic was published in a separate edition in Lima in 1840, while in 1846 both parts were published separately in La Paz.[9] Furthermore, the *Cursos* were well-known in Spain and could have been used at the *Colegio de San Felipe Neri* in Cádiz, of which Mora was headmaster, quite certainly, between 1843 and 1844, the years in which they were republished in Madrid (1842, 1845) and Seville (1845). For its part, the *Tratado*'s fortunes were mixed: it was basically circulated in Peru and was not reprinted anywhere else, although it was the vehicle through which translations of Campbell's texts first appeared in the Spanish-speaking world.

7.3 In Conservative Liberal Circles in Peru

During his time in Peru Mora's thinking—or rather, his political praxis—underwent a series of changes that need to be seen in the context of the political scene there in the early 1830s. The most significant was that he began to move in liberal circles with a conservative and authoritarian tinge, whose epicentre was the powerful General Agustín Gamarra. They advocated the pre-eminence of the executive—in short, "strong government"—over the legislative. This was a significant departure from the political path that Mora had first taken during the Liberal Triennium when

[8] Likewise, the BNE (no. 12,317) preserves a manuscript copy of this work.

[9] Macintyre (2018, 2); Medina (2022, 102–104); Mora (1840, 1846a, b).

he embraced radical liberalism; the final chapter was his imprisonment and expulsion from Chile as a result of tenacious opposition to the authoritarian government that took power after the Battle of Lircay and the fact that the influential Diego Portales, a key figure in the new government, held grudge held against him.

After the victory at Ayacucho and a brief period at the head of the government, Simón Bolívar left Peru in September 1826. Despite his enormous influence, the country's consolidation as an independent state faced a number of difficulties in areas such as the political organisation of its vast territory, the huge diversity of social groups, the dire state of public finances, the small population and the lack of one social group capable of leading the building of an independent state. In fact, it was the last issue that created the breeding ground for an on-going dispute between the military, merchants and intellectuals for control of political power. The military were in the strongest position, but, as they needed the merchants' financial and the intellectuals' ideological support, they were forced to create alliances with these groups to achieve power, which they then attempted to legitimise by means of a series of Constitutions—five were approved between 1821 and 1840 (Contreras and Cueto 2009, 79–93)—. After Bolívar's departure, General José de La Mar was elected President of the Republic, but the weakness of his position, poor political skills and the Peruvian troops' defeat in their conflict with Gran Colombia, which forced the surrender of Guayaquil, paved the way for his overthrow by General Agustín Gamarra. In an atmosphere of political and military instability in which the desire for order prevailed over the desire for freedom, the *Congreso Extraordinario*, which remained in the hands of the liberals, elected him provisional president in August 1829. After he called and won the first elections in an independent Peru in December 1829 his mandate was extended until December 1833 (Sobrevilla 2021, 61). Gamarra established a politically decentralised and economically protectionist regime whose main aim was to preserve the Cuzco *obrajes*—textile production centres—. In December 1833 he was replaced by Orbegoso, who, in contrast, developed a free trade policy and thus sowed the seeds of the civil war that broke out between the north and the south on the initiative of their respective economic elites (Contreras and Cueto 2009, 105–106).

One of the main ideological debates of the time revolved around the appropriate form of political organisation for dealing with what was basically a state of anarchy in many areas of civil life. On one side were advocates of the primacy of the legislative—*el Congreso*—over the executive, while on the other were those who considered it necessary to create a "strong government" headed by a military leader who was granted almost absolute power; two of Mora's close friends, José María de Pando and Felipe Pardo y Aliaga were in the forefront of the latter (Contreras and Cueto 2009, 94–95). The controversy between a liberal *Congreso* and an authoritarian president marked Mora's entire sojourn in Peru, which was characterised by political instability and bloody factional struggles.

According to Amunátegui (1888, 266–68), in Peru Mora may have been seeking a safe haven that was conducive to intellectual reflection and to rebuilding his life and fortune, avoiding the hardships he had undergone in Argentina and particularly Chile; if so, this might partly explain his rapprochement with authoritarian circles there. Mora was undoubtedly frustrated by his experiences in Rivadavia and Pinto's governments and expressed a certain disappointment at both leaders' lack of tenacity and determination. It was precisely these traits that he highlighted in General Gamarra, whom he admired for his "fists", that is, for his firmness and resolve to put an end to the turmoil in Peru since the end of the Bolívar regime (Monguió 1967, 157). Mora expressed his fear of the revolutionary processes that were so frequent during the Gamarra years in several articles published in the national press, opposing the results of applying the "public spirit" and "the progress of reason" of enlightened Frenchmen like Turgot to the consequences of Jacobin revolutionary currents.

However, perhaps more than his admiration for the period of stability and peace ushered in by Gamarra, it was personal relationships that brought Mora closer to Lima's conservative circles. The fact that he was fully integrated into these circles is clear from the teaching staff at the *Ateneo del Perú* and the subscribers to the *Cursos de lógica y ética*, among whom was none other than President Gamarra himself. According to the school prospectus, its board of directors included Mora's friends Pando and Pardo y Aliaga,[10] of which the former was the most influential. Secretary of State during the Liberal Triennium, protégé of Bolívar, personal friend of President Gamarra and a minister in his government on several occasions, Pando was not only on the *Ateneo*'s board of directors but was responsible for the subject of political economy. Mora probably met him in Spain during the Liberal Triennium; what is certain is that

[10] The rest of the teaching staff was made up of prestigious members of Peru's intellectual, scientific and political elite such as Hipólito Unanue and Manuel Lorenzo de Vidaurre; see Monguió (1967, 123).

Pando invited him to his famous gatherings, inspired by the eighteenth-century literary salons, at which cultural and political issues were discussed in conversations that frequently went beyond the press and reached as far as parliament itself. The closeness and warmth of the relationship between Pando and Pardo y Aliaga and Mora's deep admiration for their "reasoning" must have been a decisive factor in his slide towards political conservatism. Journalist and writer Pardo y Aliaga also participated in the gatherings of the Peruvian intellectual elite. Although born in Peru, in 1821 he had emigrated to Madrid, where he remained until 1828. It is not clear exactly when his relationship with Mora began but there was undoubtedly a strong bond between them, to the extent that it remained intact when Mora joined the service of Santa Cruz, who Pardo detested (Monguió 1967, 101, 123).

These two friends' political and journalistic facets would be of fundamental importance in Mora's career during his time in Peru. However, he insisted that his ties with the group—"Pando, Martínez, Pardo and Vivanco"—were strictly limited to friendship (Monguió 1967, 157). He reinforced this idea when he pointed out that he had never "belonged to the politics of Mr. Agustín [Gamarra] because nothing could bind me to it" (Amunátegui 1897, 168). Basadre (2002, 240) seems to confirm this relative detachment when he says that Mora, as a journalist, collaborated with Pando's group, although its members considered Gamarra a lesser evil than his predecessor La Mar.

7.4 Mora and the Economics Articles in the Peruvian Press

The numerous economics articles that Mora wrote anonymously during his stay in Lima were mainly published in the MP, *El Conciliador* (ECO, 1830–1834) and *La Verdad* (LV, 1833). All these publications had close links to Gamarra's government, the circle frequented by Mora and especially Pando and Pardo y Aliaga. The ECO, the Peruvian government's mouthpiece from January 1830 to January 1834, was the successor to a series of official titles that began with the publication of *El Peruano* in 1825. Its editor was Felipe Pardo y Aliaga, assisted by José María Pando as leader writer and author of many articles. As an official newspaper the ECO carried not only government documents and legislative texts but also had regular foreign and domestic policy sections. The "*Variedades*" and "*El Conciliador*" sections publicised news of political events in Hispanic America, Europe and North America and ran many of Mora's economics articles. The MP used one of the Peruvian press's historical titles, which had been an eminent exponent of enlightened thought during the closing decades of the eighteenth century. However, although its founders intended to preserve the connection with the original title, the new MP, which appeared from August 1827 to March 1834, adopted a conservative ideology from 1829 onwards and fostered a climate of opinion that favoured the authoritarian governments' reforms and policies, in defence of the Gamarra administration. Although Pando founded the paper and was chief editor for some time, reinforcing its analytical consistency and stylistic elegance, Felipe Pardo y Aliaga and José Antolín Rodulfo also contributed pieces later.[11] The "*Variedades*" section, which published scientific and literary articles, also occasionally carried economics articles but most of these were in the "*Mercurio Peruano*" section. Finally, the LV appeared in December 1832 in a context of growing controversy between the government and the opposition press, aiming to defending "strong government" and guiding possible constitutional reforms to establish it. Basadre (2002, 232) argues that the paper's wording and contents, including those referring to legal, political and economic issues, suggest that Pando was the main writer, but he acknowledges that there may have been other contributors. As for the economics articles, especially on public credit, there is no doubt that Mora was involved in them, albeit with help from either Pando himself, Andrés Martínez de Orihuela, who was Finance Minister in late 1832, or an unknown author.

As previously noted, it has so far been held that Mora confined his intellectual activity in Lima to the literary, law and moral philosophy spheres. The fact that he kept up his habit of not signing his articles and denied that he was contributing to the ECO in his correspondence to his friends in Chile naturally contributed to this. Admittedly, his entry into authoritarian circles in Peru must have come as a surprise to Chilean "Pipiolo" circles and Mora, shielded by his anonymity, denied taking part in the short-lived political battles that characterised Gamarra's term of office (Monguió 1967, 159). However, there is sufficient evidence to show that he was in fact the sole author of a huge number of articles on political

[11] This was a daily publication that focussed on trade and maritime information, was mainly distributed in Lima and consisted of four pages divided into different sections: "*Interior*", "*Variedades*", "*Remitidos*", "*Marítima*" or "*Avisos del día*" (Velázquez-Morales 2021).

economy in the Peruvian press and that he contributed to many others. In the first place, his authorship is likely on the basis of the written style, which bears a clear resemblance to his articles on political economy in the MUC, EMC and CPL. Two further pointers are firstly the analytical background to these articles, which is very similar to that in the EMC, and secondly the unfailing admiration for the British economic, political and colonial model that was so characteristic of his writings. However, there are more concrete data to confirm that Mora's was the pen behind many articles on political economy: the reproduction of the annotated summaries of Bentham's works that he had published in the CPL in Buenos Aires and an article he translated from McCulloch's work, whose dissemination in Spanish America in this period he appears to have monopolised. More conclusive, if possible, are elements such as the frequent recourse to works published in the ER, one of Mora's regular intellectual sources; the reference to Livorno as a model of a free port; the descriptions of the Lancasterian method of mutual teaching that he used in his educational projects and the references in the ECO to the principles of Scottish Common Sense moral philosophy taken from his monograph *Cursos de lógica y ética*. In short, there is no doubt about Mora's contribution to these journals, especially in terms of the economics articles.

7.5 Publicising Political Economy

Mora's entry into conservative political circles does not seem to have altered either the ideological or educational and literary aspects of his ideas, which retained their deep certainties and theoretical foundations, and the same can be said with regard to political economy. Although his economics works were published in the official and unofficial press of Gamarra's authoritarian government, it seems plausible that Mora had relative autonomy in the sphere of economic and political thought, at least to a similar extent to that which he had enjoyed in Buenos Aires and also perhaps in Santiago de Chile. Proof of this are the articles in which he commented on Bentham and his work, which had already been published in the CPL and which he now reproduced with few amendments in the MP.[12] As he had in Buenos Aires, Mora stressed Bentham's independent judgement and condemned the "factious" and "arbitrary" nature of sec-

[12] MP (18/VII/1832; 19/VII/1832; 24/VII/1832; 10/VII/1832; 10/IX/1832); on Bentham, see also, previously, MP (7/V/1832).

tions of the British parliament, but also the antipathy it had generated in some liberal circles in Peru. This position chimed in perfectly with the circumstances in which Mora found himself in Peru and showed that he enjoyed an unusual degree of freedom in a political climate that was characterised by limiting parliamentary power. Where Bentham's works were concerned, the articles accurately reproduced CPL summaries with an additional correction to the summary of *Defence of Usury*, which he had published in Buenos Aires under the incorrect title *Defence of the Economy*. Manoeuvring the discourse round to what most interested him, Mora interpreted the work as a defence of free trade, especially the free circulation of money, and a critique of the taxes on consumption and intervention in interest rates.

This disseminating of classical political economy was a reflection of Mora's conviction that economic prosperity would guarantee the survival of the liberal republics in Hispanic America. In fact, he stated in the ECO that all his articles there were "devoted almost exclusively to illustrating […] questions of political economy", since its "truths" were "perfectly in keeping with national interests, Peru's prosperity [and] the spread of well-being among our citizens" (ECO, no. 44, 28/V/1831). This is not to say that he did not proceed with some caution, given the political environment in which he moved. In early contributions to the ECO, he noted that he was expressing "wishes" rather than "advice" (ECO, 5/VII/1831) and, when referring to Pando's gatherings at which trade policy issues were discussed, he pointed out that "this meeting of friends (as the head of the nation has called them) has no function other than to supply the government with the fruit of their observations in an informal private discussion" (ECO, 5/VII/1831; MP, 11/II/1832).

Mora understood that popularising political economy required simplifying economic discourse. From his earliest contributions he warned readers that, although everything was "ring-fenced by principles", he would use "the common way" of reasoning to explain the theory of classical political economy (MP, 17/V/1831; ECO, 7/V/1831). He stuck to this maxim and, certain specific questions excepted, used rhetoric that was accessible to the general public, making profound economic concepts comprehensible and demonstrating once again the splendid gifts as a publicist that characterised his entire career. However, the fundamental analytical principles did not alter and an overall reading of his economics articles from this period reveals that the model of economic development for the new republics of Hispanic America, visible in the EMC and indebted to McCulloch, remained unchanged. Economic growth depended on capital accumulation, which was fed by profits whose origins lay in labour and, moreover, was conditioned by a series of institutional requirements in the sphere of taxation, monetary economics and trade policy (ECO, 17/V/1831). Within this analytical framework, Mora skilfully communicated a series of ideas which he tried to ingrain in the Peruvian public through constant references to his main intellectual sources: "the profound Smith", Malthus, Ricardo, Say, Storch, Gioja, Mill and naturally McCulloch, who played an increasingly important role in this task of dissemination. In fact, the reviews that McCulloch included in the ER, such as "On Political Economy in Russia", which basically featured Storch, were widely used as sources for the MP articles.

7.6 The Free Trade Apostle

In contrast to Mora's discourse in Chile, in Peru he began to veer clearly towards the issue that would monopolise most of his work in the political economy field from then on: free trade. This was a substantial change, as the idea of free trade came to occupy the heart of his economics rhetoric. The analysis of public finance, the monetary question, demography and economic development as a whole now became subordinate to the inescapable principle of the free circulation of goods and money. Thus, having been a free trade advocate, Mora now became a true "apostle". His work in Peru was the first genuine example of this new approach to economic problems, which years later would lead to DLC, published on his return to Spain in 1843. From this perspective, Mora's articles in the ECO, MP and LV tackled the Republic of Peru's economic problems, suggested formulas for dealing with them and set out detailed analyses of the Gamarra government's reforms and policies. Although Mora's principles were unchanged after his immersion in Peru's economic policy, he did introduce some nuances which, although significant, did not alter the substance of the agenda he had put together in Chile.

From 1826 to 1833 Peru's trade policy was decisively protectionist, with high duties levied on textiles, agricultural products and many manufactured goods. This protectionism was the result of a campaign driven by Peruvian merchants in alliance with local producers and retailers and organised because of the import oversupply crisis saturating the Peruvian market from 1826 onwards, in which foreign merchants importing European products were also competing. From 1828 in particular, on the initiative of officials responding to demands from Peruvian traders, a prohibitionist policy was launched to ban the import of products that competed with local output and tight restrictions were imposed on the activity of foreign traders, who effectively became consignees (Gootenberg 1982, 237–44, 248–51).[13] During his mandate Gamarra made a special effort to protect the *obrajes* in his native city of Cuzco.

The chief motivation behind Mora's economics articles was to persuade both readers and the Peruvian government of the merits of free trade. Although his usual intellectual influences were in evidence throughout, McCulloch's ideas also reappeared as the main lever for mobilising public opinion and underpinning his free trade strategy. McCulloch's article "On Foreign Trade", which was published in Spanish in the MP, contained the main ingredients of international trade theory and included several examples illustrating the "territorial division of labour" and the trade-derived benefits for the "reciprocal fortune and civilisation" of countries that engaged in trade relations (MP, 13, 14 and 15/II/1833). Other elements of this theory that McCulloch expressed in the text, which Mora translated, were an explanation of absolute advantage due to uneven allocation of resources—"unequal distribution of production forces"—in different geographical areas, the assumption of the internal and international mobility of production factors and the boost that free trade gave to innovation in production and mechanisation (O'Brien 1992, 193–94). To illustrate this last point and probably also to suggest applying it to the Peruvian mining industry, Mora summarised McCulloch's review of Charles Babbage's *On the Economy of Machinery and Manufactures* (1832) in the ER ("Art.II. On the Economy of Machinery and Manufactures. By Charles Babbage, Esq. A.M.", CXII, 1833, 313–32).

McCulloch's article contained the theoretical bases of free trade but Mora's free trade rhetoric, in which elements of McCulloch's concurrence with Smith's WN were also visible, followed a simple structure that adhered to the following sequence: "the growth of useful labour presupposes capital, capital presupposes accumulation, accumulation presupposes trade", and all this leads to greater prosperity. Trade thus emerged as the wellspring of production, capital and prosperity and not as a mere exchange activity. By making goods available to consumers at lower prices free trade stimulated overall consumption in the trading countries and led

[13] For the specific structure of protectionism and the role of traders, distributors (storekeepers and messengers) and state institutions see Gootenberg (1982).

to an increase in "useful labour", capital and "public happiness". Conversely, the harm done by prohibitionism did not just affect "general trade", but "in the long run it only affects domestic trade and local consumption", reducing "useful labour", capital, accumulation and prosperity (MP, 11/III/1833); even worse, the "prohibitive laws were responsible for the horrible cancer [...] of smuggling", with its consequences for honest and efficient capitalists, Treasury revenue, public morality and of course prosperity. This refutation of prohibitionism rang with Smithian echoes of the subordination of "the vast consumer class to the small producer class", of "common rights to private rights" and of "the consumer's interests [to that] of owners" (MP, 11/III/1833; ECO, 4/VI/1831)" in the same way as laws preventing religious freedom were (MP, 11/III/1833). It is worth noting that Mora referred to "prohibitionism" and generally avoided mentioning the term "protectionism", a significant nuance that may have been part of his careful strategy of persuasion in the context of a protectionism-prone conservative government.

7.7 A Free Trader in a Protectionist Environment

Mora's dissemination of a relatively radical free trade system was in contrast to its application in the specific context of 1830s Peru. He did not entirely escape the pro-protectionist atmosphere that prevailed there, particularly in Lima's conservative government circles, and, without renouncing any of his ideological principles or making concessions to the infant industry theory, he introduced a number of qualifications on the grounds that the "principle is too vague and absolute for a matter into the considerations of which so many individual circumstances must enter". Like "most economists" Mora held as a general rule that free trade should prevail when factories "do not rely on an age-old practice or national customs consolidated by time" (MP, 9/VIII/1831). In his view, between the two extremes of a consolidated industry and a "non-existent" industry, there was a "middle level" industry that could "deserve protective laws, and we do not say prohibitions because in no case do we consider them useful, [and] deserve financial incentives and other no less effective encouragements, which is what we believe has wisely been adopted in this country" (MP, 9/VIII/1831). The nuance was significant and seemed to derive from political, fiscal and economic pragmatism. The first was clear from his statement that "in the epoch of industrial development we shall no doubt find some industries that have reached the era of protection and then it is very easy to give it to them. This idea, we believe, has served as a basis for the current Congress to pass the first article of the trade regulation that it is debating" (MP, 9/VIII/1831). The second, fiscal, will be dealt with later and the third, economic, could be consistent with a pragmatic application of the theory of the stages of economic growth visible in Mora's economics writings in Chile, which advocated a gradual natural development of industry as the process of capital accumulation became consolidated.

The protecting of these industries was not the only issue with regard to which Mora referred to specific aspects of Peruvian trade policy. He argued in no uncertain terms in the LV that the transition from the current highly protective system to free trade should be gradual, while in the ECO he became involved in commenting on the trade regulations enacted by the *Congreso*. As they entailed the "annihilation of prohibitions" his verdict was on the whole positive, but he warned legislators of the need to design good specific trade rules to avoid the proliferation of two ills: smuggling, with its consequences for "capitalist merchants of good repute", on the one hand, and the corruption of government officials, a legacy of the colonial past and known as "contraband fraud", on the other.[14] However, he felt that state forces, strict regulations, severe penalties, the "large number of employees" and difficult coastal access were not sufficient if they were used with restraint, since the origins of these evils lay in government monopolies over certain goods, prohibitive laws and excessive taxes. The remedy was therefore free trade and moderate levels of taxation.

The most interesting and heated debate in which Mora was involved was sparked by a Trade Treaty between Bolivia and Peru, which was signed in Arequipa on 8 November 1831 together with a Treaty of Peace and Friendship.[15] Article 1 of the former laid down that "citizens of Bolivia shall pay the same taxes and enjoy the same commercial privileges in Peru as if they were Peruvians; and this in turn in Bolivia". In the same vein, it reduced reciprocal duties on both countries' products by 6%, declared free shipping on Lake Titicaca and established exemptions for some products, including European goods, on which the same import duties would be

[14] ECO's issues published between June 1832 and March 1832 embrace references and reflections on this Treatise and during the last 1832 months to the draft of the Commerce Regulation.

[15] For details of the negotiations and reactions in Peru and Bolivia see Basadre (2002, 205–209).

paid as in Peru but not exceeding 30% (*Tratado* 1832). However, the Bolivian government, which had accepted the Treaty of Peace and Friendship, rejected the Trade Treaty as detrimental to its interests, which included control of the strategic port of Arica. At the beginning of June 1832, the ECO published an article entitled "*Breves reflexiones sobre el Tratado de Comercio concluido en Arequipa a ocho de noviembre de 1831 entre Bolivia y Perú*", which began with a symbolic quotation from Vattel expressing the need for nations to trade with each other "for the advantage of the human race, because of people's reciprocal needs" (ECO, 9/VI/1832). Although it is impossible to say whether Mora was the sole author or not, there is no doubt that he was directly involved in producing the piece, at least as far as the theoretical bases were concerned.

The article's publication triggered an irate reaction in Bolivia, where several pamphlets in opposition to it were published. One of them, titled "*Examen sobre el Tratado de comercio ajustado en Arequipa entre el Perú y Bolivia, por sus respectivos plenipotenciarios bajo la mediación del estado de Chile*", apparently published in Arequipa on 4 January 1832 by a group of traders "between Chile and Bolivia", condemned the discriminatory treatment accorded to Bolivia in the Treaty (Anonymous 1832a). The "*Contestación a las breves reflexiones sobre el Tratado de Comercio entre Bolivia y Perú*" enjoyed wider circulation in Bolivia and possibly also in Peru; it was published in La Paz (Basadre 2002, 206), attributed it to Casimiro Olañeta, leader of the nationalist reaction to the signing of the Treaty and considered one of the main driving forces behind the creation of the Republic of Bolivia. Olañeta aimed "to demonstrate to the point of proof that of the 29 articles in the Trade Treaty, only the first is good and reciprocal for Bolivia and the remaining […] are contrary to its sovereignty or its happiness" (Anonymous 1832b, 2). The pamphlet was symbolically headed with a further quotation from Vattel urging careful examination of the terms of trade treaties. To this end it examined every article in the Treaty in detail and refuted precisely what was declared in the first: mutual benefit for Peruvians and Bolivians. Although there is no space here to dwell on the details of the refutation it should be noted that the "*Contestación*" sought to challenge the reciprocity theory in the same terrain that was ring-fenced in the "*Breves reflexiones*"; that is, the protectionism-free trade debate. The author employed "famous economists' theories" to criticise the lack of reciprocity and used quotations from Say's *Traité*, Smith's WN and the "work and dictionary" by Ganilh, who he considered as much a supporter as "the publishers of the paper we refute"—a tacit reference to Mora and the possible co-author—to "destroy the opinion that the most copious source of the wealth of nations is foreign trade", as stated in the "*Breves reflexiones*".[16] The author claimed, with Ganilh, to have "high praise for foreign trade" but did not accept that "it is more advantageous than internal trade" and while he accepted the "editors'" argument that reducing a tax—in this case customs duties—favoured consumers and increased demand for products and "useful labour", this applied to the domestic market but not to foreign markets (Anonymous 1832b, 4–5). As if this were not enough, the author of the "*Contestación*" appealed to the judgement of one "of the most celebrated writers in America [who] has proved the accuracy of these principles in his results [...] and without departing from them [...] we shall show that lowering duties on Peruvian exports to Bolivia to 6% ruins our agricultural industry". A footnote made it clear that this was "Joaquín Mora in *El Mercurio de Chile*" (Anonymous 1832b, 8). The author was naturally referring to the path of agricultural development that Mora had suggested for Chile; however, it is not clear whether this statement was directed at Mora and his possible collaborators with the aim of laying bare their contradictions, or whether, on the contrary, the author was unaware of Mora's participation in the ECO articles, which Mora himself denied to his Chilean liberal friends, as noted above. Olañeta is likely to have had a relationship with Mora and Pando, probably on a purely intellectual level, since at the end of his pamphlet he stated that "the defence into which we entered seemed to us more imperative than the voice of friendship" (Anonymous 1832b, 45), perhaps to shield himself from the hostile atmosphere that the Trade Treaty had created in Bolivia. Some comments in "*Breves reflexiones*" also hint at this relationship (ECO, 9/VI/1832).

In any event, it was a highly interesting debate with a significant degree of analysis and use of sources. The author of the "*Contestación*" stated his opposition to "restrictive systems" and balance of trade theory, while favouring private interest; however, he interpreted the classical economists as protectionists. His position, which had a clear agricultural backdrop, was the outcome of the importance he attached to the domestic economy as a wealth creator with respect to the international market. It was precisely this singular interpretation of classical theory that instigated the campaign spread over numerous ECO articles to challenge the protectionist conclusions in the "*Contestación*" and to persuade people of the

[16] Ganilh is mentioned several times in articles for ECO.

Treaty's reciprocity, a challenge that played out more in the economic than the political sphere. There is no need discuss the finer points of the challenge in the ECO here, but Mora may have had help with the details and even with the drafting. Nevertheless, the refutation of the "sophisms" in the "*Contestación*" contained all the characteristic elements of Mora's free trade rhetoric: the harm done to Bolivian consumers; the favouring of a minority group of producers; the fallacy of the "infant" industry—in this case agriculture—argument; the increase in smuggling; the reduction in useful labour; the consequences for capital accumulation and, in short, for public happiness, all peppered with quotations from Smith (ECO, 9/VI/1832). The fact that the challenge was published in the Gamarra government's official newspaper is of course significant. In the end a Peruvian politician named La Torre visited Bolivia to negotiate a new trade agreement, this time with President Santa Cruz in person, and they agreed to sign a new Treaty on similar terms to those of the Arequipa agreement, which became effective in Chuquisaca on 17 November 1832. Different articles in the ECO expressed satisfaction with the signing and announced that it had put an end to the controversy.

Once free trade had been established as the priority on Mora's economic agenda, the other parts of his economic programme differed little from the guidelines set out in Chile and were adapted to this policy. As was the case with Chile, Peru's entry into the international division of labour would require the country to specialise; in keeping with his own agrarian liberalism, Smith's theory of the stages of economic development and Peru's natural resources Mora felt that Peru should base its economic development on two sectors: agriculture and precious metal mining. However, in his view agricultural development there was hindered by two factors: the scarcity of fertile land and the meagre population. To tackle the former, he proposed in the ECO a genuine agricultural reform that would redistribute land belonging to convents and other church-owned properties in order to create a "new social class, as interested in the preservation of order and the legal regime as its predecessor class had been [...] in absolutism";[17] he warned, however, of the danger of land falling into the hands of "*agiotistas*" or speculators, evoking events in Spain during the Liberal Triennium.

As for mining, shortly after independence the English seized the investment opportunities that the sector offered in the Hispanic-American

[17] Mora approved of redistributing land to the indigenous population.

republics in a context in which the period's political instability had had a negative impact on mining (Marichal 1999). This was the case in Peru before the famous guano era, which propelled the country towards a free trade policy from the mid-nineteenth century onwards thanks to its monopoly in this organic raw material, which was excellent agricultural fertiliser (Contreras 2012). Mora may have been well-aware of British investors' interest and he included the growth of the Peruvian mining industry in the international division of labour framework: Peru produced money—precious metals—and England had the means to acquire it (ECO, 4/VI/1831). This exchange naturally meant that precious metals would flow out the Republic, the cause of some apprehension in certain influential circles, which feared an increase in the price of metals and scarcities;[18] hence Mora's great interest in showing that precious metals were a commodity like any other, which paved the way for their export, and that Peru enjoyed an absolute advantage in their production in an international economic framework (ECO, 4/VI/1831). Perhaps rather over-optimistically, he pointed out that the advantage in this specific product could lead to greater acceleration in capital accumulation than would result from following the normal path of developing agriculture, trade and manufacturing:

> Mexico and Peru are perhaps the only two points of the globe where it is not impossible [if it is permissible to say so] to improvise civilisation, that is to say, to avoid the long period of infancy, of slow transitions, of uncertainty, which lies between the rudiments of society and the age of perfection. (ECO, 26/V/1832)

To support this theory the MP carried a commentary on William Jacob's *An Historical Inquiry into the Production and Consumption of the Precious Metals* (1831), which gave a historical account of their production and trading (MP, 11, 12 and 13/III/1833). However, the

[18] Two articles in the MP, which were probably not written by Mora alone, attempted to show, with Ganilh, that the continued increase in production and the possibility of supplementing metal money with bank notes would avoid this problem (MP, 27/IV/1832). Two translations of articles from the New York *El Redactor* on deposit banks and their importance in dealing with cash shortages, together with other articles in the MP, seem to pursue this line, which continues Mora's reflections on deposit banks in Chile (MP, 26/III/1833; 24/IV/1833). On the monetary question in the early years of independence see De Haro (2016, 227–65).

commentary was written not as a result of reading the book itself but McCulloch's review of it in the ER ("Art. III. An Historical Inquiry into the Production and Consumption of the Precious Metals. By William Jacob, Esq. F.R.S.", 1832, LV, 43–61), in which he expressed confidence in the early recovery of precious metal production in Hispanic America and, with Hume, of their beneficial effects on the world economy. Despite Mora's enthusiasm for precious metal production as an instrument of Peru's economic modernisation, he was not unaware of the difficulties that developing this industry would face. No doubt with the colonial past in mind, he recognised that it was the countries with precious metal reserves "that derive the least profit from their wealth, being usually the least abundant in industrial enterprises for the sole reason that they are the least populated" (MP, 27/IV/1832).

It is therefore no coincidence that the MP itself included some observations on the population issue. As he had in the Buenos Aires CPL, Mora disagreed with the universality of the Malthusian relationship between population increase and economic scarcity, in the light of North America's experience (MP, 31/12/1832) and, as with Argentina, he believed that the population increase was the result not of plentiful resources but of emigration from European countries that were suffering the tension between population and resources (MP, 31/I/1832; 13/I/1833). Mora suggested that the Irish, hit by the "scourge of famine", could be a good source of population for Peru (MP, 15/I/1833), as he argued in several articles in the MP and LV (MP, 13/I/1833; 7/VI/1833; LV, 13/I/1833). The hypothetical reason for choosing Ireland could lie in its cultural affinities with Peru because of the influence of Catholicism, but it is more likely to have been his reading of two of McCulloch's reviews in the ER that led him to focus his attention there, especially Article V of Volume XLI, in which McCulloch discussed five papers dealing with population and poverty in 1825 ("Article V", ER, 1825, XLI, 356–410), and Art. IX of Vol. XLIX in 1829 in which he reviewed Michael Thomas Sandler's study *Ireland: Its Evils and their Remedies: being a Refutation of the Errors of the Emigration Committee and Others, Touching that Country* (1828) ("Art. IX. 1. Ireland Its Evils and their Remedies, &c.&c. By Michael Thomas Sandler" ER, XLIX, 1829, 300–17). Taking as a source some of the ideas and figures in these works, calculating the cost of transporting Irish migrants to Peru, describing the Irish peasantry's miserable situation and accepting the lack of public funds, Mora deemed it possible that "patriotic landowners" would encourage this migratory flow, a type of business based on “private interest and [the] spirit of association” (MP, 7/VI/1833; 13/I/1833). However, to be successful the project needed “the magic power that has exerted such an effective attraction” in North America: free trade (MP, 31/I/1832). In the same vein he took advantage of the population debate to defend the permanent residence of “foreigners”, including merchants, an issue that was widely debated in Peru at the time, as mentioned above. It is interesting to note that Mora expressed his admiration for the skills of English merchants on several occasions in Peru and naturally made no secret of his wish to forge stable economic links with England.

A major stumbling block for all these projects was the state of public finances. Revenue and expenditure levels in the post-independence period were meagre and tax revenue was stagnant. Most of it was raised by a sort of poll tax that was levied on the indigenous population, which Bolívar's government extended to the non-indigenous population in 1826. The other important component came from customs duties, which were especially high between 1826 and 1833 (Contreras 2012, 46–48). Mora's free trade option forced the government to replace customs revenue with other sources of state income and he wrote several articles emphasising the notion that the resulting rise in trade would generate increased customs revenue despite the lower duties and adding three alternative sources of revenue: a tax reform shifting the burden towards direct taxation, revenue from warehouses in Peru's ports and public borrowing. It is paradoxical, however, that articles on fiscal questions took very little space in his writings on political economy as a whole, since this was not only a crucial topic but there is also evidence that he participated in the tax discussions of the day. In fact, when a rumour involving the establishing of a finance board circulated in Lima, he pointed out, during June 1831 in the ECO, that “this name [a finance board] should not be given to a meeting of citizens, whose good sense and experience the President of the Republic wishes to consult in order to improve the fortunes of trade”, adding: “nothing seems more rational than to turn to those who have reason to know something about the matter”, among whom Mora himself was presumably to be found.

As is clear from these and other comments on taxation issues, Mora subscribed to the principle of tax efficiency, in that he linked income structure to advances in trade in Peru and its consequences for “public happiness”, and there are also signs that the ability to pay principle that he had formulated in Chile still held. On the basis of these premises, Mora seems to have favoured a direct taxation model to replace the form of taxation during the colonial period, as McCulloch did, and the article in which he discussed direct taxation in France and its management by the government both pointed in this direction (MP, 7/II/1833]. It is not known what influence this approach may have had on the Gamarra's government but it is more than likely to have influenced Ministry of Finance decisions, as is suggested by a series of articles published under the title *"Artículo ministerial. Contribuciones"* in the ECO, the government's official mouthpiece, which Mora is not known to have written and certainly cannot be directly attributed to him. However, leaving aside the specific details of the management of the indigenous people's contribution, the discussions on the abolishing of colonial period taxes such as tithes, the so-called "first fruits" and many others, and the reduction of customs duties by "one third", for example, show some affinity with his theory (ECO, 7/IV/1832). At the same time, many ingredients of Mora's free trade rhetoric appeared throughout these articles: the link between high duties and smuggling; the preference for the English over the French taxation model; the match between individual and national interest, the contrast between colonial and liberal administration and of course fiscal legislation's subordination to free trade and capital accumulation. The same was true of the sources, which were similar to Mora's classical favourites and included McCulloch—incorrectly referred to as "Mr Culloch"[19]—.

Transit trade was a crucial element of the economic future of a Peru that had joined the international division of labour and storage port revenue was part of this. Mora suggested establishing storage depots in the Pacific to create a trade network that could even link up with European ports, referring in particular to mercury from European mines—Almadén and Istria—which was necessary for precious metal mining (ECO, 11/V/1831). Although the creating of this trading area was his priority, he did not disregard the revenue that payments for storage would bring to the public coffers, since the "Treasury would have all the Pacific ports as taxpayers, from the state of Ecuador to the peninsula of California" (ECO, 11/V/1831). However, there were two conditions: the charges should be modest and the merchants themselves should decide how long the cargo should be stored.

Mora's third proposal for raising state revenue was public borrowing, to which he had already paid a great deal of attention in the EMC,

[19] ECO (7/IV/1832; 14/IV/1832; 18/IV/1832; 25/IV/1832; 28/IV/1832).

particularly in terms of technical and administrative details. The fiscal troubles of the early years of Peru's independence granted an important role to merchants as sources of state finance through loans of various types and other financial instruments (Contreras 2012, 46). Mora suggested a more stable and less controversial alternative, given the advantages that some merchants, especially the Consular court, obtained from decision-making bodies and conducted a thorough-going public information campaign on the advantages and benefits of debt in numerous articles in the ECO and LV,[20] whose arguments he summarised as follows:

> Public borrowing supplies the Treasury with immense resources without increasing taxes, provides for the relief of taxpayers and property owners; respecting the capital of rich and industrious men, it protects the establishment of public and private wealth, multiplies enterprises, distributes labour, guarantees subsistence and spreads well-being and happiness to even the humblest classes in society.

His benchmark was Britain, where "a speculative company" had been created, which he considered the most suitable vehicle for mediating between the Treasury and creditors. In defending this in the LV Mora used all his rhetorical weapons to show that although the company was a monopoly, the advantages it provided far outweighed the costs it generated.

Government borrowing was naturally a controversial issue, even more so in Hispanic America as a result of the vicissitudes involved in loans from the English, and Mora was at pains to persuade Peruvian public opinion of the merits of public debt. He therefore pointed out that it was clear that this gradually increased, to the point at which half of all revenue in England was devoted to debt service coverage but he also argued that agricultural and industrial production grew and prospered in the same "proportion as this debt" and thus, although the debt grew, it remained stable in real terms and was the "measure of the value of other things". Countries that were able to maintain a high level of debt proportionate to the level of their agricultural and industrial production had a powerful tool for ensuring economic prosperity. Naturally, this required two conditions: timely debt servicing and low interest rates so as not to jeopardise the flow of capital into productive activities. Mora adopted the stance taken by

[20] The main articles on this issue are ECO (30/I/1833; 6/II/1833; 9/II/1833; 20/II/1833; 23/II/1833; 2/III/1833; 13/III/1833; 4/IV/1833) and LV (25/06/1833).

McCulloch, who was not in fact in favour of high public borrowing and defended low interest rates (O'Brien 1992, 263–70). In any event, he understood the stagnation of state revenues and the difficulties of transforming the colonial tax system without harming revenue collection (LV, 25/VI/1833). Add to this mix the pressing need to build the institutions of the liberal state and the infrastructure necessary to organise an internal market that was hampered by the lamentable state of the roads and public debt was the only alternative; hence his intense campaign on the issue in the Lima press.

7.8 Political Economy in the Service of the Peru-Bolivian Confederation

In the twilight of his days, from the far-off Iberian Peninsula, Mora painfully contemplated the state of anarchy in which the Bolivian Republic was mired in the 1860s. He recalled the years spent in the service of Santa Cruz, for whom he had great admiration, as "private secretary to the president, and later [as] his consul general and trusted agent in London" with a certain nostalgia and deep sorrow in the Spanish magazine *La América*. He described the period as a model of "order, regularity, sound and pure government", which had spread "public happiness" to all spheres of Bolivian life: education, the financial system, communications and a Treasury capable of funding all state activities. Over and above these achievements, Mora felt that the task to which Santa Cruz had devoted his greatest efforts was tariff legislation, reflecting the conviction that "the most important, the most urgent and what could most effectively influence the growth of [the country's] wealth should be the exporting of its fruits", particularly the "inexhaustible precious metal deposits". In those final moments, Mora was addressing a Hispanic-American and peninsular readership with the aim of using the lessons provided by historical experience to underpin his radical free trade preaching. However, he was also doubtlessly vindicating his participation in Santa Cruz's free trade and modernising project (LA, 24/II/1862, 3–4).

Mora had forged a close friendship with Santa Cruz while they were both in Chile, keeping the relationship alive through regular correspondence, especially after Mora arrived in Lima. The letters reveal Mora's admiration for Santa Cruz's achievements in the legislative, governmental and economic spheres, but also show his intellectual authority over Santa

Cruz, whom he advised on moral philosophy, teaching and economics, among other matters (Núñez 1961, 100–102). Despite Gamarra's turbulent relationship with Santa Cruz and the fears that the latter awoke in Peru as a result of his ability to govern, Mora had publicly described his achievements in Bolivia in the Lima press, stressing the consequences of his reforms for prosperity and political stability, which he considered a panacea compared to the state of chaos in Peru.

It is therefore not surprising that given the political turmoil in Peru—there were nineteen revolutions during Gamarra's term of office—and the personal risk Mora was running there, because of the antipathy he had created among some Lima residents for publicly praising O'Higgins and among his liberal associates for his closeness to authoritarian circles in Peru (Monguió 1967, 194–95), he unhesitatingly accepted Santa Cruz's offer of working for the cause of educating the Bolivian young. He sailed from the port of Callao (Peru) on 2 September 1834, arriving in La Paz (Bolivia) on 21 October. Trease (1953) believed that after leaving Chile Mora became an opportunist who renounced his principles in order to benefit from proximity to power. Leaving aside this judgement regarding the supposed fragility of his ethical and political principles, it can be categorically stated that, apart from a few nuances imposed by the economic situation in Bolivia, his economics ideology remained unchanged, as did his aversion to despotism, to which was added a rejection of doctrinaire liberalism after his time in Lima.

Mora's activities in Bolivia mirrored the model he had previously developed in Buenos Aires, Santiago and Lima. In accordance with Santa Cruz's plan, his chief commitment was to the education of the Bolivian elite, and he took the Literature Chair at the *Universidad de San Andrés*, which he combined with foreign language lessons at the *Sociedad Filológica* as well as founding a school in La Paz based on the *Liceo de Chile* but on a more modest scale. He also made an active contribution to education planning in Bolivia by drawing up the regulations for the *Colegio Normal* and the charter for the *Universidad de San Andrés* (De Mesa-Gisbert 1965, 45; Mora 1834). As in previous stages of his Hispanic-American odyssey, his poems were published in the Bolivian press and his works on moral philosophy and law were widely circulated and read (Monguió 1967, 197–203). However, Santa Cruz soon recruited him to be his personal secretary and right-hand man to see through his grand project for the Peru-Bolivian Confederation. From early 1836 Mora worked solely as

Santa Cruz's private secretary and placed his crippled network of relationships with Gamarra, Orbegoso and De La Torre at his disposal.[21]

Following their independence from Spain, the new Hispanic-American republics were faced with the problem of establishing their borders. In Bolivia's case the territory had belonged to the Viceroyalty of Peru, but the defeat of the royalist troops at the Battle of Ayacucho put an end to Spanish rule and in 1825 Marshal Sucre founded the "Bolivar Republic" in the territories then known as "Upper Peru", which was renamed the Republic of Bolivia shortly afterwards. This created a new division that raised the issue of civil and political identities (Sobrevilla 2011, 7). Santa Cruz, who had become President of the Governing Council of Peru, considered himself Peruvian to the extent that he would not accept the presidency of the Bolivian Republic until he was assured in Lima that he could retain his Peruvian nationality. In 1828 he founded a lodge with the aim of partitioning Peru and forming a confederation between Peru and Bolivia (Basadre 2002). To this end he implemented a series of reforms to strengthen the Bolivian army and modernise legislation in general and economic legislation in particular, incorporating incentives for free trade and economic growth. In other words, Santa Cruz became a successful state builder who achieved the creation of a strong and well-administered Bolivian Republic that would be the germ of the confederation that was his dream (Sobrevilla 2011, 2–3, 112–26). To protect the Republic of Bolivia, Peru had to be divided into two republics: North Peru and South Peru. Santa Cruz had a group of extraordinary collaborators working on this grand project, among whom Mora stood out; he became the champion and advocate of his policies in many areas such as law—through his famous pioneering *Códigos*—, religion, charity and the economy (EEP, no. 88, 23/VIII/1837; Basadre 2002, 366).[22]

Mora was the author of the manifesto *Exposición de los motivos que justifican la cooperación del Gobierno de Bolivia en los negocios políticos del Perú*, signed by Santa Cruz on 15 June 1835, which outlined the motives driving the Republic of Bolivia to intervene in Peruvian politics (Basadre 2002, 320). The quest for a legal basis in the principles of international

[21] Santa Cruz recognised Mora's crucial role by awarding him the *Legión de Honor del Perú* on 11 September 1836 at the rank of Commander and the *Legión de Honor de Bolivia* on 30 November of the same year (Sobrevilla 2011, 243–44).

[22] All the details about the political and administrative set-up of the Confederation, its assemblies and congresses, can be found in Peralta (2020).

law and political law and the equating of anarchy with despotism are proof that the document was Mora's work (Monguió 1967, 237). Santa Cruz's dream finally materialised with the founding of South Peru, the organising of North Peru and ultimately in the decree setting up the Peru-Bolivian Confederation on 28 October 1836, although the new political reality did not achieve institutional status until 1 May 1837 with what is known as the Pact of Tacna (Sobrevilla 2011, 242).

Prior to that date, shortly after the Constitution of the newly created state of North Peru was approved, the first issue of *El eco del Protectorado* (EEP, 1836–1839) was published on 20 August 1836. It was the Peru-Bolivian Confederation's official mouthpiece and channel for disseminating the decrees, official documents and principles on which the new government was based.[23] The publication's size enabled "the editor to include scientific, political and literary articles, chosen from the plentiful materials at his disposal" (EEP, no. 1, 20/VIII/1836). The editor, as some sources have suggested and careful reading of the texts confirms, was none other than Mora.

The journal was divided into sections such as "*Artículos de Oficio*", "*Interior*", "*Exterior*" and "*Variedades*". Mora used the editorial section named "*El eco del Protectorado*" to support Santa Cruz's policies in the Confederation and it was this section that also carried most of his economics articles. As in Peru, he did not apply his economic ideology in a rigid or doctrinaire fashion, instead adapting it to the Confederation's particular economic and political circumstances, and undoubtedly to Santa Cruz's political and economic interests as well. The EEP and its editor thus became the main vehicle for spreading the principles on which the Peru-Bolivian Confederation project was based, which were naturally those of its instigator, Supreme Protector Andrés de Santa Cruz. The main economic issues addressed in the paper were the funding of the Confederation's new political conglomerate, the consolidating of its public accounts and free trade, which was linked to the desire to create an economic space in the Pacific area that was free of barriers to trade.

The overriding issue, on the resolving of which the Confederation's survival depended, was the parlous state of its public accounts. As noted

[23] The Constitution of North Peru named Santa Cruz "Supreme Protector of the state of North Peru" and granted him political power over the northern and southern Peruvian states. He had previously been named "Protector of the state of South Peru" and it was from this title that the EEP took its name.

above, Santa Cruz's policies had stabilised the Republic of Bolivia's income and expenditure, but when the Confederation was consolidated it took on the financial problems that the Peruvian republics had struggled with after years of political disorder and poorly controlled public accounts; it is no wonder that Santa Cruz had an ineffable desire for centralisation. The first issues that the EEP addressed were the debt moratorium and how to fund it. In raising these issues Mora faithfully reproduced the approach he had taken in the EC and LVD a few years previously; these were clearly the same problems manifesting themselves in the same context. However, he now had a new and valuable tool for solving them at his disposal: Santa Cruz's prestige and his efficient management of the public accounts. Hence, as soon as the Constitution of North Peru had been approved, the Bolivian Finance Ministry issued two decrees establishing "inflexible severity" with regard to collections and payments. Mora suggested that the measure would increase lenders' confidence and allow a temporary moratorium on debt servicing (EEP, no. 2, 24/VIII/1836). Although he acknowledged the need to provide the federal authority with its "own exclusive purse" to pay for the Confederation's functions, he did not discuss the structure of taxation and public expenditure, possibly because it was not one of the confederal government's powers (EEP, no. 28, 23/XI/1836). On the contrary, Mora still believed the best instrument for financing the Confederation and its constituent states to be government borrowing, so from his privileged position as editor of the Confederation government's official publication he attempted to influence the use of this fundamental means of raising money. The fact that a good deal of the time that Mora spent reflecting on economic issues during his final period in Lima was taken up with this "great matter of government borrowing" has already been discussed (EEP, no. 17, 15/X/1836). In Bolivia he did not deviate one iota from the approach he had adopted in the Lima newspapers: the consolidating of an increasing public debt in line with economic growth was a sign of economic prosperity, the sound managing of public finances guaranteed payment and the managing of state borrowing was entrusted to an efficient "national bank". He went into some detail on the institutional architecture of the national bank in the EEP, announcing that the Confederation government was busy analysing various projects "drawn up by intelligent men and friends of the country", which would serve as the basis of an institution that was needed "so badly by the state of our industry" (EEP, no. 17, 15/X/1836).[24] Although he did not specify whether he was personally involved in the project, he devoted no less than three special articles to detailed discussions on creating the bank, which would be modelled on the Bank of England. This new institution would be responsible for interest payments and debt servicing in exchange for a fee for managing the debt and the sums that it advanced. Mora pointed out from the start that the project's theoretical basis was to be found in the "best political economy book that we know of", undoubtedly a reference to Smith's WN, with Chapter II of Book II specifically containing the theoretical frame of reference for the proposal. Mora agreed with Smith's argument that banks organised credit but did not create it, since it was the result of "public confidence". Also, from Smith came confidence in the issuance of bank notes, since they were misused only occasionally, and the national bank was thus no less stable than the government.[25] This was because, unlike banks, governments issued paper money in unlimited quantities, without convertibility, in order "to cope with 'difficulties'" in a way that did not adapt to the "needs of the market" and upset the "price balance" resulting in the dreaded inflation (EEP, no. 20, 26/X/1836).[26] He also suggested complementing the national bank with a savings bank along the lines of those in England and France in order to attract the savings of the humbler classes and contribute to capital accumulation in the Confederation. In his opinion this second bank would be a storming success in the new republics because of the high interest rates and the low propensity to consume in their economies (EEP, no. 29, 26/XI/1836).

The second issue that figured prominently in Mora's economic articles was the adopting of two sets of regulations, one for trade and the other for customs. The Pact of Tacna (1836), which provided the legal basis for the

[24] It is not possible to be sure whether Mora raised this question of public debt at confederal level or at the level of each of the confederated republics. However, there is no doubt that he argued that "under the wing of the protectorate government" the Confederation as a whole had gained enough confidence to develop a public credit system either separately or jointly (EEP, no. 17, 15/X/1836).

[25] Smith; EEP (no. 17, 15/X/1836; no. 18, 19/X/1836; no. 20, 26/X/1836).

[26] To solve the problem of the cash shortage at the dawn of the Republic, the *Banco Auxiliar de Papel Moneda* was established in Peru, the first experience of issuing paper money in Hispanic America, whose theoretical source was the *Ensayo económico sobre el sistema de la moneda papel y el crédito* by José Alonso Ortiz; it was published in Madrid in 1796 and reprinted in Lima in 1822. The book shows an undeniable Smithian influence, which is unsurprising since his author had translated WN into Spanish (De Haro 2013).

Confederation, gave the general authorities responsibility for trade legislation and its governmental ramifications, in other words, customs management.[27] Should there be any doubts in this regard Mora put forward a series of economic arguments to underpin the centralisation of these powers. In his view, unlike the United States, where manufacturing was concentrated in the north and agriculture in the south, the Peru-Bolivian Confederation had a uniform economic structure such that production and consumption shared common economic patterns. It was therefore only necessary to enact a single trade law—"one system"—to establish relations with all the countries operating under free trade premises in the Pacific. In order to argue that if "the supreme authority from which the precept must spring is subdivided into unconnected portions" the progress derived from free trade would be snuffed out, he drew on McCulloch's October 1836 ER piece discussing John Bowring's *Report on the Commerce and Manufactures of Switzerland* ("Art. IX. Report on the Commerce and Manufactures of Switzerland. By John Bowring, LL.D. Printed by Order of the House of Commons", ER, CXXIX, 168–76), which he purposely mistranslated *as "De los maravillosos efectos que produce un sistema liberal de comercio"*.[28] Mora highlighted the passages in the review in which McCulloch, following Bowring, underlined the benefits deriving from the "liberal system of commercial policy" which made Switzerland "the most prosperous of manufacturing nations"; but he also highlighted the fact that legislative power in foreign trade matters was centralised in the hands, not of the cantons, but of the Swiss people as a whole (ER, LXIV, no. CXXIX (1836–1837), 171–72).

The Trade Regulation and Internal Customs Regulation provided the practical means for carrying out such a plan. In Mora's view both were indebted to the principles of classical economics, in that the Protectoral government "has enlisted in the ranks of the most enlightened cabinets and the most deep-thinking economists of this century, has openly adopted the system of freedom and frankness which Smith timidly announced at the dawn of political economy, which McCulloch has already made into

[27] In the economic sphere, Art. 30 of the Pact of Tacna set out the Protector's power to manage all aspects of foreign trade, general customs and postal administration, as well as the appointment of these departments' employees (Basadre 2002, 365). From this point on, Santa Cruz was established in Lima and the same could perhaps be said of Mora.

[28] ER (LXIV, no. CXXIX (1836–1837), 168–176); EEP (no. 61, 20/V/1837).

the dogma of political science, which Minister Huskisson began to implement in England" (EEP, no. 61, 20/V/1837).

As with the national bank project, it is impossible to be sure of the extent of Mora's participation in the design of the draft Trade Regulation, which was approved on 3 September 1836 and which he considered the "cornerstone" of Santa Cruz's liberal economic policy (EEP, no. 6, 7/IX/1836). However, Mora used the EEP to show that the project fulfilled his expectations and was exactly in line with the requirements deriving from the new approach in his economic thought, already clear in his writings in the Lima newspapers, in which free trade had come to occupy a prominent place. He therefore emphasised that the new Regulation would bring about "mild duties", simplified trade bureaucracy and trust in merchants.[29] In his opinion the outcomes would be the disappearance of smuggling, benefits for consumers through lower prices, the availability of previously prohibited goods, the safeguarding of individual interest and, ultimately, economic prosperity. Relying on McCulloch's authority, he repeated that the root of the smuggling problem lay in "the tyranny of tariffs" and that the criminal laws were not the means of preventing it (EEP, no. 6, 7/IX/1836; no. 14, 5/X/1836).

However, Mora left some room for pragmatism, as he had in Lima—now even more so because in Bolivia he was at the heart of political decision-making—. Although he continued to uphold the Smithian principle that in any kind of protection, subsidy or monopoly "the good of all is sacrificed to the aggrandisement of a few", he proposed retaining duties on some articles "whose production should be encouraged in domestic industry because it already has a certain consistency that only needs this kind of stimulus [duties] to advance" (EEP, no. 28, 23/XI/1836), and he defended the prizes for discovering mercury mines, a fundamental raw material in silver production, by arguing that the market was in the hands of "one of the most affluent houses in Europe", no doubt referring to the Rothschilds and the exploitation of the Spanish mines of Almadén (EEP, no. 12, 28/XI/1836).

The third major theme of the economics articles in the EEP was the economic analysis of the war that broke out between the Peru-Bolivian

[29] Although Mora does not mention it, the Regulation established Callao as a deposit port, one of the concerns he had raised during his time in Peru.

Confederation and the Republic of Chile.[30] Chile's early institutional and political consolidation had enabled it to dominate trade in the Pacific area. When the conservatives came to power at the end of the 1820s they built up the merchant navy and Valparaíso consolidated its position as the main Pacific port in Hispanic America, a process that was made easier by the port of Callao's decline, partly as a result of Peru's political instability. The creation of the Confederation under Santa Cruz's leadership naturally aroused huge concern in Chile, which saw its trade dominance as under threat. This was compounded by the revoking of the Treaty of Friendship, Commerce and Navigation (1835) between the two countries in February 1836, the well-founded suspicions of mutual political destabilisation and the rivalry of the respective political leaders.[31] The assassination of Diego Portales, the real power behind the scenes in the Republic of Chile and Mora and Santa Cruz's bitter enemy, triggered the war, declared on 10 October 1837, by which means Chile intended to dissolve the Peru-Bolivian Confederation.

As Santa Cruz's personal secretary, Mora naturally played a crucial role in the conflict. Moreover, his enmity with Portales, who had expelled him from Chile, must have increased his personal involvement. In addition to embarking on a full-throated defence of the Confederation in the EEP, he explained the war in economic terms. Before it broke out, following suspicions that Portales might blockade Peruvian ports, Mora had interpreted the tensions in commercial terms and attributed them to the desire of "a few individuals" to retain their monopoly over the Pacific port of Valparaíso (EEP, no. 33, 10/XII/1836). In his opinion this monopoly was the result, not of the port's "advantages", but "of the negligence of our past governments"; in other words, the profound political turmoil in Peru. A few months before the war began, Mora had pointed out that "Valparaíso's mercantile superiority" was threatened precisely by the reform of the Confederation's trade legislation and the setting up of storage facilities in Peruvian ports (EEP, no. 72, 28/VI/1837).

In this context Mora compared the commercial projects of Chile and the Confederation, seeking possible analogies with the examples of the Swiss Confederation and the Zollverein, the German states' customs

[30] Santa Cruz's aim was to avoid war at any price and to this end he entrusted Mora with a delicate mission to the Chilean Admiral Blanco de Encalada, which ultimately failed to produce results.

[31] On the Treaty see Burr (1974, 30–32).

union under the leadership of Prussia. Mora believed Chilean trade policy to be the result of ignorance of the principles of political economy, which "teaches that a people's 'industrial income' is nourished and grows with those of other peoples with whom it has trading relations" (EEP, no. 72, 28/VI/1837). The conservative Chilean government subsequently sought to monopolise trade with Peru by promoting a trading area in which it supplied wheat and imported sugar, developing a trade model that Mora likened to the Zollverein; he used the expression "Prussian-Pacific" and considered the policy mistaken in that "all the markets of the world are mutually dependent on each other" (EEP, no. 72, June 1837; no. 75, 8/VII/1837; Cavieres-Serrano del Pozo 2018). The Confederation's trading model was indeed derived from this principle; that is, the integration of the Pacific countries into a single trading system that aimed to extend to both the United States and European markets, which were able to supply wheat and import sugar from the Confederation. The model of the Mora-Santa Cruz commercial project thus envisaged a Pacific trading organisation, which, following McCulloch, Mora assimilated to that of the Swiss Confederation, based on the principle of multilateral trade (EEP, no. 61, 20/V/1837). Once again, Mora emerged as a true free trade apostle.

This project manifested itself in Mora's support for the American merchant Wheelwright's plan to introduce steamships into Pacific trade to connect its ports with Britain via Panama and Jamaica, as well as in his promotion of meetings between English and local merchants to establish permanent commercial dialogue between the west coast of South America and Britain (EEP, no. 13, 1/X/1836). The Confederation's advantages over the Republic of Chile were obvious in this new scenario and Mora believed that they underlay the declaration of war.

7.9 Final Remarks

On 26 March 1838, Mora sailed from the port of Arica to London, where he served as Consul for the Confederation with the mission of advocating for the Confederation as a diplomat with the British authorities in the face of Chile's ambitions. Santa Cruz's defeat at the Battle of Yungay in January 1839 ended the war with Chile and led to the dissolution of the Confederation and Santa Cruz's exile to France. Now his trusted agent in London, Mora continued in Santa Cruz's service, acting as an intermediary in his correspondence with the Foreign Office and introducing numerous exiles from Peru and Bolivia into life in Britain (Monguió 1967, 279–319). In this context Mora began to devote much of his time to his private affairs, opening a parenthesis for political economy that would close in Spain in 1843 with the publication of his work DLC.

His time in Bolivia, therefore, put an end to his Spanish-American journey. During those intense years, Mora carried out a series of activities in the four countries of the southern cone of Hispanic America that had a common pattern as they were deployed in four areas: literature, education, journalism and political action. Political economy played a central role in the last three, demonstrating Mora's profound belief in the transformative potential of economic science. Reforms and policies stemming from the economic principles of classical political economy were the best path to economic prosperity for him, guaranteeing the new republics' survival and consolidation.

Mora demonstrated deep loyalty to the leaders who called him to contribute to the institutional building of the liberal state and to implement liberal policies in the new republics. As a result, Mora linked his fortune and the fate of his liberal agenda to the permanence in the office of these "*caudillos*", since his public visibility at the core of political power, advanced agenda, high intellectual stature and persuasive ability to support reforms and policies through his massive journalistic work, made him a major target of his political and intellectual rivals. The fall of his benefactors, indeed, determined the pattern of his itinerancy in the Spanish-American republics and the successive thwarting of his modernising plans in the four republics in which he carried out his intense activity. Viewed from this perspective, it might seem that his modernising agenda was frustrated, and Mora's legacy was wiped out by his successive departures from the republics that were accompanied by a conservative turn that sought to undo the liberal policies that Mora had encouraged, but the legacy of his teachings and his political and economic thought, like a seed that bears fruit later, remained intact in the minds and consciousness of later generations of liberals, equipping them for the eventual reception of innovative political and economic ideas. This is proved by the acknowledgement of intellectuals—such as Lastarria—, who played a significant role in the development of liberalism in Chile and other countries from the 1840s onwards, and undoubtedly by the intense circulation of Mora's works long after his departure from Hispanic America.

Bibliography

Books[32]

Mora, José Joaquín de. 1832. *Cursos de lógica y ética según la escuela de Edimburgo por José Joaquín de Mora*. Lima: Imprenta de José Masías.

Mora, José Joaquín de. 1834. *Discurso pronunciado en la Universidad Mayor de S. Andrés de la Paz de Ayacucho el 5 de diciembre de 1834, por el Dr. José Joaquín de Mora*. La Paz: Imprenta del Colegio de artes.

Mora, José Joaquín de. 1840: *Elementos de lógica escritos por D. José Joaquín de Mora, según la escuela de Edimburgo. Impreso en Lima y reimpreso en Sucre*. Sucre: Imprenta del Congreso.

Mora, José Joaquín de. 1846a. *Curso de ética según la escuela de Edimburgo por José Joaquín de Mora*. La Paz: Imprenta Paceña.

Mora, José Joaquín de. 1846b. *Curso de lógica según la escuela de Edimburgo por José Joaquín de Mora*. La Paz: Imprenta Paceña.

Translations and Reeditions

Campbell, George. 1846. *Tratado de la evidencia escrito en inglés por Jorge Campbell, de la Real Sociedad de Edimburgo, traducido al castellano con notas por José Joaquín de Mora*. Lima: Imprenta del Comercio.

Primary Sources

Anonymous. 1832a. *Examen sobre el Tratado de comercio ajustado en Arequipa entre el Perú y Bolivia, por sus respectivos plenipotenciarios bajo la mediación del Estado de Chile*. Arequipa.

Anonymous. 1832b. *Contestación a las breves reflexiones sobre el Tratado de comercio entre Bolivia y Perú*. La Paz: Imprenta de Educandas.

Anonymous. 1838. *Reimpresión del artículo impreso en la Miscelánea denunciando el curso de derecho que enseña el Señor Mora; y de las cartas con que se ha refutado la defensa publicada por este en los Mercurios del 16, 17 y 19 del noviembre del año pasado*. Lima: Imprenta accesoria de la casa de ejercicios de Santa Rosa.

[32] On the prolix reprints of the *Catecismos*, *Cursos* and other works of Mora in the Hispanic world, see Roldán (2003), Macintyre (2018) and Medina (2022).

Secondary Sources

Amunátegui, Domingo. 1897. *Mora en Bolivia*. Santiago de Chile: Imprenta Cervantes.

Amunátegui, Miguel Luis. 1888. *Don José Joaquín de Mora. Apuntes biográficos*. Santiago de Chile: Imprenta Nacional.

Basadre, Jorge. 2002. *La iniciación de la República*, vol. I. Lima: UNMSM.

Bradford Bow, Charles. 2018. *Common Sense int the Scottish Enlightenment*. Oxford: OUP.

Burr, Robert N. 1974. *By Reason or Force: Chile and the Balancing of Power in South America, 1830–1905*. Berkeley and Los Angeles: University of California Press.

Cavieres, Eduardo and Gonzalo Serrano. 2018. "La guerra de Chile contra la Confederación Perú-Boliviana (1836–1839): el trigo y la agricultura como bases de un proyecto nacional". *América Latina en la historia económica* 25–1, 136–64.

Contreras, Carlos. 2012. *La economía pública en el Perú después del guano y del salitre: crisis fiscal y élites económicas durante su primer siglo independiente*. Lima: Instituto de Estudios Peruanos.

Contreras, Carlos and Marcos Cueto. 2009. *Historia del Perú contemporáneo*. Lima: Instituto de Estudios Peruanos.

De Haro, Dionisio. 2013. "Papel para un Perú independiente: el pensamiento económico español y la creación del Banco Auxiliar de Papel Moneda". *Revista Complutense de Historia de América* 39, 203–27.

De Haro, Dionisio. 2016. "Plata y guerra en el Perú. La Casa de Moneda de Lima en tiempos de la independencia, 1808–1830". In *Historia de la moneda en el Perú*, edited by Carlos Contreras, 227–65. Lima: Banco Central de Reserva del Perú and Instituto de Estudios Peruanos.

Gootenberg, Paul. 1982. "The Social Origins of Protectionism and Free Trade in Nineteenth-Century Lima". *Journal of Latin American Studies* 14, 329–58.

Ibarz, Virgili and Ramón León. 2009. "José Joaquín de Mora (1783–1864): un introductor de la escuela escocesa del Sentido Común en el Perú, Bolivia y España". *Revista de historia de la psicología*, 30–2/3, 145–52.

Macintyre, Iona. 2018. "An Exponent of Scottish Common Sense Philosophy in Revolutionary South America". *Journal of Scottish Historical Studies* 38–2, 219–37.

Marichal, Carlos. 1999. *La bancarrota del Virreinato. Nueva España y las finanzas del imperio español, 1760–1810*. México: FCE.

Medina, Sara. 2022. *José Joaquín de Mora and Britain: Cultural Transfers and Transformations*. Berlin: Peter Lang.

Mesa, José de and Teresa Gisbert. 1965. *José Joaquín de Mora secretario del Mariscal Andrés de Santa Cruz*. La Paz: Academia Nacional de Ciencias de Bolivia.

Monguió, Luis. 1967. *Don José Joaquín de Mora y el Perú del ochocientos*. Madrid: Castalia.

Núñez, Estuardo. 1961. *D. José Joaquín Mora en el Perú. Cartas al Mariscal Santa Cruz*. Lima: Editorial San Marcos.

O'Brien, Denis Patrick. 1992. *J. R. McCulloch. A Study in Classical Economics*, London and Aldershot: Gregg Revivals and Routledge.

Peralta, Víctor. 2020. "Parlamentos y soberanías durante la *Confederación* del General Andrés de Santa Cruz. Chile, Perú y Bolivia". *Historia* 53–1, 155–81.

Sobrevilla, Natalia. 2011. *The Caudillo of the Andes, Andrés Santa Cruz*. Cambridge: CUP.

Sobrevilla, Natalia. 2021. "Disputando el poder de la fuerza con la ley: los liberales en la temprana república peruana y la guerra civil de 1834". *Jahrbuch für Geschichte Lateinamerikas/Anuario de Historia de América Latina* 58, 45–76.

Trease, B. David. 1953. *José Joaquín de Mora: A Spaniard Abroad*. PhD. Michigan, University of Michigan.

Velázquez, Marcel and Gustavo Morales. 2021. "El mercado de esclavos en la ciudad de Lima desde el *Mercurio Peruano*". *Desde el sur* 13–3, 1–25.

PART III

Maturity

CHAPTER 8

Back in Spain: The Free Trade Debate in *Moderate* Spain (1844–1853)

8.1 Introduction: Back in Spain

The Spain that greeted Mora after his long exile of over twenty years was very different from the country that he had left in 1823, in flight from the restoration of absolutism.[1] Ferdinand VII's death in 1833 had ushered in the decisive phase of the liberal reforms that had been attempted during the short-lived constitutional periods of the *Cortes of Cadiz* and the Liberal Triennium, during which political power shifted backwards and forwards between the moderate liberal—for longer periods—and progressive factions. After the vast majority of liberals abandoned the Constitution of Cadiz model once and for all, these factions' basic differences stemmed from their views on the political role of the Crown in a constitutional monarchy; while the latter recognised no representation other than the elected *Cortes*, to the former, national sovereignty lay in the *Cortes* together with the Crown, which had very wide-ranging powers (Artola 1973, 180–82; 1977, I, 218–54). At the same time, however, the progressive factions supported more radical reforms in social and economic terms and speedier implementation, and a more decisive opening up of political life to the middle and popular classes (Fernández Sebastián 2012b, 282–90). Following the revolution of July and August 1836, the 1837

[1] A first and shorter version of this chapter can be found in Astigarraga et al. (2023).

J. Astigarraga et al., *The Economic Legacy of José Joaquín de Mora*, Palgrave Studies in the History of Economic Thought,
https://doi.org/10.1007/978-3-031-49446-8_8

Constitution was approved by a *Cortes* in which there was a progressive majority. However, the constitutional text was "transactional", in that it included a series of concessions to moderate—or doctrinaire—liberalism, so that the political regime would be accepted by a large majority (Varela 1983–1984). The progressive majority prioritised freedom of the press, however, and abolished the preventive censorship regime, although some limits were set on freedom of expression throughout this period. A few years later in 1845 a new and more moderate Constitution reversed much of this progressive legislative work, including freedom of expression. Before the progressives' brief period in power during what is known as the *Bienio Progresista* (1854–1856), moderate liberalism enjoyed a longer political cycle, which lasted throughout the so-called Moderate Decade from 1844–1854 (Carr 1968, 211–53). These ten years coincided exactly with Mora's unwavering commitment to journalism following his arrival in the country of his birth, the main backdrop to which was the debate over free trade and its possible application to Spain.

The long-awaited liberal measures were passed from 1836 onwards, when Spain was in fact in the midst of the civil war (1833–1839) between the liberal *Isabelinos* and the *Carlists*, who supported the Ancien Régime. The reforms took a more moderate approach than the two previous phases. These measures ushered in a relatively rapid transition to a liberal society. The establishment of basic free market structures (freedom of pricing, employment, industry and labour, with the dissolution of the guilds in 1834–1836) was accompanied by others that were especially apparent in the agricultural framework and which involved significant changes in the land ownership regime and secular feudal structures. Wastelands were privatised; entailed estates were broken up; feudal estates and the *Mesta* were dismantled; church tithes were abolished and, of particular relevance, church lands were confiscated—the confiscation of common land began in 1855—[2] (Artola 1973, 107–12; Fontana 1973b, 147–84). The mobilisation of capital for the economy, the slow emergence of the financial market—the creation of the stock exchange and

[2] Finance Minister Juan A. Mendizábal was responsible for the 1836 confiscation of church land, which aimed to create a farming middle class by auctioning church-entailed estates. Later on, during the *Bienio Progresista* (1854–1856), Pascual Madoz carried out a new round of confiscation; both were at the heart of the liberal revolution in Spain. The consequences of the takeovers depended on the structure of the property, and in southern Spain they made a significant contribution to consolidating landlordism, as the land ended up in the hands of wealthy landowners; see Fontana (1985a).

growth in the number of banks—improvements in internal communications and the first steps towards industrial mechanisation also contributed to boosting demographic renewal—at relatively modest rates and accompanied by intense urbanisation (Artola 1973, 60–77)—. Spain began to emerge from the economic stagnation to which it had been condemned from 1808 to 1840 by wars, treasury bankruptcy and absolutism, paving the way for the first stable industrialisation processes, first in the Catalan textile industry and later in the Basque iron and steel industries. Mora's return to Spain thus coincided with a period of both considerable economic growth and the consolidation of liberal institutions under moderate liberal leadership.

This was accompanied by two more essential reforms. The first involved the 1841 tariff reform and effectively amounted to the beginning of the end for prohibitionism, fostering the opening up of foreign trade in 1841 and reducing prohibitions (Velasco 1989). Shortly, after, in 1849, a new tariff reform was approved, which definitively abolished prohibitionism; in the same year, the issuance monopoly was established (Vallejo 2018, 69–72). The abolition of prohibitionism meant that the struggle between protectionism and free trade came to the forefront of public debate. The second, Mon-Santillán's 1845 tax reform, marked the treasury's definitive transition from an absolutist to a liberal institution (Estapé 1971). While the reform retained certain monopolies and customs charges, it introduced, with its flaws, the budget's legality, the universality of taxes now levied on all classes—direct taxation on immovable property, crops and livestock was established—, simplified and rationalised the tax system, and established the liberal principle of legal equity under the law (Comín 2000a, 648–60); however, by prioritising excise taxes, the reform did not achieve tax equity. Moreover, although it was rolled out through formally regulated parliamentary and budgetary activity (Beltrán 1977, 219–37), the reform failed to lift the treasury out of the dire situation that it had been in since the end of the eighteenth century and which was the root cause of the crisis in absolute monarchy (Fontana 1973a): enormous inherited debt, lower revenues as a result of confiscating church property and insufficient income due to the 1845 reform all meant resorting to public debt was inevitable and impeded the true maturation of the liberal state (Comín 2000a). Furthermore, after Ferdinand VII these reforms were subject to public opinion on economic issues, which had been revived partly by parliamentary activity and partly by other institutional factors such as the emergence of a specialist press, the increase in the publishing of economics textbooks and the creation of a new network of cultural institutions with a deep political dimension.

On his return to Spain, Mora settled in his native Cadiz, becoming head of the *Colegio de San Felipe*, which had been run by prestigious liberals such as Antonio Alcalá Galiano and Alberto Lista and where he created the *Libro de la Escuela* or *Catecismo de conocimientos útiles destinados a la primera enseñanza*, which was published anonymously. It was a short catechism of scientific and geographical subjects for use in elementary schools following the *Lancasterian* method and the example of English and Prussian schoolbooks to encourage from childhood the "love for useful things" (Mora c.1844b, IV, VI), and was accompanied by the publication of an anthology of literary texts (Mora 1845). After living in Seville for a time—there, his law degree was officially recognised in July 1843—,[3] he moved to Madrid. Due to his moderate pragmatic views, he soon found a place in Madrid's institutions. The city to which Mora returned had regained the political and cultural momentum in the public sphere that had been lost after the Liberal Triennium came to an end. From 1833 onwards, cafés and literary clubs, innovative reading rooms and lending libraries blossomed in the city, which had well over 200,000 inhabitants by the mid-nineteenth century. The press emerged as an organ of opinion, reflecting the voices of political parties and factions. It was in this cultural ecosystem, in which journalists, teachers and other cultural agitators operated as promoters of relatively free debate in an urban context. This was all made possible by the slow reassertion of bourgeois society, with a legal framework that reduced censorship, freedom of the press (1834 and 1836) and copyright recognition (1847), which not only increased the oral spread of knowledge, but also instigated a qualitative leap in publishing, including works with economics content (Martínez Marín 2009, 38–40, 66–68; see Ch. 9).

But writing was not his only occupation at the time. Being a prominent figure in the elites of the reign of Isabel II, Mora held several positions connected to the moderate Party (González 1984, 355–56). In May 1847 was appointed as vice-president of the *Consejero Provincial de Madrid* and in June 1847 as *Consejero Real de Agricultura, Industria y Comercio*—he left the first post in 1851, and there is no official record of the second one—. Likewise, in three different stages, he was Spanish Consul in London (1850–1851, 1853–1854, 1856–1858) and in 1848 he was

[3] AHN, *Consejos*, bundle 13,173.

named a Fellow of the *Real Academia de la Lengua* in recognition of his long literary career. A few years earlier, in 1844, before settling in Madrid, Mora had begun what turned out to be a short-lived collaboration with the *Sociedad Matritense*, of which he had been a member since the days of Liberal Triennium. While the economic societies had not closed during the Ominous Decade (1823–1833), they had been condemned to inaction; the granting of new statutes in 1834 and 1835 enabled them to revive their traditional economic, educational and social activities, which included the managing of political economy chairs, with the aim of achieving greater independence from political power. However, although the *Matritense* was run by leading liberals such as Juan Álvarez Guerra, Antonio Sandalio de Arias and Eusebio María del Valle, it remained a stagnant bastion of old ruling class sociability.

This was not the case with the *Ateneo Científico y Literario*, in whose 1835 revival the *Matritense* itself was fundamental. One of the *Ateneo*'s four sections was devoted to moral and political sciences and it hosted prominent debates on political economy, including several on protectionism and free trade[4]; it was also responsible for the political economy, social economy, public borrowing and public finance chairs, which were established from 1836 onwards. This dynamic institution was based on dialogue and education; the breeding ground for literary elites and professional politicians, it was the best expression of both the liberal cultural ecosystem of the day and its close relationship with official political power (Villacorta 1980, 26–40). While far removed from the Triennium's elated liberalism, the *Ateneo* increasingly came under the control of both moderate and radical liberal sectors when they were not in power, although the influential political law chair reflected its closeness to the former (Garrorena 1974). It is not surprising, then, that Mora soon found a niche there.[5] Since the late 1940s he was head of the literature and fine arts section and taught both philosophy of history and English; however, as with so many

[4] *The Asociación para la reforma de los aranceles de aduanas*, which was founded in 1859 to defend free trade interests, adopted the *Ateneo* as its main propaganda centre.

[5] He may also have frequented the *Liceo artístico y literario*, which was founded in 1837 to foster literature, although there is no record of his participation there, perhaps due to the fact that his arrival in Madrid coincided with the institution's decline (Pérez Sánchez 2005).

other aspects, all trace of his presence there vanished after the Moderate Decade drew to a close, most likely due to their diplomatic duties.[6]

This revitalised institutional network facilitated the establishing of political economy as a discipline, which was particularly apparent in the emergence of a specialised economics press and the proliferation of chairs and textbooks, as detailed below.[7] While Mora is unlikely to have taught political economy in Spain, he did witness the way in which the education laws decreed in 1836, 1842 and 1845 fulfilled the long-standing liberal aspiration to set up university chairs in the subject. The main reform was the 1845 "Pidal plan", the brainchild of Interior Minister Pedro José Pidal, which enshrined the teaching of political economy in law and philosophy faculties. However, chairs in other institutions also played their part in creating a specialised teaching circuit: the *Matritense*—and other economic societies—and the *Ateneo* were veritable breeding grounds for teachers and textbooks.

The 1836 and 1842 laws allowed teachers to choose their own textbooks, thus respecting the principle of academic freedom, although a list of recommended textbooks was provided. The 1841 version included Spanish texts—Flórez Estrada (1828), Torrente (1835) and Valle Santoro (1830)—and translations of French treatises—Rossi (1840) and Droz (1842)—. The thirty-year period from 1807 to 1836 during which Say's *Traité* held sway in education thus came to an end, albeit only ostensibly as the work continued to be widely used. Flórez Estrada's *Curso* was undoubtedly key in the headway made by political economy in Spain from the 1830s to the 1860s (Almenar 1980, 2000a). Published seven times between 1828 and 1852, this brilliant treatise—as seen, was conceived in London, during the author's exile—whose roots lay in Ricardo, Say and their disciples, as well as other classical economists such as Smith, Malthus and Sismondi, contributed more than any other Spanish textbook of the day—Del Valle (1842), Paso y Delgado (1841), Borrego (1844) and Colmeiro (1845, 1859)—to ending Say's long period of dominance.

[6] Ruiz Salvador (1971, 82–85). According to details in the AAM, in 1847 Mora resigned from the presidency of the literature and fine arts section of the *Ateneo* due to new duties that he had committed himself to and health problems. Nevertheless, he accepted to do so the following year and held that post at least until 1850 (ES 28079, 01.03–033, 037; 01.04–18, 19, 20; 01.06–12). In 1855, the *Ateneo* invited him to run some of its chairs, but he declined (ES 28079, 01.03–079).

[7] The line taken by Martín Rodríguez (1989), Almenar (2000a) and Lluch and Almenar (2000) has been followed on this issue.

While the "Pidal Plan" upheld the principle of academic freedom, Blanqui (1837, 1840), Garnier (1848) and Colmeiro were added to the list of recommended textbooks. In short, the French economy had a more profound influence on Spain than the British, as is clear from the fact that Ricardo's influence there was only indirect and secondary, and interpretations of his *Principles* were often less than faithful (Almenar 2014). The many translations of Bastiat's works in the 1840s and 1850s further accentuated the tendency to look to France for inspiration.

Mora's preparations for his arrival in the *moderate* Spain of 1843 to 1854 were nothing if not enthusiastic. In 1840, while still in London, he published a translation of a new text by Holbach, closely connected to the one published in the Liberal Triennium (Mora 1840). In 1844 he edited the *Revista ecléctica Española* (REE, 1844).[8] From 1843 to 1845 he compiled a collection of Cadiz press articles by moderate liberal Alberto Lista (1844), to which he contributed the preface, and also circulated several of his own writings including the textbook for the Cadiz *Colegio de San Felipe*, a treatise on Scottish moral philosophy and a lecture in defence of *iusnaturalism* given at the *Ateneo* in 1821 (Mora 1821). Some of these writings appeared thanks to the prestigious publisher Mellado, and helped to make his presence in Spain more visible. However, all this activity was merely designed to lay the groundwork for his real goals. Although he registered to practise as a lawyer at the Seville Bar Association, there is no indication that he actually did so; however, he continued to combine his previous activities as an adviser, politician, diplomat, educator and journalist.

8.2 *De la Libertad del Comercio* (1843)

Mora showed renewed interest in economic issues as soon as he set foot in Spain, and quickly picked up on the mood in economic circles there. He wrote and published the *De la libertad del comercio* (DLC) in Seville in 1843 as a letter of introduction to these circles for his economic ideas. On the basis of the citations in the DLC, Schwartz subdivides Mora's sources as follows: McCulloch's *The Principles of Political Economy* (1825); Pebrer's *Cinco Proposiciones* (1837); Mengotti's *Il Colbertismo* (1819); the British Anti-Corn Law League and, finally, incidents in British

[8] Three issues were published in July, August and September. We have not found any copies of this journal.

economic history. To this mix Schwartz also adds a theory of international trade, to which he attributes a weak analytical foundation because it is based on absolute advantage; a theory of economic growth, the first stage of which involves agrarian development against a backdrop of free trade and competition; and, finally, what he interprets as a theory of public choice, in that Mora analyses the effects of trade policy on economic groups in dispute in cost/benefit terms (Schwartz 1999, XXXI, XXXVII–XXXIX, XLI–XLII). Schwartz also points out that Mora seems to be writing more for England than for Spain, given his relative lack of familiarity with Spanish economic literature in comparison with his mastery of British literature and economics. Although Schwartz's work is the most comprehensive current interpretation of the DLC (Schwartz 1970, 1999), it needs revising thoroughly, as it takes into account neither Mora's previous career nor the enormous influence that the book had on his journalism in the 1840s.

Schwartz's perception that Mora's work lacked firm roots in Spain's scenario can be put down to the fact that the DLC is closely related to the economics texts he produced in London, Buenos Aires and Santiago de Chile, in which, as seen, he proposed an economic model for the new Hispanic-American republics. As a recent arrival to Spain, Mora aimed to leave cultural and economic circles in no doubt as to this "deep conviction, matured over many years of study and experience and fortified by personal work that has crowned a happy result" (Mora 1843, 209). To this end, he based his book on free trade as the main goal of Spanish economic policy.

The DLC continued to be of great interest to Hispanic-American readers and was reissued in Mexico in 1853. Nevertheless, it was originally aimed at readers in Spain, who saw the free trade-protectionist debate once again becoming central to political discussion from the early 1840s and this would soon be the case in the parliamentary arena as well. Mora had been familiar with McCulloch, Pebrer and Mengotti's texts since the 1820s, and a detailed examination of the intellectual sources of the book highlights its continuity with earlier phases of his work.

These sources reveal that the DLC was probably sketched out between 1837 and 1843, towards the end of Mora's second sojourn in London when, as seen, he was an agent and diplomat for Bolivian politician Andrés de Santa Cruz. There are numerous pointers to support this hypothesis. The DLC contains many extracts from Pebrer's *Cinco proposiciones*, which was published in London in 1837 (Pebrer 1837), but Mora cites only one work by a Spanish economist, and then only the odd extract: *De la influencia del sistema prohibitivo* (1842) by free trader Manuel Marliani, who was also a diplomatic agent in London during the 1840s. While living in London, Mora must have followed the debates in parliament and uses them to show the positive effects of free trade; a speech given by Lord Palmerston on 19 May 1841, which argued that free trade promoted peace, takes up nine pages in the DLC (Mora 1843, 81–88). And while Mora's free trade rationale varies little from the previous period, in the DLC he draws on arguments from articles appearing in the early 1840s in English journals such as *The Examiner* as well as French publications, although to a lesser extent, such as the *Revue des deux mondes*. The DLC's main influence, however, is McCulloch's article "Political Economy", but not the version that Mora had read during his first London exile, but one that appeared in the seventh edition of the *Encyclopaedia Britannica*, which was published in 1842 (Mora 1843, 258–307). Hence, when Mora cites or summarises texts by Mun, Mercier de la Rivière and James Mill (*Commerce Defended*, 1807), he transcribes quotations from McCulloch's article (McCulloch 1842, 268–70; Mora 1843, 58–60), and the work also reflects McCulloch's admiration for Huskisson's reforms. This is a natural intellectual debt, especially in a work on free trade, as McCulloch had been Mora's author of reference since the 1820s and, according to O'Brien, was a "radical and uncompromising advocate of free trade" (O'Brien 1992, 191). This was all in direct contrast to the economic culture of the day in Spain, where, as seen, the influence of Flórez Estrada's treatise was all-pervasive and Say's authority had been replaced by that of his disciples Blanqui, Rossi and Droz (Almenar 1980, 2000b; Lluch and Almenar 2000). Mora also included his own experience as an advisor to Santa Cruz as proof of the soundness of free trade policies: in short, the DLC was built on theoretical foundations from his periods of exile in Britain and Hispanic America which he brought up to date by including material gathered during his second London sojourn.

Mora's starting point in the DLC is the continuing existence in the "structure of the new [liberal] society" of "remnants" and "errors of the old one" (Mora 1843, V). He identifies the main problem in the foreword, entitled "To the Reader": the anachronism of having a treasury based on tariff revenues, which should be replaced by a "system that combines the treasury's interests with the taxpayers', and that above all facilitates, strengthens, protects and broadens the *caput mortuum* from which the prosperity of both taxpayers and the treasury must exclusively flow: production" (Mora 1843, VI).

The issue for Mora was pinning down the principle in the new legislation that promoted economic development, either protectionism or free trade. In his opinion the former mainly favoured Catalan industry, while also fulfilling the need to raise revenue (Mora 1843, 26). He naturally tried to join the deregulation and liberalisation that Spanish liberals had been proposing since the *Cortes de Cádiz* and had promoted from 1836 onwards, but which lacked crucial aspects. It is important to recall that Mon-Santillán's liberal tax reform of 1845 was pending at this point, and that the 1841 Tariff Law, which made moderate progress on tariff liberalisation, had been enacted shortly before Mora's book appeared. Mora condenses these two central issues of liberal reform into the expression "free trade", and they were inseparable from the economic agenda that he sets out in the DLC, as can be seen from the following statement, which has Benthamite overtones:

> free trade, applicable to the countries whose happiness this work seeks to promote, shall be taken to mean the unlimited ability to export and import all kinds of natural and manufactured products, with the lowest duties compatible with the needs of the tax office, and with no other obligations, requirements or formalities than those that are absolutely indispensable to guarantee that these taxes are paid. (Mora 1843, 36)

On the basis of other countries' experiences Mora felt that tariffs should not exceed 15% and that they should be uniform and *ad valorem*, avoiding specificity, a conviction that was based on discussions in the British Parliament, especially a debate tabled by President of the Board of Trade Henri Labouchère (Mora 1843, 89). Mora had already shown similar signs of pragmatism when he declared that "unlimited civil liberty would be incompatible with public safety and the administration of justice" (Mora 1843, 26), and this attributing of ends relating to order, justice and market conditions to the state shows a notable parallel with Book V of Smith's WN, as well as with McCulloch's 1842 work. Several passages in the text indicate that Mora advocated a "liberal, generous" public finance system that was essentially funded by consumption, which would be bound to increase notably "as a result of the price reductions that a liberal generous customs system must necessarily produce" (Mora 1843, 128, 132). However, he does not go into the details here, which would take shape shortly afterwards in Mon-Santillán's 1845 reform, confining himself to underlining the connection between free trade and rising tax revenues.

Having set out the book's framework, Mora structures the content around free trade's "advantages" (Chap. II to VII) and "drawbacks" (Chap. VIII to XI). Among the former are improvements in capital accumulation, progress in economic sectors, relations between peoples, the prevention of smuggling and public finances. He refutes the disadvantages that protectionists attributed to the free trade system almost symmetrically; these are encapsulated in economic dependence on foreign countries, the balance of trade deficit, the outflow of money and the destruction of domestic industry.

The "capital creation and accumulation" issue contains the elements of the economic growth model that Mora set out in Santiago de Chile in EMC in the late 1820s. Profit—the expression "net product" is used in 1843—plays a central role as the "infallible principle" of capital accumulation (Mora 1843, 55). Mora confirms his debt to McCulloch here by defining capital as "the part of the product of labour which is not intended for immediate consumption", which McCulloch had used in *The Principles of Political Economy* (McCulloch 1842, 279). The four ways in which capital accumulation contributes to prosperity come from this work, especially from the section on "The Accumulation and Employment of Capital":

> 1st by facilitating the division of labour; 2nd by supplying means without which it would not be possible to produce many of the most necessary objects for life's comforts; 3rd by saving a large part of labour for this production; 4th by putting capitalists in a position to improve the products and to shorten the time spent handling them. (Mora 1843, 40; McCulloch 1842, 279–80)

Having established profit's crucial importance and its relationship with capital accumulation, Mora goes on to address the Spanish economy's specialisation in an international division of labour system such as that proposed in the DLC. In Chapter II he suggests that in Spain the net product must come from agriculture, but it is not until Chapter IX that he theoretically underpins this by means of an example from McCulloch's *The Principles of Political Economy* (Mora 1843, 147–50). This is the exchange of Polish grain for British cloth, which McCulloch used to illustrate the theory of absolute advantage, attributing absolute cost advantage to the former. The approach has analytical weaknesses with respect to proving that the exchange will actually materialise, as it does not explain how prices will bring this about. However, leaving aside these and other theoretical issues, McCulloch follows Smith's conviction that nations seek the lowest supply price, which in his terms means that they will not produce what they can import more cheaply (O'Brien 1992, 192–94). This results in a "territorial division of labour" in which countries specialise in producing goods that have an absolute cost advantage. Mora uses this argument repeatedly throughout the DLC to justify the specialisation of the Spanish economy and shares McCulloch's view that differences in costs stem from the uneven provision of natural resources, a factor that determines each country's specialisation. According to Mora Spain's advantages are

> our soil and climate; the excellence, abundance and variety of all the fruits that draw their nourishment from our blessed land, the opportunities it provides for livestock breeding [...] the excellence of its wines and oils, the richness of its mines. (Mora 1843, 65)

The wording of this extract is similar to McCulloch's in the *Encyclopaedia Britannica*. However, wealth creation does not generate prosperity without flow: "the circulation of products, services and ideas is as important in political and economic life as the circulation of blood is in physical life". Mora repeatedly refers to physical obstacles to circulation and stresses the beneficial effects of roads and public works on production and business creation (Mora 1843, 70). At the same time, he also alludes to the legal and institutional impediments to this circulation, grouping the measures that result in their removal under the term "free trade". All the elements of the Smith-McCulloch development model are here again: division of labour, capital accumulation and market scope.

Mora proposes a development strategy for Spain that combines free trade and agrarian specialisation, in line with what he had previously advocated for the Hispanic-American republics and with the aspirations of free traders in Spain (Almenar 2000b). However, he invokes the principle of non-universality of economic laws established in the CEP to address the differences between the situations in Spain and Hispanic America, which involve different strategies. There are accounts of Mora writing about entailed estates, and the harm that they caused to the economy when he was in Chile (Smith 1968, 600); in 1843, on the other hand, his views on the issue are more ambiguous, which is consistent with his economic growth theory, based on McCulloch and experiences in Britain. Along with defending private property, Mora discusses the optimal size of farms in terms of their economic yield—"net product"—which fuels capital accumulation. His conclusion is clear: "A hundred adjacent pieces of land distributed among a hundred different owners do not produce as much fruit, nor so varied nor perfect, as if they were united under a single owner" (Mora 1843, 48).

Farm size is therefore a key element in agricultural development and economic prosperity. Although Mora does not explicitly refer to technical change and innovations, as he explained in the MUC, he had undoubtedly accepted the Classical economists' canonical position and invoked Say to argue that machinery reduced prices, increased the "net product", contributed to capital accumulation and need not be confined solely to the industrial sector (MUC, 1825–1826, II, 44). Only larger farms were capable of incorporating technical improvements and consequently contributing more to economic prosperity. What could be done in mid-nineteenth-century Spain to encourage these more productive agricultural units, especially bearing in mind the fact that Minister Mendizábal's 1836 promotion of disentailment had actually encouraged the old nobility and the merchant bourgeoisie to hoard land? In line with his agrarian growth model and drawing on the British experience, Mora, ever a pragmatist, advocated changes in Spanish legislation that

> should instead apply themselves to acclimatising these conditions, rather than to destroying the *caput mortuum* which the conditions could vitalise; or, if they lacked the means to do so, wait for time and the progress of the enlightened to fill this void, and put the Medinacelis, Osunas and Infantados in a position to do what the Metternichs, Russells and Northumberlands do. (Mora 1843, 47–48)

Mora is referring to the lack of free trade, the "exclusive cause of the palpable disproportion between the extent of possessions and the scarcity of income" (Mora 1843, 48). As a result, he modifies his view of large seigniorial estates: their inefficiency is due not to the institution itself, but to "collateral circumstances" (Mora 1843, 47). In his view, eliminating tariff barriers would create incentives to stimulate the transformation of manorial property into productive units that promoted economic prosperity.

This is another sign that Mora's position became more moderate after he returned to Spain, as his concern for private property and large-scale farming also shows. The early 1840s witnessed a number of reform projects, including property distribution and the quest for efficient farm size. While progressive liberals such as Flórez Estrada advocated property distribution and small farms, more moderate perspectives such as that represented by Juan Álvarez Guerra's *Proyecto de ley agraria. Código rural* (1841), which was sponsored by the *Sociedad Económica Matritense*, attributed a stabilising role to large agricultural holdings, with guaranteed property rights, an approach which later became popular among moderate circles (Robledo 1993, 55–59). Mora therefore joined the movement, which, according to economists such as Andrés Borrego and Vicente Vázquez Queipo, was keen to integrate the landed gentry into the new social order, believing that free trade would provide the catalyst for this process. This is all further proof of the complexity of the protectionism-free trade debate in the mid-nineteenth century, in that behind the discussions over trade lay deep discord between the social groups that were in dispute and over the development of capitalism.

Population, which is to say the labour factor, is the other component in Mora's growth model, which relies on the important role of the population-agriculture binomial in boosting the export of agricultural surpluses by making the most of the Spanish economy's absolute advantages. As seen, Mora had devoted several articles in London and Buenos Aires to refuting the Malthusian population thesis in order to show that population increases, especially in the United States, were not only directly related to increased food supplies, but also to European emigration. There is no explicit mention of the Malthusian model in the DLC but Mora reaches a similar conclusion: encouraging Europeans to emigrate to Spain as a complement to capital accumulation (Mora 1843, 69). He leaves some question marks hanging over the proposal, however, such as the nature of the link between free trade and the promoting of emigration beyond the free mobility of labour. Nor does he specify the destinations of foreign migrants: would they work on large farms? And where would Spanish colonisers settle? In the context of the agrarian reforms in Spain at the time, Mora's proposal contains many unknowns.

The DLC is not, strictly speaking, an economics treatise. The work presents a rather disorganised series of ideas, with aims that are more rhetorical than systematic. There are rambling arguments about the evils of the "mercantile system", balance of trade theory and identifying wealth with precious metals. Mora had pointed out in earlier writings that reducing import duties did not entail "taking money out of the country", a claim that characterised the "mercantilist" doctrine, which, in Smith's view, held that a country's wealth consisted in accumulating precious metals through a positive balance of trade, achieved through prohibitions and restrictions that affected imports in particular.

Mora refutes this theory in the DLC by revisiting an idea with clear classical roots which he had already put forward in the MUC when he argued that money was equivalent to any other commodity and so accumulating it over and above one's needs was useless (Mora 1843, 166–67). However, he offered a new critical perspective on the issue, stipulating that every "nation should take in [the] money it needs: what it does not need must go out one way or another, and no power can stop it. Excessive increases in the quantity of money lower its price as a commodity", in such a way that it produces "the admirable distribution of money all [...] over the earth" (Mora 1843, 169).

This is essentially the Hume-Ricardo "price-specie flow" or self-correcting precious metal mechanism, which represented the theoretical defeat of the "mercantile system". Should any doubts remain, Mora points out that "where raw materials, wages and manufactured goods rise in price, preference is given to foreigners who produce more cheaply. Money's attempt to flow outwards and seek the goods that attract it is thus inevitable" (Mora 1843, 171).

While this is Mora's strongest analytical argument against the "mercantile system", much of his work also draws on historical experience. This relentless and methodical critique was merely a precursor to the overt censure of protectionism in the Catalan textile industry that he unfolds in Chapter XI, in which he states that the "system called manufacturing, the deformity of which is now disguised under the title of *protection system* [...], is not a present-day invention" (Mora 1843, 175). This explains why he uses a text that was already somewhat anachronistic almost halfway through the nineteenth century: Mengotti's *Il Colbertismo* (1819), a reissued work that had been awarded a prize by the Florentine *Accademia dei Georgofili* in 1792. Mora introduces it in Chapter X in order to show the continuity between the "mercantile system" and industrial protectionism.

Mora had avoided the "fledgling industry" debate in Buenos Aires and Santiago de Chile, as the issue was practically superfluous in the context of agrarian specialisation in the Hispanic-American republics. However,

1840s Spain was familiar with the development of industry in Catalonia, supported by a protectionist strategy with roots in the late eighteenth century and structured around the Barcelona Board of Trade by the emerging cotton-manufacturing bourgeoisie (Lluch 1973). He therefore provides a detailed analysis of the advantages of free trade to promote the "domestic manufacturing industry" (Mora 1843, Ch. V). This was of course one of his main reasons for writing the DLC and a *filo rosso* through which he tried to establish himself in the Spanish liberal circles of the 1840s, at the height of the debate over the 1841 Tariff Law. During the Liberal Triennium Mora had pinpointed the Catalan cotton industry as the chief beneficiary of the protectionist framework; however, at that time the industrial explosion of the 1830s had not yet taken place, nor had the protectionist doctrine become so deeply rooted in industrial circles in Catalonia.

Revealing the harmfulness of protection is thus a central element of the DLC, and Mora uses Pebrer's *Cinco proposiciones* (1837) to do so. Pebrer's work was published in Spanish during Mora's second exile in London, but the two men had met in the 1820s during his first sojourn there. The choice of Pebrer's work as a reference for criticising Catalan protectionism was highly symbolic, as it had been severely censured and was naturally challenged in Catalonia, as is clear from the *Refutación de las Cinco proposiciones del Señor Pebrer contra el sistema prohibitivo* (1838), which was written at the *Sociedad Económica Barcelonesa*. A second noteworthy and well-known refutation was written by Manuel María Gutiérrez (1837), a prominent convert to protectionism who became a defender of Catalan protectionist practices in Madrid's economic circles. Manuel Inclán, a member of the Tariff Review Board, made an unsuccessful attempt to mediate in the controversy from positions that Mora considered were close to his own (Reeder 2003; Mora 1843, 225). In addition to these writings, Mora used McCulloch's ideas and British parliamentary speeches from the 1840s, through which Anti-Corn Law League criteria filtered.

Mora follows Pebrer to refer to the "incompatibility of Catalan interests with those of the vast majority of the nation" (Mora 1843, 77). Catalan protectionism benefits "a privileged class, smoothing the path to fortune for its members, who enrich themselves from our deprivations and, with the price they want to demand from us, increase their speculations" (Mora 1843, 185). Imposing "protective rights" is an "abuse of power" against the liberal state and destroys "legal equality", for while it "condemns thirteen million men to ignorance and deprives them of the fruits of labour", it benefits the "protective law of 50,000 men" (Mora 1843, 179). Furthermore, some sectors such as agricultural producers and, evoking Smith, consumers are particularly hard-hit, while there are harmful effects for the whole system, since "the majority are essentially consumers and consumption is an overriding daily need" (Mora 1843, 213). These points are complemented in the DCL with typical free trader arguments such as the lack of incentives for productivity, the administrative and political costs of overseeing protection measures, the encouragement of smuggling and the moral degradation of prosecuting the non-payment of tariffs (Mora 1843, 114, 119–10, 191–92). In short, Mora equates free trade with economic stimulus and competition based on individual interest, and interprets protectionism as privilege and monopoly, which lends his arguments a Smithian tone, via McCulloch (Salvadori and Signorino 2013).

Mora's forceful refutation of Catalan protectionist ideas probably obliged him to argue that this did not imply an anti-industry approach. In an aside entitled "Del origen natural y de los progresos de la industria manufacturera", in Chapter XII of the DLC, he explains that he is not against encouraging industry:

> The first thing to observe from this emerging development of labour is that its use is primarily directed at the raw materials within easiest reach [...] and therefore as long as [...] there are uncultivated lands on which crops and abundant grasses can grow; [...] as long as there are no workers for these useless wastelands and food is therefore scarce [...], it seems foolhardy to remove capital and labour from the agricultural sphere. (Mora 1843, 195–97)

Recent literature has cast doubt on Eltis, Hollander and Meek's claims that Smith accepted "stadial theory" as a taxonomy of the relationships between modes of production and social, political and legal institutions, rather than an evolutionary model of economic development; however, it is referred to frequently in Books III and V of WN (Smith 1776 [1976b]; Paganelli 2022). Irrespective of these divergences, Mora shared this theory of development in stages, which unfolded naturally through the process of capital accumulation (Mora 1843, 199). The aside in Chapter XIII ultimately makes the point that he is neither exclusively an industrialist nor an agrarianist, but in fact seeks the spread of capitalism. This should begin in the agrarian sector, as he suggested with regard to the Hispanic-American republics, and then address the physical and institutional transformations that would lead "naturally" to the development of other economic sectors; that is, without the need to protect industry specifically.

8.3 The *Memoria Sobre los Puertos Francos* (1844)

Unlike the DLC, which engaged in debates about foreign trade, the *Memoria de los puertos francos* (MPF) was written for a competition organised by the *Sociedad Económica Matritense* on 17 April 1843 on the subject of "the benefits or harm to Spain if it offered all its ports free to other nations". Mora spied an opportunity to enter Madrid's economic circles and sent the Society an anonymous paper as the announcement stipulated, doubtlessly spurred on by the prize of free Society membership.

The competition aroused not a little controversy. The *Matritense* awarded its prize on 30 April to a paper, "whose author's views it neither accepted nor rejected", and which appeared in its official journal *El Amigo del País* (EAP, 1844–1847; Mora 1844). Two weeks later the Society reported that as the prize-winner's identity was still unknown, they were unable to give the customary speech of thanks, but that the winning text would be published in issue seven of the Society's journal, ignoring the fact that it had already appeared in print (EAP, I, no. 6, 15/VII/1844, 316). However, instead of Mora's paper, another prize-winning study appeared in the issue; it discussed whether it was advisable to sign trade treaties only with less advanced nations and was written by José María Ibáñez, Secretary of the Statistics Commission, a discipline in which he held the chair at the *Matritense* Society (Ibáñez 1844a). The work criticised "theoretical economists" for not applying "absolute principles" in practice: defending industries that were in "their infancy" did justify only signing trade treaties with less developed nations. When Mora's identity was finally revealed a row broke out in the Society, the outcome of which was Ibáñez's *Impugnación a la memoria sobre los puertos francos* (1844b). This only added to the confusion, because while it maintained that the Society recognised a certain literary merit and "good intentions and patriotism" of the prize-winning author—Mora—, it did not take responsibility for the practical applications, which "influenced its members not to award this text the prize" (EAP, I, no. 10, 15/VII/1844, 316). Prize-winning or otherwise, according to several contemporary publications,

Mora's work also created controversy outside the *Matritense*. In the end the Society published a note in its journal in which it declared the debate fruitful and stated that it did not incline towards either point of view (EAP, I, no. 13, 1/IX/1844, 397). Mora's work was eventually published in 1844 as a monograph, in which he was appearing as a lawyer in Seville (Mora 1844).

Free ports were created by Modern Age absolutist states with the aim of gaining trading advantages and economic supremacy over other powers, something which was consistent with the "mercantile system". However, there is no unanimity as to how these institutions should be interpreted: while various historiographical currents consider them to be purely "mercantilist" (Kliesser 2021), others assume that they actually instigated the theorising surrounding free trade (Tazzara 2017, 255–57). Mora, of course, supported the second interpretation from the outset. He adopted a particularly emphatic position in a passage in the EMC, reproduced verbatim in the MPF, in which he uses French prohibitionist François Ferrier's panegyric on Colbert's creation of three free ports in France (Bayonne, Dunkirk and Marseilles; Ferrier 1803; Mora 1844, 15–16, 31–34). The link established here between free ports and free trade is unique in Spanish economic literature, at least during the era of Classical economics.[9]

Mora's interest in free ports stemmed from personal experience. As seen, in 1819–1820 he was sent on a royal mission to study the port of Livorno, as a result of which he suggested creating a free port in Cadiz. Livorno (Tuscany) was a perfect example of a free trade enclave in Europe, originating in a Mediterranean state's reaction to the rapid economic growth around the Atlantic during the sixteenth century. From 1566 Livorno had enjoyed special status, with its own customs system and other privileges. Due to the political and trading instability in the Mediterranean region—the frontier with the Muslim world—, the port became a centre for the warehousing and transit of goods that crossed the Mediterranean, and its success was widely recognised in the eighteenth century (Tazzara 2017). Mora first refers to it in the CEP and an article published in Buenos Aires' CPL, and subsequently in the EMC.

[9] The exception was Pío Pita Pizarro's work on free trade and the free port of Cadiz (1834), in which, as well as linking free ports to free trade, he supported the establishing of a free port there.

However, over and above these preliminaries, the MPF's roots were in the DLC. Its content is essentially confined to DLC argument, but this is succinctly reworked for a "public that is uninitiated in the precepts of social science" (Mora 1844, 21). The only exception to this, as noted previously, are the paragraphs that Mora reproduces from an EMC article, which includes a quotation from Say's *Traité*'s. This is, undoubtedly, an exercise in empty rhetoric and opportunism: empty, as these paragraphs do not alter his fundamental premise; and opportunistic because they were written with the *Matritense* competition in mind. In the light of MPF content, it is clear that Mora considered free ports to be anachronisms in the mid-nineteenth century, and nowhere in his work does he propose their creation. When he speaks of "providing free ports", therefore, he is in fact referring to free trade (Mora 1844, 8).

Free trade is Mora's objective from the outset, and he equates it with "opening up ports to other nations" and not with the actual creation of free ports (Mora 1844, 11). During his stay in Argentina, he had suggested creating a free port in Buenos Aires, speculating, like Smith, on the possibility of turning the whole republic into a free port. [10] The MPF is, moreover, structured around the "advantages" and "drawbacks" of free trade on the basis of "the direction that society is pointing us in", and Mora reproduces the organisation of "influences" and "objections" in the DLC. He divides the advantages into economic, moral and political, including the increase in imports, population, capital and the "movement of wealth" in the first category (Mora 1844, 15). Moral advantages include the creation of useful jobs and eradicating of smuggling, and he goes on to state that the prosperity brought by free trade will guarantee social order and increased clout for Spain in "the grand jury of European cabinets". The drawbacks are limited to "the fear that free exporting will greatly reduce the mass of money needed for internal circulation, and our manufacturing will collapse if we open our doors to foreign goods" (Mora 1844, 29).

In certain respects, Mora waters down his views on some of the objections expressed in the DLC. This is true of his attack on protecting Catalan industry, which was one of the main reasons for writing the work. Catalan protectionism is not even mentioned in the MPF, and there is also a

[10] Smith expressed this view in his lectures to students in Glasgow (Tazzara 2017, 529). Mora is unlikely to have been aware of this, and what is being pointed out here is simply a parallel.

suggestion that the "mercantile system" contained trading institutions which contributed to the prosperity of absolutist states, among them free ports.

The MPF's theoretical underpinning is still the Smith-McCulloch model in the DLC, which is introduced in a simplified and more succinct form and centres on production, the division of labour and the circulation of goods as the linchpins of economic prosperity, with free trade acting as the catalyst for the whole process. There is also a brief reference to monetary theory and the self-correcting mechanism of precious metals, but on the whole greater weight is given to other countries' free trade experiences and their consequences for economic prosperity. The origins of Spain's economic woes are attributed to ignorance of economic science, especially Smith's theories.

The controversy surrounding the MPF in the *Matritense* Society has already been noted. Ibáñez's *Impugnación* was originally handwritten, signed on 27 June 1844 and eventually published in the EAP (Ibáñez 1844b). Ibáñez stated that he was motivated by the fact that Mora was offered "another prize for this year's competition", so that he could show how tariff revenues would be replaced in the event of free trade in greater depth than in the MPF. There is no record of Mora completing this work, but Ibáñez interpreted the commission as proof that although the *Matritense* declared itself neutral, it actually supported Mora's "doctrines". Ibáñez's *Impugnación* accepted the classic prohibitionist arguments to reveal "the errors of the free trade system in its application to Spain"; in the MPF's case, these arose from the adopting of abstract "school" principles, which Ibáñez identifies with Smith, whose theories he deemed anachronistic and already overtaken by the forward march of economic science (Ibáñez 1844b, 303–305). Ibáñez also countered Mora's information with the link that he believed existed between Britain's prosperity and its protectionist policies. Taking as a premise the notion that free trade would destroy national output, the remainder of the *Impugnación* attempted to refute the "advantages" that the MPF attributed to this system. To sum up, the most fatal blow to Spanish industry would be to establish free ports, naturally, an allusion to a free trade system.

The controversy in the EAP rumbled on, this time in a pamphlet entitled *Reflexiones sobre la cuestión del comercio libre* (1844) by José Arias de Miranda, which was written in defence of Mora. Ibáñez himself wrote a reply in which he suggested a happy medium between "exaggerated restrictions" and "abusive freedom" (Ibáñez 1844c); it was inspired, like his previous writings, by Manuel María Gutiérrez's prohibitionism (Almenar 2020). Somewhat later Juan Antonio Seoane, a contributor to the journal and the guiding light of its theoretical articles, joined the fray with an article in defence of Mora and his general free trade principle, albeit suggesting some "special modifications", especially a gradual liberalisation that would enable domestic industry to take root (Seoane 1844). There are no signs that Mora was involved in the aftermath of the controversy sparked by the MPF.

8.4 The Economics Press

The publication of the DLC and the MPF opened the door to Madrid journalism for Mora. According to his biographers the first link was forged when he joined *El español* as a contributor (EED, 1835–1837, 1845–1848). Unlike the *Eco del comercio* (EDC, 1832–1848), which was in progressive liberal hands, the EED was the major national and international daily newspaper for moderate monarchist constitutional liberalism. It was founded and edited by Andrés Borrego, a former liberal expatriated in Paris and who had taken advantage of the transition to the liberal state to set up a moderate liberal alternative publication. In 1846, Mora probably also contributed to *El Heraldo de Madrid* (EHM, 1842–1854), the mouthpiece of the moderate party which also was another publication representative of the Hispanic conservatism, then led by Ramón María Narváez.

However, the true hallmark of Mora's career in journalism was his participation in other distinguished newspapers in 1840s Madrid. He is associated with two types of periodicals, cultural and economic, and, as part of Spanish liberalism's moderate and pragmatic currents, his work reflected common criteria. His contributions tended to be succinct interpretative essays rather than book reviews or publishing news, a sign of the new forms of journalism that dominated the mid-nineteenth century. Mora was an enormously versatile writer on a range of subjects, from literature and philosophy to politics and political economy, although once again his contributions are not particularly original. He tends to cover familiar ground such as free trade and university studies in Spain. His articles were published at the height of the liberal university reforms, particularly in the far-reaching 1845 "Pidal Plan", which provided the opportunity to modernise philosophy and law teaching, an issue that was at the very heart of his concerns.[11] Lastly, the fact that he also had links with journals that were oriented towards the Hispanic-American world suggests that he wished to continue influencing the region from Spain. The titles of the magazines he edited or contributed to during those years are clear reflections of this topic: the *Revista de España, de Indias y del extranjero* (REIE, 1845–1848), the *Revista Hispano-Americana* (RHA, 1848) and the *Revista española de ambos mundos* (REAM, 1853–1855).[12]

Mora witnessed the boom in the economics press during the 1840s (Almenar 1996), yet he was not involved in an extremely prominent initiative, the short-lived *Revista económica de Madrid* (REM, 1842, 1847). The first issue appeared in 1842, when Mora was not in Spain. It was edited by Eusebio María del Valle, professor of political economy at the *Universidad Literaria de Madrid* and author of a *Curso de economía política* (1846), who had connections with political economy professors at other universities and was the leader of the new generation of protectionist economists—Andrés Borrego (1844), Manuel Colmeiro (1845, 1859) and Manuel María Gutiérrez (1837)—. Mora did not participate in the REM's second phase either, even though it leaned towards moderate free trade (Almenar 2020), perhaps because this phase was as brief as the first—a single volume in 1847, headed by Valle's disciples, specifically Ruperto Navarro Zamorano and José Álvaro de Zafra and prestigious teachers such as Manuel Colmeiro and Manuel de Azpilicueta—.

However, Mora was involved in EAP. As seen, the fortnightly journal was an arm of the *Sociedad Matritense*; while it reported on the Society's

[11] As a result of this spirit of renewal, Mora reissued the *Cursos de ética y lógica* in Madrid in 1845, which had originally appeared in Lima in 1832. He also produced a brief synthesis of John Stuart Mill's *System of Logic* (1843), one of the first accounts of the work to be published in Spain (RHA, 1848, 5–17, 59–71), so that it could be used in universities. Mill was presented as a "disciple of the immortal Bentham" and as the "first who has concentrated all the rules applicable to all the aptitudes of the human soul in a single vast system" (RHA, 1848, 9). On this basis, his book would enable a "true and compact school" of philosophy to be established in Spain, which, according to Mora, "disastrous scholasticism" had failed to do. The current "teaching anarchy" and "lack of system" would be resolved by the treatise written by Mill, whose "service to the sciences in general" was similar to Bentham's service to jurisprudence (RHA, 1848, 71).

[12] Mora also actively contributed to the foundation and first steps of the *Revista universal de la administración* (RUA, 1848–1850), and he also drafted some economic articles. All the evidence suggests that these articles followed his usual subjects, but the impossibility of finding a complete journal series makes it difficult to ascertain the precise scope of his contributions.

activities, it also had a theoretical side, which was expressed through speeches given by officials and its own members, and prize-winning papers. However, Mora's involvement was limited to the controversial MPF, and the fact that he kept his distance from the journal is likely to have been because of the prize, which in the end did not lead to his newly nomination as a member of the Society—Mora had already belonged to it during the Liberal Triennium—. However, there may have been other reasons for his relative absence, perhaps connected with the profile of the publication, which tackled subjects that Mora did not usually cover, such as the emerging "social issue" (pauperism and charity) and the applied arts (agronomy, chemistry, natural history, etc.). It may also have been motivated by the Society's need to maintain multiple ideological positions, evident from the outset in the tension between the first editor Eusebio del Valle's moderate liberalism and the fact that the secretary and a major theoretical reference, Juan Antonio Seoane, was closer to the general principle of free trade (Almenar 2020). Although the second position increasingly gained ground, the EAP never fully embraced it. The contrast between Mora's warm reception of Bastiat's *Sophismes économiques* in 1846 and the deeply critical translation of the work, attributed to Ángel Justo Pasarón and published in the EAP in 19 instalments between January and October 1847, is striking. The journal's distance from the radical free trader that Mora was in those years and from other journals that shared this stance, specifically the *Guía de comercio y Boletín de fomento* (GDC, 1842–1851), could not be clearer.

It was precisely because Mora had always considered this publication to be the genuine defender of "free trade ideas" that he chose it as a means of influencing public opinion on economics during the 1840s. The weekly GDC had been founded in January 1842 with the aim of revealing the early benefits of the 1841 Tariff Law and to continue removing obstacles to trade (GDC, no. 1, 5/I/1842). Its ideological orientation was initially in the hands of Casimiro Rufino, an enthusiastic free trader who edited the magazine during the ten or so years that it was active; from mid-1843, however, Ramón de la Sagra, a progressive liberal and one of the first to introduce "social economics" in Spain outside Say's tradition, had more sway (Sagra 1840).

Mora's contributions to the GDC were infused with great significance and a sense of opportunity, appearing at key moments for maintaining the journal's genuine free trade orientation. His first contribution was in January 1844, the month in which the GDC also published José Montilla's review of Mora's DLC, in which he called the paper "misguided" because it rejected the thesis that the balance of trade was the best measure of national wealth (GDC, no. 106, 10/I/1844). Within two weeks Mora had produced a point-by-point reply from Seville (GDC, no. 108, 24/I/1844), which began by mentioning Barbon, North, Say, Ricardo, Mill, McCulloch and Storch in order to discredit Montilla's claim that Mora was one of the first writers to defend free trade. He then recommended that Montilla should read Vadillo so as to understand the benefits of exporting money and, finally, he asked Montilla to choose between free trade and balance of trade theory, thus calling into question his rhetorical practice—extremely common in the protectionist tradition—of defending anti-free trade positions while at the same time appealing to its benefits. All this had little effect on Montilla, who quickly replied to Mora, accusing him of being "too rigorous" in his treatment of the balance of trade theory and insisting that it could be reconciled with free trade (GDC, no. 99, 31/I/1844; n. 100, 7/II/1844).

Mora replied with a brief note (GDC, no. 109, 28/II/1844). However, much more importantly, he took advantage of this juncture to breathe new life into free trade theories. He did so by means of a forceful strategy that reflects the fact that by early 1844 his activity as journalist in Spain had been completely restored to its former glory. Between 6 March and 19 April, the GDC published a series of five issues with a lengthy summary of Pebrer's *Cinco proposiciones*, which Mora had used extensively in the DLC, and just a month later carried a long excerpt from his "award-winning" MPF (GDC, no. 142, 13/V/1844). In the mid-1840s Spanish free trade circles were thus functioning like a well-oiled lobby, in which Mora was a key player.

Pinning down Mora's role in the GDC in subsequent years is not easy, as many of his articles were published anonymously. In any event, throughout 1844 and 1845 the publication was a battleground for disputing authors and lobbies against the backdrop of the pending tax and tariff reforms, giving a voice to protectionist opinions—on several occasions, those of the Barcelona Board of Trade and the region's textile producers—and free traders alike. However, the GDC's inclination towards the latter became clear when under Casimiro Rufino it became the unofficial mouthpiece for the *Sociedad Mercantil Matritense*, a body that had been created in mid-1844 as a lobby for pro-free trade legislation—though not radical free trade—and a year later its national counterpart, the *Confederación Mercantil Española*, of which Rufino was appointed

Secretary and whose mainly Madrid-based members received the GDC. Both institutions played a notable role in the ideological reflection and militant agitation campaign in the run-up to the 1849 Tariff Law.

Mora fervently embraced this campaign, gradually moving away from his classical foundations, especially McCulloch, in favour of French economist Bastiat's radical and idealised liberalism (Baslé and Gélédan 1991), which would shape his ideological position in the years to come. Mora first met Bastiat in May 1846 when he was starting to gain popularity in Spain[13]; he wrote a review of the first French edition of the *Sophismes économiques* (1846) in the same month, presenting free trade as a

> principle of reasoning, a clear, indisputable, inalienable right, a primitive natural law, which protests against the oppression it has suffered and claims the superiority [...] which has been proved by error and violence for so many centuries. (GDC, no. 229, 20/V/1846)

A succession of anonymous articles appeared over the next three months, perhaps instigated by Mora himself; as their expressive titles show, the author or authors attacked the protectionist system head-on,[14]

[13] At least fourteen of Bastiat's works were translated and published in the cycle from 1846 to 1870, notably the *Sophismes économiques* (1846) and the *Harmonies économiques* (1851), which were also published in Hispanic America (Cabrillo 1978). Among the series of translations was one from French, produced by Elías Bautista Muñoz in 1847 for the *Biblioteca de la Revista Económica de Madrid*, which contained a detailed history of the English League, including speeches by Cobden and Peel, with the aim of applying its principles to France. Its starting point was that political economy "was not an art, but a science" (Bastiat 1847, XV). Nevertheless, Mora's economic thought during this period is a construction based on Say's ideas; its core is classical political economy, particularly McCulloch, and Bastiat is the summit. Therefore, rather than making a theoretical shift, Mora evolved towards Bastiat's rhetoric without renouncing the classical economic principles on which he based his policy and reformist agenda. The entries written by Mora between 1852 and 1855 in the *Enciclopedia Moderna* proved this, as they relied on the consecutive theoretical sources he had used (Say, Mill, McCulloch and Bastiat), although Mora's shift towards Bastiat should not be interpreted as the result of vested interests. For the relationships between vested interests and political economy in nineteenth-century Britain, see Grampp (1960).

[14] See among others: "*Efectos de la libertad de comercio*" (no. 231, 3/VI/1846); "*Perjuicios que causan las aduanas y utilidad de su abolición*" (no. 232, 10/VI/1846); "*España más que ninguna otra nación prosperaría en todos ramos con la abolición completa de sus aduanas*" (no. 233, 17/VI/1846; no. 234, 21/VI/1846); "*Los estancamientos corrompen las buenas costumbres y además de ser injustos por muchos conceptos y perjudiciales, son contrarios a los derechos del ciudadano*" (no. 234, 21/VI/1846); "*Farsas del sistema vigente protector de nuestra industria y comercio*" (no. 236, 8/VII/1846).

borrowing extensively from Flórez Estrada's *Examen imparcial* (1812), evoking Bastiat and lamenting that Vadillo, Preber, Marliani and Mora's works had not even had "the honour of rebuttal".

These writings appeared during the run-up to Cobden's visit to Spain as part of a European tour that began a few months after Robert Peel had abolished the Corn Laws in Britain and the Anti-Corn Law League was dissolved. The visit was a key moment in the free trade offensive in Spain (Almenar and Velasco 1987; Lluch 1988). In September 1846 the GDC initiated the founding of a pro-free trade association along similar lines to the body led by Cobden in England. This was followed by reports of Cobden's visit to France (GDC, no. 246, 16/IX/1846), while similar associations to the entity that the GDC had proposed were founded in Paris, Bordeaux and Marseille (GDC, no. 248, 30/IX/1846), and finally an in-depth account of Cobden's trip to Spain in October and November 1846 appeared. The visit began with an excellent "banquet" in Madrid, organised by the *Confederación Mercantil Española* and which Mora attended (GDC, no. 251, 21/X/1846), and continued with events in Seville and Cadiz. The GDC also encompassed a biographical account of Cobden (GDC, no. 253, 4/XI/1846), to be rounded off by the glowing coverage of this "triumphal tour" that appeared in the British press.[15] Against this background, the GDC republished a paper by Mora in which he refuted a common argument among those who had argued, in the presence of Cobden himself, that free trade was no use to "backward" nations such as Spain (GDC, no. 253, 4/XI/1846).

Meanwhile, the free trade agitation sparked off by Cobden's trip to Spain led to local initiatives to create institutions and a press in support of this trade option. A prime example of this was Cadiz, where in 1847 sectors linked to export agriculture created the *Asociación española para propagar las doctrinas del libre comercio* and its sister newspaper *El propagador del libre comercio* (PLC, 1847–1848). Mora was involved in this publication from the outset; it ran from January 1847 to October 1848 and aimed to combat "the sophistry of protectionist and prohibitionist parties" (PLC, no. 1, 1/I/1847; no. 3, 16/I/1847). The magazine's orientation was left in the hands of a Cadiz free trader who Mora knew very well, José María Vadillo, head of the *Sociedad Económica de Cádiz*, and Antonio de Zulueta, who was secretary; Mora's influence was

[15] On the effects of Cobden's journey in *El clamor público*, *El eco del comercio* and other journals that were contemporaries of the GDC, see Lluch (1988, 74–76).

ultimately marginal, however, as he contributed with only one article, which had already appeared in the GDC (PLC, no. 75, 3/11/1847; no. 76, 10/11/1847).

Mora continued to contribute to the GDC at least until the end of 1847. His writings contained new pro-free trade harangues arguing that trade and tax legislation should be separated once and for all, and he intermingled his old Smithian convictions that the protective system generated monopolies that pushed up prices and punished consumers with the dazzling new theory based on Bastiat and his conviction that current legislation amounted to a "real attack on natural laws" (GDC, no. 308, 21/XI/1847). To Mora, the fact that the "immortal Cobden" had visited Spain had contributed to the "triumph of sound ideas"; now they had to be put into practice. His reform agenda was revealed in 1848 during the lead up to the 1849 Tariff Law (REIE, VIII, 19–31; GDC, no. 269, 21/II/1847), although it was actually nothing more than a slightly better-organised version of what had already been proposed in the DLC: abolishing prohibitionism, internal customs and the costly systems for supervising transport and collecting duty. Meanwhile, tariffs should be *ad valorem*, as in 1843, and not exceed 15%, which guaranteed "the domestic producer a considerable advantage", and any resulting loss of revenue would be made up by a tax on profits ("net product"), rather than by taxing consumption, as suggested in the DLC. However, they contained scant reference to the Anti-Corn Law League, despite he was living in London when it was created.[16]

These articles also revealed Mora's interest in distribution. In a commentary on a paper by Scottish politician Henry Brougham he argued that trade was the best means of dissolving concentrations of economic and political power—a kind of "counter-poison to the property-owning oligarchy"—, that it promoted more equal wealth distribution and, as the example of Britain showed, when combined with good education and the spread of useful knowledge, it guaranteed social order and material improvements for the poorer classes (GDC, no. 287, 30/VI/1847).

Mora's involvement in the GDC appears to have waned from late 1847, although he is more than likely to have authored other anonymous texts, as stated in his articles. However, once Ramón de la Sagra was restored to a leading role in 1848 and the 1849 Tariff Law was finalised, the GDC itself

[16] In any event, the differences between authors on a suitable tariff level seem smaller at this time. While Mora set customs duty at 15%, Seoane set it between 12% and 20% in the EAP. Cobden advocated a rate of 20% on imported foreign goods and tariff-free imports of the raw materials needed for domestic industry (Lluch 1988, 80).

underwent a certain decline. Under the new title of *Guía del comercio, industria y agricultura*, it became a publication for official information and statistics until its closure in February 1851. In any event, as Mora noted, the GDC's free trade orientation was not matched by other journals of its time, including the EAP, which barely mentioned Cobden's trip—even though he was welcomed by the leaders of the *Sociedad Matritense* during his stay in Madrid, which honoured him with membership—.

Mora's key contribution to the GDC was his journalism. His economic stance also cast a shadow—albeit a faint one—over the cultural journals, which either reprinted earlier articles as the REIE did (REIE, VIII, 19–31), or carried original work like the REAM. The latter expressed a preference for "the English school presided over by Peel" (REAM, no 1, VII), although its review section revealed its clear leanings towards French authors Blanqui, Coquelin and Guillaumin, and Chevalier, whose work on "the progress and future of civilisation" opened the journal. However, in his only article with economics content and the last of his contributions to *moderate* Spain, still in 1853, Mora once again lashed out against the mercantile and prohibitive system. As a symbol of the intellectual journey that he had taken since the publication of the DLC ten years earlier, his source was now Bastiat, who tacitly inspired him with the idea of free trade as an "indisputable" law, based on "eternal, unalterable, all-embracing" principles, and also marked the deeply anti-statist tone of his article: "the lesser the individual sacrifice for society's ends, the more perfect the legislation" (REAM, I, 561–70).[17]

8.5 Final Remarks

Spain's gradual reception of classical economics began with the arrival of Smith's WN in the late eighteenth century and was a key factor in the relentless battle waged by supporters of free trade and protectionism throughout the following century. Free trade's limited success as regards reforms is one of Spain's most obvious fault lines where classical ideas were concerned: Figuerola's 1869 Tariff Law, the most "free trade" tariff in the nineteenth century, was still moderately protectionist (Comín 2000a,

[17] Mora also contributed to Revista universal de la administración (RUA, 1848–1849), especially during 1848, writing articles that brought very few changes concerning his previous contributions. The journal focused on the amelioration of public administration under a liberal environment, paying particular emphasis on the Treasury. The journal was edited by José de Olona and involved very prominent members of moderate liberalism, such as Antonio Alcalá Galiano, Eusebio María del Valle and Manuel María Gutiérrez.

639). However, the fact that the free trade option had only minority appeal in Spain did not prevent it from having significant influence. Leaving aside its Enlightenment forerunners, this alternative had a major theoretical basis as early as 1812, set out in Flórez Estrada's *Examen imparcial* (Almenar 1976), and had emerged distinctly during the constitutional periods of the *Cortes de Cadiz* and the Liberal Triennium. However, due to a confluence of multiple factors (liberal economic reforms, regular parliamentary activity, greater institutionalisation of the political economy and an increase in the number of supporters of free trade), it was in the 1840s when free trade shifted from the intellectual to the political sphere; the decade was marked by debates on the 1841 and 1849 tariff reforms and these eventually spread beyond academic discussion and entered the political arena, against a backdrop of growing social discord (Costas 2000, 471). Given this scenario it is not surprising that anti-prohibitionist literature found a new lease of life in works by authors such as Pita Pizarro, Pebrer, Vadillo, Marliani and Mora. The latter played an outstanding role in setting up this alternative.[18] His untiring work as a journalist from 1843 to 1853, which has been thoroughly covered in this chapter, shows his leading role in spreading free trade ideology. However, his extensive work as one of the great Spanish propagators of the ideas of the classical school cannot be properly understood without taking into account his previous career during the long years of exile in London and the Hispanic-American republics. His eventual return to Spain brought about a gradual shift from an economic model akin to Smith-McCulloch to one that was closer to Bastiat.

[18] Mora's commitment to spreading free trade in Spain and Hispanic America can be compared to the global advocacy of trade liberalisation by the Board of Trade official John Bowring. Both were firmly committed to spreading free trade across national borders, had close contact with McCulloch, were convinced of the "intellectual persuasiveness of abstract theory", considered free trade a concept that could be adapted to different political and cultural contexts and used the printing press as a means of forming public opinion and persuading the government to adopt free trade policies. Nevertheless, unlike Mora during these years, Bowring had clear economic interests and was an agent of Lord Palmerstone; see Todd (2008, 376–77).

Bibliography

Books[19]

Mora, José Joaquín de. 1821. *Discurso inaugural que pronunció en el Ateneo español D. José Joaquín de Mora, uno de sus socios, al abrir un curso de Derecho Natural, el día 7 de marzo de 1821*. Madrid: Imprenta del censor. Reed. 1843. Sevilla; Establecimiento tipográfico.

Mora, José Joaquín de. 1840. *Elementos de lógica escritos por D. José Joaquín de Mora, según la escuela de Edimburgo. Impreso en Lima y reimpreso en Sucre*. Sucre: Imprenta del Congreso.

Mora, José Joaquín de. 1843. *De la libertad de comercio, por José Joaquín de Mora*. Sevilla: Establecimiento tipográfico, Imprenta de Carlos Rubio y compañía.

Mora, José Joaquín de. 1844. *Memoria sobre los puertos francos, por José Joaquín de Mora*. Madrid: Imprenta de Benito Lamparero y compañía.

Mora, José Joaquín de. c.1844b. *El libro de la escuela o Catecismo de conocimientos útiles destinado a la primera enseñanza*. Sevilla: Establecimiento tipográfico, Plaza del silencio.

Mora, José Joaquín de. 1845. *Ejercicios de lectura, o Extractos de literatura moderna en prosa y verso, para el uso de los alumnos del Colegio de S. Felipe Neri de Cádiz*. Cádiz: Imprenta de la viuda e hijo de Bosch.

Translations and Reeditions

Lista, Alberto. 1844. *Ensayos literarios y críticos por D. Alberto Lista y Aragón, con un prólogo por D. José Joaquín de Mora*. Seville: Calvo Rubio y compañía.

Primary Sources

Álvarez Guerra, Juan. 1841. *Proyecto de una ley agraria o código rural*. Madrid: Miguel de Burgos.

Bastiat, Frédéric. 1846. *Sophismes économiques*. Paris: Guillaumin.

Bastiat, Federico. 1847. *Cobden y la Liga o la agitación inglesa en favor de la libertad de comercio, obra escrita en francés por Don M. Federico Bastiat*. Madrid: Imprenta y Establecimiento de Grabados de Don Baltasar González.

Bastiat, Frédéric. 1851. *Harmonies économiques*. Paris.

[19] On the prolix reprints of the *Catecismos*, *Cursos* and other works of Mora in the Hispanic world, see Roldán (2003), Macintyre (2018) and Medina (2022).

Blanqui, Jérôme-Adolphe. 1837. *Histoire de l'économie politique en Europe, depuis les anciens jusqu'à nos jours suivie d'une bibliographie raisonnée des principaux ouvrages d'économie politique*. Paris: Guillaumin.

Blanqui, Adolphe. 1840. *Compendio elemental de economía política*. Paris: Rosa.

Borrego, Andrés. 1844. *Principios de economía política con aplicación a la reforma de aranceles de aduanas*. Madrid: Imprenta Soc. de oper. del mismo Arte.

Colmeiro, Manuel. 1845. *Tratado elemental de economía política ecléctica*. Madrid: Calleja.

Colmeiro, Manuel. 1859. *Principios de economía política*. Madrid: G. Alhambra.

Droz, Joseph. 1842. *Economía política o principios de la ciencia de las riquezas*. Madrid: Viuda de Calleja e hijos.

Ferrier, François-Louis-Auguste. 1803. *Essai sur les ports francs*. Bayonne: Chez Fauvet.

Flórez Estrada. Álvaro. 1812. *Examen imparcial de las disensiones de la América con la España, de los medios de su reconciliación y de la prosperidad de todas las naciones*. Cádiz: Imprenta Manuel Ximena de Carreño.

Flórez Estrada, Alvaro 1828. *Curso de economía política*. Londres: D.M. Calero.

Garnier, Joseph. 1848. *Elementos de economía política, por José Garnier*. Madrid: Imprenta y librería de la publicidad.

Gutiérrez, Manuel María. 1837. *Impugnación a las cinco proposiciones de Pebrer sobre los grandes males que causa la ley de aranceles a la nación en general, a la Cataluña en particular, y a las mismas fábricas catalanas*. Madrid: Imprenta de Don Marcelino Calero.

Ibáñez, José María. 1844a. "Memoria premiada [...] sobre si es o no conveniente a una nación celebrar tratados de comercio con otras más adelantadas en industria". *El Amigo del País*, vol. I, no. 7 (1/6/1844), 193–223.

Ibáñez, José María. 1844b. "Impugnación a la memoria sobre los puertos francos". *El Amigo del País*, vol. I, no. 10 (15/VII/1844), 301–316.

Ibáñez, José María. 1844c. "Sobre los puertos francos". *El Amigo del País*, vol. II, no. 14 (9/15/1844), 17–20.

Marliani, M. (1842). *De la influencia del sistema prohibitivo en la agricultura, industria, comercio y rentas públicas*. Madrid: D. J. Cuesta.

McCulloch, John Ramsay. 1825. *The Principles of Political Economy, with a Sketch of the Rise and Progress of the Science*. Edinburgh and London: Adam and Charles Black-Longman, Brown, Green and Longmans.

McCulloch, John Ramsay. 1842. "Political Economy". In *The Encylopedia Britannica or Dictionary of Arts, Science, and General Literature*. 7th ed, vol. XVII, 258-307. Edinburgh: Adam and Charles Black.

Mengotti, Francesco. 1819. *Il Colbertismo*. Florence: Piatti.

Paso y Delgado, Nicolás. 1841. *Elementos de economía política*. Granada: Imprenta de Benavides.

Pebrer, Pablo. 1837. *Cinco proposiciones sobre los grandes males que causa la ley de aranceles a la nación en general, a la Cataluña en particular, a las mismas fábricas catalanas.* London and Madrid: Imprenta española de D. V. Torras.

Rossi, Pellegrino. 1840. *Curso de economía política (año escolar de 1836–1837).* Madrid: Boix.

Sagra, Ramón de la. 1840. *Lecciones de economía social dadas en el Ateneo científico y literario de Madrid.* Madrid: Ferrer y C.

Smith, Adam. 1776 [1976b]. *An Inquiry into the Nature and Causes of the Wealth of Nations*, edited by Roy H. Campbell, Andrew S. Skinner and William B. Todd. Oxford: OUP.

Sociedad Económica Barcelonesa de Amigos del País. 1838. *Refutación de las cinco proposiciones del Señor Pebrer contra el sistema prohibitivo.* Barcelona: Juan Francisco Piferrer.

Torrente, Mariano. 1835. *Revista general de la economía política*, 3 vols. La Habana: Jordán.

Valle Santoro, Marqués de. 1830. *Memoria sobre la balanza de comercio y examen del estado actual de la riqueza de España.* Madrid: Imprenta R. Vergés.

Secondary Sources

Almenar, Salvador. 1976. "Agrarismo y librecambio en la crisis del Antiguo Régimen". *Información Comercial Española* 517, 58–81.

Almenar, Salvador. 1980. "Estudio Preliminar". In Álvaro Flórez Estrada, *Curso de economía política*, edited by Salvador Almenar, vol. I, XXXV–CXXIII. Madrid: IEF.

Almenar, Salvador. 1996. "Economic Thought in Spanish Periodical Publications of the 18th and 19th Centuries: an Introduction". *History of Economic Ideas* IV–3, 119–47.

Almenar, Salvador. 2000a. "El desarrollo del pensamiento económico clásico en España". In *Economía y economistas españoles. Vol. IV. La economía clásica*, edited by Enrique Fuentes, 7–92. Barcelona: Galaxia Gütenberg and Círculo de Lectores.

Almenar, Salvador. 2000b. "Flórez Estrada y la economía política clásica". In *Economía y economistas españoles. Vol. IV. La economía clásica*, edited by Enrique Fuentes, 369–411. Barcelona: Galaxia Gütenberg and Círculo de Lectores.

Almenar, Salvador. 2014. "The Reception and Dissemination of David Ricardo's Ideas in Spain". In *The Reception of David Ricardo in Continental Europe and Japan*, edited by Gilbert Faccarello y Masashi Izumo, 152–77. London and New York: Routledge.

Almenar, Salvador. 2020. *El fulgor de la libertad. Bastiat, el librecambio, el progreso y la democracia en España (1846–1850)*, Madrid: RACMP.

Almenar, Salvador and Rogelio Velasco. 1987. "Una etapa en la consolidación del librecambio en España: el viaje de Richard Cobden por Andalucía". In *Andalucía en el pensamiento económico*, edited by Gumersindo Ruiz, 105–18. Málaga: Arguval.

Artola, Miguel. 1973. *La burguesía revolucionaria (1808–1869)*. Madrid: Alianza.

Artola, Miguel. 1977. *Partidos y programas políticos (1808–1936)*, 2 vols. Madrid: Aguilar.

Astigarraga, Jesús, Javier Usoz and Juan Zabalza. 2023. "José Joaquín de Mora and the Debates on the Free Trade Policy in Spain (1843–1853)", *History of Economic Ideas* XXXI-1, 11–39.

Baslé, Maurice and Alain Gélédan. 1991. "Frédéric Bastiat, théoricien et militant du libre-échange". In *L'économie politique en France au XIXe siècle*, edited by Yves Breton and Michel Luftalla, 83–110. Paris: Economica.

Beltrán, Miguel. 1977. *Ideologías y gasto público en España (1814–1860)*. Madrid: IEF and Ministerio de Hacienda.

Cabrillo, Francisco. 1978. "Traducciones al español de libros de economía política (1800–1880)". *Moneda y Crédito* 147, 71–103.

Carr, Raymond. 1968. *España, 1808–1939*. Barcelona: Ariel.

Comín, Francisco. 2000a. "Los economistas clásicos y los políticos liberales ante los problemas de la economía española". In *Economía y economistas españoles. Vol. IV. La economía clásica*, edited by Enrique Fuentes, 621–703. Barcelona: Galaxia Gütenberg and Círculo de Lectores.

Costas, Antón. 2000. "Industrialización y cuestión arancelaria en España. Reflexiones en torno al librecambismo de Laureano Figuerola". In *Economía y economistas españoles. Vol. IV. La economía clásica*, edited by Enrique Fuentes, 459–481. Barcelona: Galaxia Gütenberg and Círculo de Lectores.

Del Valle, Eusebio María. 1842. Curso de Economía Política, Madrid, Imp. del Colegio Nacional de Sordo-Mudos.

Estapé, Fabián. 1971. *La reforma tributaria de 1845*. Madrid: IEF.

Fernández Sebastián, Javier. 2012b. "Liberalismo en España (1810–1850). La construcción de un concepto y la forja de una identidad política". In *La aurora de la libertad. Los primeros liberalismos en el mundo iberoamericano*, edited by Javier Fernández Sebastián, 236–301. Madrid: Marcial Pons.

Fontana, Biancamaria. 1985a. Rethinking the Politics of Commercial Society: The *Edinburgh Review, 1802–1832*. Cambridge: CUP.

Fontana, Josep. 1973a. *Cambio económico y actitudes políticas en la España del siglo XVIII*. Barcelona: Ariel.

Fontana, Josep. 1973b. *Hacienda y Estado en la crisis final del Antiguo Régimen español, 1823–1833*. Madrid: IEF.

Garrorena, Ángel. 1974. *El Ateneo de Madrid y la teoría de la monarquía liberal, 1836–1847*. Madrid: IEF.

González Pizarro, José Antonio. 1984. "Don José Joaquín de Mora, Cónsul español en Londres (1850–1858)". *Boletín de la Academia Chilena de Historia* 51, 353–67.

Grampp, William Dyer. 1960. *The Manchester School of Economics.* Stanford and London: Stanford University Press and OUP.

Kliesser, R. Grant. 2021. "An Empire of Free Ports. British Commerce Imperialism in the 1776 Free Port Act". *The Journal of British Studies* 60–2, 334–61.

Lluch, Ernest. 1973. *El pensament econòmic a Catalunya (1760–1840)*. Barcelona: Edicions 62.

Lluch, Ernest. 1988. "La 'gira trionfal' de Cobden per Espanya (1846)". *Recerques* XXI, 71–90.

Lluch, Ernest and Salvador Almenar. 2000. "Difusión e influencia de los economistas clásicos en España (1776–1870)". In *Economía y economistas españoles. Vol. IV. La economía clásica*, edited by Enrique Fuentes, 93–170. Barcelona: Galaxia Gütenberg and Círculo de Lectores.

Martín Rodríguez, Manuel. 1989. "La institucionalización de los estudios de Economía Política en la universidad española (1784–1857)". In *Elementos de economía política con aplicación particular a España*, by Marqués de Valle Santoro, XI–CCXXXIV. Madrid: IEF.

Martínez Marín, Jesús A. 2009. *Vivir de la pluma. La profesionalización del escritor, 1836–1936*. Madrid: Marcial Pons.

O'Brien, Denis Patrick. 1992. *J. R. McCulloch. A Study in Classical Economics*, London and Aldershot: Gregg Revivals and Routledge.

Paganelli, Maria Pia. 2022. "Adam Smith and Economic Development in Theory and Practice: A Rejection of the Stadial Model?". *Journal of the History of Economic Thought* 44–1, 95–104.

Pérez Sánchez, Aránzazu. 2005. *El Liceo artístico y literario de Madrid (1837–1851)*. Madrid: Fundación Universitaria Española.

Reeder, John. 2003. "Nota bibliográfica sobre un economista español decimonónico". In *Estudios de historia y de pensamiento económico. Homenaje a Francisco Bustelo García del Real*, 295–99. Madrid: Universidad Complutense.

Robledo, Ricardo. 1993. *Economistas y reformadores españoles: la cuestión agraria (1760–1935)*. Madrid: Ministerio de agricultura, pesca y alimentación.

Ruiz Salvador, Antonio. 1971. *El Ateneo científico, literario y artístico de Madrid.* Londres: Tamesis Books.

Salvadori, Neri and Rodolfo Signorino. 2013."The Classical Notion of Competition Revisited". *History of Political Economy* 45–1, 149–75.

Seoane, Juan Antonio. 1844. "Sobre el uso de los puertos españoles", EAP, II, n. 19, 30/11/1844, pp. 174–191.

Schwartz, Pedro. 1970. "*De la libertad del comercio*, por Joaquín de Mora: una defensa del libre-cambio a mediados del siglo XIX". *Anales de economía* 5–8, 189–224.

Schwartz, Pedro. 1999. "Estudio Preliminar". In *De la libertad del comercio*, by José Joaquín de Mora, VIII–XLIX. Madrid: IEF.

Smith, Robert Sidney. 1968. "El pensamiento económico de José Joaquín de Mora", *Humanitas* IX, 595–607.

Tazzara, Corey. 2017, *The Free Port of Livorno and the Tranformation of the Mediterranean World*. Oxford: OUP.

Todd, David. 2008. "John Bowring and the Global Dissemination of Free Trade". *The Historical Journal* 51–2, 373–297.

Vallejo, Rafael. 2018, "La política comercial liberal desde 1820 a 1869. Entre la apertura exterior y las resistencias prohibicionistas". *Áreas. Revista Internacional de Ciencias Sociales* 37, 61–77.

Varela, Joaquín. 1983–1984. "La Constitución española de 1837: una Constitución transaccional". *Revista de derecho político* 20, 95–106.

Velasco, Rogelio. 1989. "El debate de la ley de reforma de aranceles de 1841: librecambistas frente a proteccionistas". *Revista de historia económica*, 7, extra 2, 95–98.

Villacorta, Francisco. 1980. *Burguesía y cultura. Los intelectuales españoles en la sociedad liberal, 1808–1931*. Madrid: Siglo XXI.

CHAPTER 9

Mora and the *Enciclopedia Moderna* (1851–1855)

9.1 Introduction: Initiating the Trade in Ideas

Between 1851 and 1855 Granada-born printer and publisher Francisco de Paula Mellado produced the main volumes of the *Enciclopedia moderna* (EM), the first general knowledge encyclopaedia to appear in Spain. That it was an ambitious project is clear from the number of volumes—there were eventually 39—the range of subjects covered—around 50, including political economy and public finance—and the list of contributors, which included distinguished university teachers and intellectuals of the day.[1] As this chapter discusses in some detail, the economics entries were written by Mora and constitute one of the pinnacles of his writings on economics as a whole.[2]

Over and above its content and authors, Mellado's project was a vivid reflection of the maturing of significant underlying processes in Spanish society which directly affected the demand and supply structure in the

[1] The authors included José María Antequera (responsible for the Legislation, Public Finance, and Government section), Facundo Goñi (Socialism) and Augusto de Burgos (Agriculture), along with Antonio Ferrer del Río, Modesto Lafuente and other renowned liberals of the day (Mellado 1851–1855).

[2] A first interpretation of the issue of this Chapter appears in Astigarraga and Zabalza (2007) and a re-edition of some of the EM's most important economics entries, in Astigarraga et al. (2022a). Mora had expressed his support for the spreading of knowledge through dictionaries and encyclopaedias while in Chile (EMC, no. 1, 1/IV/1828, 50–51).

J. Astigarraga et al., *The Economic Legacy of José Joaquín de Mora*, Palgrave Studies in the History of Economic Thought,
https://doi.org/10.1007/978-3-031-49446-8_9

publishing market (Brotel 1993, 179–331). On the demand side, a work like the EM can only be understood in the context of a social fabric such as that in Spain, which was gradually becoming more urbanised and had a population to whom literacy was no longer just for minorities but extended to artisans, small traders and other sectors of the working classes: by the mid-nineteenth century, the literacy rate in Spain it is estimated to have been between 25% and 40% of the population, depending on whether the context was rural or urban, and rising to 50% in Madrid. The rise in income levels and consequent emergence of a stable and thriving middle class created a market with a steadily growing demand for works such as the EM; that is, educational publications whose goal was to promote general knowledge to a larger and more diverse audience. In Madrid itself, the appearance of cafés and taverns, "talk societies" and reading groups brought about a change in reading habits and the exchange of ideas, encouraging free debate and a cultural revival when the dark years of absolutism had been left behind and the right to free expression and press freedom gradually re-established.

Changes on the publishing side were no less significant. The dismantling of the guilds (1834–1836) established freedom of industry, and this was accompanied by advances in printing techniques—the introduction of continuous paper, mechanical presses and new letter casting systems—which led to reduced costs and increased output. During the 1840s the old artisanal printing presses inherited from the Ancien Régime were gradually replaced by modern printing companies, which were both more productive and more capable of adapting to the new demand. The increase in the availability of subscriptions, delivery services and public libraries fostered the rise of new non-specialist publishing formats such as dictionaries, handbooks, guides and encyclopaedias, aimed at spreading knowledge of all kinds. It is no coincidence, then, that the early 1840s witnessed the first attempts to publish a general encyclopaedia in Spain, and that some of the most prestigious publishers of the day competed in this sector of the industry.[3] Encyclopaedia-type works covering economic issues, which appeared in the wake of the "rapid, widespread and enduring" dissemination of the writings of Say and his disciples (Lluch and Almenar 2000; Menudo and O'Kean 2005, 2019), experienced a notable upsurge

[3] Ignacio Boix attempted this ten years before the EM appeared, but his project never progressed beyond the letter A (12 vols.). It also carried entries on economics due to José Morales Santisteban (Boix 1842–1845).

during the 1820s and 1830s, when dictionaries covering trade, politics, technology and agriculture with substantial economics content began to multiply (Astigarraga et al. 2001, 28–38). In fact, this "golden age" of Spanish encyclopaedias was effectively brought an end by the publication of the EM; the successful enterprise not only reached its peak via the subscription system, but also had a remarkable print run for its time. Although it is not known how many copies were published or who their recipients were, the fact that it is still found in many libraries in Spain bears witness to its importance as a publishing venture.[4] Estimates place the number of copies in circulation in 1863 at around 4000.[5]

9.2 Francisco de Paula Mellado and the *Enciclopedia Moderna*

The EM's publisher Francisco de Paula Mellado (Granada, 1807-Madrid, 1876) is known to have left his home town and settled in Madrid at the beginning of the *Sexenio Absolutista*.[6] However, it was in the early 1830s that he began to carve out a niche in the Madrid literary scene as a publisher of his own works and translations within the emerging romanticism movement. After the death of Ferdinand VII in 1833, he made the most of the new laws of freedom of the press and printing to begin a fruitful and uninterrupted career as an entrepreneur and publisher of literary and cultural newspapers, albeit on a small scale as guild regulations were still in force and technical progress was rather slow. Mellado was very close to his brother-in-law, the historian Modesto Lafuente, and from then on operated within the moderate currents of liberalism, contributing to the emergence of liberal and cultural social activities in Madrid in the second half of the 1830s through his participation in the *Ateneo* and the *Liceo Artístico* and the promotion of reading groups.

Mellado's career path took a radical turn in the 1840s when he embarked on the modernisation of his publishing house, following the lead of other local publishers such as *Casa Boix*, which was owned by his

[4] According to the *Catálogo Colectivo del Patrimonio* (CCPB) it is kept by over a hundred libraries in Spain.

[5] The EM did not match the figures of Mellado's extremely widely circulated *Biblioteca popular económica*, which had a print run of 11,000 copies, but Lafuente's successful *Diccionario de historia española* attracted 1600 subscribers (Martínez Marín 2018, 193).

[6] The details are taken from Martínez Marín's excellent biography of Mellado (2018).

chief competitor Ignacio Boix (Peñas 2018). Inspired by French publishing house Didot, in 1843 he set up one of the first companies in Spain to cast letters for printing, creating a mechanical typography that could be used in printing, engraving, stereotyping and lithography. The *Establecimiento tipográfico de Don Francisco de Paula Mellado* became one of the most prosperous print shops in Madrid, and although he also made numerous forays into the world of banking, finance and insurance, Mellado became a journalist, bookseller, printer and distributor, ending up as a "fully-fledged publisher" who, by milking the subscription and delivery systems, "published everything" and left no title or subject untouched (Martínez Marín 2018, 149). One of the business activities closest to his heart was publishing educational books, both written in Spanish and translated from French, in the form of either popular economics or Spanish collections as well as handbooks, guides, dictionaries and encyclopaedias covering all disciplines, from history—he published Lafuente's successful *Historia general de España* (1850–1867)—to geography, statistics and arts and crafts. Of all these projects the EM was undoubtedly his most ambitious, as well as the main one to deal with economic issues.[7]

Mellado was thus the architect of the process by which the typographical Ancien Régime was transformed into the modern literature and publishing market. This was clearly apparent during the 1840s, in a context of increased demand—including for the first time Hispanic- American countries, where Mellado owned bookshops and attempted to reduce the prevalence of French books—and the gradual professionalisation of the figure of the author and publisher (Martínez Marín 2018, 37–44; Peñas 2018). There was open competition between ambitious publishing houses (Boix, Gaspar and Roig, Maristany, etc.), all heavily influenced by French models (Brotel 1993, 229–33), many of which—Mellado included—had workshops in Paris. Mellado had to learn to operate within the market economy, and at the same time he became aware of the opportunities it provided for the spreading of knowledge as a key element in the consolidation of a liberal society. More specifically, it was about the figure of the journalist, publisher and printer who is committed to the ideas that he propagates in his books, which he uses to shape and guide public opinion in support of the liberal cause (Villacorta 1980, 323). There can be no

[7] Mellado also published the applied arts work *Diccionario de artes* (1856–1857), which in reality was a translation of the *Dictionnaire des arts* (1845–1847) complied by Laboulaye (1856–1857).

doubt that, over and above the specific business interests that it may have awakened, the EM was also a response to the desire to circulate a body of accurate technical and theoretical knowledge. Above all Mellado sought to fulfil the two main maxims of his publishing enterprises, to entertain and to educate, in accordance with a civilising vision in which general education and the circulation of knowledge were prerequisites for attaining the public good (Mellado 1851). At the same time, however, the EM illustrated the impact of the introduction of a system of "general freedom" in Spain, based on the principles of free competition and free trade. In this sense it does not seem unrelated to the strategy of the Spanish free trade movement, which, not without difficulty, in the midst of a liberal reform process that would put an end to the legacy of the Ancien Régime, had entered a period of optimism as a result of Cobden's visit to Spain.

9.3 The *Enciclopedia Moderna*'s Formal Features and Production Stages

Producing the finished version of the EM was a long and drawn-out process. The first 33 volumes were published between 1851 and 1855 and two new volumes with the title of "Supplement" were added in the latter year. Four more volumes appeared from 1865 to 1867, all containing economics entries, although they were less interesting and, more importantly, had limited analytical scope. The most significant economics content is therefore to be found in the original volumes.

The EM's formal features are remarkably modern compared to those of other Spanish encyclopaedias of the day (Martínez Marín 2018, 189–93). Entries are arranged alphabetically, usually include a carefully compiled and up-to-date bibliography and are grouped according to topic. There are approximately fifty core topics, which can be classed under the following disciplines: history and geography; moral philosophy and religion; law and legislation; literature and language; logic and mathematics, and political economy.

The EM's relative modernity with respect to questions of form is likely to have been a reflection of the *Encyclopédie moderne. Dictionnaire abrégé des sciences, des lettres, des arts, de l'industrie, de l'agriculture et du commerce*, published between 1846 and 1851 by Firmin Didot's sons Ambroise and Hyacinthe and edited by Léon Renier. Having analysed various encyclopaedic collections of the day—including the latest edition of the *Encyclopaedia*

Britannica and the collections published in German by Friedrich Arnold Brockhaus and Joseph Meyer—, Mellado felt that the most complete publication was Didot's second edition (Mellado, 1851–1855, 37 vols.). In fact, he set up business contacts with Didot so that he would allow him to translate various entries and include them in the EM, as eventually happened, and also to buy the 360 geographical plates illustrating the *Encyclopédie moderne*, which were published in the EM in an *Atlas* supplementing the main volumes (Mellado 1851–1855, I, IX). In spite of this close relationship, however, the EM was in no way a translation of Didot's *Encyclopédie moderne*. Mellado believed scientific principles to be universal, although their specific application varied from country to country (Mellado 1851–1855, I, VII), and the EM thus aimed to be original—a "truly Spanish" work—in which special attention was paid to the country's circumstances. This meant incorporating a new added value into many entries, including those that covered economics issues.

The relative weight of the economics entries in the EM as a whole is by no means negligible: even without taking into account the economics ideas scattered among the entries on borderline disciplines such as moral philosophy and rural economics, there are over a hundred political economy entries, taking up around 900 pages. They are classified under three main headings: political economy, which undoubtedly includes the most relevant entries, trade and industry and, finally, public finance. All the entries were published anonymously, so it is not possible to be absolutely certain who wrote the economics texts. There was probably more than one author, and the entries also correspond to three very distinct stages in the EM's production.

The first stage is admittedly very short and is essentially limited to Volume I. It includes several political economy entries but they are of little academic value; moreover, most of them are taken from Didot's *Encyclopédie*. This is probably because there was no overall planning for the economics content; while Mellado introduces many of the authors of the entries covering specific topics in the "*Prólogo*", he omits to mention the writer responsible for the economics content. In any event, whatever the author's identity, he did far more than simply translating articles from the *Encyclopédie*. Not only are several of the entries in Volume I original, but they are specifically geared towards Spanish circumstances; the "Customs" entry, for example, contains a well-argued defence of the application of free trade principles in Spain. Although several authors may have contributed the economics entries, there is no shift in the ideological framework that seems to have been adopted from the very beginning of the work.

The second stage runs from Volume II to XXVII and is fundamental from the point of view of economic thought, as it includes the largest number of entries and the most significant from an analytical and applied perspective. It is important to appreciate the fact that although some ideas are repeated because of the strict alphabetical order used, the entries retain a tight internal logic and together create a coherent economic discourse with its own personality. The fact that these entries were undoubtedly carefully planned endows them with an unquestionable unity, discernible not only in their common analytical basis, but also in their defence of the same economic policy guidelines. Mora was responsible for this overall design, and he also wrote these entries. His subsequent departure from the EM for reasons that are unknown—perhaps related to his new post of Spanish consul in London—would explain why there was a noticeable change in the economics content in later volumes.

In fact, Mora seems to have had no connection whatsoever with the economics entries in the work's third stage, which runs from Volume XXVIII to XXXIII. Although these entries are unimportant in terms of their number and quality, they introduce a political orientation to the EM that had previously been somewhat lacking: concern with the "social question". In short, what is absolutely clear is that the EM's economic core lies in Volumes II to XXVII and was written by Mora.

9.4 The Author of the Economics Entries: Mora

There can be no doubt that Mellado and Mora were close; not only did they socialise in the same places in Madrid, but Mellado had published several of Mora's works on his return from exile, as Ignacio Boix had also done. However, there is no documentary evidence of the relationship between the two men with regard to the creation of the EM, as noted in some previous studies and clearly shown more recently (Astigarraga and Zabalza 2007).

Mellado probably chose Mora because of their undoubted ideological affinities. Like Mora, Mellado did not hold political office, nor did he operate as a party man, fitting in with moderate liberal currents and publishing Thiers and Guizot's works in Spain. He supported the idea of exploring a third way between moderates and progressives and had no sympathy with revolutionary tendencies and was highly critical of the

Revolution of 1854, which put the working classes behind the barricades in Madrid, ended the Moderate Decade and ushered in the *Bienio Progresista* (Artola 1973, 222–28). These affinities extended to the economics sphere: Mellado admired Tory Robert Peel's liberal free trade policies (Martínez Marín 2018, 298–301) and there were signs of this in his previous works, which could be considered precursors to the EM. Mora backed the free trade journal GDC and Mellado had included articles from it supporting Spanish tariff reform in the *Revista enciclopédica* (RE, 1846–1847), a monthly publication that was free to subscribers to the successful *Biblioteca popular económica* (1844–1863; RE, no. 3, XII/1846, 93–95). There are clearer points of continuity with the EM in a later venture: the *Instrucción para el pueblo* (IPEP; Mellado 1851), an ambitious but ultimately doomed project that involved the weekly publication of treatises, which were usually translations, covering a broad range of subjects and essentially aimed at a general audience (Martínez Marín 2018, 187–89). In the end the project produced only 100 hundred treatises, including "*Principios de economía política*", "arranged from the French original" and no doubt a summary of a handbook by one of Say's disciples, and a second instalment about statistics (Mellado 1851, II, 2913–44, 2945–76).[8] Mora did not feature among the IPEP authors, but other writers who joined the EM staff later did, among them Augusto de Burgos, author of lengthy contributions on agronomy and rural economy in both works, and José María Antequera. The latter was responsible for the first of the political economy treatises mentioned above, but his conservative jurist background did not seem altogether suitable for injecting the liberal content that Mellado wanted into the EM, so that he put Antequera in charge of the Legislation, Finance and Administration entries and was then able to turn to Mora.

The signs that Mora wrote the economics contributions in the EM's second and strongest stage could not be clearer. It has already been noted that these entries were planned by a single author; moreover, the consistency of their written style seems to imply that they were also the work of one writer. It is important to underline that, along with the financial survival guaranteed by participating in the *Enciclopedia*—Mellado paid his contributors by the column—, Mora's involvement can be explained by

[8] The work also contained treatises on accountancy, public works, railways, statistics and numerous tracts on rural economics, as well as industrial and commercial legislation, also in a rural context.

his continued interest in producing entries for a future dictionary of political economy. It is only necessary to recall the noteworthy set of Mora's articles published in the EMC in Santiago de Chile in 1828–1829—that is, a quarter of a century before the EM—in which he addressed some of the same issues. However, there is even more conclusive evidence of Mora's involvement. Several pieces that he had written previously appeared in the EM, such as a manuscript that had been kept in Argentina and was published by Siegrist de Gentile (1992), which became the EM's "Spain" entry, one of the main economics entries in the entire work.[9] Likewise, long extracts from Mora's 1843 DLC monograph also appear in other important entries such as "Capital" or "Trade" (Mellado 1851–1855, VII, 82–95; IX, 782–824).[10] The 1844 MPF is a similar case: it was transferred in its entirety to the entry on "Free (ports)" (Mellado 1851–1855, XX, 222–34).

Mora's crucial role in the EM is also visible in smaller details. "Economists. Economics Bibliography" (Mellado 1851–1855, XV, 374–414), another outstanding entry, includes one of the work's most comprehensive lists of economics texts and was taken entirely from the "*Économie politique*" entry in Coquelin and Guillaumin's *Dictionnaire d'économie politique* (1852–1853, I, 666ff.),[11] with the exception of three references, two written by Mora himself—DLC and MPF—and a third—the *Sumario de la España económica* (1843)—by Vadillo, who Mora deemed one of the leading Spanish authorities in the free trade economics field and with whom he had established a close relationship during the Liberal Triennium and his period of exile in London.

To sum up, there is every reason to believe that Mora was the author of the economics entries in the EM's second stage, and that some of them—when they were not straightforward copies—came from a range of previous works by Mora himself, especially from the intellectual phase of his career that began with his economics articles for the EMC in 1828–1829. It is important to bear this in mind when assessing some of the analytical anachronisms in EM entries, as well as the way in which Mora updates his own writings by adding new content to old.

[9] This was found in the *Archivo General de la Nación* in Buenos Aires and was written after 1851.

[10] This is particularly true of the "Trade" entry, which has a very similar structure to the DLC, with the aim of refuting protectionist economists' most common objections to free trade: external dependence, a negative balance of trade, encouraging infant industry, etc.

[11] This bibliography is grouped according to country in the EM.

9.5 The Sources

Like all encyclopaedia-type works the EM mentions innumerable authors and political economy texts from a wide range of geographical areas and time frames. Although references to nineteenth-century authors and texts naturally abound, Mora often uses earlier sources, frequently referring to Smith, Bentham, the Physiocrats and other economists and European schools of political economy from the 1750s to 1800. Likewise, although British and French sources clearly predominate, there are also references to Italian, Swiss, German and, of course, Spanish authors. The Spanish sources frequently go back to the sixteenth- and seventeenth-century *arbitristas* and eighteenth-century Enlightenment economists, as was the norm in dictionaries with economics content about Spain.

While the aim is not to make a comprehensive study of the EM's enormously rich range of sources, what follows is an attempt to cover their main structure. This is an issue of some importance, as it may be useful for gauging the ideas and economic currents circulating in Spain in the mid-nineteenth century, a fundamental issue given that Spain was a net importer of knowledge. At the same time, as the EM's *raison d'être* was to inform, reconstructing its sources helps to understand not only the economics concepts, but also the authorities that it aimed to make available to an audience that was literate but lacked expert knowledge.

The first types of sources that occur frequently in the EM are general encyclopaedias and dictionaries of political economy and commerce. The two major works in the first group are Didot's *Encyclopédie moderne* (1846–1851) and recent editions of the *Encyclopaedia Britannica* (1768–1771), while from the second there are many references to key works of European economic thought from the 1820s and 1830s: Canga Argüelles' two *Diccionario de Hacienda* (1826–1827; 1833–1834), McCulloch's *Dictionary of Commerce* (1832) and Guillaumin's dictionaries, both the *Dictionnaire du commerce et des marchandises* (1839) and especially the essential *Dictionnaire de l'économie politique* (1852–1853), which he compiled with Coquelin. In the same group, although less significant, are dictionaries produced by other disciples of Say, Blanqui's seminal *Dictionnaire du commerce et de l'industrie* (1837–1840) and Ganilh's *Dictionnaire analytique* (1826), which was the more important of the two. Mora also consulted various eighteenth-century encyclopaedias and dictionaries of commerce, in particular Denis Diderot and Jean le Rond D'Alembert's *Encyclopédie* (1751–1772), as well as the volumes on

"*Économie politique et diplomatique*" in Charles-Joseph Panckoucke's *Encyclopedie méthodique* (1784–1788) and the Anglo-French series that began with Jacques Savary's *Dictionnaire* (1723–1730): André Morellet, Thomas Mortimer and Malachy Postlethwayt (Perrot 1992; Astigarraga and Zabalza 2007). He also seems to have used dictionaries with contents that were closer to economic statistics, such as those compiled by the Scotsman John Sinclair and the Frenchman Jacques Peuchet, although to a lesser extent. Finally, it is interesting to note that Mora omits any reference to the dictionaries of commerce that had appeared in Spain in the 1820s and 1830s after the publication of the Canga Argüelles' influential works, clearly illustrating the different ideological positions to emerge in the wake of the controversy over protectionism and free trade (Astigarraga et al. 2001, 31–33).

The second major group of sources consists of writings on political economy and includes treatises, university textbooks and books on the history of political economy and other informative texts—summaries, glossaries, etc.—or designed to promote the teaching of "popular lessons". Most of the items in this important body of sources are either English or French. From the British tradition Mora used all the main economics texts produced by the classical school, from Smith to John Stuart Mill, including Malthus, Ricardo, Torrens, West, James Mill and McCulloch, and others with content that touched on political economy, especially Bentham. The French sources cover a broader spectrum, in both chronological and ideological terms; the works of Montesquieu, Turgot and the Physiocrats—Pierre Paul Mercier de la Rivière and Pierre Samuel Dupont de Nemours—are at one end and Bastiat is at the other.

Mora knew Sismonde de Sismondi and various utopian socialists, mainly Claude Henri de Saint-Simon and Charles Fourier, although he cites them very little. In this respect it is important to recall that the core socialist group in Spain, which occasionally allied with democratic and republican groups, benefitted from a greater capacity for organising and spreading their ideas through their own publications, especially in the 1840s. Mora's own disaffection from socialism must have been profoundly influenced by his deep liberal convictions and also by the experience of the French Revolution of 1848; mentioned repeatedly in the EM, along with its leaders—particularly Louis Blanc—, it was overtly referred to as a frustrated revolutionary experiment that was harmful to society. Moreover, the turbulent years of the mid-nineteenth century in Europe probably exacerbated the dichotomy between Mora's relatively radical defence of free trade on the one hand and his more moderate conservative defence of political and moral freedoms on the other, a legacy from his time in Hispanic America. While eternally respectful of parliamentarianism and representative democracy, he went so far as to invoke Catholic beliefs to argue in favour of imposing coercive measures and restrictions on society in order to avoid the ills that could result from a surfeit of political and moral freedom.

In spite of the EM's vast range of sources, Mora's main link with French political economy is through the influential line connecting Say with his disciples—Chevalier, Garnier and Rossi—and these with Bastiat's "optimistic" school and the founders of the *Journal des économistes* (1841). Blanqui, his main cornerstone in reconstructing the evolution of the history of political economy, is part of this line, although there are also benchmark British authors such as McPherson. The "History of Political Economy" entry especially is based on Blanqui's *Histoire de l'économie politique* (Mellado 1851–1855, XV, 307–66; Blanqui 1860 [1837]). However, Mora does not merely translate this and the other entries, but reworks his contributions, partly in order to include references to Spain and the *arbitrista* and Enlightenment economists. In doing so he provides ample proof of two questions: firstly, that he has read in depth and understood the political economy texts he quotes, which enables him to furnish his readers with a well-informed and well-reasoned history of political economy; and secondly, he shows an intense interest in history as an essential element in legitimising ideas and public policies. His entries burst with references and long historical passages, which frequently go back to the Holy Scriptures and the republics of ancient Greece and Rome.

The relative unimportance of German, Italian and Spanish sources is striking when compared to Mora's widespread use of classical British and French currents. The main Russian reference is the *Cours*, by Storch (1823), a distinguished follower of Say. As for Italian sources, besides Mengotti, one of Mora's major references in his critique of the "protective" system, his mentions of various Milanese and Neapolitan Enlightenment authors such as Pietro Verri, Antonio Genovesi and Gaetano Filangieri, and indeed of the Italian *Risorgimento*—Melchiorre Gioja—are relatively marginal (Astigarraga 2001; Zabalza 2001). As noted above, where Spain is concerned Mora makes use of the sixteenth- and seventeenth-century *arbitristas* and eighteenth-century Enlightenment thinkers, sometimes simply for rhetorical reasons, and establishes a clearer line of continuity with the last generation of the late

Enlightenment—Jovellanos, Sempere, etc.—. However, his main focus of attention is undoubtedly the free trade economists, especially Flórez Estrada, Vadillo and Pebrer, sources of the utmost importance in his tireless criticism of protectionism.

Thirdly and lastly, the EM also includes references to the periodical press and journals, mainly from Britain—chiefly *The Economist*, *The Scotsman* and the ER—and France—such as the *Revue des Deux Mondes* and the *Journal des Debats*—as well as to European laws and government reforms which could be useful to Spain. The most important is undoubtedly the British reform that repealed the Corn Laws in 1846 as a result of the famous Cobden-Bright campaign; this was the work of Robert Peel, who Mora repeatedly praised in his entries.

Mora handles these sources in a variety of ways in his careful compilation of the economics entries. First of all, he generally includes long extracts from the works of featured authors. Despite the fact that many of these works would have been translated into Spanish (Cabrillo 1978), Mora seems to use the original texts without needing to approach them through secondary sources, which confirms that he had no difficulty in accessing the main books he consults—McCulloch, Bastiat, Chevalier, Vadillo, Pebrer and Say—. However, there is one notable exception: Smith's WN is normally cited through McCulloch's *Principles.*

Secondly, as well as habitually including excerpts, the EM bristles with mentions and specific citations of economics writers and treatises, along with authors from related disciplines such as law, politics and moral philosophy. It should not be assumed that there is a perfect match between the number of citations and the authors' real impact on Mora's thought, however; for instance, although he cites McCulloch and Bastiat less often than Quesnay or Mercier de la Rivière, they undoubtedly had far greater influence on him.

The bibliographical references included at the end of some entries make up the third type of citation. In the case of four of the most important entries in the EM—"Capital", "Trade", "Political Economy" and "History of Political Economy" (Mellado 1851–1855, VII, 95; IX, 824; XV, 307, 366)—,[12] these references have been shown to be faithful reflections of

[12] A further entry of great importance has been excluded from this analysis: "Economists. Economics Bibliography" (Mellado 1851–1855, XV, 407–13). As noted later, the bibliography was copied almost word for word from the entry "*Économie politique*" by Coquelin and Guillaumin 1852–1853, I, 667ff.).

Mora's influences when writing the economics entries. Smith, McCulloch, Bastiat, Pebrer, Vadillo and Mengotti's books are central to Mora's economic thought, as well as to the mark he made on the EM. There are other bibliographical references, some of which were almost obligatory in Spain at that time, such as Say, Blanqui and Storch from among the foreign economists and Canga Argüelles and Flórez Estrada from among the Spanish writers.

All these points paint a clear picture of the essential features of the economic sources Mora used in his contributions to the EM. On the whole they are relatively up-to-date—they cover Bastiat and Coquelin and Guillaumin's *Dictionnaire* (1852–1853) from the French sphere and John Stuart Mill from the British, although less so—and are an accurate reflection of the geographical and ideological diversity characterising the circulation of economic ideas in Mora's day. However, British political economy is given relatively more weight than usual and more than hitherto ascribed to it, mainly due to McCulloch's ubiquitous presence.

9.6 Classification of the Economics Entries

The economics entries in the EM have been grouped under five headings: doctrine and theory; international trade and economics; financial economics; public finance, and authors and history of political economy.

Like any attempt at taxonomy this classification is both partial and open to argument, but it is largely based on the criteria Mora chose to write his entries. It is clear from their content that he followed the Smithian tradition and prioritised *Ordnungspolitik* over *Prozesspolitik*, arguing for the greatest possible individual freedom in a framework of law and order (Coats 1971, 6–7). Furthermore, there is a strong permanent link between the theoretical and political aspects of his writings; the topics are not dealt with solely for the purpose of spreading knowledge, but there is a deliberate attempt to relate theory to its specific application to Spanish economic policy and it is not easy to distinguish between analytical and strictly descriptive entries. Moreover, some topics are naturally more important than others and the most significant group for reasons of length and relative weight in the work's internal structure would consist of entries such as "Capital", "Trade", "Political Economy", "Economists. Economics Bibliography", "Spain" and "History of Political Economy". Some of these, such as "Political Economy", "Trade" and "Spain", are so long that they could almost be classed as small treatises.

To turn to the five headings' specific content, "Doctrine and Theory" brings together a set of core points which form the backbone of the work's theoretical content; they are undoubtedly the crucial entries and the most space is therefore devoted to them. Taken as a whole they make up a kind of textbook, if not exactly theory-based then certainly ideological, as together they comprise a tightly knit body of ideas. The next section of this chapter focuses on this group of entries.

Although the limited number of entries on "Authors and the History of Economic Thought" may appear to suggest that the EM lacks biographical or strictly historical articles, this impression is only superficial. It is true that a single entry is devoted to an economist—"Bentham"—which Mora may have written with someone else, but there are two other very long entries with historical content: "History of Political Economy" and "Economists. Economics Bibliography". As already noted, both contain short treatises comparing and evaluating a number of economists, although the quality is rather patchy.

The first entry, "History of Political Economy" (Mellado 1851–1855, XV, 307–66), appears to have been written with the aim of providing an overall view of the history of economic ideas, as it contains an extremely thorough survey of economic theory from Aristotle to Mora's contemporaries, firstly McCulloch and John Stuart Mill, secondly Bastiat and the French "optimistic" school, and finally the Spanish free trade economists of Mora's generation, all from a markedly critical perspective. While Mora describes a wide spectrum of economists and arguments during his journey through history, the *filo rosso* is his account of the development of economic science from what he calls the "protective" system, which he identifies with the "mercantile system" and Colbertism, to a more modern economic analysis, underpinned by a new theory of value that justifies and provides a basis for the system of economic freedom. The economists and economic schools are judged according to this central criterion, in such a way that the history of economic science is interpreted as a forward movement towards doctrines that defend free trade and minimal state intervention in the private sector.

The second entry, "Economists. Economics Bibliography" (Mellado 1851–1855, XV, 374–414), is more interesting from the point of view of Mora's own thought. He focuses on thinkers that he considers to be "founders of economic systems, authors of important discoveries and leaders of authoritative schools". These are essentially reduced to Physiocracy, Smith, Malthus, Ricardo, Say and Bastiat; rather surprisingly, McCulloch is not mentioned here. Mora's intellectual path emerges more clearly in this entry, which ends with two French economists, the ultra-liberal Bastiat and the more moderate Chevalier, to whom the last few pages are devoted.

Bastiat certainly had a profound influence on Mora's thinking, so much so that when much of the EM had already been written he stated unequivocally that the remaining economics entries, especially "Property", "Wealth", "Value" and so on should simply be based on his ideas, specifically the *Harmonies économiques* (1851; Mellado 1851–1855, XV, 400).[13] The fact that Mora left the EM meant that these entries were never published, and so Bastiat's influence, which was visible in certain nuances and rhetorical turns of phrase in several entries, was essentially based on the *Sophismes économiques* (1846). In the 1850s Mora turned to Chevalier as an authority through which to criticise the "protective" system, inspired by the idea of philanthropic internationalism and brotherhood between all countries; in other words, the liberal Chevalier joined the ranks of authors such as Mengotti, Pebrer and Vadillo, who were so important in Mora's earlier writings criticising the countless evils of the "mercantile system". In essence, Mora once again identified the development of political economy with the evolution of ideas about economic freedom (Mellado 1851–1855, XV, 406).

The "Trade and International Economics" heading contains the entries that directly address the defence of free trade in both the domestic and international market.[14] On the whole it is this group that shows the greatest continuity with Mora's previous works, in particular the DLC and MPF, lengthy excerpts from which are included in the EM. As reflected in the entry titled "Trade", the common thread running through these articles is firstly the defence of trade in all kinds of goods, including luxury items, on the grounds that commercial activity is a powerful factor in promoting human development, intelligence and knowledge (Mellado 1851–1855, IX, 791–93), as well as civilisation and better practices, which ties in with the old Enlightenment "*doux commerce*" tradition embodied by authors such as Hume and Montesquieu (Mellado 1851–1855, IX, 782–87). Furthermore, the critique of the "mercantile system" and the "protective" state once more comes to the

[13] In these comments Mora is simply copying from the work's index.

[14] There is a detailed analysis of EM content covering trade crises and credit in Astigarraga and Zabalza (2011).

fore in these ideas. Mora uses two analytical instruments for this: refuting both the balance of payments theory and the absolute advantage theory (Mellado 1851–1855, IV, 446–450; XVIII, 33–41). While the former was based on the current ideas of post-Smithian economics in its rejection of the "mercantile system", the latter mainly focussed on McCulloch's work. Mora found absolute advantage theory sufficient to justify the origin of trade between nations.

McCulloch's influence is fundamental here. Although the EM used sources with a very broad range of geographical and ideological bases, it was undoubtedly McCulloch to whom Mora turned most frequently, particularly in this group of entries on international economics. Mora uses his "Political Economy" article (1842) for the *Encyclopaedia Britannica*, *The Principles of Political Economy* (1825)—which he cites as *The Elements*—, *A Practical, Theoretical and Historical Dictionary of Commerce and Commercial Navigation* (1832) and his renowned articles for *The Scotsman* and the ER to nuance a range of conclusions reached by other classical economists who were McCulloch's contemporaries, as reflected in entries such as "Company", "Political Economy" and "Manufacturing" (Mellado 1851–1855, IX, 907–49; XVIII, 258–78). However, Mora's ideas naturally draw on other sources, which he had used in 1843 and are of some importance in his justification of economic freedom from an ideological point of view (Schwartz 1999, 33): Mengotti's *Il Colbertismo* (1819); Pebrer's *Cinco proposiciones sobre los grandes males que causa la Ley de Aranceles* (1837); and a short work by the controversial Pebrer and Vadillo's *Sumario de la España económica de los siglos XVI y XVII* (1843). There are also continuous references to British liberal economic reforms, with particular attention paid to the Peel government's 1846 repeal of the Corn Laws, as noted above.

This group of entries also contains other arguments which had already formed part of Mora's intellectual development. One of them is anti-colonialism, which is set out in the "Colonies" section (Mellado 1851–1855, IX, 558–690). Mora was critical of both the Spanish and British colonial systems, accusing Britain of exercising an inefficient and unjust trade monopoly that was largely beneficial to the country itself but had a devastating impact on its overseas territories. He found the example of the prosperity attained by the United States, now an independent republic, enough of an argument in favour of the economic advantages of independence for colonies. The source of all these ideas is clear: Bastiat and his firm commitment to the ideas of peace and the international brotherhood of nations which modifies his stance on British colonialism which he had addressed more favourably in previous writings (Baslé and Gélédan 1991, 91–92). These notions and their ramifications in the area of international trade are one of the themes that cut across the EM's economics content, especially the international trade and economics entries—"Economists. Economics Bibliography", "Exports", "Imports"—in which the shadow cast by the influential Bastiat appears time and again (Mellado 1851–1855, XV, 374–414; XVIII, 41–42; XXIII, 937–43).

The final groups of entries cover "Financial Economics" and "Public Finance". Where the former is concerned, entries such as "Credit", "Public Loan" and "Public Debt" express ideas of considerable economic significance, once again drawn from McCulloch and no doubt from Bastiat as well. Mora attributes a primary function as means of transaction to money, banknotes and credit. The economic purpose of the money supply is therefore to facilitate the circulation of goods, in accordance with the classical theory of the limited effect of money on the real economy and wealth creation, whose source is labour (Mellado 1851–1855, XI, 561). However, also in line with classical orthodoxy, Mora understands that lack of liquidity slows down economic growth because it hinders the circulation of goods; on the other hand, as the "Trade Crises" entry reflects, surplus liquidity is a major cause of trading problems (Mellado 1851–1855, XI, 620–25).

The "Public finance" entries are longer than the previous ones, which may be related to the importance attached by this aspect of economics in the Spain's liberal programme following the approval of Mon-Santillán's tax reform in 1845. All these entries are based on similar taxation principles, following Smith and Sismondi, which can ultimately be summed up in just two: the simplification and fairness of taxing activities that create larger economic surpluses and thus facilitate capital accumulation. The tax burden should therefore be shared out among the different sectors of society, with the aim of respecting the criteria of equality and efficiency. Mora puts forward a detailed argument in favour of and against adapting the different types of taxation to these criteria, then opts for a tax system based on direct contribution, which is universal and certain, difficult to defraud and promotes social justice. In entries such as "Contribution" and "Public Finance", he seems to argue for something along the lines of the McCulloch's "ability-to-pay principle". Therefore, he opposed consumption excises and suggested the direction that should take taxation when pointing out the introduction of Income Tax in England, which contrast with the ambiguity that he demonstrated in DLC about this issue (Mellado 1851–1855, X, 982–1013; XXII, 432–47). Nevertheless, this group of entries is generally in line with ideas in the long classical tradition linking Smith's work with McCulloch's. On the revenue side the entries advocate a tax system that respects the maximisation of the rate of return (O'Brien 1992, 230) and on the expenditure side, a substantial reduction in the state's economic weight and its broad areas of public intervention. The EM's over-arching aim is to gradually achieve a state with functions similar to those envisaged in the WN, which, however, entails a somewhat broader public agenda than the classic trio of justice, defence and infrastructure (O'Brien 1992, 380ff.; Coats 1971, 7ff.). Nevertheless, Mora, who was aware of the growing public wants of the liberal state, gave central significance to the public credit in the entry "Public Loan" following the footprints that Mora imprinted in EMC in the late 1820s in which he supported the public credit. The entry describes the mechanics of the public loans, gives a historical account of the British, the French—including the Law experiment and the Necker and Turgot reforms—and the Spanish experiences (Mellado 1851–1855, XVI, 262–83).

9.7 The Analytical Core

As previously mentioned, the EM includes a central set of entries that define clearly the analytical and theoretical foundations of its economics content. The most important of these is undoubtedly "Political Economy". In keeping with his times Mora draws a distinction between the "scientific or theoretical" branch of political economy and the "applied or art" branch, arguing that there is a set of universal economic laws dealing essentially with wealth. He underlines political economy's moral sense in several passages and is strongly opposed to authors like Sismondi who propose an overly mechanistic view of wealth production which would make it possible to separate political economy from morality. Economic laws must be discovered by means of a fundamentally speculative rather than empirical methodology and to defend this abstract method, for the first time in his career, Mora resorts to the "methodological revolution" represented by John Stuart Mill's famous standpoints, which were little known in Spain. Mora seems to have learned Mill's arguments—which were actually far more hybrid than he was willing to admit—in favour of a "specific deductive method", which operated through logic on the basis of premises arrived at via introspection and observation (O'Brien 1995, 110–12; Sowell 1977, 122ff.). As reflected in "History of Political Economy", he draws mainly on French sources, particularly Rossi and Bastiat, who he considered Mill's successors in the field (Mellado 1851–1855, XV, 307–66).

Mora understands political economy as the science that "deals with the creation, distribution and consumption" of wealth, and the "Political Economy" entry, the backbone of the economic entries in the EM, is organised around this idea. He probably chose this structure because of its predominance in economics handbooks and textbooks in Spain at the time, the result of the enormous popularity of the writings of Say and his disciples. However, although this structure does not match that in the *Principles*, everything points to the fact that McCulloch was fundamental in the way Mora organises specific content on these three aspects of political economy, as innumerable passages from his work are summarised in this entry. That is not to say that Mora relies exclusively on McCulloch's writings; on the contrary, his achievement in selecting and refining ideas is remarkable[15]; for example, his definition of political economy's scope of analysis omits free goods on the basis of similar ideas to those used by McCulloch and Coquelin and Guillaumin in their recently published *Dictionnaire* (1852–1853, I, 652).

The analysis of output is based on the notion of the labour factor's key role in the wealth creation process. Mora stresses this time and again, aiming to combat the "legacies" of the "mercantile system", which were still highly visible in economic debates in mid-nineteenth-century Spain.[16] This idea is also vitally important in his formulation of growth theory. In his view, the chief task of economists is to identify the "conditions" and "circumstances" that make the labour factor more productive—that is, that reduce the cost of production—, lower its price and, in short, favour capital accumulation processes. In tackling these issue Mora addresses one of the problems at the heart of classical political economy in very similar terms to the "requirements" and "conditions" McCulloch used in his *Encyclopaedia Britannica* article on "Political Economy"; hence, in a way

[15] It is also enlightening that, as seen, in the 1825 CEP Mora should have chosen a structure similar to that used in McCulloch's *Principles* and to James Mill.

[16] This issue heavily conditioned the WN's reception in Spain; see Astigarraga et al. (2022b), Menudo (2015), Usoz (2022) and Zabalza (2022).

that O'Brien (1992, 278) understands as being closer to Smith's work than to Ricardo's. McCulloch, in particular, is used as an intellectual source to make some nuances to Smith's theories, exemplified by the entry "Manufacturing" where Mora points out how McCulloch demonstrated the superior productivity of industry in high contrast to Smith's view. Nevertheless, Mora continued supporting the Smithian theory of the stages of development and advocated that agriculture must be fully developed in a country before it becomes industrialised (Mellado 1851–1855, XVIII, 919–30). This is consistent with the agrarian path of development that he advocated for agriculture in Spain and Hispanic-American countries, and the opposition to state interventionism in the promotion of industry, mainly through tariff protection, which was characteristic of Mora's approach. In entries such as "Bentham", "Circulation" and "Manufacturing", Mora argues that the price reduction that would accompany a fall in production costs would increase the overall economic surplus and thus impact on individual and collective prosperity: society would be closer to the utilitarian principle of "the greatest welfare for the greatest number of people", whose popularisation owed so much to Bentham (Mellado 1851–1855, VIII, 703; V, 9–29). Monopolies, trade restrictions and all state intervention in markets are therefore to be rejected, not only because they have unwanted consequences on economic prosperity and growth, but also because of their negative effects on individual and collective welfare from a utilitarian perspective.

On the basis of the content of entries such as "Political Economy", "Division of Labour", "Division of Property" and "Luxury", Mora identifies the "conditions" for economic development in two main factors: capital accumulation and the structure of property. The "circumstances" for economic development are the division of labour and the "association of capital" (Mellado 1851–1855, XIV, 618–30). This is nothing more than a return to the old ideas in Smith's WN, but once again filtered through McCulloch, especially his "Political Economy" article. While McCulloch adapted the article for inclusion in the *Principles* (O'Brien 1992, 274), Mora, on the other hand, did not do so for the EM.

The structure of property is analysed in the context of general growth theory. Mora devotes special attention to the size of property, in a similar vein to his fellow free trader Flórez Estrada. Although he appears to favour an intermediate formula, like almost all Spanish economists, he finally opts for small properties, basing his choice on the example of Britain, whose prosperity he did not believe to have been caused by *la grande culture*

(Almenar 1980). However, his main concern was agricultural productivity, to the extent that he had not opposed large estates in the 1840s if they were sufficiently productive. Likewise, according to the contents of entries such as "Political Economy" and "Division of Property", of equal importance to the scale of productive units was solving the problem of the vast amount of uncultivated land or "mortmain" in the hands of "non-productive" classes such as the nobility and the clergy, which were still powerful in the Spanish economy; hence his defence of the liberal agrarian reforms enacted in Spain in the 1820s and 1830s (Mellado 1851–1855, XIV, 608–18; XV, 285–86).

Where the division of labour is concerned Mora adopts criteria similar to those used by Smith in Chapters 1 to 3 of Book I of the WN, albeit once again through the medium of McCulloch. If Mora is highly aware of the importance of the division of labour as a positive factor in increasing capital accumulation, he is also very critical of "labour associations" and the various forms of working class organisation for precisely the opposite reason; that is, because of their negative impact on such accumulation. This is a highly significant issue given that the EM was written in a context of public demonstration of the power of such associations, which demanded better working conditions and higher wages (Artola 1973, 227). Another striking aspect is that while the volumes of the EM written by Mora contain a well-argued defence of producing luxury goods, the "social question" is barely touched on (Mellado 1851–1855, XIV, 414–22; XV, 300–307). In fact, Mora is openly critical of the more socially oriented economists—led, in his opinion, by Sismondi, whose ideas he refutes by means of the French liberal economist Droz—and he also mounts a forceful attack on one of the main starting points of Catholic-social economics, Alban de Villeneuve de Bargemont's *Économie politique chrétienne* (1834), even refusing o acknowledge its scientific nature.

Having specified the factors determining output the EM's analytical framework shifts to a discussion of the distribution of production between consumption and saving, in which the latter variable is identified with a high rate of profit (Mellado 1851–1855, XV, 300–307; VII, 82–95). Accepting as axiomatic the notion that greater capital accumulation is consistent with greater prosperity, Mora embarks on an analysis of one of the EM's core issues: the varying levels of productivity attributable to different economic sectors. This is ultimately a question of ascertaining which capital destination produces higher "net profits" and therefore contributes most effectively to capital accumulation and thus to national prosperity. In fact Mora does not opt for any particular sector, understanding that the choice is subject to each country's production structures and specific circumstances, especially with regard to the practical expression of the laws of productivity in each one (Mellado 1851–1855, VII, 82–95; IX, 782–824; XIV, 49–57). In Spain this issue was still bogged down by an age-old debate as to whether agriculture or industry should take the lead in economic development. The question had surfaced among the seventeenth-century *arbitristas* and Mora had echoed it in his previous work. He believes that industry will obtain higher returns in the long term, but also feels that the law of diminishing returns has not yet begun to take effect in Spanish agriculture, and therefore follows Blanqui's *Dictionnaire* (1840) and advocates introducing specialisation criteria (Mellado 1851–1855, IX, 782–824). However, in the EM Mora seems to abandon his previous stances and deliberately sidesteps an exclusive choice between "agricultural" and "industrial" development strategies,[17] attempting to find common ground between the two in the notion that both would be hampered if the instruments of the "protective" system were used to boost the economy. Thus, the theory of economic growth based on free trade once again prevails as the central argument in the EM.

Mora's analysis of distribution uses arguments which, had he not consulted McCulloch's *Principles* in detail, would appear to be drawn from Smith's work: a theory of value based on the cost of production in which the market price fluctuates around the factor price. Mora expressly criticises the subjective theory of value, which was so influential in pre-Smithian literature and is based on the criteria of "utility" and abundance and scarcity. Although he handles several of Ricardo's concepts such as the theory of differential rent—which he does not consider applicable to Spain, however—, his theory of distribution is incomplete and is moreover contradictory in the same terms as Smith's is (Mellado 1851–1855, XV, 276–80); the only clear idea to emerge from it is that agriculture is not the only sector that creates net product. Likewise, Mora understands that the distribution process is determined by two specific factors: competition and money (Mellado 1851–1855, X, 22). The former causes output costs to fall and therefore leads to rises in surplus; the latter, meanwhile, boosts trade. Underlying everything is a profound criticism of the "mercantile

[17] This represents a certain departure from the free trade mainstream in Spain, which had unequivocally linked the defence of free trade with that of industrial interests since the 1840s (Costas 2000).

system", and all the arguments for rejecting protectionism and state interventionism raise their heads once more. These criteria are also extended to the labour market, which should simply be regulated according to the laws of demand and supply of labour, as Mora had already stated in other writings.

Finally, entries such as "Luxury", "Consumption" and "Political Economy" devote long passages to the question of consumption, especially to discussions about the hoary debate over productive and unproductive consumption. Mora's argument that all consumption is beneficial is undoubtedly a defence of luxury goods production taken from Say and, to a lesser extent, Droz, but is also compatible with the analytical criteria used by McCulloch, a great advocate of luxury as a factor in economic growth (Mellado 1851–1855, XXVI, 441–42; McCulloch 1825, Part. IV, Ch. I; O'Brien 1992). If all these ideas are taken into account, it is clearly no accident that Mora criticises the negative treatment of luxury in Panckoucke's *Encyclopédie méthodique* and the differentiation between productive and unproductive labour from a Christian perspective. He considers Smith's differentiating criterion to be too narrow and resorts to Say in some passages to justify the notion that all work that produces useful goods or services for society is productive; he does so to the same end in other passages, using Part IV of McCulloch's *Principles* and perhaps also Bastiat's authority (Mellado 1851–1855, X, 837–38; XV, 343; XXVI, 414–22).[18]

It will be clear from everything said so far that "Political Economy" is the entry that lies at the heart of the EM's economics content and embodies the organisational framework of the economic entries of the Encyclopaedia, lending them a unitary nature. Although there is no high-level analysis, the EM's organisational coherence and the scope of its economics content make it a key work in economic science and also in the spread of analytical progress in the discipline in Spain at that time. Meanwhile, the rich rhetoric used to defend free trade ideology and criticise the "mercantile system", based on sources as diverse as works by Mengotti, Rossi, Chevalier, Pebrer and Vadillo, is a transversal axis that runs through all the entries and also makes it unique for its time and place. In short, the EM is structured in defence of a development strategy whose main argument is the advocacy of free trade as the basis of national wealth, and for which McCulloch's book is fundamental.

[18] On the divergent positions of classical economists on luxury see Eltis (1999).

9.8 Stage Three: The "Social Question"

It has already been noted that the economics entries in the last six volumes of the EM (Vols. XXVII–XXXIII) were probably written by someone other than Mora and whose identity is unknown due to lack of documentary information. Although Mora frequently referred to entries such as "Credit", "Population", "Production", "Protection of Industry", "Protectionism", "Income", "Wealth", "Wages", "Labour" and "Value" throughout the previous volumes (Vols. II–XXVI), most were not actually included in the EM, while the few that were, such as "Property" and "Labour", had their own ideological guidelines and were based on entirely different sources from Mora's. This change of authorship occurred in 1854 and may have been related to the July Revolution which swept the progressive liberals to power as well as to his new post of Spanish Consul in London.

The entries in the third part of the EM are less interesting than those written by Mora. Although on the whole they maintain the same pro-free trade content (Mellado 1851–1855, XVIII, 456–58), as can be seen from entries such as "Wages" or "Labour", their sources are now mainly the French classics and especially Say, in itself a real anachronism even for an intellectual milieu like Spain, which constantly lagged behind other countries (Mellado 1851–1855, XXXII, 698–701; XXIII, 406–10). This is why the set of entries is analytically inferior to those in the previous stage; however, these volumes introduce an argument that had hitherto scarcely been addressed in the EM as a whole and which became the core theme of the economics content: the social consequences of industrialisation; in other words, the "social question".

In previous entries of the EM, especially "History of Political Economy" (Mellado 1851–1855, XV, 307–66), Mora had expressed his disquiet over the problems of pauperism and the "the workers' fate", although he showed no affinity whatsoever with the emerging socialist currents. In stage three of the work this topic is openly addressed from a purely Catholic perspective in entries such as "Pauperism" or "Labour". Sources such as Villeneuve de Bargemont (1834) are used, certainly filtered through influential Spanish academic and economist Manuel Colmeiro's *Tratado elemental de economía política ecléctica* (1845, Book II, Part. II, Chap. VIII; Mellado 1851–1855, XXXIII, 406–10; XXIX, 989ff.). It is more than a little significant that this Catholic approach extends to entries covering "Saint-Simonianism" and "Socialism"; while the first is purely descriptive and displays overt tolerance of the social conclusions of Saint-Simon's theories (Mellado 1851–1855, XXXII, 74–86), the second, contributed by Facundo Goñi, Professor of International Law at the *Ateneo de Madrid*, is a harsh critique of socialism from a Catholic perspective (Mellado 1851–1855, XXXII, 528–36).

The most interesting economics entry in this part of the EM is "Property", which tackles the question of property ownership following the debate in mid-nineteenth-century France, specifically between Proudhon and Thiers (Mellado 1851–1855, XXX, 665–76). Without in any way disputing the legitimacy of individual ownership of land and other property, it is Thiers' influential work *De la Propieté* (1848) that carries the most weight here. This is a clear contrast with the positions adopted by Mora, who had attributed serious analytical errors to Thiers and questioned his ideas on the basis of Chevalier's anti-protectionist line of thinking in previous volumes (Mellado 1851–1855, XV, 400–401; XXX, 665–76).

In short, the EM's final volumes lack the interest of previous sections from an analytical and normative point of view. Moreover, they use criteria that are clearly more cautious—linked to the emergence of Catholic economic currents and the "social question"—and are penned in a less combative spirit than Mora's entries.[19]

9.9 Final Remarks: A *Machine à Guerre* in Support of the Liberal Cause and Free Trade

The publication of the EM was a real landmark in the context of mid-nineteenth-century Spanish culture. In terms of its political economy content, the work highlights the fact that Spanish political and cultural elites attributed a similar status to that of the classical sciences to the discipline. The economics entries were written with the overall aims of disseminating political economy among a well-read but non-specialist audience, contributing to the training of the elites responsible for the future development of fledging Spanish capitalism and influencing the design of contemporary

[19] The third part of the EM may have represented a bridge to the *Diccionario enciclopédico hispano-americano* (1887–1898), the second major milestone in encyclopaedia-type works in nineteenth-century Spain, in which the "social question" was a central theme. This is because it was produced by the Krausists, mainly José Manuel Piernas Hurtado; see Astigarraga and Zabalza 2021, 219–42).

economic policy. The many pages devoted to these issues, their internal coherence and the work's extremely broad distribution made it a key player in the spread of European economic thought, particularly ideas that were aligned with liberal and free trade ideology, throughout mid-nineteenth-century Spain. In any event, the EM stands out from other institutional and publishing ventures with roots in this ideological pattern and which were also circulated among the elites and the educated public, from entrepreneurs to civil servants and policy makers.

It is in this context that the importance of Mellado's initiative should be underlined. Some academics have suggested that what makes economic theories more powerful is their transformation into popular mythology. If this idea is accepted, "the propagators of economic ideas might play a more important role in the formulation and acceptance of economic policy than the original authors" (Sockwell 1994, 99). In the case in question, Mora used the EM to defend a free trade programme for Spain, but he was also an outstanding propagator of scientific knowledge and a firm believer that education for all social classes was crucial in consolidating liberal institutions. The analytical weakness and anachronisms discernible in various passages of his entries can be mitigated by the fact that their main aim was to popularise economic ideas, especially free trade ideology, a substantial element of a conception of economic science that has always had its moral and civilising aspect very much in mind. It is thus important to stress that members of the highly influential "economist school" in the 1860s, such as Laureano Figuerola, Gabriel Rodríguez, Segismundo Moret and Manuel Colmeiro, all followers of Bastiat and free trade advocates, were trained during the 1850s; that is, when the EM was published.

Stage two of the EM provides a magnificent mirror in which the circulation of economic knowledge in the mid-nineteenth century in Spain is reflected. Mora undoubtedly consulted works by Say and his followers, but the fact that he was also palpably influenced by Smith and Ricardo's disciples, especially McCulloch, contradicts the notion that British economic thought was almost unknown in Spain at the time due to the marked ascendancy there of French economists. At the same time, however, Bastiat, whose writings had recently been translated five times—in 1845, 1847, 1848, 1853 and 1854—, was also a key author in the EM's economics content. In fact, the EM was one of the first vehicles to spread his ideas in Spain, even before they began to appear in eminent works such as Benigno Carballo's *Curso de economía política* (1855–1856) and Colmeiro's *Principios de economía política* (1859).

From the perspective of the interpretation proposed here it is no accident that the EM took the same anti-statist free trade direction as Coquelin and Guillaumin's *Dictionnaire de l'économie politique* (Le Van-Lemesle 1985), which was designed to become the Spanish dictionary of political economy, and that it was the most representative collective economic work in mid-nineteenth-century Spain, as it was in France. In turn, its wide circulation throughout Spain, together with that enjoyed by the texts written by the main authors of the *Dictionnaire* entries—Garnier, Chevalier, Molinari, etc.—, may explain why the *Dictionnaire* was never translated. Nevertheless, it was a widely consulted work, as is clear from the fact that substantial extracts from it were included in the Spanish university textbooks written by Carballo (1855–1856) and Mariano Carreras y González (1865; Almenar 2000a).

Bibliography

Books[20]

Mora, José Joaquín de. 1825. *Catecismo de economía política.* London: R. Ackermann.

Mora, José Joaquín de. 1832. *Cursos de lógica y ética según la escuela de Edimburgo por José Joaquín de Mora.* Lima: Imprenta de José Masías.

Mora, José Joaquín de. 1834. *Discurso pronunciado en la Universidad Mayor de S. Andrés de la Paz de Ayacucho el 5 de diciembre de 1834, por el Dr. José Joaquín de Mora.* La Paz: Imprenta del Colegio de artes.

Mora, José Joaquín de. 1842: *Curso de derecho natural.* Santiago de Chile: Imprenta liberal.

Mora, José Joaquín de. 1843. *De la libertad de comercio, por José Joaquín de Mora.* Seville: Establecimiento tipográfico, Imprenta de Carlos Rubio y compañía.

Primary Sources

Bastiat, Frédéric. 1846. *Sophismes économiques.* Paris: Guillaumin.

Bastiat, Frédéric. 1851. *Harmonies économiques.* Paris.

Blanqui, Adolphe. 1860 [1837]. *Histoire de l'économie politique en Europe.* Paris: Guillaumin.

[20] On the prolix reprints of the *Catecismos, Cursos* and other works of Mora in the Hispanic world, see Roldán (2003), Macintyre (2018) and Medina (2022).

Boix, Ignacio. 1842–1845. *Enciclopedia española del siglo diez y nueve, o Biblioteca completa de ciencias, literatura, artes y oficios, etc. por una Sociedad de literatos españoles y de hombres especiales en diversas ciencias y profesiones,* 12 vols. Madrid: Imprenta y librería de Ignacio Boix.

Canga Argüelles, José. 1826–1827 *Diccionario de Hacienda para el uso de los encargados de la suprema dirección de ella*, 2 vols. London: Imprenta española de M. Calero.

Canga Argüelles, José. 1833. *Elementos de la ciencia de la Hacienda*. Madrid: J. Palacios.

Carballo, Benigno. 1855–1856 *Curso de economía política*, 2 vols. Madrid: P. Montero.

Carreras y González, Mariano. 1865. *Tratado didáctico de economía política*. Madrid: Imprenta y librería de Miguel Guijarro.

Colmeiro, Manuel. 1845. *Tratado elemental de economía política ecléctica*. Madrid: Calleja.

Colmeiro, Manuel. 1859. *Principios de economía política*. Madrid: G. Alhambra.

Coquelin, Charles and Gilbert Urbain Guillaumin. 1852–1853. *Dictionnaire de l'économie politique*. Paris: Librairie de Guillaumin et Cie.

Guillaumin, Gilbert-Urbaine. 1839. *Encyclopédie du commerçant. Dictionnaire du commerce et des marchandises*, 2 vols. Paris: Guillaumin et Cie.

McCulloch, John Ramsay. 1825. *The Principles of Political Economy, with a Sketch of the Rise and Progress of the Science*. Edinburgh and London: Adam and Charles Black-Longman, Brown, Green and Longmans.

McCulloch, John Ramsay. 1832. *A Dictionary, Practical, Theoretical, and Historical, of Commerce and Commercial Navigation*. London: Longman, Rees, Orme, Broen, Green & Longman.

Mellado, Francisco de Paula. 1851. "Prólogo". In *Enciclopedia moderna. Diccionario universal de literatura, ciencias y artes, agricultura, industria y comercio,* VI–XXIV. Madrid: Establecimiento Tipográfico de Mellado.

Mellado, Francisco de Paula. 1851–1855. *Enciclopedia Moderna: diccionario universal de literatura, ciencias, artes, agricultura, industria y comercio*, 37 vols. Madrid, Establecimiento Tipográfico de Mellado.

Pebrer, Pablo. 1837. *Cinco proposiciones sobre los grandes males que causa la ley de aranceles a la nación en general, a la Cataluña en particular, a las mismas fábricas catalanas*. London: Imprenta española de D. V. Torras.

Storch, Heinrich Friedrich von. 1823. *Cours d'économie politique*. Paris: J. P. Aillaud.

Thiers, M. Adolphe. 1848. *De la propriété*. Paris: Paulin et L'Heureux.

Secondary Sources

Almenar, Salvador. 1980. "Estudio Preliminar". In Antonio Flórez Estrada, *Curso de economía política*, edited by Salvador Almenar, vol. I, XXXV–CXXIII. Madrid: IEF.

Almenar, Salvador. 2000a. "El desarrollo del pensamiento económico clásico en España". In *Economía y economistas españoles. Vol. IV. La economía clásica*, edited by Enrique Fuentes, 7–92. Barcelona: Galaxia Gütenberg and Círculo de Lectores.

Artola, Miguel. 1973. *La burguesía revolucionaria (1808–1869*). Madrid: Alianza.

Astigarraga, Jesús. 2001. "The Light and Shade of Italian Economic Thought in Spain (1750–1850)". In *From Economists to Economists. The International Spread of Italian Economic Thought, 1750–1950*, edited by Piero F. Asso, 227–53. Firenze: Polistampa.

Astigarraga, Jesús and Juan Zabalza. 2007. "Political Economy in the First Spanish General Encyclopaedia: *The Enciclopedia Moderna* (1852–1855)". *History of Economic Ideas* XV–2, 79–108.

Astigarraga, Jesús and Juan Zabalza, eds. 2022. *Adam Smith and 'The Wealth of Nations' in Spain. A History of Reception, Dissemination, Adaptation and Application, 1778–1840.* London and New York: Routledge.

Astigarraga, Jesús, Juan Zabalza and António Almodovar. 2001. "Dictionaries and Encyclopaedias on Political Economy in the Iberian Peninsula (18th, 19th and 20th Centuries)". *Storia del Pensiero Economico* 41, 25–63.

Astigarraga, Jesús, Zabalza, Juan. 2011. "Commercial Crisis and Credit in the First Spanish General Encyclopaedia (1851–1855)" In Besomi, Daniele (ed.) Crises and Cycles in Economic Dictionaries and Encyclopaedias., London and New York: Routledge, 220–232.

Astigarraga, Jesús, Javier Usoz and Juan Zabalza. 2022a. "Estudio preliminar". In *Voces económicas en la 'Enciclopedia Moderna'*, by José Joaquín de Mora, edited by Jesús Astigarraga, Javier Usoz and Juan Zabalza, 11–80. Madrid: IEF.

Astigarraga, Jesús, José Manuel Menudo and Javier Usoz. 2022b. "Nuancing Adam Smith. *The Wealth of Nations'* Reception and Influences in Spain, 1800–1820". In *Adam Smith and 'The Wealth of Nations' in Spain*, edited by Jesús Astigarraga and Juan Zabalza, 121–37. New York and London: Routledge.

Baslé, Maurice and Alain Gélédan. 1991. "Frédéric Bastiat, théoricien et militant du libre-échange". In *L'économie politique en France au XIX*[e] *siècle*, edited by Yves Breton and Michel Luftalla, 83–110. Paris: Economica.

Brotel, Jean-François. 1993. *Libros, prensa y lecturas en la España del siglo XIX*. Madrid: Pirámide.

Cabrillo, Francisco. 1978. "Traducciones al español de libros de economía política (1800–1880)". *Moneda y Crédito* 147, 71–103.

Coats, Alfred W. 1971. "Editor's Introduction". In *The Classical Economists and Economic Policy*, edited by Alfred W. Coats, 1–32. London: Methuen and Co.

Costas, Antón. 2000. "Industrialización y cuestión arancelaria en España. Reflexiones en torno al librecambismo de Laureano Figuerola". In *Economía y economistas españoles. Vol. IV. La economía clásica*, edited by Enrique Fuentes, 459–81. Barcelona: Galaxia Gütenberg and Círculo de Lectores.

Eltis, Walter. 1999. "Does luxury consumption promote growth?". In *From Classical Economics to the Theory of the Firm: Essays in Honour of D. P. O'Brien*, edited by Roger E. Backhouse and John Creedy, 87–103. Cheltenham: Edward Elgar.

Le Van-Lemesle, Lucette. 1985. "Guillaumin, éditeur d'économie politique, 1801–1864". *Revue d'économie politique* XCV–2, 134–49.

Lluch, Ernest and Salvador Almenar. 2000. "Difusión e influencia de los economistas clásicos en España (1776–1870)". In *Economía y economistas españoles. Vol. IV. La economía clásica*, edited by Enrique Fuentes, 93–170. Barcelona: Galaxia Gütenberg and Círculo de Lectores.

Martínez Marín, Jesús A. 2018. *Los negocios y las letras. El editor Francisco de Paula Mellado (1807–1876)*. Zaragoza: Prensas universitarias.

Mengotti, Francesco. 1819. Il Colbertismo, Florencia, Piatti.

Menudo, José Manuel; O'Kean, José María. 2005. "La recepción de la obra de Jean-Baptiste Say en España: la teoría económica del empresario", Revista de Historia Económica, Año XXIII primavera, 1, 117–142.

Menudo, José Manuel. 2015. "Correspondencia y economía política en España (1809–1831). La relación epistolar con Jeremy Bentham y Jean-Baptiste Say". *Cuadernos de Ilustración y Romanticismo* 21, 109–20.

Menudo, José Manuel and José María O'Kean. 2019. "Ediciones, reimpresiones y traducciones en español del *Tratado de economía política* de Jean-Baptiste Say". *Revista de historia económica* 37–1, 169–92.

O'Brien, Denis Patrick. 1992. *J. R. McCulloch. A Study in Classical Economics*, London and Aldershot: Gregg Revivals and Routledge.

O'Brien, Denis Patrick. 1995. "Introduction". In *The Collected Works of J. R. McCulloch. Vol. VIII. Articles in the Edinburgh Review*. London: Routledge and Thoemmes Press.

Peñas Ruiz, Ana 2018. "Un «editor infatigable»: la trayectoria biográfica, editorial y empresarial de Ignacio Boix". Cuadernos De Ilustración Y Romanticismo, (24), 133–171.

Perrot, Jean-Claude. 1992. *Une histoire intellectuelle de l'économie politique (XVIIe–XVIIIe siècles)*. Paris: EHESS.

Schwartz, Pedro. 1999. "Estudio Preliminar". In *De la libertad del comercio*, by José Joaquín de Mora, VIII–XLIX. Madrid: IEF.

Siegrist de Gentile, Nora. 1992. *José Joaquín de Mora y su manuscrito sobre la industria y el comercio de España hacia 1850*. Cádiz: Universidad de Cádiz.

Sockwell, William D. 1994. *Popularizing Classical Economics. Henry Brougham and William Ellis*. New York: St. Martin's Press.

Sowell, Thomas. 1977. *Classical Economics Reconsidered*. Princeton: PUP.

Usoz, Javier. 2022. "Adam Smith and the *Cortes de Cádiz* (1810–1813): More than Enlightened Liberalism". In *Adam Smith and 'The Wealth of Nations' in Spain*, edited by Jesús Astigarraga and Juan Zabalza, 186–204. New York and London: Routldege.

Villacorta, Francisco. 1980. *Burguesía y cultura. Los intelectuales españoles en la sociedad liberal, 1808–1931.* Madrid: Siglo XXI.

Zabalza, Juan. 2001, "The Spread of Italian Economic Thought in Spain 1850–1950: from Historicism to Corporatism". In *From Economists to Economists. The International Spread of Italian Economic Thought, 1750–1950*, edited by Pier F. Asso, 227–53. Firenze: Polistampa.

Zabalza, Juan. 2022. "Adam Smith in the Economic Debates during the Liberal Triennium (1820–1823): the Second Liberal Exile and Hispanic America". In *Adam Smith and 'The Wealth of Nations' in Spain*, edited by Jesús Astigarraga and Juan Zabalza, 205–21. New York and London: Routledge.

CHAPTER 10

A Last (Free Trade) Look at Hispanic America: *La América*

10.1 Introduction

After his collaboration with the EM ended in 1854, Mora held his peace on political economy for a few years. This was undoubtedly due to other professional commitments. As noted, he was appointed Consul General of Spain in London three times during the 1850s (1850–1851, 1853–1854, 1856–1858). Mora was certainly well-qualified for the post: he had experience as Santa Cruz's agent in London; he knew the ins and outs of British culture, politics and government, and he was also extremely familiar with London institutions, as shown by the contacts he kept up after his return to Spain. However, his appointment was not entirely uncontroversial: he was not a career civil servant and had been a front-line participant in *General* Juan José Flores' 1846 expedition to Ecuador, which was organised with the aim of establishing a monarchical regime there and had left an aura of distrust in some of the Hispanic-American republics. More than these experiences, the decisive factor in his first two periods as Consul in London (1850–1851, 1853–1854) must have been his membership of moderate liberal circles from the mid-1840s. After two years of progressive governments in Spain (1854–1856) and the accession to power of the *Unión Liberal*, a party that sought to bring together all the liberal groups (Carr 1968, 254–60), Mora took charge of the London Consulate again (1856–1858). Diplomatic correspondence increased greatly during his

J. Astigarraga et al., *The Economic Legacy of José Joaquín de Mora*, Palgrave Studies in the History of Economic Thought,
https://doi.org/10.1007/978-3-031-49446-8_10

terms there,[1] and this may explain his silence in the intellectual fields that interested him. His work—"prickly and sometimes compromising"—obliged him to maintain a regular, detailed and laborious correspondence with Spain to keep the authorities up to date with every last detail of affairs in England. As an essential part of this concerned "trade management", he was required to keep abreast of official statistics relating to the economy and regularly sent Madrid news on prices, goods, imports, exports and tariffs, the prices of products such as copper, gold and silver, as well as advances in production techniques in an England that was in the midst of the Second Industrial Revolution. He also acted as a go-between for reports, books and all kinds of news from Hispanic America, including developments that could affect the Spanish economy such as the discovery of nitrate of soda in Chile and guano deposits in Cuba.[2] Mora's enthusiasm for his work was clearly reflected in the reports on the Bank of England's economic and monetary situation that he sent almost weekly to the Ministry in order to protect Spanish commercial interests.[3]

By the end of the decade Mora was settled in Spain and had resumed his publishing activities in a range of fields that included literature, history, classical culture and book reviews. He also worked as a journalist, reporting on international politics and of course on political economy, especially economic policy. As this chapter goes on to discuss, the main launching pad for his new phase as an information provider was *La América. Crónica Hispano-Americana* (LA, 1857–1886). This important activity was a reflection of the political instability and profound economic and cultural changes that were taking place in mainland Spain at the time. The Spanish economy was characterised by a sort of schizophrenia in which a traditional agricultural sector with low productivity and huge weight in the economy overall coexisted with an industrial sector that was located in peripheral regions such as the Basque Country, Catalonia and Andalusia to a lesser extent (Sánchez Albornoz 1968). However, this industry was never sufficiently strong to bring about a structural transformation

[1] The full documentation is in the AHN, *Ministerio Exteriores*, bundles H1,942 and H1,943; PP619, bundle 8,183. Many of the details appear in González Pizarro (1984).

[2] AHN, *Ministerio Exteriores*, bundle H1,943, letters dated 15 and 16/IV/1857.

[3] See by way of example AHN, *Ministerio Exteriores*, bundle H1,943, letters dated 30/IV/1858 and 1/VII/1858. Mora slipped significant economic ideas into his reports only occasionally, such as when he criticised "protectionists, preoccupied with the old idea that money alone constitutes real wealth" (AHN, *Ministerio Exteriores*, bundle H1,943, letter dated 25/1/1857).

capable of modernising the country, as had happened in industrialised economies in Europe. Nevertheless, neither the economy nor the industrialisation process was actually stagnant;[4] moreover, the economy grew during a period of railway expansion and the consolidation of liberal institutional reforms such as the Mon-Santillán tax reform (1845) and a tariff reform (1849). After a decade of moderate liberal governments (1844–1854) the 1854 Revolution swept the progressive faction to power; this was a more radical liberalism that was wary of any reconciliation between the interests of the liberal bourgeoisie and the Crown. During the *Bienio Progresista* (1854–1856) the progressives were joined by the group of democrats which also included radical republicans and initially embraced the incipient labour movement. However, the fall of the progressives in 1856 ceded the alternative to the moderates, who were replaced shortly afterwards by O'Donnell's government (1858–1863); his party, the *Unión Liberal*, aimed, as noted, to be a bridge between the two liberal factions, with the ultimate goal of uniting them. It was precisely during this period that Mora became one of the LA's main writers and the magazine became extremely popular, partly thanks to the *Unión Liberal*, which, via a Royal Order, recommended that it should be read throughout the last remaining vestiges of the empire: Cuba, Puerto Rico and the Philippines (Escolano 2018, 112). O'Donnell's party embraced an interventionist foreign policy that included expansionist ventures in Morocco and military action in Hispanic America, which in fact amounted to unsuccessful attempts to recover some former overseas territories. As the party ultimately failed to live up to the expectations of regeneration, democrats and progressives withdrew their support in 1863, ushering in a long period of political instability (Chato 2011).

10.2 A Fresh Look at Hispanic America

It was in this context of economic growth and reforms after the new republics had been recognised in 1835 that the emerging Spanish trading and industrial bourgeoisie glimpsed their enormous economic opportunities in Hispanic America. Despite the inevitable distancing of the post-independence period, cultural and language links had been maintained; by

[4] GDP figures show a growth of 1,04% per annum between 1855 and 1866, while industrial output increased at an annual rate of 3,91% between 1850 and 1870 (Prados de la Escosura 2000, 70, 151).

then, however, Hispanic-American markets had been infiltrated by foreign merchants—particularly from England—who had begun to introduce their own products into these countries, a strategy they had been pursuing since independence. The United States' expansionist ambitions in the Americas also heralded commercial and political colonisation, and all these factors prompted Spain to adopt a new strategy of rapprochement with the Hispanic-American republics. After independence the absolutist elites, anchored in their imperialist and colonial mentality, had completely ignored the emerging countries; however, the new generations of liberals proposed a different strategy based on establishing mutually beneficial economic, commercial and cultural ties and respect for liberal ideas: as expressly endorsed in the LA (8/VI/1857, 3), the "era of domination" had been forced to give way to one of "association".

To support this political and economic manoeuvring, a series of journals appeared in mainland Spain during the 1840s and 1850s. They provided a fresh look at the former colonies—and of course at those that still existed, which Spain aimed to hang onto—and also at their economic and cultural elites. Mora was unquestionably a leading figure in this shift. Although his relentless free trade campaigning continued, it took up less space in the new publications than articles, essays and book reviews relating to philosophy, morals, history and law (See Chap. 8). While the works provided a line of continuity with Mora's Hispanic-American publications in these disciplines, which were always at the heart of his concerns, they were also an opportunity to modernise the way in which these subjects were taught in Spain following the enactment of the liberal reforms of Spanish universities and the decisive 1845 "Pidal Plan". As seen, these two aspects converged in a series of titles which Mora produced before devoting himself fully to the LA: the RHA, the REIE and the REAM.

The RHA was probably the sole publication that Mora founded during those years, and he did so in partnership with the chameleon-like politician and moderate journalist Pedro de Madrazo. A fortnightly journal specialising in literature, the arts and philosophy, the RHA in fact lasted less than a year, soon succumbing to the printing crisis in the late 1840s. Intent on ploughing his own furrow, Mora published three issues on James Mackintosh's work (RHA, 1848, 167–77, 215–24, 258–70) and, which was more of a departure, a lengthy article on John Stuart Mill's *System of Logic* (1843), one of the first to appear on the work in Spain (RHA, 1848, 5–17, 59–71). Rather than a simple review, it was actually a summary of the book, probably for use in universities, and described Mill as a "disciple of the immortal Bentham" and the "first who has concentrated all the rules applicable to all the aptitudes of the human soul in a single vast system" (RHA, 1848, 9). Because of this, the book would promote the establishing of a "true and compact school" of philosophy in Spain, which in Mora's view had not existed since scholasticism, which he found nefarious. In the face of the current "teaching anarchy" and "lack of system", the Mill's *System* provided "the sciences in general" with a service that was akin to Bentham's contribution to jurisprudence (RHA, 1848, 71).

Mora's participation in the REIE was similar to his work for the RHA. During the journal's four-year existence its Hispanic-American focus was reflected in long pieces on the republics' history, economy, politics and culture. Among other topics Mora submitted contributions on natural history and *oeconomie* (REIE, 1846, VI, 166–81), politics—in defence of a majority government (REIE, 1846, V, 364–73)—and history—a lengthy commentary on Juan de Mariana's work (REIE, 1846, VI, 258–321)—. At the same time, he turned his attention once again to university studies in Spain, highlighting certain grounds for hope such as the presence in classrooms of the enlightened juridical tradition of Beccaria, Filangieri, Brissot, Bentham and Rossi (REIE, 1845, IV, 43–53), and later Romagnosi, to whose work he devoted an entire article (REIE, 1845, IV, 246–63). In the same vein, he stressed that the "simple introduction of courses in commerce and political economy is an honourable tribute to the needs of the century and the new turn that ideas have taken" (REIE, 1847, VIII, 320). These were offset by the teaching of philosophy, especially moral philosophy and logic, which Mora considered essential for training good jurists (REIE, 1845, III, 358–65; IV, 281–99). He attacked the disastrous consequences of scholasticism's secular survival and clearly stated his alternative in terms that were repeated again and again in other articles. In keeping with Bacon's empiricist tradition, Mora distanced himself from what he considered the two "main currents" of philosophy: the sensualist tradition whose roots were in France, which he identified with authors such as Condillac, Cabanis and Tracy—to adopt the latter's work would be "a wretched choice, which will seem very strange in Europe"—and the ontological tradition, which prevailed in the German states and was especially embodied by Hegel. Mora's rejection of these two schools of thought can be attributed to what he saw as their excessive reliance on sensory experiences and abstract hypotheses and deduction; in short, in neither case did the philosophy take any account of experience and factual observation. In the face of these "two dire extremes", Mora again showed his preference for the Common Sense school, giving REIE readers very specific information so that they could be introduced to it not only by Stewart, Abercrombie, Campbell and Smith—he recommended consulting his *Theory of Moral Sentiments*, "of which there is a very acceptable French translation"—but also by their French disciples (REIE, IV, 297–98). The stamp of Mora's two monographs on law, logic and ethics that were first published in Chile and Lima, and which he republished in Madrid in 1845 (Mora 1832), was evident throughout.

Mora may have been encouraged to collaborate on the REAM by its multidisciplinary and moderate approach (Rubio 2013). Edited by Mellado, the journal's catholic and liberal identity was evident in contributions from politicians and intellectuals such as Cánovas del Castillo, Gayangos and Ferrer del Río. Mora empathised with the journal's broad cultural content and wrote a lengthy commentary on Machiavelli (REAM, I, 143–57) and a piece on the situation of Hispanic-American countries for the first volume (REAM, I, 29–43, 257–79). Adopting a historical and political approach, he defended their republican systems and held up Chile and Peru as examples, but also urged the countries' rulers to study European parliamentary systems so that they could leave their authoritarian regimes behind; he also ventured to predict that free trade would shortly advance throughout the region and "in a few short years will become the public and general law of those states" (REAM, I, 43). Nevertheless, Mora's radical free trade views, whose stamp on the journal was clear, also marked his fate there and his contributions dwindled,[5] in all likelihood due to the paper's shift towards Krausism and historicism with contributors such as Julián Sanz del Río and Lucas Mallada.[6]

[5] Mora published just one review, devoted to German historian Federico Schlegel, in the second volume (REAM, II, 454–65) and nothing in the final volumes.

[6] In its economic aspect, Krausism was one of the most influential schools in Spain to criticise classical economics in the second half of the nineteenth century. It was inspired by the German philosopher K. C. Friedrich Krause and attributed a protective function to the state which resulted in interventionism aimed at eliminating the negative effects of industrialisation.

10.3 Mora and *La América*

The founding of the LA in 1857, two years after the REAM's closure, was also part of the rapprochement strategy vis-à-vis former overseas territories in an attempt to recover lost ground in the spheres of culture and, above all, trade. Conceived through the lens of liberal ideas, the strategy was formulated in entirely new terms of equality and mutual benefit in these two areas. Eduardo Asquerino, a prominent writer and the LA's editor, was an outstanding example of this new relationship. His works were very popular in Cuba and Mexico and a visit to the two countries in 1853 was marked by banquets held in his honour and praise for his literary work in the press. Asquerino had political links to Spanish liberalism's progressive faction and in January 1855, during the *Bienio Progresista*, the government appointed him Chargé d'Affaires and Consul General in Chile and he subsequently held similar posts in Venezuela. His time in Chile was particularly interesting from this book's point of view as it enabled him to establish a close friendship with the Chilean writer, intellectual and politician José Victorino Lastarria, as seen, a former student of Mora's at the *Liceo de Chile* (see Chap. 6), whose expulsion from the country had pushed him towards radical and combative positions vis-à-vis the conservative government. In the 1840s, with other intellectuals, many of whom had also been Mora's students, he was head of the *Sociedad Literaria* (1842), which aimed to construct a literary and national identity for Chile and to modernise the Republic (Cancino and Cancino 2014). In addition to his political and literary activities, Asquerino had economic interests as a result of his marriage to Peregrina La-Cave, a member of a powerful bourgeois family devoted to wine production in Sanlúcar de Barrameda, a strategic port in the Cadiz area for trading with Hispanic America during the colonial period. Asquerino himself made it clear that the LA would act as an advertising vehicle for Spanish trading and finance companies, as well as a "free agency" for dealing with administrative matters overseas (López-Ocón 1982, 142–44).

Like its editor, the LA and its contributors had close links with Spanish liberalism's progressive and democratic factions. Following the failure of the *Bienio Progresista* in 1856, the progressives themselves were compelled to rearm ideologically, and the LA was one of the main tools of their regeneration (López-Ocón 1982, 140–41). Although its extraordinary list of contributors reveals intellectuals with all types of liberal tendencies, it was the progressives that took centre stage. The LA had a rather encyclopaedic air, with articles on politics, government, political economy, trade, industry and agriculture, yet also covering literature, the arts and science. Particular attention was paid to international political issues related to the European liberal movements that threatened the unity of empires and which the contributors supported enthusiastically. Issues concerning the Hispanic-American world and the Spanish islands of Cuba, the Philippines and Puerto Rico where liberation movements had already emerged, naturally took pride of place, and the LA's new approach to this issue meant that it was the most suitable mouthpiece for Spanish liberalism's colonial reformism (López-Ocón 1982).

The LA appeared fortnightly—the price per quarter was 24 reals on the mainland and 12 pesos a year overseas—. The broadsheet format, which was unusual at the time in Spain, followed the pattern set by the London *Times* and the *New York Herald*. It is important to note here that the publishers were determined to ensure rapid circulation in Hispanic-American countries, in a way that was almost simultaneous with the Madrid edition, which was facilitated by telecommunications advances in the 1850s.[7] Surprised by "the positive reception that our publication has received throughout the Americas", the publishers tried to ensure that the latest news would reach Hispanic America before the European newspapers did, and not much later than the Spanish edition, in order to "keep the spirit of Spain alive on the new continent" (Escolano 2018, 116, 123, 129).

Mora's participation in a journal that was anchored in progressive liberalism requires a brief explanation, given his affinity with the moderate governments of the previous two decades. Although it is true that during the years of his collaboration with the LA a serious attempt was being made to unite the different liberal currents—O'Donell's *Unión Liberal*—and that, despite its undoubtedly progressive origins and bias, the journal had contributors from all these currents, this is not enough to justify Mora's involvement. According to González Pizarro (1984), the reason may lie in the LA's need for writers that would contribute to the strengthening of ties with Hispanic America, and Mora had unquestionable qualities in this respect. As Spanish Consul in London he had resumed his relationships with Hispanic America by producing reports on matters such

[7] The publishers decided to send handwritten "autograph sheets" containing telegram reports from Madrid about "the general interests of politics and commerce" and "the latest news from the stock exchange" to Paris, from where they would be forwarded to the steamers leaving for America (LA, 24/VI/1857).

as copper and Chile's railways, dealing with dispatches to Madrid from Lima and providing up-to-date information on the guano market. He also had wide experience editing and contributing to magazines for the region, most of which was acquired during his periods of exile in London and Hispanic America and then in Spain in the 1840s and 1850s. However, over and above all this, the network of personal and intellectual links he built up in Hispanic-American countries must have played a major role in his recruitment, and the relationship that Asquerino established during his stay in Chile with Lastarria, who he brought in as a regular contributor to the magazine, is a prime example.[8]

Mora's contributions to the journal began on 24 September 1859 with an article on guano, a poultry by-product used as organic fertiliser in of which Peru had large reserves. The article described guano's chemical properties in minute detail, with information from analyses carried out by English and French chemists as well as experiments by leading agronomists, some in Spain, which showed that it enhanced soil fertility. This was especially true for damp soils such as that in England, and Mora therefore concluded that it was unlikely to be used in Spain because the soil there contained less water. The piece was reminiscent of the scientific articles in the MUC in London to spread advanced English production techniques throughout Hispanic America. However, on this occasion, Mora had chosen a topic that was closely related to his term as Consul in London; as noted above, in 1857 he sent Madrid several reports on the discovery of guano deposits in Cuba, analysing their quality and the repercussions that such a discovery could have for both the guano market and the Peruvian economy and the country's ability to repay its loans from England.

Mora was not yet one of the LA's regular contributors in late 1859, nor did his name appear on the journal's masthead. However, following the appearance of his article "*Moralidad de la economía política*" on 8 March 1861, he began to publish there regularly and figured among its contributors almost uninterruptedly until the final phase of the illness that caused his death in October 1864. His last article was an account of the pampas of Argentina, published posthumously on 27 November 1864. For almost four years his involvement with the magazine was total, continuous and essential; he contributed to three areas and wrote the opening "*Revista Extranjera*" section anonymously from 24 November 1861 to 8 May

[8]The fact that in 1860 Lastarria proposed Mora as a staff member in the Philosophy and Humanities Faculty at the Universidad de Chile has already been noted (see Chap. 6).

1862, almost without exception signing his articles simply "M". When the section began to include information on domestic issues it was renamed "*Revista General*" and Mora also wrote it uninterruptedly until 27 July 1864. He also penned at least twenty-three articles on contemporary political issues in Europe under the name Jacinto Beltrán, perhaps using a pseudonym so as to be able to dispense with the discretion necessary for pieces that carried his by-line, and to be able to express his interpretations of political events in the Western world in a freer and more open—even stark in some passages—manner, always from a liberal perspective. The articles carrying his full name contained news about publications in Spain and abroad: they brought together information on and analyses of geographical and historical aspects of the politics, culture and economies of stateless territories in Europe such as Hungary and Transylvania; they also covered legal, historical and economic aspects of the Hispanic-American countries in which Mora had spent his years of exile—Argentina, Chile, Peru and Bolivia—and dealt with multiple legal, literary and historical issues. Almost all Mora's economics writings in the LA fell into the last group, the only exception being an article on free trade in Belgium, which he signed Jacinto Beltrán.

10.4 Mora on the Wave of Progressive Liberalism

The "*Revista Extranjera*" section was a fortnightly account of the main political and military events that took place during the early 1860s, especially in Europe. To some extent it mirrored the "*Revista Política*" section at the beginning of each issue of the REAM, to which Mora also contributed, although it had a more international stamp in the LA. The "*Revista Extranjera*" carried news from chiefly British sources with which he was in close contact, as well as information from foreign newspapers, mainly French and English, which were key founts of information for his articles in the LA. However, rather than being mere political or military accounts, Mora's pieces were imbued with views on the courses taken by events, which he interpreted from the perspective of an unequivocally advanced, progressive and Anglophile liberalism, in contrast to his recent affiliation to more moderate circles.

One indication of a certain return to the more radical roots of his youth was his review of John Stuart Mill's *Considerations on Representative Government* (1861). Sticking to his customary pattern, Mora condensed Mill's highly detailed analysis of the practice and doctrinal principles of parliamentary government by means of summaries and reviews from the British press. In line with contemporary interpretations of Mill's theory of democracy, and either because he had read the book and agreed with it, or as a result of his own reflections, Mora identified the two somewhat contradictory principles on which Mill based representative government: the principle of the maximum possible participation of citizens in governance and the principle of competence, which stated that as it was impossible for "numerous bodies" to carry out legislative and administrative tasks, decision-making powers should be vested in "competent persons [...] men of learning and vast knowledge and not deprived of experience" (LA, 6/VI/1861). This was a categorical defence of the institution of parliament, but also an appeal for the establishing of rules to facilitate its proper functioning and guarantee efficiency, including the abolition of the aristocratic principle; the election of the executive by representatives; regular renewal of the chamber and, finally, the need to debate proposals, for which Mora invoked Bentham *Essay on Political Tactics* (1843), deeming Bentham to have inspired Mill.[9] Like Mill, Mora warned of the dangers of the right to vote in elections reverting to those who were "notable for their wealth" and the imposition of "interests and tendencies opposed to those of the nation as a whole" in the chambers, which he felt the history of France was proof of (LA, 8/VI/1861, 9–10).

Mora's ideological shift towards progressive liberalism was also visible in his regular reports on the political unification of Italy. He was highly sympathetic to this cause and its leaders, particularly Garibaldi and Cavour, in their quest to free their country from the yoke of European absolutist powers. He also expressed support for national liberation movements in regions such as Denmark and Hungary, which sought to break away from the great Prussian and Austrian empires. As he did with Italy, Mora explained these processes in terms of the dialectic between tradition and liberalism and was highly critical of the authoritarianism of the Second French Empire and its interference in Italy and Mexico, all of which was bound to awaken enormous sympathy among republican elites in Hispanic America. However, he showed a certain ambiguity with regard to the American Civil War, the result of an acute ideological conflict. On the one hand, he was adamant about the need to end slavery, and from this perspective would seem to align himself with Lincoln's abolitionism. On the

[9] According to Mora, Mill made progress on the issue of female franchise following ideas that had already been put forward by Bentham.

other, he sympathised with the Southern States' free trade policy and disapproved of Lincoln's policy of blockading ports to prevent the export of cotton to England. The fact that Mora gave equal priority to the principles of economic and political liberalism and believed them both to be indispensable is shown by his ambivalent view of Chevalier and Cobden. While he considered them both genuine champions of economic freedom, Chevalier's support for France's meddling in Mexico and Cobden's support for Napoleon III provoked harsh criticism on his part, as is clear from the following comment:

> M. Chevalier is an eminent economist: but as a deep thinker and eloquent writer, his reputation is not enviable… We would fill volumes were we to set ourselves the task of dissecting M. Chevalier's work and making an inventory of the errors, misrepresentations, reservations and boasts it contains. (LA, 8/VI/1862, 12)

These articles rekindled Mora's deeply Anglophile spirit and his admiration for the development of political and economic liberalism in Argentina, Chile, Peru and Bolivia. He linked this achievement to the process initiated by Rivadavia, Pinto and Santa Cruz, the presidents with whom he had worked on these republics' institutional construction. In addition to advances in political freedom there, he naturally emphasised their adopting of free trade policies (González Pizarro 1987). A particularly revealing piece of writing was his article "*El Código civil chileno*", in which he stated that the "most effective, most active, most powerful reason why […] the transition has been so quick and so complete […] is free trade" (LA, 12/XII/1862, 7). He also gave a detailed description of the process of institutional transformation in the economic, education and legal spheres—the Civil Code itself—that arose from free trade, as well as of some of its supporters, such as Andrés Bello, with whom he had argued while in Chile.

Mora was obviously seeking recognition in Spanish progressive liberal circles for his contributions to economic and political liberalism, given his links—now weakened—with moderate circles since his return to Spain in 1843. His LA articles once again showed a controversial thinker, a militant liberal who was at ease in the tense atmosphere of Isabel II's Spain. In his view moderate liberalism had been "absorbed" by "neo-Catholicism" and had subdued "the printing press, stifling the spirit of scrutiny, restricting all the prerogatives of free men", ignoring the "legitimacy of the kingdom of Italy" and supporting the French occupation of Rome (LA, 12/XII/1863),[10] all elements of Spanish progressive ideology. Precisely as a result of the moderates' manoeuvres to prevent the progressives gaining access to power by legal and direct means, Mora endorsed the *Manifiesto del Partido Progresista a la nación* (1863) announcing the end of cooperation with the moderates and the beginning of a breakaway strategy which called for a new constituent *Cortes* (LA, 12/IX/1863, 3), although he did not sign it. His radicalism had its limits, however, mainly related to the economic models associated with certain economic utopias that were beginning to spread through Spain at that time.

10.5 Mora's Political Economy in *La América*

Political economy figured prominently in the articles Mora wrote for the LA. These were concentrated into the first year of his regular collaboration from March 1860 onwards, and in several he unveiled his aim of spreading the principles and beneficial consequences of the abolition of customs tariffs, a commitment based on the experience of the Anti-Corn Law League, the instigator of the 1846 repeal of the Corn Laws in England. In his opinion the success of Cobden's organisation was the result of an orchestrated strategy by means of speakers, or lecturers, that were qualified to present the basics of the case for abolishing the Corn Laws in "energetic but clear language within the reach of all intelligences"; to "multiply the announcements concerning the enterprise in all the newspapers"; to "pay distinguished writers" and, finally, to promote the famous "meetings" in defence of free trade throughout the country (LA, 7/X/1862, 12). There is no question that Mora had returned to the path that he first trod in the late 1840s and was calling on Spanish free traders, who had already begun to organise themselves, to promote a similar strategy.

The event that prompted Mora to introduce economic issues into the LA was undoubtedly the signing of the Cobden-Chevalier Treaty between France and Great Britain on 23 January 1860, two months before he

[10] In Spain the Catholic thinkers Jaime Balmes and Donoso Cortés, influenced by Joseph De Maistre, Louis de Bonald and, more generally, by the conservative intellectual reaction that followed the French Revolution, had laid the foundations of what was known as "neo-Catholicism", which during Isabel II's reign pursued an illiberal and traditionalist political project (González Cuevas 2020). The LA had in fact been criticised by Spanish neo-Catholic organs, especially the journal *El pensamiento español* (EPE, 1860–1874), to which Mora replied in the LA.

joined the journal's editorial staff. The Treaty was a well-known turning point in nineteenth-century trade policy as it introduced the "Most Favoured Nation" clause extending trade agreements to third countries, and thus heralded a period of free trade in Western economies, at least in relation to previous eras (Tena-Junguito et al. 2012). In fact, true to his own intellectual journey, free trade was the backbone of all Mora's political economy articles for the LA. They were the epigone of his contributions on the discipline and interwove the legacy of his previous writings with other elements and nuances, derived both from events in the 1860s and new-found intellectual influences.

Mora's contributions barely mentioned the theoretical bases of political economy. He himself made it clear that the journal was not a suitable place in which to dwell on the theoretical aspect of classical economics and although he mentioned some of its principles—such as wealth being "the work of labour" and that the theory of value is "regulated by the cost of production"—he focused on different arguments. Nevertheless, he argued in no uncertain terms that classical economics, particularly British economics, formed the theoretical underpinning of free trade, with Smith as its initiator. He did not overstep the theoretical boundaries of the ideological position that he had almost set in stone in the EM. Free trade meant cheaper goods and increased competition and hence better-quality products, leading to prosperity and enhanced welfare. He made few changes to the list of authors who he believed to have developed the discipline's theoretical foundations and who continued to be habitual sources for his writings: Smith, Ricardo, Storch, Torrens, Say, Mengotti, Bastiat and, especially, as "they deserve a special mention", McCulloch and James Mill, who he often cited in his LA articles, adding a few familiar Spanish authors such as Vadillo, Pebrer and Flórez Estrada.

The new arrivals, while few, were certainly noteworthy: John Stuart Mill and Michel Chevalier (LA, 8/VI/1860, 6). He cited two of Mill's economics works: *Essays on Some Unsettled Questions of Political Economy* (1844) and especially the *Principles of Political Economy with some of their Applications to Social Philosophy* (1848). He also gave a brief account of his methodology, stressing the importance of the new interpretation of inference, which, in contrast to Aristotelian syllogism, used empirical evidence to broaden the field of human knowledge (LA, 24/I/1861, 7–8).[11] Indeed, he highlighted the methodological shift that Mill had introduced into political economy by transforming it into a deductive science that inferred its propositions from specific facts. On the basis of these premises, he continued to uphold his empirical and inductive methodological approach, as he believed Mill's methodology to be a complement that set up the ideal models of economic organisation that should act as references for practical economics and economic policy.[12] However, as will be seen later, Mill was also highly important in the nuancing—or, rather, enriching—of some aspects of his approach to free trade. Mora used Chevalier's *Examen du système commercial connu sous le nom de système protecteur* (1849) as an inexhaustible supply of statistical resources on which he based much of his free trade rhetoric and criticism of protectionism.

In his quest to put forward a comprehensive and multi-faceted argument for free trade Mora rolled out his economic discourse in the LA on several levels, the first of which was moral. Following a row that erupted in the public sphere in Spain about political economy's moral nature he published two articles entitled "*Moralidad de la economía política*", aimed at refuting the notion that it was "an immoral science (if it merits the name)", since its "doctrines tend to nothing less than the supremacy of matter over the spirit" (LA, 8/III/1860, 5). Mora did not specify the school, "widely disseminated in our days", that supported this theory, but it is safe to surmise that it was neo-Catholicism, since he aimed to show that political economy and liberalism were compatible with religion and the precepts of the Gospels. His possible conversion to Protestantism adds weight to this argument, as does the certainty that he wrote an

[11] Although he did not expressly cite it, Mora clearly relied on Mill's description of his method in *A System of Logic*, which had been published in Spain in the 1850s and with which he was probably familiar (Mill 1853). However, he also pointed out that the critique of Mill's syllogistic method had been put forward in the works of Thomas Reid and Dugald Stewart, members of the Common Sense school, with which Mora was very familiar, as previously noted (LA, 24/1/1861, 7–8).

[12] In the EM he had echoed the innovative nature of these two works by Mill, which he learned about through a critical note in the French journal *Revue des deux mondes*. Mora attributed to Mill the modernising or updating of classical doctrine via the introduction of a deductive and abstract methodology, heir to Ricardo. In the LA he reiterated the importance of this new approach, which he nevertheless considered compatible with his empirical-practical viewpoint.

anti-Catholic treatise during his second term as Consul in London: *Roman Catholicism in Spain* (Mora 1855; Medina 2022, 219).[13]

Furthermore, probably because speculation was one of the focal points for criticism from political economy's opponents, Mora put forward a fierce defence of government borrowing, drawing on the authority of Chapter XII of John Stuart Mill's *Principles* as well as the adequacy of finance institutions.[14] He also revisited old ideas from his *Cursos de lógica y ética según la escuela de Edimburgo* (1832) to argue that "the urges and feelings which guide men in all life's actions are the same as those which lead them to acquire goods", and if the former "contribute to their perfection", the latter "cannot tend to the opposite", an approach which in his view Smith had perfected in the *Theory of Moral Sentiments* (1759; LA 8/III/1860, 5; 24/III/1860, 5). Having established political economy's moral nature Mora shifted the debate to laying bare the immorality of protectionism, in that high duties produced "shortages of goods" and the "paralysis of productive labour", while promoting illicit trade and smuggling, two ills that he felt could be classed as immoral.

The second level was historical analysis, which unfolded in a series of articles on trade in the empires of ancient times and more recent experiences in Europe. In two articles entitled "*Del comercio en la antigüedad*" Mora undertook a historical exploration on the basis of incidents in the Old Testament in order to draw a series of lessons from them, which he summarised in the following enlightening hypotheses:

> 1. Among all the creative and propagative agents of civilisation, trade is the most effective, the most enduring and the most analogous to man's moral condition. 2. Trade is the indispensable ally, the indispensable companion to

[13] However, his conversion to Protestantism has never been fully documented. His relationship with it dates back to his time in London and his involvement with the BFBS.

[14] Mora was referring specifically to lending institutions, which, contrary to the popular belief that they were a source of speculation, constituted a formidable vehicle for economic prosperity. In the wake of the publication of a report by the General Meeting of Shareholders of the *Banco de España*, which explained "the monetary conflict" caused by the withdrawal of currency "destined mainly for the country's exports", Mora fully supported the Bank's policy of purchasing precious metals abroad in order to preserve "the basis of its circulation and credit" (Banco de España 1862, 12–14). Classical aspects of his financial thinking such as the need for fiat money once again came to the fore in his defence; on the other hand, more explicitly than in previous writings, Mora favoured "increasing the capital circulating in a nation without increasing its metallic wealth" in order to face financial crises (LA, 8/V/1862, 7–8).

all other sources of useful work. 3. Free trade is the soul of commerce. (LA, 24/VII/1862, 11)

Mora's analysis of France and England's experiences also enabled him to extol free trade's superiority. Unsurprisingly, he opposed the interventionist and protectionist French model and supported the British free trade model with which he had become acquainted during his long exile in London. Now, moreover, his admiration extended to the trade policy that followed the victory of the Anti-Corn Law League's abolitionist stance. In three articles entitled "Colbert", Mora reviewed France's economic and trading history from the time Colbert took over the management of the Treasury under Louis XIV until the 1860 Cobden-Chevalier Treaty, adding a fourth article that discussed how French economic circles had reacted to the signing of the Treaty (LA, 8/11/1860, 6–7). Mora turned to his traditional sources to describe Colbert's political acts, especially Mengotti's *Il Colbertismo*, using extracts from the work to describe Colbert's policies and reforms, whose principles he essentially reduced to three: the balance of trade doctrine, "the preference for manufacturing over all other kinds of useful work" and the "high duties imposed on foreign goods" in order to promote national industry (LA, 8/VIII/1860, 5–6). It was this artificial expansion of industry under the aegis of an interventionist and protectionist system that was the main focus of his criticism. Although Mora mentioned Mengotti's examples of various Italian cities' failed attempts to industrialise, the influence of Smith's "natural progress of opulence" model was clear when he pointed out that manufacturing industry "develops gradually, in the manner of the human body, moving naturally from childhood to puberty", as well as in his enduring adherence to early Spanish liberalism's agricultural development model (LA, 24/VIII/1860, 5–6; Mengotti 1819; Paganelli 2022). Other excerpts contained comments that also evoked Smith: the welfare theory that argued that it was "a great injustice to condemn the many to enrich the few", the reliance on "private interests" as a factor in wealth creation and the fallacy of protectionism as a means of enrichment and industrialisation, all intertwined with contemporary debates on trade policy (LA, 24/VIII/1860, 5–6).

According to Mora it was the entrenchment of *Colbertiste* policies in France that lay behind the Cobden-Chevalier Treaty's unpopularity there (LA, 8/XI/1860, 5–6). In his view the backwardness caused by these policies over time and their lasting legacy in protectionist terms, particularly in the textile sector, explained the inefficiency of French industry vis-à-vis British "large-scale establishments", whose greater division of labour resulted in visibly higher production. Mora pointed out the paradox of the contrast between this tradition and the advances in French political economy, which were fuelled by authors such as Say, Bastiat and Chevalier, all champions of economic and trading freedom. However, in his opinion, in contrast to England, these ideas had not penetrated French public opinion sufficiently, which endorsed the importance of spreading political economy, as well as its most practical outcome: free trade. This explains why Chevalier was treated as a free trade hero who was launching a new policy in France that aimed to break away from the *Colbertiste* legacy.

Mora described the progress of English political economy in two series of articles entitled "*La economía política en Inglaterra*" (LA, 8/V/1860; 8/VI/1860; 24/VI/1860; 8/VII/1860) and "*Los economistas modernos*" (LA, 7/X/1862; 27/X/1862), paying particular attention to "the institutions on which these theories make their mark and the general movement of industry, trade and, above all and more than everything, the public's welfare" (LA, 8/V/1860, 6). He pointed out that not only had extraordinary "progress" been made in economic theory in England, but political and civil liberties such as "the unlimited impact that can be achieved by voting", the "freedom of the press" and the "public meetings and assemblies" were also more advanced. The latter institutions were crucial for changing legislation, as they provided points of communication between political economy and economic and trade legislation, mediated by a favourable "general" public opinion, to such an extent that "this statement is manifested by the means authorised by law" (LA, 8/VI/1860). This could be seen from the innovations passed by the two chambers in cases such as "Catholic emancipation, parliamentary reform, the abolition of slavery, the repeal of the Corn Laws [and] the improvement of tariffs" (LA, 8/V/1860).

On the basis of these premises, Mora set out a historical overview of British administrative practices and trade legislation since Cromwell's Protectorate, mentioning the parallel advance of political economy, whose remote origins he located in Mun, Petty, Child, North, Hume, Harris and Bentham. This body of theory converged in the figure of Smith, the starting point for political economy and "the most sublime propagator of free trade ideas" (LA, 24/VI/1860, 5). Mora went on to discuss familiar names from his writings, among them McCulloch and James Mill, to which he made the significant addition of John Stuart Mill. In contrast to the ideas of his youth, in which he stressed the inadequacy of Ricardo's deductive method, Mora now intentionally sidestepped any methodological or theoretical differences among economists—especially where Ricardo was concerned—to emphasise the way in which they converged in a common defence of free trade.

Where economic facts were concerned, Mora, of course, highlighted the events that had brought about advances in economic and trade freedom such as those during Walpole, Huskisson and especially Peel's ministries and the Anti-Corn Law League campaign. He interpreted free trade victory as being the outcome of the combination of a set of diverse factors: the strength of classical economic arguments, the highly effective movement to spread them via the lecturers, press advertisements, popular subscriptions and meetings, as well as the way in which the arguments were received by a society "as positive and logical as the English", who "became free traders". The political decision-making structure favoured the legislative implementation of abolitionist laws and the entire sequence led to the Cobden-Chevalier Treaty, whose leading players were treated as true champions of economic freedom (LA, 7/X/1862, 12–13).

The third level was an empirical analysis of the outcomes of contemporary experiences. As mentioned previously, in 1847 Mora was appointed *Consejero Real de agricultura, industria y comercio*, a post that he juggled with his three terms as Spanish Consul in London. As he himself said, these responsibilities gave him access to numerous statistical sources, from which he obtained "copies of irrefutable data, which we consider to be the most solid support and the most victorious arguments in favour of the doctrine that we profess" (LA, 21/III/1860, 5). Among these sources were the British Board of Trade, the French *Direction Générale des Douanes* and Spanish customs statements, and Mora also drew on data in works by economists such as Chevalier (LA, 8/VIII/1860, 5), thus equipping himself with statistical information that enabled him to underpin three ideas. The first was the link between lowering customs duties and the consequent growth in state revenue from them due to increased international trade, which in turn was the result of the reduction in the price of goods and the increase in tax bases in all spheres of tax administration (LA, 8/XII/1860, 5). The second was a drop in smuggling, a direct effect of lower tariffs (LA, 21/III/1860, 5), and, finally, there were the positive results for France in terms of exports to England because of the Cobden-Chevalier Treaty.

These three lines of argument were aimed indiscriminately at readers in mainland Spain, the Hispanic-American republics and the last remaining overseas territories, but in some respects, there was a particular and unequivocal target audience: the Spanish public. In his articles in the LA Mora revived his criticism of the protectionism that stemmed from the Catalan textile industry in similar terms to those set out in the DLC in 1843, that is, he linked protectionism and mercantilism along the lines laid down by Mengotti. However, he now extended this criticism to protectionism of all types, whether agricultural—grain imports—or industrial, both of which existed in Spain at the time. These principles were behind his debate with Joan Güell i Ferrer, the main Catalan protectionist theoretician and activist, whose ideas were based on Carey and List; this was a dispute that Güell i Ferrer had already begun with other Spanish free traders such as Luis María Pastor and in which he decried Bastiat's service-value theory (Artal 1979, 229). Güell i Ferrer, a Catalan textile manufacturer, had also criticised Mora's articles "*Sobre la moralidad de la economía política*", prompting Mora to respond with another entitled "*Contestación a un proteccionista*" (LA, 24/V/1860, 4–5). Mora entered the fray with a certain lofty air of disdain with respect to Güell's arguments, considering him completely ignorant of economic history, the most basic economic principles and the benefits generated by free trade policies in the countries that had adopted them. In spite of this he made it clear that free trade benefited both consumers, by guaranteeing low prices and, albeit indirectly, producers, whose markets grew due to increased demand; these were not new arguments for Mora but they acquired another dimension during this decade. He also accused Güell's protectionism of favouring a minority of producers at the expense of a majority of consumers and general welfare. Mora's favourite Smithian theory of welfare cropped up again in this critique, this time expressed in very plain terms: protectionist tariffs were a privilege that favoured a single industry—he was referring mainly to the Catalan cotton sector—resulting in "bad distribution of taxes, [which dries up] the wellsprings of useful work and public happiness" (LA, 24/V/1860, 5–6).

The free trade-protectionist debate in Spain effectively entered a new phase from 1859 onwards. The boost from Spanish free traders in the wake of Cobden's "triumphal tour" in late 1846 virtually fizzled out during the 1850s (See Chap. 8), when the *Sociedad de Economía Política* was founded with the aim of spreading economic knowledge throughout Spain. However, in 1859 they banded together in the *Asociación para la*

Reforma de los Aranceles de Aduanas which, following the pattern set by similar reform associations in Europe, especially France, now focused on promoting free trade and abolishing tariffs. The *Asociación* brought together university professors, traders and some of the most important businessmen in the finance, property, railway and mining sectors; that is, the leading Spanish industries of the day. The main Spanish free traders all had liberal tendencies ranging from moderate to democrat and were led by the *Asociación* President Luis María Pastor and the secretary Gabriel Rodríguez; their meetings at the Madrid Stock Exchange to discuss free trade-related economic issues formed part of a publicity campaign that included the press and seemingly mirrored various aspects of the Anti-Corn Law League's strategy. Their views finally triumphed in 1869 when Finance Minister Laureano de Figuerola, a prominent member of the *Asociación*, pushed through a free trade tariff law, the *Ley de Bases Arancelarias.*

Mora was of course aware of the *Asociación*'s activities. He praised it in the LA, reporting on some of the meetings and detailing the interventions of its most prominent members such as Luis María Pastor and Segismundo Moret (LA, 8/VIII/1861, 7; 12/I/1864, 11–12). Furthermore, other leading economists of the institution such as Manuel Colmeiro, Félix Bona and Andrés Borrego were regular contributors to the journal and expressed a pro-free trade point of view which Mora deemed "the same doctrine" as Chevalier's (LA, 27/X/1862). However, despite their common interests, aims and intellectual sources there is no evidence that Mora took part in the *Asociación*'s meetings or had any particular relationship with its members, and he is not mentioned in the *Asociación*'s minutes (*Asociación* 1860). He did not contribute to the *Gaceta Economista* (GE, 1860–1863), the *Asociación*'s informative publication, or participate in the successful lectures held at the *Ateneo de Madrid*, an institution to which he had close links and in which practically all the propagandists for liberalism played a part (*Asociación* 1863). Firmly anchored in the generation of Flórez Estrada, Vadillo and Pebrer,[15] Mora chose to ignore the works of the latest batch of Spanish free trade economists as intellectual sources for his articles, all of which gives the impression that while his support for free trade in the LA

[15] He included a citation from *Influencia del sistema prohibitivo en la agricultura, comercio y rentas públicas* (1842) by Manuel Marliani in the LA (, 21/III/1860, 5). Marliani was another first-generation free trader to whom Mora had, however, paid little attention in earlier works.

ran parallel to the mainstream of Spanish economists grouped around the *Asociación*, their two separate routes towards it did not actually overlap. In short, instead of speculating on the motivation and circumstances behind Mora's estrangement from the most representative organisation of Hispanic free trade, it seems preferable at this point to focus on the path Mora chose to take in the early 1860s. In a poem published in the LA in late 1863 he seemed to refer to this intellectual solitude when he wrote that those who "devote themselves to the pursuit of knowledge live alone and quietly in their attics; let the lay gang triumph at ease, since everything in Spain today is a gang" (LA, 12/X/1863, 13).

Although most of the rhetoric and arguments Mora used in his contributions to the LA varied little from his previous writings, the fact that some new elements and nuances nevertheless appeared shows that he never failed to grasp changes in political economy and that his thinking was not watertight but open to new ideas which he adapted to an analytical structure whose essence remained intact. The most significant of these new developments was the link between free trade, social justice and universal peace. The repeal of the Corn Laws in England was not only a reaction to the interests of a pressure group that pursued specific economic benefits brought about by the reduction in labour costs, but also to a radical, ideological approach to international relations that responded to the dream of universal peace pursued by Cobden and his followers (Howe 1998). Furthermore, the Anti-Corn Law League was extremely popular with the middle and working classes because it satisfied their demand for cheaper consumer goods. Linked to this approach was a change of strategy in the practice of free trade. In 1846 the League had proposed repealing the Corn Laws on a unilateral basis; however, this strategy was gradually modified and both Cobden and Gladstone himself accepted that free trade should be extended on a reciprocal basis, on the grounds that this would guarantee a climate of peace in international relations, cut defence spending and allow for lower taxes (Cain 1999). Mora, who always had an ear open for economic and political developments in Britain, would have picked up on this ideological mood during his London sojourns and undoubtedly embraced both the strategy of trade reciprocity and the ideology of universal peace. This can be seen from his knowledge of the activities of the International Peace Society founded by John Bright, joint leader with Cobden of the Anti-Corn Law League, as well as his constant references to free trade's peace-making role, which he believed would also guarantee mutual prosperity (LA, 7/X/1862, 12; 8/III/1861). The traditional Smithian demand regarding the benefits of the cheap consumer goods that free trade produced, which Mora raised time and again in the LA, must now have found complementary practical support in the demands of the Cobdenites and the English working classes. The fact that in the 1840s Mora moved closer to Bastiat, when his influence in France was at its height, has already been mentioned, as has his somewhat later proximity to John Stuart Mill's approach, especially his methodology. Mora now interpreted Mill through the prism of free trade and Mill was the authority on whom he based his peace-making, civilising approach to free trade when introducing an extract from Chapter XVII of the *Principles* in which he argued that increased international trade was the "main guarantee of world peace" (LA, 27/IV/1864, 6).[16]

The fact that Mora attached great importance to free trade's new dimension as the guarantor of a new international order at the level of morality and social justice is confirmed by a series of citations from other authors such as the Swiss Fourierist economist M. H. Dameth (*Le juste et l'utile,* 1959), a work that underlined the economy's leading role in achieving maximum welfare and resolution of conflicts (LA, 21/III/1860, 6), and Brussels-based German jurist Heinrich Ahrens and the *Curso de Derecho Natural* (1841), one of the main channels through which Krausism was introduced into Spain. Also, highly significant in this respect were the two articles in which Mora discussed the monograph *Della economia pubblica e delle sue attinenze con la morale e col diritto* (1859) by Marco Minghetti, President of the Council of Ministers and Minister of Finance in Italy. Mora linked Minghetti with Gladstone to explain that economics had succeeded in placing two erudite people who had "broadened their intelligence by means of solid doctrines" in the highest political spheres. Mora's interest in Minghetti's book, which he read in French—it was published in 1863 by the "economist" publishing house Guillaumin et Cie, Librairie—, is not surprising, considering that it attributed to free trade policies the ability to bring about radical change in international relations towards a new peaceful order (Gherardi 2001). Mora's free trade reading of the book was similar to his interpretation of Mill's *Principles* and led him to underline the notion that "the contest or rivalry which

[16] However, there is no mention of the theoretical debate on the benefits and drawbacks of either free trade unilateralism or reciprocity, which had been introduced by Torrens, a reciprocity advocate and author known to Mora (Irwin 1996, 101–15).

economists call competition", which opened up "an endless race towards progress", resulted from free trade (LA, 12/I/1864).

The repeal of the Corn Laws in England raised the issue of replacing the tax revenue previously obtained from customs duties. In order to temporarily compensate for this loss of government revenue Peel introduced income tax in 1842, which was completed in 1860, with Gladstone as Chancellor of the Exchequer. Both men were confident that reduced rates of taxation would lead to an increase in overall revenue and that this would make new taxes unnecessary; however, Gladstone was forced to lower the minimum exempt income threshold in the early 1860s (Cain 1999). Despite this, free trade was very popular in Britain and the abolition of tariffs and introduction of income tax had the support of the middle and working classes. Mora shared Peel and Gladstone's confidence in the positive impact of tariff reduction on total revenue but, like them, he understood the need to build a tax system that would raise the funds necessary to sustain the liberal state. Always aware of economic developments in Britain, Mora echoed Gladstone's "total emancipation of trade" project and introduction of income tax to abolish customs duties (LA, 8/VII/1860, 6), although there is no subsequent mention in the LA of the possibility of introducing income tax in Spain. As previously noted, in the DLC Mora had leaned—not without some ambiguity—towards a tax on consumption, although he did not delve very deeply into the debate surrounding direct and indirect taxation. His position was based on Smith's taxation principles, headed by the "ability to pay" principle, a reference from his time in Chile and his articles for the EMC. However, as also mentioned previously, in the EM he took the bull by the horns and criticised indirect taxation in no uncertain terms. Enlightened by British innovations in taxation, he stressed in the LA that fiscal theory should resolve the debate between direct and indirect taxes, going on to wonder whether "duties on consumption, besides being harmful to labourers because they reduce their ability to buy the articles necessary for their subsistence and that of their families, are not equally harmful to capitalists who employ labour, obliging them to raise wages and the price of their products" (LA, 8/VII/1860, 7). In doing this he took up a position that was consistent with the progressive circles in which he now moved, which advocated the abolition of excise duties—later restored when the moderates acceded to government in 1856—given that, as Figuerola argued in parliamentary discussions to this effect, they adversely affected commercial transactions in the domestic market (Martín Rodríguez 2009, 285).

The fiscal nuances that Mora introduced revealed his concern for the material and moral conditions of the populace as a whole, in line with British abolitionists, an interest that led him to explore various utopian approaches that had penetrated certain Spanish circles at that time.[17] More significant than Dameth was Mora's critical commentary on P. J. Proudhon's *Du principe féderatif et de la nécessité de reconstituer le parti de la révolution*, which was published in 1863 (LA, 12/IV/1863, 6–7), the same year as the French edition appeared and almost a decade before the book was translated by Pi i Margall, who was the main advocate of Spanish federalism. Mora did not considered federalism any guarantee of a competitive system, since the most powerful and populous cities and regions would dominate the weaker ones, creating a situation of poverty and inequality. More generally, Mora was clearly sceptical about the ability of economic utopias, which now began to permeate Spanish progressive and democratic circles, to remedy the ills they denounced: "All the panaceas that have been invented up to now to suppress misery at a single stroke have been nothing more than the follies of visionaries or the secrets of charlatanism" (LA, 12/I/1864, 11).

10.6 Final Remarks

Mora distrusted both revolutionary utopias and the rehabilitation of the old mercantilist policies, now normalised in the protectionism of "vested interests"—that is, those of Catalan industry—to promote the prosperity that their sponsors promised. On the contrary, his articles for the LA expressed an unquestionable confidence in the doctrines and policies of classical economics, particularly free trade, as a means of combining national wealth and a new international moral order. It was therefore imperative for state authorities to promote economic science in academic circles and to spread its principles among civil servants and public opinion so that they could be translated into good policies which would contribute to paving the way to prosperity as they had in Britain. The recipients of this message were not only elites in mainland Spain, but also those in the Hispanic-American republics and the remaining colonies. Mora's economics articles for the LA fairly bristled with signs of his conviction that if

[17] Mora's openness to the advances in economics is demonstrated by the book review he published to *Recherches sur les principes mathematiques de la theorie de la richesse* by Cournot (LA 27/08/1864, 8–9).

reforms were to become enshrined in law, it was first necessary to provide plenty of information in order to sway public opinion in their favour. There is no question that he devoted himself to this task with great passion over the last years of his life. Few details are known about how Mora spent those last years. According to Ferrer del Río (1864, 6), Mora "worked many hours a day, entertained himself with long walks, and in the evenings he chatted with friends on science and literature". In late winter of 1864, his health began to weaken seriously. After trying to recover fruitlessly during the summer in the pleasant French town of Saint Jean de Luz, he died in Madrid on 3 October of the same year.

Bibliography

Books[18]

Mora, José Joaquín de. 1832. *Cursos de lógica y ética según la escuela de Edimburgo por José Joaquín de Mora*. Lima: Imprenta de José Masías.

Mora, José Joaquín de. 1855. *Roman Catholicism in Spain*. Trans. Thomas Parker. Edinburgh: Johnstone and Hunter.

Primary Sources

Banco de España. 1862. *Memoria leída en la Junta General de accionistas del Banco de España el día 8 de marzo de 1862*. Madrid: Imprenta y librería de D. Eusebio Aguado.

Mengotti, Francesco. 1819. *Il Colbertismo*. Florence: Piatti.

Mill, John Stuart. 1853. *Sistema de Lógica demostrativa e inductiva: o sea, exposición comparada de los principios de evidencia y los métodos de investigación científica*. Madrid: Imprenta M. Rivadeneyra.

Secondary Sources

Artal, Françesc. 1979. "Guëll i Ferrer, Joan". In *Ictineu. Diccionari de les ciències de la societat als Països Catalans (segles XVIII–XX)*, edited by Françesc Artal et alii. Barcelona: Edicions 62.

Cain, Peter. 1999. "British Free Trade, 1850–1914: Economics and Policy". *Refresh. Recent Findings of Research in Economics&Social History* 29, 1–4.

[18] On the prolix reprints of the *Catecismos*, *Cursos* and other works of Mora in the Hispanic world, see Roldán (2003), Macintyre (2018) and Medina (2022).

Cancino, Hugo and Rita Cancino. 2014. "El movimiento generacional e intelectual de 1842 y la irrupción de un proyecto de modernidad en Chile". In *Pensamentos, contextos y instituicôes: Dos processsos de independencia a globalizacao*, edited by Lená Medeiros de Menezes, Hugo Cancino Troncoso and Rogelio de la Mora, 250–66. Rio de Janeiro: Universidade do Estado do Rio de Janeiro.

Carr, Raymond. 1968. *España, 1808–1939*. Barcelona: Ariel.

Chato, Ignacio. 2011. "La Unión Liberal y la renovación del sistema de partidos (1858–1863)". *Revista de Estudios Políticos* 153, 75–111.

Escolano, Luis Alfonso. 2018. "*El Museo Universal* y *La América* (1857–1860): dos estilos periodísticos diferentes y una misma perspectiva americanista al servicio de la burguesía liberal española". *Tzintzun. Revista de Estudios Históricos* 68, 105–35.

Gherardi, Raffaela. 2001. "La scienza, il capitale e la libertà: *l'economia publica* (1859) e le 'relazioni pacifiche dei popoli'". *Scienza&Política* 24, 39–55.

González Cuevas, Pedro Carlos. 2020. "Neocatolicismo, carlismo y democracia". *Memoria y Civilización. Anuario de Historia* 23, 229–57.

González Pizarro, José Antonio. 1984. "Don José Joaquín de Mora, Cónsul español en Londres (1850–1858)". *Boletín de la Academia Chilena de Historia* 51, 353–67.

González Pizarro, José Antonio. 1987. "José Joaquín de Mora y *La América, Crónica hispanoamericana* (1859–1864)". *Revista de literatura* 97, 95–114.

Howe, Anthony. 1998. *Free Trade and Liberal England, 1846–1946*. Oxford: OUP.

Irwin, Douglas A. 1996. *Against the Tide. An Intellectual History of Free Trade*. Princeton: PUP.

López-Ocón, Leoncio. 1982. "*La América. Crónica hispano-americana*. Génesis y significación de una empresa americanista del liberalismo democrático español". *Quinto Centenario* 4, 137–74.

Medina, Sara. 2022. *José Joaquín de Mora and Britain: Cultural Transfers and Transformations*. Berlin: Peter Lang.

Paganelli, Maria Pia. 2022. "Adam Smith and Economic Development in Theory and Practice: A Rejection of the Stadial Model?". *Journal of the History of Economic Thought* 44–1, 95–104.

Prados de la Escosura, Leandro. 2000. *El progreso económico de España (1850–2000)*. Bilbao: Fundación BBVA.

Rubio Cremades, Enrique. 2013. "Hispanoamérica y España a mediados del siglo XIX: el editor Francisco de Paula Mellado y la *Revista española de ambos mundos*". *Anales de literatura española* 25, 317–39.

Sánchez Albornoz, Nicolás. 1968. *España hace un siglo: una economía dual*. Madrid: Península.

Tena-Junguito, Antonio, Markus Lampe and Felipe Tâmega. 2012. "How Much Trade Liberalization Was there in the World Before and after Cobden-Chevalier?". *The Journal of Economic History* 72, 708–40.

A Catalogue of Mora's Journalistic Articles and Encyclopaedic Entries on Political Economy and Allied Sciences (1825–1864)

Compiling this Catalogue, the only one to date has had to face multiple and diverse difficulties. Mora's work was very lengthy and was carried out in six different countries, so, as mentioned in Chap. 1, it is by no means certain that we have been able to identify and recognise the entire body of Mora's writings, in particular, those published in the printing press. At the same time, it was not always possible to find the newspapers in which he wrote, and, in some cases, we have only access to incomplete collections of them. In addition, most of the texts published by Mora in the press and encyclopaedic collections appeared anonymously or unsigned, so attributing him their authorship is ambiguous and tremendously tricky. As seen in Chap. 1, the criterion adopted here has been to attribute writings to Mora indirectly based on intellectual affinity; content—he used the same magnificent written style in Spanish in all his writings, not only the strictly literary pieces—; intellectual development; the use of similar sources and the position he occupied in the hierarchy of the journal or publication in which the texts in question were published. We have opted to attribute the political economy articles in journals at which he was editor, co-editor or a leading journalist to him. Finally, in this Catalogue, articles and encyclopaedic entries with a title of their own are enclosed in quotation marks. The main subjects of untitled works are enclosed in square brackets and works with a possible pseudonym are enclosed in dashes.

J. Astigarraga et al., *The Economic Legacy of José Joaquín de Mora*, Palgrave Studies in the History of Economic Thought, https://doi.org/10.1007/978-3-031-49446-8

Museo universal de ciencias y artes (London, 1825–1826)

"Comercio de la Gran Bretaña", I (1825), 79–85; "Economía Política", I (1825), 91–94; "Leyes prohibitivas del comercio", I (1825), 94–96; "Agricultura. De los medios de mejorar la condición de un país", I (1825), 96–105; "Economía Política. Ideas sobre la balanza de comercio", I (1825), 148–51; "Economía Política. Nuevas empresas en Inglaterra", I (1825), 232–34; "Economía Política. Las máquinas", I (1825), 234–39; "Economía Política. De los impuestos sobre granos extranjeros. Memoria leída en la sociedad de los Georgofilos de Florencia, por el Comendador Lappo di Ricci", I (1825), 239–43; "Instituciones de Beneficencia", I (1825), 254–56; "Población", I (1825), 257–62; "Agricultura", I (1825), 277–83; "Comercio. Del comercio de Inglaterra y de los trabajos debido a su influjo", I (1825), 283–89; "Estadística. Utilidad de los datos estadísticos, y medios de adquirirlos con seguridad", I (1825), 290–96; "Enseñanza económico-moral. Bosquejo de un curso de economía y de moral", I (1825), 302–308; "Pensamientos sueltos sobre la industria y la moral", I (1825), 308–14; "Economía política. Ideas sobre este asunto", II (1826), 43–45; "De la Lógica", II (1826), 97–103; "Pensamientos sobre el bien público, por un alemán", II (1826), 115–19; "Observaciones sobre el informe acerca de aumentar los derechos de exportación de plata y oro", II (1826), 143–52; "De la enseñanza escolástica de la moral", II (1826), 152–56; "Bibliografía extranjera o examen de algunas obras importantes publicadas recientemente en Europa" (Book review to *Tratado de legislación, o exposición de las leyes generales según las cuales los pueblos prosperan, decaen, o permanecen estacionarios, por Carlos Comte*), II (1826), 157–61; "Bibliografía extranjera o examen de algunas obras importantes publicadas recientemente en Europa" (Book review to *Cinco preguntas sobre la actual crisis mercantil de Inglaterra, por P. Pebrer*), II (1826), 161–64; "Bibliografía extranjera o examen de alguna obras importantes publicadas recientemente en Europa" (Book review to *Bosquejos políticos, históricos y civiles de Argel, que contienen datos sobre la geografía, la población, el gobierno, las rentas, el comercio, la agricultura, las costumbres, &c., de aquel país, por Guillermo Shaler, Cónsul general de los Estados Unidos en Argel*), II (1826), 164–67; "Bibliografía extranjera o examen de algunas obras importantes publicadas recientemente en Europa" (Book review to *Catecismo de economía política; publicado por R. Ackermann en Londres, y en sus establecimientos de México, Guatemala, Colombia, Buenos Aires, Chile y Perú*), II (1826), 217–26; "De la crisis comercial que sufre actualmente la Inglaterra, y de su reacción en Francia", II (1826), 226–29.

Correo literario y político (London, 1826)

"Cartas sobre Inglaterra, por el barón de Stael Holstein", 70–75, 110–16, 201–209, 305–12; "Cartas de un americano sobre las ventajas de los gobiernos federativos", 352–56; "Algunas ideas sobre los progresos de la ciencia política", 357–61.

Crónica política y literaria de Buenos Aires (Buenos Aires, 1827).[1]

"Economía política. De la población", no. 4, 8/III/1827; [Public debt], no. 4, 8/III/1827; "Agricultura", no. 7, 17/III/1827; "Economía política. De la población. Artículo segundo", no. 8, 29/III/1827; "Del espíritu de asociación", no. 12, 19/III/1827; [On Flórez Estrada's *Reflexiones*], no. 13, 21/III/1827; [On Say's *Traité*], no. 14, 3/IV/1827; [Book review of *Lettres sur l'administration de Bresil*], no. 16, 7/IV/1827; "Casa de Moneda", no. 17, 17/IV/1827; "Del espíritu de asociación. Artículo 2", no. 20, 21/IV/1827; [On Flórez Estrada's *Reflexiones*], no. 21, 26/IV/1827; "Economía política. De los bancos particulares de Escocia", no. 23, 1/V/1827; "Emigración", no. 30, 17/V/1827; "Federalismo", no. 33, 29/V/1827; "Del espíritu de asociación. Tercer y último artículo", no. 43, 26/VI/1827; "Variedades" [On the spirit of commerce], no. 49, 11/VII/1827; "Revista sumaria de los progresos de la economía política", no. 56, 19/VII/1827; [On Huskisson's policy], no 57, 20/VII/1827; "Fallecimiento de Mr. Fallenberg en Hofwyl (Suiza)", no. 60, 25/VII/1827; "Economía política. Sobre las opiniones de Mr. Mac Culloch", no. 61, 26/VII/1827; "Establecimiento de Mr. Fallenberg en Hofwyl (Suiza)", no. 62, 27/VII/1827; "Economía política. Sobre los impuestos moderados", no. 63, 28/VII/1827; "Economía política. Bosquejo histórico del Banco nacional", no. 69, 4/VIII/1827; "Economía política. Crédito público", no. 71, 7/VIII/1827; "Obras de Jeremías Bentham", no. 72, 8/VIII/1827; "Obras completas de Jeremías Bentham", no. 73, 9/VIII/1827; "Economía política. Bosquejo histórico del Banco nacional", no. 74, 10/VIII/1827; "Obras completas de Jeremías Bentham", no. 74, 10/VIII/1827; "Obras completas de Jeremías Bentham", no. 75, 11/VIII/1827; "Banco. Continuación de los artículos insertos en los números 69, 71 y 74", no. 81, 20/VIII/1827; [On the free trade], no. 83, 22/VIII/1827; "Banco", no. 96, 7/IX/1827; "Aduanas", no. 97, 10/IX/1827; "Sistema de empréstitos", no. 99, 12/IX/1827; "Aduanas",

[1] Nos. 34–35, 37, 47, 53–54, 73, 95, 101, 110 and from 112 onwards have not been found.

no. 100, 13/IX/1827; "Aduanas", no. 103, 17/IX/1827; "Sistema de contribuciones", no. 104, 18/IX/1827.

El mercurio chileno (Santiago de Chile, 1828–1829)

"Del crédito público, de su naturaleza, de sus ventajas y de sus principios", no. 1, 1/IV/1828, 5–25; "De los sistemas de hacienda", no. 2, 1/V/1828, 53–62; "Legislación comercial. Almacenes de depósito", no. 2, 1/V/1828, 99–100; "Contribuciones", no. 3, 1/VI/1828, 101–16; "De los bancos de descuento y circulación", no. 4, 1/VII/1828, 149–71; "Hacienda de los Estados Unidos", no. 4, 1/VII/1828, 196; "Aduanas. Art.1°", no. 5, 1/VIII/1828, 197–207; "Estadística económica. Comercio de trigo en Inglaterra", no. 5, 1/VIII/1828, 242; "Aduanas. Artículo segundo", no. 6, 1/IX/1828, 245–68; "Banco nacional", no. 7, 1/X/1828, 327–33; "Variedades. Estadística económica", no. 7, 1/X/1828, 331–32; "Comercio. Importaciones y exportaciones de la Gran Bretaña", no. 7, 1/X/1828, 336; "Variedades. Empréstitos. Restricciones mercantiles", no. 8, 1/XI/1828, 386–88; "Puertos Francos", no. 9, 1/XII/1828, 389–403; "Crédito público", no. 9, 1/ XII/1828, 403–408; "Correspondencia a un ciudadano de los Estados Unidos", no. 9, 1/XII/1828, 427–32; "Variedades. Contribuciones en Inglaterra", no. 9, 1/XII/1828, 432; "Aduanas. Observaciones sobre la organización de las aduanas en Francia", no. 10, 1/I/1829, 466–70; "Aranceles de los Estados Unidos", no. 10, 1/I/1829, 474–76; "Bancos", no. 14, 15/V/1829, 662–69; "Variedades. España. Situación económica", no. 14, 15/V/1829, 668–69; "Comercio. Interés del dinero", no. 14, 15/V/1829, 673–74; "Comercio. Juicio de esta obra. Artículo primero", no. 15, 15/VI/1829, 677–84; "Aplicación de algunas verdades de esta ciencia a la situación de Chile", no. 16, 15/VII/1829, 725–35; "El comercio en el siglo XIX&C. Juicio de esta obra. Artículo segundo", no. 16, 15/VII/1829, 757–65.

Mercurio peruano (Lima, 1827–1834)[2]

"Mercurio peruano. Economía Política. ¿Cómo desaparece la riqueza de los pueblos?", no. 1104, 17/V/1831; "Mercurio peruano. Prohibiciones (Art. Tercero)", no. 1170, 9/VIII/1831; "Mercurio peruano. Pormenores sobre el Banco de Inglaterra", no. 1191, 5/IX/1831; "Exterior. Crédito público en España y en Francia"—Signed by EE—, no.

[2] In the collections that we have consulted of the *Mercurio Peruano*, some issues are missing. Quite certainly, Mora published, in the missing issues, two articles in the section "Mercurio Peruano" entitled respectively "Prohibiciones Art. I" and "Prohibiciones Art. II".

1210, 3/X/1831; "Mercurio peruano" [Definitions and theoretical issues in economics], no. 1249, 15/XI/1831; "Variedades. Obras de Jeremías Bentham", no. 1445, 18/VII/1832; "Variedades. Obras de Jeremías Bentham. Continuación del número anterior", no. 1446, 19/VII/1832; "Variedades. Obras de Jeremías Bentham. Continuación del número anterior", no. 1450, 24/VII/1832; "Variedades. Obras completas de Jeremías Bentham. Continuación del número 1450", no. 1453, 1/VIII/1832; "Variedades. Obras completas de Jeremías Bentham. Continuación del número 1453", no. 1463, 10/VIII/1832; "Crédito público"—Signed by "Los imparciales"—, no. 1471, Suplemento al *Mercurio Peruano*; "Obras completas de Jeremías Bentham. Conclusión", no. 1486, 10/IX/1832; "Variedades. Estado de la industria en Francia y en Inglaterra", no. 1491, 15/IX/1832; "Variedades. Estado de la industria en Francia y en Inglaterra. Conclusión del núm. anterior", no. 1492, 17/IX/1832; "Mercurio peruano" [On *Curso de Derecho Natural y de Gentes* and Dugald Stewart. Debate with an author from *La Miscelánea*], no. 1542, 16/XI/1832; "Mercurio peruano" [On *Curso de Derecho Natural y de Gentes* and Dugald Stewart. Debate with an author from *La Miscelánea*], no. 1543, 17/XI/1832; "Mercurio peruano" [On *Curso de Derecho Natural y de Gentes* and Dugald Stewart. Debate with an author from *La Miscelánea*]", no. 1544, 19/XI/1832; "Mercurio peruano" [On the Trade Treatise Peru-Ecuador], no. 1565, 14/XII/1832; "Variedades. De las relaciones comerciales de la Francia con la América del Sur", no. 1763, 28/VIII/1833; "Variedades. De las relaciones comerciales de la Francia con la América del Sur", no. 1765, 31/VIII/1833; "Mercurio peruano" [On Bowring's spread of free trade], no. 1772, 9/IX/1833; "Variedades. Industria" [On Charles Babbage], no. 1805, 18/X/1833; "Variedades. De la Economía política en Rusia", no. 1860, 24/XII/1833; "Mercurio peruano" [On prohibitions], no. 1299, 17/I/1832; "Mercurio peruano" [On prohibitions], no. 1311, 31/I/1832; "Mercurio peruano" [On prohibitions], no. 1320, 11/II/1832; "Variedades. Pormenores sobre la circulación de metales", no. 1365, 7/IV/1832; "Variedades. Pormenores sobre la circulación de metales", no. 1368, 11/IV/1832; "Variedades. Pormenores sobre la circulación de metales", no. 1369, 12/IV/1832; "Mercurio peruano" [On depopulation], no. 1379, 27/IV/1832; "Mercurio peruano" [On Bentham and his works on criminal jurisprudence], no. 1387, 7/V/1832; "Variedades. Obras de Jeremías Bentham", no. 1445, 18/VII/1832; "Variedades. Obras de Jeremías Bentham", no. 1446, 19/VII/1832; "Variedades. Obras de Jeremías Bentham", no.

1450, 24/VII/1832; "Variedades. Obras completas de Jeremías Bentham", no. 1463, 10/VIII/1832; "Obras completas de Jeremías Bentham (Conclusión)", n. 1486, 10/IX/1832; "Mercurio peruano. Economía política" [Letter on depopulation], no. 1578, 3/I/1833; "Variedades. Bien Público" [On the education of the deprived], no. 1588, 15/I/1833; "Mercurio peruano. Economía política. De las contribuciones directas en Francia", no. 1607, 7/II/1833; "Mercurio peruano. Del comercio extranjero por Mac-Culloch", no. 1612, 13/II/1833; "Mercurio peruano. Continuación del número anterior", no. 1613, 14/II/1833; "Mercurio peruano. Continuación del número anterior", no. 1614, 15/II/1833; "Mercurio peruano. Economía política" [Book review of the ER to W. Jacob's book], no. 1632, 11/III/1833; "Mercurio peruano. Economía política. Continuación del artículo inserto en el número 1632″, no. 1633, 12/III/1833; "Mercurio peruano. Economía política. Continuación del artículo inserto en el número 1633″, no. 1634, 13/III/1833; "Variedades. El jurisconsulto Bentham", no. 1641, 22/III/1833; "Variedades. Bancos de depósito", no. 1642, 23/III/1833; "Variedades. Bancos de depósito (Continuación del número anterior)", no. 1643, 26/III/1833; "Mercurio peruano. Libertad de comercio", no. 1662, 22/IV/1833; "Economía política. Compañías de comercio privilegiadas", no. 1663, 23/IV/1833; "Variedades. Economía política. Compañías de comercio privilegiadas (Conclusión del núm. 1663)", no. 1664, 24/IV/1833; "Variedades. Progreso de las poblaciones en Estados Unidos", no. 1664, 24/IV/1833; "Exterior. Situación comercial de la Europa", no. 1678, 10/V/1833.

El conciliador (Lima, 1830–1833)

[Public wealth and franchising], II (1831), no. 36, 4/V/1831, no. 37, 7/V/1831; [Warehousing depots], II (1831), no. 38, 11/V/1831; [Suppression of friaries and church property], II (1831), no. 39, 14/V/1831, no. 40, 18/V/1831; "Un gobierno solo debe administrar bienes del estado", II (1831), no. 41, 21/V/1831; [Political economy], II (1831), no. 44, 28/V/1831, no. 46, 4/VI/1831; [Credit], II (1831), no. 50, 19/VI/1831; [Merchant shipping], II (1831), no. 55, 6/VII/1831; [Commerce], II (1831), no. 59, 20/VII/1831; [Council properties], II (1831), no. 60, 23/VII/1831; [Population], II (1831), no. 30/VII/1831; [Slavery], II (1831), no. 63, 3/VIII/1831; [Public finances], II (1831), no. 65, 10/VIII/1831; [Scottish philosophy], II (1831), no. 67, 17/VIII/1832, no. 70, 24/VIII/1831; [Statistics], II (1831), no. 75, 10/IX/1831; [The economy in Mexico], II (1831), no.

76, 14/IX/1831; [Peru's natural and economic advantages], II (1831), no. 82, 5/X/1831; [Commerce], II (1831), no. 85, 15/X/1831; [Commerce Regulation], II (1831), no. 86, 19/X/1831; [On prohibitions], II (1831), no. 89, 29/X/1831, no. 90. 2/XI/1831; [Foreign trade barriers], II (1831), no. 95, 19/XI/1831; [Political economy is not a brilliant utopia], II (1831), no. 96, 23/XI/1831; [Government is no substitute for private initiative], II (1831), no. 104, 21/XII/1831; [Political economy], III (1832), no. 1, 4/I/1832; [Treasury boards], III (1832), no. 10, 4/II/1832; [Causes of US wealth], III (1832), no. 41, 26/V/1832; [Foreign trade as a source of wealth], III (1832), no. 45, 9/VI/1832; [Peru-Bolivia Trade Treaty], III (1832), no. 50, 27/VI/1832, no. 51, 30/VI/1832, no. 52, 4/VII/1832; no. 53, 7/VII/1832, no. 55 14/VII/1832, no. 57, 21/VII/1832, no. 60, 1/VIII/1832, no. 61, 4/VIII/1832, no. 62, 8/VIII/1832, no. 64, 15/VIII/1832, no. 76, 29/IX/1832, no. 87, 10/XI/1832, no. 96, 12/XII/1832; IV (1833), no. 4, 12/I/1833, no. 13, 16/II/1833, no. 24, 30/III/1833; [Coca and tithes], III (1832), no. 66, 22/VIII/1832; [Corn dealers], III (1832), no. 72, 12/IX/1832; [Bailout bank], III (1832), no. 73, 15/IX/1832; [Consulate of trade], III (1832), no. 74, 19/IX/1832; [Public finance improvement measures], III (1832), no. 83, 27/X/1832; [Commerce Regulation], III (1832), no. 86, 7/XI/1832, no. 87, 10/XI/1832, no. 88, 14/XI/1832, no. 89, 17/XI/1832, no. 90, 21/XI/1832, no. 91, 24, XI/1832, no. 92, 28/XI/1832, no. 93, 1/XII/1832, no 95, 8/XII/1832, no. 96, 12/XII/1832, no. 97, 15/XII/1832, no. 98, 19/XII/1832, no. 99, 22/XII/1832; [Prohibitions system], IV (1833), no. 1, 3/I/1833, no. 2, 5/I/1833; [Rate of interest], IV (1833), no. 3, 9/I/1933; [Usury], IV (1833), no. 6, 19/I/1833; [Equality], IV (1833), no. 8, 26/I/1833; [Public credit and its effects], IV (1833), no. 9, 30/I/1833, no. 10, 6/II/1833, no. 11, 9/II/1833, no. 14, 20/II/1833, no. 15, 23/II/1833, no. 17, 2/III/1833, no. 19, 13/III/1833, no. 25, 4/IV/1833; [Rate of interest], IV (1833), no. 33, 1/V/1833, no. 34, 4/V/1833.

La verdad (Lima, 1833)[3]

"Política exterior", no. 9, 5/I/1833; "Hacienda", no. 28, 8/III/1833; "Constitución", no. 50, 4/VI/1833; "Agricultura", no. 51, 7/VI/1833; "Constitución", no. 55, 23/VI/1833; "Constitución (Continuación del

[3]The attribution to Mora of articles not directly concerned with public credit is particularly doubtful.

número anterior)", no. 56, 28/VI/1833; "Crédito público (Continuación del número anterior"), no. 57, 2/VII/1833; "Crédito público" (Continuación del número anterior"), no. 58, 5/VII/1833; "Crédito público", no. 62, 19/VII/1833.

El eco del Protectorado (Lima, 1836–1839)

"El eco del Protectorado" [On Public Finances and Santa Cruz's commercial reforms], no. 2, 24/VIII/1836; "Economía política" [On Custom Duties Regulation], no. 5, 3/IX/1836; "El eco del Protectorado" [On Custom Duties Regulation], no. 6, 7/IX/1836; "Variedades. Progresos del crédito público", no. 7, 10/IX/1836; "El eco del Protectorado", no. 8, 14/IX/1836; "El eco del Protectorado" [On the Organization of Public Charity], no. 9, 17/IX/1836; "El eco del Protectorado" [On the American merchant Wheelwright's plan to introduce steam power in the Pacific trade], no. 11, 24/IX/1836; "El eco del Protectorado" [On prizes to support mercury mining], no. 12, 28/IX/1836; "El eco del Protectorado" [On the Amercian merchant Wheelwright's plan to introduce steam power in the Pacific trade], no. 13, 1/X/1836; "El eco del Protectorado" [On Domestic Custom Duties Regulation], no. 15, 8/X/1836; "Variedades. Estadística" [Populationist trends in the US and Britain], no. 15, 8/X/1836; "Bancos. Artículo Primero", no 17, 15/X/1863; "El eco del Protectorado" [Commercial relationships with Chile], no. 18, 19/X/1836; "Bancos Artículo Segundo", no. 18, 19/X/1836; "Bancos Artículo Tercero", no. 20, 26/X/1836; "El eco del Protectorado" [On public credit], no. 22, 9/XI/1836; "El eco del Protectorado" [Commercial relationships with Chile], no. 26, 16/XI/1836; "El eco del Protectorado" [On the centralization of the foreign trade legislation of the Peru-Bolivian Confederation], no. 28, 23/XI/1836; "El eco del Protectorado" [On commerce and public finances Regulations], no. 29, 26/XI/1836; "Economía Política. Bancos de Ahorro", no. 29, 26/XI/1836; "El eco del Protectorado" [On the Protectorate commercial policy outcomes], no. 34, 14/XII/1836; "El eco del Protectorado" [News about the public Budget], no. 39, 31/XII/1836; "El eco del Protectorado" [Private Banker Rotschild biographical sketch], no. 40, 4/I/1837; "El eco del Protectorado" [On Chile's public debt and Peru's public credit], no. 41, 7/I/1837; "El eco del Protectorado" [Ignorance of the principles of political economy by the Chilean government], no. 42, 11/I/1837; "El eco del Protectorado" [Announcement of the first steps towards the foundation of the National Bank], no. 44, 18/I/1837; "El eco del Protectorado" [Policy of centralising legislation of commerce], no. 61, 20/V/1837; "El eco del Protectorado" [Economic causes behind the war undertaken by Chile against Peru], no.72, 28/VI/1837; "El eco del Protectorado" [Protectoral Administration's achievements in the management of public finances and credit], no. 74, 5/VII/1837; "El eco del Protectorado. Trigo y azúcar", no. 75, 8/VII/1837; "El eco del Protectorado. Deuda de Chile en Inglaterra", no. 81, 29/VII/1837; "Variedades. Economía Política. Prohibiciones absolutas", no. 86, 16/VIII/1837.

Guía de comercio y Boletín de fomento (Madrid, 1843–1851)

"Extracto de la memoria premiada de los puertos francos", no. 142, 13/V/1844; "Sofismas económicos, por Federico Bastiat. París 1846", no. 229, 20/V/1846; "De la economía política propia de las sociedades atrasadas", no. 253, 4/XI/1846; "Sobre la aplicación práctica de las doctrinas económicas", no. 269, 21/II/1847; "Educación popular. Observaciones prácticas dirigidas a los jornaleros y menestrales", no. 287, 30/VI/1847; "Hechos económicos", no. 308, 21/XI/1847.

Revista española de Indias y del extranjero (Madrid, 1845–1848)

"Del estudio de la filosofía como preparación al del Derecho", III (1845), pp. 358–65, IV (1845), 281–99; "La justicia y la venganza", IV (1845), 43–53; "Economía de la tierra", IV (1845), 222–45; "Romagnosi", IV (1845), 246–63; "Del estudio de la filosofía en España", IV (1845), 318–49; "Gobierno de mayorías", V (1846), 364–73; "El hombre americano", VI (1846), 166–81; "Opiniones políticas de Juan de Mariana", VI (1846), 258–321; "Sobre la aplicación práctica de las doctrinas económicas", VIII (1847), 19–31.

El propagador del libre comercio (Cádiz, 1847–1848)

"De la economía política propia de las naciones atrasadas", no. 75, 3/11/1847, no. 76, 10/11/1847.

Revista Universal de la Administración (Madrid, 1848–1850).[4]

"De los bancos de emisión", I, no. I, 15/1/1848; "De las industrias fundamentales", I, no. III, 15/II/1848; "Política comercial de Sir Roberto Peel", I, no. V, 15/III/1848; "De los bancos de emisión (segundo artículo)", I, no. VII, 15/IV/1848.

Revista Hispanoamericana (Madrid, 1848)

"Estudios filosóficos. La *Lógica* de Mill", 5–17, 59–71; "Estudios filosóficos. Aspecto general de los progresos de la filosofía moral,

[4] No complete series of this journal has been found.

especialmente durante los siglos XVII y XVIII, por Sir James Mackintosh", 167–77, 215–24, 258–70.

Enciclopedia moderna (Madrid, 1852–1855)[5]

"Balanza de comercio (Economía política)", IV (1851), 446–50; "Bélgica (Comercio e industria)", IV (1851), 954–63; "Banca, Banquero", IV (1851), 521–24; "Banco", IV (1851), 524–28; "Bancos españoles", IV (1851), 528–39; "Bancos extranjeros. Economía política", IV (1851), 539–59; "Bentham (Filosofía, legislación, economía política)", V (1851), 10–29; "Caja de Amortización (Hacienda)", VI (1851), 439–41; "Cajas de ahorros", VI (1851), 441–65; "Capital (Economía política)", VII (1851), 82–95; "China (Agricultura, industria y comercio)", VIII (1851), 380–425; "Circulación. (Economía política)", VIII (1851), 700–705; "Colonias (Economía política, historia, legislación)", IX (1851), 558–616; "Comercio (Economía política)", IX (1851), 782–835: "Compañía (Comercio, economía política), IX (1851), 907–12; "Compañía Inglesa de la India (Historia)", IX (1851), 907–49; "Concurrencia (Economía política)", X (1851), 226–39; "Consumo (Economía política)", X (1851), 831–42; "Contrabando", X (1851), 907–22; "Contribución (Economía política)", X (1851), 982–1015; "Crédito (Economía política)", XI (1852), 560–69; "Crisis comercial (Economía política)", XI (1852), 620–29; "Déficit", XII (1852), 838; "Depósito (Almacenes de, Hacienda, Economía política), XIII (1852), 43–48; "Deuda pública (Economía política, Hacienda), XIII (1852), 810–34; "División del trabajo (Economía política)", XIV (1852), 618–30; "División de la propiedad (Economía política y legislación), XIV (1852), 608–18; "Economía política", XV (1852), 257–307; "Economía Política (historia de la)", XV (1852), 307–66; "Economía pública", XV (1852), 366–68; "Economía moral", XV (1852), 371–72; "Economistas (Bibliografía económica)", XV (1852), 374–413; "Empréstitos públicos (Economía política)", XVI (1852), 262–83; "España (Industria y comercio)", XVII (1852), 792–862; "Exportación (Economía política)", XVIII (1852), 33–42; "Fabril (Industria, economía política)", XVIII (1852), 919–30; "Francos (Puertos), (Economía Política)", XX (1853), 222–39; "Ganancia" (Economía política), XX (1853), 910–16; "Hacienda pública" (Economía política, Administración)", XXII (1853), 432–47; "Importación", XXIII (1853), 937–43; "Industria (Economía política)", XXIV (1853), 49–57;

[5] Medina (2022, pp. 223–24) also attributes to Mora the entries "Comercio de cabotaje" and "Escasez", both in Vol. XXXIV (Supplement).

"Inglaterra (Industria y comercio)", XXIV (1853), 270–313; "Interés del dinero (Economía política)", XXIV (1853), 733; "Lujo (Economía política)", XVI (1853), 414–22; "Tratados comerciales", XXXIII, 456–58.

Revista española de ambos mundos (Madrid, 1853–1855)

"De la situación actual de las repúblicas sur-americanas", I (1853), 29–43, 257–79; "Machiavelli. Sus obras y su carácter", I (1853), 143–57; "La lógica del tráfico libre", I (1853), 561–70; "Historia. Lecciones sobre la historia moderna, por Federico Schelegel. Juicio de esta obra", II (1854), 454–65.

La América. Crónica Hispano-Americana (Madrid, 1857–1886)

"Moralidad de la economía política (art. 1)", IV (1860), no. 1, 8/III/1860, 5–6; Moralidad de la economía política (art. 2)", IV (1860), no. 2, 24/III/1860, 5–6; "De las doctrinas económicas en Francia", IV (1860), no. 3, 8/IV/1860, 5–6; "La economía política en Inglaterra. Art. I", IV (1860), no. 5, 8/V/1860, 6–7; "Contestación a un proteccionista", IV (1860), no. 6, 24/V/1860, 5–6; "De la economía política en Inglaterra. Art. II", IV (1860), no. 7, 8/VI/1860, 5–6; "De la economía política en Inglaterra. Art. III", IV (1860), no. 8, 24/VI/1860, 5–6; "De la economía política en Inglaterra. Art. IV", IV (1860), no. 9, 8/VII/1860, 5–7; "Bibliografía" [Reference to the reprinting of *Il Colbertismo* by Mengotti], IV (1860), no. 10, 24/VII/1860, 2–4; "Colbert", IV (1860), no. 11, 8/VIII/1860, 5–6; "Colbert. Art. 2", IV (1860), no. 12, 24/VIII/1860, 5–6; "Colbert. Art. 3", IV (1860), no. 13, 8/IX/1860, 5–6; "Nuevo Arancel francés", IV (1860), no. 17, 8/XI/1860, 6–7; "Variedades económicas. Art. 1", IV (1860), no. 19, 8/XII/1860, 5–6; "Variedades económicas. Art. 3", IV (1861), no 21, 8/I/1861, 6–7; "Bibliografía" [Book review to 'Lógica" by Dr. Whately], IV (1861), no. 22, 24/I/1861, 7–8; "Inglaterra y Estados-Unidos de América", IV (1861), no. 23, 8/II/1861, 6; "El derecho internacional y la economía política", V (1861), no. 1, 8/III/1861, 5; "España y los estados del Río de la Plata", V (1861), no. 2, 24/III/1861, 5; "Los aranceles de los Estados Unidos", V (1861), no. 3, 8/IV/1861, 2–3; "El arancel de la Confederación Argentina", V (1861), no. 4, 24/IV/1861, 5; "Bibliografía. Consideraciones sobre el gobierno representativo, por Juan Stuart Mill (Juicio de esta obra)", V (1861), no. 7, 8/VI/ 1861, 9–10; "Dos palabras sobre el algodón"—as Jacinto Beltrán—, V (1861), no. 7, 8/VI/1861, 9; "De la enseñanza pública"—as Jacinto Beltrán—, V (1861), no. 9, 8/VII/1861, 5; "Banquete de economistas", V (1861), no. 11, 8/VIII/1861, 7; "La diplomacia economista", V (1862), no. 23,

8/II/1862, 17; "Bolivia", V (1862), no. 24, 24/II/1862, 3–4; "Poder colonial de Inglaterra", año VI (1862), no. 2, 24/III/1862, 8–9; "El papel", VI (1862), no. 3, 8/IV/1862, 7; "El Banco de España", año VI (1862), no. 5, 8/V/1862, 7–8; "Del comercio en la antigüedad. Art. I", VI (1862), no. 10, 24/VII/1862, 11[6]; "El Perú y la influencia europea", VI (1862), no. 10, 24/VII/1862, 11–13; "El Austria y la Unión Aduanera de Alemania", VI (1862), no. 12, 24/VIII/1862, pp. 9–10; "Los economistas modernos. Art. 1", VI (1862), no. 14, 24/IX/1862, 6–7; "Los economistas modernos. Art. 2", VI (1862), no. 15, 7/X/1862, 12–13; "Los economistas modernos. Art. 3", VI (1862), no. 16, 27/X/1862, 8–9; "El Código Civil de Chile", VI (1862), no. 19, 12/XII/1862, 7–8; "Bibliografía extranjera. Art. 1" [Book review to P.-J. Proudhon, *Du principe federatif et de la nécessité de reconstituer le parti de la revolution*], VII (1863), no. 7, 12/IV/1863, 6–7; "Bibliografía extranjera" [Book review to *Recherches sur les príncipes mathematiques de la theorie de la richesse, par Mr. Cournot*], VII (1863), no. 16, 27/VIII/1863, 8–9; "Almacenes generales de depósito (Docks)", VII (1863), no. 23, 12/XII/1863, 8; "Bibliografía extranjera. Artículo primero" [Book Review to Minghetti's *Relaciones de la economía política con la moral y el derecho*, part. I], VIII (1864), no. 1, 12/I/1864, 11–12; "La alhóndiga", VIII (1864), no. 2, 27/I/1864, 11; "Bibliografía extranjera. Art. segundo" [Book Review to Minghetti's *Relaciones de la economía política con la moral y el derecho*, part. II], VIII (1864), no. 3, 12/II/1864, 10–11; "Los libre-cambistas belgas"—as Jacinto Beltrán—, VIII (1864), no. 8, 27/IV/1864, 5–6.

[6] The missing issue of 8 August 1862 in the collection of *La América* in the BNE probably contains Mora's article "Del comercio en la Antigüedad. Art. 2".

Bibliography

Works of José Joaquín De Mora

Books[1]

Mora, José Joaquín de. 1821. *Discurso inaugural que pronunció en el Ateneo español D. José Joaquín de Mora, uno de sus socios, al abrir un curso de Derecho Natural, el día 7 de marzo de 1821*. Madrid: Imprenta del censor. Reed. 1843. Sevilla; Establecimiento tipográfica.

Mora, José Joaquín de. 1824a. *Cartas sobre la educación del bello sexo por una señora americana*. London: R. Ackermann.

Mora, José Joaquín de. 1824b. *Gimnástica del bello sexo, o Ensayos sobre la educación física de las jóvenes*. London: R. Ackermann.

Mora, José Joaquín de. 1824c. *Mémoires historiques sur Ferdinand VII, roi des Espagnes, et sur les événemens de son règne. Par Don****, avocat près des tribunaux espagnols. Traduits en anglais sur le manuscrit espagnol, par Michael J. Quin, et en français par M. G. H*****. Paris: Librarie Universelle de P. Mongie aîné.

Mora, José Joaquín de. 1825. *Catecismo de economía política*. London: R. Ackermann.

[1] On the prolix reprints of the *Catecismos*, *Cursos* and other works of Mora in the Hispanic world, see Roldán (2003), Macintyre (2018) and Medina (2022).

J. Astigarraga et al., *The Economic Legacy of José Joaquín de Mora*, Palgrave Studies in the History of Economic Thought, https://doi.org/10.1007/978-3-031-49446-8

Mora, José Joaquín de. 1828. *Respuesta a la Memoria sobre los mayorazgos de Chile publicada en Santiago el 9 de junio de 1828.* Santiago de Chile: Imprenta de Rengifo.

Mora, José Joaquín de. 1830a. *Curso de derechos del Liceo de Chile, por José Joaquín de Mora, director de aquel establecimiento. Tomo único. Derecho penal y Derecho de gentes.* Santiago de Chile: Imprenta republicana.

Mora, José Joaquín de. 1830b: *Oración inaugural del curso de oratoria del Liceo de Chile, pronunciada el 20 de abril de 1830 por José Joaquín de Mora, director de aquel establecimiento.* Santiago de Chile: Imprenta de Rengifo.

Mora, José Joaquín de. 1832. *Cursos de lógica y ética según la escuela de Edimburgo por José Joaquín de Mora.* Lima: Imprenta de José Masías.

Mora, José Joaquín de. 1834. *Discurso pronunciado en la Universidad Mayor de S. Andrés de la Paz de Ayacucho el 5 de diciembre de 1834, por el Dr. José Joaquín de Mora.* La Paz: Imprenta del Colegio de artes.

Mora, José Joaquín de. 1840: *Elementos de lógica escritos por D. José Joaquín de Mora, según la escuela de Edimburgo. Impreso en Lima y reimpreso en Sucre.* Sucre: Imprenta del Congreso.

Mora, José Joaquín de. 1842: *Curso de derecho natural.* Santiago de Chile: Imprenta liberal.

Mora, José Joaquín de. 1843. *De la libertad de comercio, por José Joaquín de Mora.* Sevilla: Establecimiento tipográfico, Imprenta de Carlos Rubio y compañía.

Mora, José Joaquín de. 1844a. *Memoria sobre los puertos francos, por José Joaquín de Mora.* Madrid: Imprenta de Benito Lamparero y compañía.

Mora, José Joaquín de. c.1844b. *El libro de la escuela o Catecismo de conocimientos útiles destinado a la primera enseñanza.* Sevilla: Establecimiento tipográfico, Plaza del silencio.

Mora, José Joaquín de. 1845. *Ejercicios de lectura, o Extractos de literatura moderna en prosa y verso, para el uso de los alumnos del Colegio de S. Felipe Neri de Cádiz.* Cádiz: Imprenta de la viuda e hijo de Bosch.

Mora, José Joaquín de. 1846a. *Curso de ética según la escuela de Edimburgo por José Joaquín de Mora.* La Paz: Imprenta Paceña.

Mora, José Joaquín de. 1846b. *Curso de lógica según la escuela de Edimburgo por José Joaquín de Mora.* La Paz: Imprenta Paceña.

Mora, José Joaquín de. 1849. *Lecciones elementales de Ideología.* In *Curso de derechos del Liceo de Chile por Don José Joaquín de Mora, director de aquel establecimiento. Tomo único. Derecho natural y derecho de gentes,* 1–60. La Paz de Ayacucho: Imprenta del Pueblo.

Mora, José Joaquín de. 1855. *Roman Catholicism in Spain.* Trans. Thomas Parker. Edinburgh: Johnstone and Hunter.

Mora, José Joaquín de. 1865. *Curso de derecho romano, extractado de la famosa obra de Heinecio [...]. Texto adoptado por las tres universidades de la República para la enseñanza del derecho romano.* Cochabamba: Tipografía de Gutiérrez.

Translations and Reeditions

Bentham, Jeremy. 1820. *Consejos que dirige a las Cortes y al pueblo español Jeremías Bentham: traducidos del inglés por José Joaquín de Mora*. Madrid: Repullés.

Blanco-White, José. 1844. *Cartas sobre Inglaterra dirigidas a don Alberto Lista, por don José Blanco-White y continuadas por don José Joaquín de Mora*. Santiago de Chile: Imprenta del Siglo.

Campbell, George. 1846. *Tratado de la evidencia escrito en inglés por Jorge Campbell, de la Real Sociedad de Edimburgo, traducido al castellano con notas por José Joaquín de Mora*. Lima: Imprenta del Comercio.

Chateaubriand, François-René de. 1814. *De Buonaparte y de los Borbones, por F. A. de Chateaubriand. Traducido al castellano por José Joaquín de Mora*. Cadiz: Imprenta de R. Howe.

Clavijero, Javier. 1826. *Historia antigua de México, sacada de los mejores historiadores españoles y de los manuscritos y de las pinturas antiguas de los indios*, 2 vols. London. R. Ackermann.

Fénelon, François. 1825. *Compendio de las vidas de los filósofos antiguos, escrito en francés por Fenelon, y traducido al castellano por J. J. de Mora*. Paris: Librería de Cormon y Blanc.

Holbach, Paul-Henri-Thirty d'. 1823. *Ensayo de las preocupaciones, escrito en francés por el barón de Holbach, y traducido con correcciones y adiciones por José Joaquín de Mora*. Madrid: Imprenta de don José del Collado.

Holbach, Paul-Henri-Thirty d'. 1840. *La moral universal o los deberes del hombre, fundados en su naturaleza por el Barón de Holbach. Aumentada con el interesante discurso que publicó este célebre escritor sobre el origen y estado de las preocupaciones. Traducido por el literato D. J. J. de Mora*. Madrid: Oficinas del establecimiento central.

Lista, Alberto. 1844. *Ensayos literarios y críticos por D. Alberto Lista y Aragón, con un prólogo por D. José Joaquín de Mora*. Seville: Calvo Rubio y compañía.

Parkes, Samuel. 1824. *Catecismo de química*. London: R. Ackermann.

Pinnock, William. 1824. *Catecismo de geografía, o Introducción al conocimiento del mundo y de sus habitantes*. London: R. Ackermann.

Robinson, William Davis. 1824. *Memorias de la revolución de Méjico y de la expedición del General D. Francisco Javier Mina: a que se han agregado algunas observaciones sobre la comunicación proyectada entre los dos océanos, Pacífico y Atlántico, escritas en inglés por William Davis Robinson; y traducidas por José Joaquín de Mora*. London: R. Ackerman.

Primary Sources

Alonso Ortiz, José. 1796. *Ensayo sobre el sistema de la moneda-papel y sobre el crédito público*. Madrid: Imprenta Real.

Álvarez Guerra, Juan. 1841. *Proyecto de una ley agraria o código rural.* Madrid: Miguel de Burgos.

Anonymous. 1824. *Catecismo de industria rural y doméstica.* London: Ackermann.

Anonymous. 1828. *Memoria sobre los mayorazgos de Chile dedicada al público por algunos sucesores inmediatos.* Santiago de Chile: R. Rengifo.

Anonymous. 1832a. *Examen sobre el Tratado de comercio ajustado en Arequipa entre el Perú y Bolivia, por sus respectivos plenipotenciarios bajo la mediación del Estado de Chile.* Arequipa.

Anonymous. 1832b. *Contestación a las breves reflexiones sobre el Tratado de comercio entre Bolivia y Perú.* La Paz: Imprenta de Educandas.

Anonymous. 1838. *Reimpresión del artículo impreso en la Miscelánea denunciando el curso de derecho que enseña el Señor Mora; y de las cartas con que se ha refutado la defensa publicada por este en los Mercurios del 16, 17 y 19 del noviembre del año pasado.* Lima: Imprenta accesoria de la casa de ejercicios de Santa Rosa.

Asociación para la reforma de los aranceles de aduanas. 1860. *Actas de las sesiones de la Asociación para la reforma de los Aranceles de Aduanas.* Madrid: Imprenta de los Sres. Arcas y Montoya.

Asociación para la reforma de los aranceles de aduanas. 1863. *Conferencias librecambistas: discursos pronunciados en el Ateneo Científico y Literario de Madrid, por varios individuos de la Asociación para la Reforma de los Aranceles de Aduanas en el curso de 1862 a 1863.* Madrid: Imprenta de Manuel Galiano.

Banco de España. 1862. *Memoria leída en la Junta General de accionistas del Banco de España el día 8 de marzo de 1862.* Madrid: Imprenta y librería de D. Eusebio Aguado.

Bastiat, Frédéric. 1846. *Sophismes économiques.* Paris: Guillaumin.

Bastiat, Federico. 1847. *Cobden y la Liga o la agitación inglesa en favor de la libertad de comercio, obra escrita en francés por Don M. Federico Bastiat.* Madrid: Imprenta y Establecimiento de Grabados de Don Baltasar González.

Bastiat, Frédéric. 1851. *Harmonies économiques.* Paris.

Bentham, Jeremy. 1821. *Cartas de Jeremías Bentham, al señor Conde de Toreno, sobre el proyecto de Código penal presentado a las Cortes.* Madrid: Imprenta de Diego García Campoy.

Bentham, Jeremy. 2012. *On the Liberty of the Press, and Public Discussion, and other Legal and Political Writings for Spain and Portugal.* In *The Collected Works of Jeremy Bentham*, edited by Catherine Pease-Watkin and Phillip Schofield. Oxford: Oxford Clarendon Press.

Bentham, Jeremy. 2015. Colonies, Commerce, and Constitutional Law. In *The Collected Works of Jeremy Bentham*, edited by Phillip Schofield. Oxford: OUP.

Blanqui, Adolphe. 1840. *Compendio elemental de economía política.* Paris: Rosa.

Blanqui, Adolphe. 1860 [1837]. *Histoire de l'économie politique en Europe.* Paris: Guillaumin.

Boix, Ignacio. 1842–1845. *Enciclopedia española del siglo diez y nueve, o Biblioteca completa de ciencias, literatura, artes y oficios, etc. por una Sociedad de literatos españoles y de hombres especiales en diversas ciencias y profesiones*, 12 vols. Madrid: Imprenta y librería de Ignacio Boix.

Borrego, Andrés. 1844. *Principios de economía política con aplicación a la reforma de aranceles de aduanas.* Madrid: Imprenta Soc. de oper. del mismo Arte.

Canga Argüelles, José. 1825. *Elementos de la ciencia de la Hacienda Pública.* London: Macintosh.

Canga Argüelles, José. 1826–1827 *Diccionario de Hacienda para el uso de los encargados de la suprema dirección de ella*, 2 vols. London: Imprenta española de M. Calero.

Canga Argüelles, José. 1833. *Elementos de la ciencia de la Hacienda.* Madrid: J. Palacios.

Carballo, Benigno. 1855–1856 *Curso de economía política*, 2 vols. Madrid: P. Montero.

Carreras y González, Mariano. 1865. *Tratado didáctico de economía política.* Madrid: Imprenta y librería de Miguel Guijarro.

Chevalier, Michel. 1849. *Examen du système commercial connu sous le nom de système protecteur.* Paris.

Colmeiro, Manuel. 1845. *Tratado elemental de economía política ecléctica.* Madrid: Calleja.

Colmeiro, Manuel. 1859. *Principios de economía política.* Madrid: G. Alhambra.

Condorcet, Jean-Antoine-Nicolas de Caritat, Marquis of. 1792 *Compendio de la obra inglesa intitulada Riqueza de las naciones, hecho por el Marqués de Condorcet, y traducido al castellano, con varias adiciones del original por don Carlos Martínez de Irujo.* Madrid: Imprenta Real.

Constitución política del Estado de Chile. 1823. Santiago: Imprenta Nacional.

Constitución política de la República de Chile. 1828. Santiago: Imprenta de R. Rengifo.

Coquelin, Charles and Gilbert Urbain Guillaumin. 1852–1853. *Dictionnaire de l'économie politique.* Paris: Librairie de Guillaumin et Cie.

Destutt de Tracy, Antoine-Louis-Claude. 1826. *Elementos de Ideología por Destutt-de-Tracy, incluidos en diez y ocho lecciones, e ilustrados con notas críticas, por el Catedrático D. Mariano S.* Paris: Casa de Masson e hijo.

Droz, Joseph. 1842. *Economía política o principios de la ciencia de las riquezas.* Madrid: Viuda de Calleja e hijos.

Dufresne Saint-Leon, Louis-Cesar-Alexandre. 1824. *Étude du crédit public et des dettes publiques.* Paris: G. de Bossange.

El mercurio chileno. 2009. Edited by Gabriel Cid. Santiago de Chile: Centro de investigaciones Diego Barros Arana.

Encyclopédie moderne. Dictionnaire abrégé des sciences, des lettres, des arts, de l'industrie, de l'agriculture et du commerce. 1846–1851. 3rd ed., Paris: Didot Frères.

Ferrier, François-Louis-Auguste. 1803. *Essai sur les ports francs.* Bayonne: Chez Fauvet.

Flórez Estrada. Álvaro. 1811. *Examen imparcial de las disensiones de la América con la España, de los medios de su reconciliación y de la prosperidad de todas las naciones.* Cádiz: Imprenta Manuel Ximena de Carreño.

Flórez Estrada, Álvaro. 1819. *Representation to H. C. M. Ferdinand VII, King of Spain, in defence of the Courts.* London.

Flórez Estrada, Álvaro. 1827. *Reflexiones acerca del mal extraordinario que en el día aflige a la Inglaterra y que más o menos incomoda ya a las naciones más industriosas de la Europa.* London: Imprenta española de M. Calero.

Flórez Estrada, Álvaro. 1828 [1980]. *Curso de economía política,* edited by S. Almenar, 2 vols. Madrid: IEF.

Ganilh, Charles. 1815. *La théorie de l'économie politique.* Paris: Deterville.

Garnier, Joseph. 1848. *Elementos de economía política, por José Garnier.* Madrid: Imprenta y librería de la publicidad.

Guillaumin, Gilbert-Urbaine. 1839. *Encyclopédie du commerçant. Dictionnaire du commerce et des marchandises,* 2 vols. Paris: Guillaumin et Cie.

Gutiérrez, Manuel María. 1837. *Impugnación a las cinco proposiciones de Pebrer sobre los grandes males que causa la ley de aranceles a la nación en general, a la Cataluña en particular, y a las mismas fábricas catalanas.* Madrid: Imprenta de Don Marcelino Calero.

Hennet, Albert-Jospeh-Ulpien. 1816. *Théorie du crédit public.* Paris: Testu et C.

Herrera Dávila, José and Antonio Alvear. 1827. *Lecciones de economía política.* Sevilla: Imprenta de Mariano Caro.

Ibáñez, José María. 1844a. "Memoria premiada [...] sobre si es o no conveniente a una nación celebrar tratados de comercio con otras más adelantadas en industria". *El Amigo del País,* vol. I, no. 7 (1/6/1844), 193–223.

Ibáñez, José María. 1844b. "Impugnación a la memoria sobre los puertos francos". *El Amigo del País,* vol. I, no. 10 (15/VII/1844), 301–16.

Ibáñez, José María. 1844c. "Sobre los puertos francos". *El Amigo del País,* vol. II, no. 14 (9/15/1844), 17–20.

Jaumeandreu, Eudaldo. 1816. *Rudimentos de economía política.* Barcelona: Oficina de D. Antonio Brusí.

Jaumeandreu, Eudaldo. 1836. *Curso elemental de economía política con aplicación a la legislación económica de España,* 2 vols. Barcelona: Imprenta de Gaspar.

Laboulaye, Charles-Pierre Lefèbvre de. 1856–1857. *Diccionario de artes y manufacturas, de agricultura y minas,* 4 vols. Madrid: Establecimiento tipográfico de Mellado.

Labra, Rafael María de. 1878. *El Ateneo de Madrid*. Madrid: Imprenta de Aurelio J. Alaria.

Le Bas, M.-Ph. 1840–1845. *Dictionnaire encyclopédique*. Paris: Didot Frères.

Marliani, M. (1842). *De la influencia del sistema prohibitivo en la agricultura, industria, comercio y rentas públicas*. Madrid: D. J. Cuesta.

McCulloch, John Ramsay. 1825. *The Principles of Political Economy, with a Sketch of the Rise and Progress of the Science*. Edinburgh and London: Adam and Charles Black-Longman, Brown, Green and Longmans.

McCulloch, John Ramsay. 1832. *A Dictionary, Practical, Theoretical, and Historical, of Commerce and Commercial Navigation*. London: Longman, Rees, Orme, Broen, Green & Longman.

McCulloch, John Ramsay. 1842. "Political Economy". In *The Encylopedia Britannica or Dictionary of Arts, Science, and General Literature*. 7th ed., vol. XVIII, 258–307. Edinburgh: Adam and Charles Black.

Mellado, Francisco de Paula. 1842. "Mora, José Joaquín". In *Diccionario universal de historia y geografía*, vol. V, 543–44. Madrid: Establecimiento Tipográfico.

Mellado, Francisco de Paula. 1851. "Prólogo". In *Enciclopedia moderna. Diccionario universal de literatura, ciencias y artes, agricultura, industria y comercio*, VI–XXIV. Madrid: Establecimiento Tipográfico de Mellado.

Mellado, Francisco de Paula. 1851–1855. *Enciclopedia Moderna: diccionario universal de literatura, ciencias, artes, agricultura, industria y comercio*, 37 vols. Madrid, Establecimiento Tipográfico de Mellado.

Mengotti, Francesco. 1819. *Il Colbertismo*. Florencia: Piatti.

Mill, James. 1821. *Elements of Political Economy*, London: Baldwin, Cradock and Joy.

Mill, James. 1827. *Elementos de economía política por J. Mill*, 2 vols. Paris: J. Smith.

Mill, John Stuart. 1844. *Essays on Some Unsettled Questions of Political Economy*. London: Longmans, Green, Reader and Dyer.

Mill, John Stuart. 1848. *Principles of Political Economy with some of their Applications to Social Philosophy*. London: John W. Parker.

Mill, John Stuart. 1853. *Sistema de Lógica demostrativa e inductiva: o sea, exposición comparada de los principios de evidencia y los métodos de investigación científica*. Madrid: Imprenta M. Rivadeneyra.

Paso y Delgado, Nicolás. 1841. *Elementos de economía política*. Granada: Imprenta de Benavides.

Pastor, Esteban. 1825. *Catecismo de agricultura*. London: Ackermann.

Pebrer, Pablo. 1826. *Five Questions on the Actual Mercantile Distress*. London: Effingham Wilson.

Pebrer, Pablo. 1837. *Cinco proposiciones sobre los grandes males que causa la ley de aranceles a la nación en general, a la Cataluña en particular, a las mismas fábricas catalanas*. London and Madrid: Imprenta española de D. V. Torras.

Rocafuerte, Vicente. 1826. *Cartas de un americano sobre las ventajas de los gobiernos republicanos federativos.* London: Imprenta española de M. Calero.

Rossi, Pellegrino. 1840. *Curso de economía política (año escolar de 1836–1837).* Madrid: Boix.

Sagra, Ramón de la. 1840. *Lecciones de economía social dadas en el Ateneo científico y literario de Madrid.* Madrid: Ferrer y C.

Say, Jean Baptiste. 1821. *Tratado de economía política o exposición sencilla del modo con que se forman, se distribuyen y se consumen las riquezas.* Madrid: Fermín Villalpando.

Smith, Adam. 1759 [1976a]. *The Theory of Moral Sentiments*, edited by D. D. Raphael and A. L. Macfie. Oxford: OUP.

Smith, Adam. 1776 [1976b]. *An Inquiry into the Nature and Causes of the Wealth of Nations*, edited by Roy H. Campbell, Andrew S. Skinner and William B. Todd. Oxford: OUP.

Smith, Adam. 1794. *Investigación de la causa y la riqueza de las naciones. Obra escrita en inglés por Adam Smith, doctor en leyes.* Valladolid: Viuda e hijos de Santander.

Sismonde de Sismondi, Jean-Charles-Léonard. 1834. *Nuevos principios de economía política*, 2 vols. Granada: Imprenta de Benavides.

Sociedad Económica Barcelonesa de Amigos del País. 1838. *Refutación de las cinco proposiciones del Señor Pebrer contra el sistema prohibitivo.* Barcelona: Juan Francisco Piferrer.

Storch, Heinrich Friedrich von. 1823. *Cours d'économie politique.* Paris: J. P. Aillaud.

Thiers, M. Adolphe. 1848. *De la propriété.* Paris: Paulin et L'Heureux.

Torrente, Mariano. 1835. *Revista general de la economía política*, 3 vols. La Habana: Jordán.

Tratado de comercio con Bolivia. 1832. https://www.leyes.congreso.gob.pe/.

Urcullu, José. 1825. *Catecismo de aritmética comercial.* London: Ackermann.

Vadillo, José Manuel. 1821. *Discurso sobre los medios de fomentar la industria española y contener o reprimir el contrabando.* Madrid: Imprenta de la Calle de Greda.

Vadillo, José Manuel. 1842. *Breves observaciones sobre libertad y prohibiciones de comercio.* Madrid: Imprenta de Alegría y Charlain.

Valle, Eusebio María del. 1846. *Curso de economía política.* Madrid: C. N. SordoMudos.

Valle Santoro, Marqués de. 1830. *Memoria sobre la balanza de comercio y examen del estado actual de la riqueza de España.* Madrid: Imprenta R. Vergés.

Secondary Sources

Acevedo, Carlos Alberto. 1949. "La enseñanza de la ciencia de las finanzas en la Universidad de Buenos Aires desde su fundación hasta 1830". *Revista del Instituto de Historia del Derecho* 2, 11–46.

Almenar, Salvador. 1976. "Agrarismo y librecambio en la crisis del Antiguo Régimen". *Información Comercial Española* 517, 58–81.

Almenar, Salvador. 1980. "Estudio Preliminar". In Antonio Flórez Estrada, *Curso de economía política*, edited by Salvador Almenar, vol. I, XXXV–CXXIII. Madrid: IEF.

Almenar, Salvador. 1996. "Economic Thought in Spanish Periodical Publications of the 18th and 19th Centuries: an Introduction". *History of Economic Ideas* IV–3, 119–47.

Almenar, Salvador. 2000a. "El desarrollo del pensamiento económico clásico en España". In *Economía y economistas españoles. Vol. IV. La economía clásica*, edited by Enrique Fuentes, 7–92. Barcelona: Galaxia Gütenberg and Círculo de Lectores.

Almenar, Salvador. 2000b. "Flórez Estrada y la economía política clásica". In *Economía y economistas españoles. Vol. IV. La economía clásica*, edited by Enrique Fuentes, 369–411. Barcelona: Galaxia Gütenberg and Círculo de Lectores.

Almenar, Salvador. 2014. "The Reception and Dissemination of David Ricardo's Ideas in Spain". In *The Reception of David Ricardo in Continental Europe and Japan*, edited by Gilbert Faccarello y Masashi Izumo, 152–77. London and New York: Routledge.

Almenar, Salvador. 2020. *El fulgor de la libertad. Bastiat, el librecambio, el progreso y la democracia en España (1846–1850)*, Madrid: RACMP.

Almenar, Salvador and Vincent Llombart. 2001. "Spanish Societies, Academies and Economic Debating Societies". In *The Spread of Political Economy and the Professionalisation of Economists*, edited by Massimo M. Augello and Marco E. L. Guidi, 109–25. London: Routledge.

Almenar, Salvador and Rogelio Velasco. 1987. "Una etapa en la consolidación del librecambio en España: el viaje de Richard Cobden por Andalucía". In *Andalucía en el pensamiento económico*, edited by Gumersindo Ruiz, 105–18. Málaga: Arguval.

Amunátegui, Domingo. 1897. *Mora en Bolivia*. Santiago de Chile: Imprenta Cervantes.

Amunátegui, Miguel Luis. 1888. *Don José Joaquín de Mora. Apuntes biográficos*. Santiago de Chile: Imprenta Nacional.

Arias de Saavedra, Inmaculada. 2007. "La Universidad de Granada en la época moderna: estudio y estado de la cuestión". In *Universidades hispánicas: modelos territoriales en la Edad Moderna*, edited by Luis Enrique Rodríguez San Pedro, 237–68. Salamanca: Universidad de Salamanca.

Artal, Françesc. 1979. "Guëll i Ferrer, Joan". In *Ictineu. Diccionari de les ciències de la societat als Països Catalans (segles XVIII–XX)*, edited by Françesc Artal et alii. Barcelona: Edicions 62.

Artola, Miguel. 1973. *La burguesía revolucionaria (1808–1869*). Madrid: Alianza.

Artola, Miguel. 1977. *Partidos y programas políticos (1808–1936)*, 2 vols. Madrid: Aguilar.

Asensio, María Pilar. 2011. "Mora en Londres: aportaciones al Hispanoamericanismo". In *Londres y el liberalismo hispánico*, edited by Daniel Muñoz y Alonso García, 111–24. Madrid and Frankfurt am Main: Iberoamericana and Verbuet.

Astigarraga, Jesús. 2001. "The Light and Shade of Italian Economic Thought in Spain (1750–1850)". In *From Economists to Economists. The International Spread of Italian Economic Thought, 1750–1950*, edited by Piero F. Asso, 227–53. Firenze: Polistampa.

Astigarraga, Jesús. 2020. *An Unifying Enlightenment. Institutions of Political Economy in Eighteenth-Century Spain (1700–1808)*. Leiden and Boston: Brill Publishers.

Astigarraga, Jesús and Juan Zabalza. 2007. "Political Economy in the First Spanish General Encyclopaedia: *The Enciclopedia Moderna* (1852–1855)". *History of Economic Ideas* XV–2, 79–108.

Astigarraga, Jesús and Juan Zabalza. 2017. "José Joaquín de Mora y la divulgación de la doctrina económica liberal en Latinoamérica en los inicios del siglo XIX". *Revista de historia industrial* 67, 39–68.

Astigarraga, Jesús and Juan Zabalza, eds. 2021. *Adam Smith and 'The Wealth of Nations' in Spain. A History of Reception, Dissemination, Adaptation and Application, 1778–1840.* London and New York: Routledge.

Astigarraga, Jesús, Juan Zabalza and António Almodovar. 2001. "Dictionaries and Encyclopaedias on Political Economy in the Iberian Peninsula (18th, 19th and 20th Centuries)". *Storia del Pensiero Economico* 41, 25–63.

Astigarraga, Jesús, Javier Usoz and Juan Zabalza. 2020. "Entre la economía, la política y la opinión pública: el nacimiento de las reseñas económicas en España (1737–1805)". *Revista de estudios políticos* 190, 259–88.

Astigarraga, Jesús, Javier Usoz and Juan Zabalza. 2022a. "Estudio preliminar". In *Voces económicas en la 'Enciclopedia Moderna'*, by José Joaquín de Mora, edited by Jesús Astigarraga, Javier Usoz and Juan Zabalza, 11–80. Madrid: IEF.

Astigarraga, Jesús, Javier Usoz and Juan Zabalza. 2023. "José Joaquín de Mora and the Debates on the Free Trade Policy in Spain (1843–1853)", *History of Economic Ideas* XXXI–1, 11–39.

Astigarraga, Jesús, José Manuel Menudo and Javier Usoz. 2022b. "Nuancing Adam Smith. *The Wealth of Nations'* Reception and Influences in Spain, 1800–1820". In *Adam Smith and 'The Wealth of Nations' in Spain*, edited by Jesús Astigarraga and Juan Zabalza, 121–37. New York and London: Routledge.

Augello, Massimo M. and Marco E. L. Guidi, eds. 2001. *The Spread of Political Economy and the Professionalisation of Economists.* London: Routledge.

Augello, Massimo M. and Marco E. L. Guidi, eds. 2019. *Economisti e scienza economica nell'Italia liberale (1848–1922). Una storia istituzionale*, vol. 1. Milano: Franco Angeli.

Ausejo, Elena. 2000. "L'émergence de la science dans la fureur absolutiste: la Crónica Científica y Literaria (1817–1820)". Sciences et Techniques en Perspective 4–2, 207–20.

Basadre, Jorge. 2002. *La iniciación de la República*, vol. I. Lima: UNMSM.

Baslé, Maurice and Alain Gélédan. 1991. "Frédéric Bastiat, théoricien et militant du libre-échange". In *L'économie politique en France au XIXe siècle*, edited by Yves Breton and Michel Luftalla, 83–110. Paris: Economica.

Baumol, William J. 1977. "Say's (at least) Eight Laws, or What Say, and James Mill May Really Have Meant". *Economica* 174: 145–61.

Beltrán, Miguel. 1977. *Ideologías y gasto público en España (1814–1860).* Madrid: IEF and Ministerio de Hacienda.

Bradford Bow, Charles. 2018. *Common Sense int the Scottish Enlightenment.* Oxford: OUP.

Braun-Llona, Juan, et al. 1998. "Economía Chilena 1810–1995. Estadísticas Históricas". WP no. 187. Pontificia Universidad Católica de Chile. Instituto de Economía.

Breña, Roberto. 2011. "El primer liberalismo español y su proyección hispanoamericana". In *Liberalismo y poder. Latinoamérica en el siglo XIX*, edited by Iván Jaksic and Eduardo Posada, 63–88. Santiago de Chile: FCE.

Brotel, Jean-François. 1993. *Libros, prensa y lecturas en la España del siglo XIX.* Madrid: Pirámide.

Burr, Robert N. 1974. *By Reason or Force: Chile and the Balancing of Power in South America, 1830–1905.* Berkeley and Los Angeles: University of California Press.

Bustos, Manuel. 2005. *Cádiz en el sistema atlántico. La ciudad, sus comerciantes y la actividad mercantil, 1650–1830.* Madrid: Sílex.

Cabrillo, Francisco. 1978. "Traducciones al español de libros de economía política (1800–1880)". *Moneda y Crédito* 147, 71–103.

Cain, Peter. 1999. "British Free Trade, 1850–1914: Economics and Policy". *Refresh. Recent Findings of Research in Economics&Social History* 29, 1–4.

Cancino, Hugo and Rita Cancino. 2011. "El movimiento generacional e intelectual de 1842 y la irrupción de un proyecto de modernidad en Chile". In *Pensamentos, contextos y instituicões: Dos processsos de independencia a globalizacao*, edited by Lená Medeiros de Menezes, Hugo Cancino Troncoso and Rogelio de la Mora, 250–66. Rio de Janeiro: Universidade do Estado do Rio de Janeiro.

Carr, Raymond. 1968. *España, 1808–1939.* Barcelona: Ariel.

Cavieres, Eduardo and Gonzalo Serrano. 2018. "La guerra de Chile contra la Confederación Perú-Boliviana (1836–1839): el trigo y la agricultura como bases de un proyecto nacional". *América Latina en la historia económica* 25–1, 136–64.

Chato, Ignacio. 2011. "La Unión Liberal y la renovación del sistema de partidos (1858–1863)". *Revista de Estudios Políticos* 153, 75–111.

Chiaramonte José Carlos. 2004. *Nación y Estado en Iberoamérica. El lenguaje político en tiempos de las independencias*. Buenos Aires: Editorial Sudamericana.

Coats, Alfred W. 1971. "Editor's Introduction". In *The Classical Economists and Economic Policy*, edited by Alfred W. Coats, 1–32. London: Methuen and Co.

Comín, Francisco (1977), *Hacienda y economía en la España contemporánea (1800–1936)*, Madrid: IEF.

Comín, Francisco. 2000a. "Los economistas clásicos y los políticos liberales ante los problemas de la economía española". In *Economía y economistas españoles. Vol. IV. La economía clásica*, edited by Enrique Fuentes, 621–703. Barcelona: Galaxia Gütenberg and Círculo de Lectores.

Comín, Francisco. 2000b. "Canga Argüelles: un planteamiento realista de la Hacienda liberal". In *Economía y economistas españoles. Vol. IV. La economía clásica*, edited by Enrique Fuentes, 413–39. Barcelona: Galaxia Gütenberg and Círculo de Lectores.

Contreras, Carlos. 2012. *La economía pública en el Perú después del guano y del salitre: crisis fiscal y élites económicas durante su primer siglo independiente*. Lima: Instituto de Estudios Peruanos.

Contreras, Carlos and Marcos Cueto. 2009. *Historia del Perú contemporáneo*. Lima: Instituto de Estudios Peruanos.

Conway, Stephen, ed. 1989. *The Collected Works of Jeremy Bentham. The Correspondence of Jeremy Bentham, Vol. 9*. Oxford: OUP.

Conway, Stephen, ed. 1994. *The Collected Works of Jeremy Bentham. The Correspondence of Jeremy Bentham, Vol. 10*. Oxford: OUP.

Costas, Antón. 2000. "Industrialización y cuestión arancelaria en España. Reflexiones en torno al librecambismo de Laureano Figuerola". In *Economía y economistas españoles. Vol. IV. La economía clásica*, edited by Enrique Fuentes, 459–81. Barcelona: Galaxia Gütenberg and Círculo de Lectores.

De Ávila Martel, Alamiro. 1982. *Mora y Bello en Chile*. Santiago: Universidad de Chile.

De Haro, Dionisio. 2013. "Papel para un Perú independiente: el pensamiento económico español y la creación del Banco Auxiliar de Papel Moneda". *Revista Complutense de Historia de América* 39, 203–27.

De Haro, Dionisio. 2016. "Plata y guerra en el Perú. La Casa de Moneda de Lima en tiempos de la independencia, 1808–1830". In *Historia de la moneda en el Perú*, edited by Carlos Contreras, 227–65. Lima: Banco Central de Reserva del Perú and Instituto de Estudios Peruanos.

De Rosa, Nicolás Andrés. 2019. "La *Crónica política y literaria de Buenos Aires* (1827). Una aproximación de Mora y De Angelis en sus años rivadavianos". In *Prensa y política en Iberoamérica*, edited by Fabián Herrero and Alejandra Pasino, 249–75. Buenos Aires: Universidad de Buenos Aires.

Di Pasquale, Mariano. 2011. "La recepción de la *Idéologie* en la Universidad de Buenos Aires". *Prismas. Revista de historia intelectual* 11, 63–86.

Dome, Takuo. 2004. *The Political Economy of Public Finance in Britain (1767–1873)*. London and New York: Routledge.

Durán López, Fernando. 2015. *Versiones de un exilio. Los traductores españoles de la Casa Ackermann (Londres, 1823–1830)*. Madrid: Escolar y Mayo.

Durán López, Fernando. 2018. "José Joaquín de Mora contra el romanticismo en la *Crónica científica y literaria* (1817–^#-1820)". In *José Joaquín de Mora o la inconstancia. Periodismo, política y literatura*, edited by Salvador García and Alberto Romero, 179–225. Madrid: Visor.

Durán, Fernando and Daniel Muñoz. 2016. "Periódicos españoles en Londres: prensa 'en' y 'desde' el exilio". In *La prensa hispánica en el exilio de Londres (1810–1850)*, edited by María José Ruiz Acosta, 45–77. Salamanca: Comunicación social.

Edwards, José. 2018. "Historia del pensamiento económico en Chile, 1790–1970". In *Historia política de Chile, 1810–2010. Tomo III. Problemas económicos*, edited by Claudio Robles, 369–95. Santiago de Chile: FCE.

Eltis, Walter. 1999. "Does luxury consumption promote growth?". In *From Classical Economics to the Theory of the Firm: Essays in Honour of D. P. O'Brien*, edited by Roger E. Backhouse and John Creedy, 87–103. Cheltemham: Edward Elgar.

Entin, Gabriel. 2014. "Libertad: Argentina/Río de la Plata". In *Diccionario político y social del mundo iberoamericano*, edited by Javier Fernández, vol. II, 49–68. Madrid: UPV-CEPC.

Escolano, Luis Alfonso. 2018. "*El Museo Universal* y *La América* (1857–1860): dos estilos periodísticos diferentes y una misma perspectiva americanista al servicio de la burguesía liberal española". *Tzintzun. Revista de Estudios Históricos* 68, 105–35.

Estapé, Fabián. 1971. *La reforma tributaria de 1845*. Madrid: IEF.

Fernández Sarasola, Ignacio. 2012. "La Constitución de Cádiz en Inglaterra". *Historia Constitucional* 13, 1–21.

Fernández Sarasola, Ignacio. 2015. "Constitution Projects during the Spanish Enlightenment". In *The Spanish Enlightenment Revisited*, edited by Jesús Astigarraga, 129–47. Oxford: Voltaire Foundation.

Fernández Sebastián, Javier, ed. 2009. *Diccionario político y social del mundo iberoamericano. La era de las revoluciones, 1750–1850*. Madrid: Sociedad Española de Conmemoraciones Culturales and CEPC.

Fernández Sebastián, Javier. 2012a. "Introducción. En busca de los primeros liberalismos iberoamericanos". In *La aurora de la libertad. Los primeros liberalismos en el mundo iberoamericano*, edited by Javier Fernández Sebastián, 9–35. Madrid: Marcial Pons.

Fernández Sebastián, Javier. 2012b. "Liberalismo en España (1810–1850). La construcción de un concepto y la forja de una identidad política". In *La aurora de la libertad. Los primeros liberalismos en el mundo iberoamericano*, edited by Javier Fernández Sebastián, 236–301. Madrid: Marcial Pons.

Fernández Sebastián, Javier, ed. 2014. *Diccionario político y social del mundo iberoamericano*, 10 vols. Madrid: UPV-CEPC.

Ferrer del Río, Antonio. 1864. "Necrología. Don José Joaquín de Mora". *La América*, VIII–21 (12/XI/1864), 5–6.

Folchi, Mauricio. 2001. "La insustentabilidad de la industria del cobre en Chile: los hornos y los bosques durante el siglo XIX". *Revista Mapocho* 49, 149–75.

Fontana, Biancamaria. 1985a. Rethinking the Politics of Commercial Society: The *Edinburgh Review, 1802–1832.* Cambridge: CUP.

Fontana, Josep. 1971. *La quiebra de la monarquía absoluta, 1814–1820.* Barcelona: Ariel.

Fontana, Josep. 1973a. *Cambio económico y actitudes políticas en la España del siglo XVIII.* Barcelona: Ariel.

Fontana, Josep. 1973b. *Hacienda y Estado en la crisis final del Antiguo Régimen español, 1823–1833.* Madrid: IEF.

Fontana, Josep. 1979. *La crisis del Antiguo Régimen, 1808–1833.* Barcelona: Crítica.

Fontana, Josep. 1985b. "La desamortización de Mendizábal y sus antecedentes". In *Historia agraria de la España contemporánea. Vol. 1. Cambio social y nuevas formas de propiedad (1800–1850),* edited by Ramón Garrabou, 219–24. Barcelona: Crítica.

Fradera, Josep Maria. 2005. *Colonias para después de un imperio.* Barcelona: Bellaterra.

Freni, Giuseppe and Salvadori, Neri. 2019. "Ricardo on machinery: an analysis of Ricardo's examples". *The European Journal of the History of Economic Thought*, 26–3, 537–53.

Fuentes, Juan Francisco. 1994. "Estructura de la prensa española en el Trienio Liberal: difusión y tendencias". *Trienio* 24, 165–96.

Gallo, Klaus. 2002. "Jeremy Bentham y la 'feliz experiencia'. Presencia del utilitarismo en Buenos Aires (1821–1824)". *Prismas. Revista de historia intelectual* 6, 79–96.

Gallo, Klaus. 2004. "En búsqueda de la 'República ilustrada'. La introducción del utilitarismo y la *Idéologie* en el Río de la Plata a fines de la primera década revolucionaria". In *Revolución, política e ideas en el Río de la Plata durante la década de 1810*, edited by Fabián Herreo, 85–100. Buenos Aires: Ediciones Cooperativas.

Garrorena, Ángel. 1974. *El Ateneo de Madrid y la teoría de la monarquía liberal, 1836–1847*. Madrid: IEF.

Gayer, Arthur D., Rostow, W. W. and Schwartz, Anna Jacobsin. 1953. *The Growth and Fluctuation of the British Economy, 1790–1850*, 2 vols. Oxford: Clarendon Press.

Gherardi, Raffaela. 2001. "La scienza, il capitale e la libertà: *l'economia publica* (1859) e le 'relazioni pacifiche dei popoli'". *Scienza&Política* 24, 39–55.

Giacomin, Alberto. 2007. "Paper-Money: A Reassessment of Adam Smith's Views". In *Money and Markets: A Doctrinal Approach*, edited by Alberto Giacomin and Maria Cristina Marcuzzo, 181–89. London and New York: Routledge.

Gil Novales, Alberto. 1975. *Las sociedades patrióticas (1820–1823)*. Madrid: Tecnos.

Gil Novales, Alberto. 1980. *El Trienio Liberal*, Madrid: Siglo XXI, edited by Ramón Arnabat. Zaragoza, Prensas de la Universidad, 2020.

Gil Novales, Alberto. 1986. *El primer Ateneo de Madrid, 1820–1823*. Madrid: Ateneo.

Gil Novales, Alberto. 2010. "Mora, José Joaquín de". In *Diccionario biográfico de España (1808–1833). De los orígenes del liberalismo a la reacción absolutista*, edited by Alberto Gil Novales, vol. II, 2054–57. Madrid: Fundación Mapfre.

Goldman, Noemí. 2000. "Libertad de imprenta, opinión pública y debate constitucional en el Río de la Plata (1810–1827)". *Prismas. Revista de historia intelectual* 4, 9–20.

Goldman, Noemí. 2009. "Constitución: Argentina-Río de la Plata". In *Diccionario político y social del mundo iberoamericano. La era de las revoluciones, 1750–1850*, edited by Javier Fernández, 325–37. Madrid: Sociedad Española de Conmemoraciones Culturales and CEPC.

González, Carlos. 1961. *Francisco de Paula González Vigil: el precursor, el justo, el maestro*. Lima: Escuela de artes gráficas del Politécnico Nacional Superior José Pardo.

González Bernaldo de Quirós, Pilar. 2003. "Sociabilidad y opinión pública en Buenos Aires (1821–1852)". *Historia contemporánea* 27, 663–94.

González Cuevas, Pedro Carlos. 2020. "Neocatolicismo, carlismo y democracia". *Memoria y Civilización. Anuario de Historia* 23, 229–57.

González Hermoso, Alfredo. 2018. "Fernández Sardino y María del Carmen Silva: periodismo y exaltación". *Cuadernos de Ilustración y Romanticismo* 24, 669–700.

González Pizarro, José Antonio. 1984. "Don José Joaquín de Mora, Cónsul español en Londres (1850–1858)". *Boletín de la Academia Chilena de Historia* 51, 353–67.

González Pizarro, José Antonio. 1987. "José Joaquín de Mora y *La América, Crónica hispanoamericana* (1859–1864)". *Revista de literatura* 97, 95–114.

Gootenberg, Paul. 1982. "The Social Origins of Protectionism and Free Trade in Nineteenth-Century Lima". *Journal of Latin American Studies* 14, 329–58.

Grampp, William Dyer. 1960. *The Manchester School of Economics*. Stanford and London, Stanford University Press and OUP.

Guerra, François-Xavier. 1992. *Modernidad e independencias. Ensayos sobre las revoluciones hispánicas*. Madrid: Mapfre.

Hollander, Samuel. 2005. *Jean-Baptiste Say and the Classical Canon in Economics*. Abingdon-New York: Routledge.

Howe, Anthony. 1998. *Free Trade and Liberal England, 1846–1946*. Oxford: OUP.

Hurtado, Celso. 1984. "La economía chilena entre 1830 y 1930: sus limitaciones y sus herencias". *Colección de Estudios CIEPLAN* 12, 37–60.

Ibarz, Virgili and Ramón León. 2009. "José Joaquín de Mora (1783–1864): un introductor de la escuela escocesa del Sentido Común en el Perú, Bolivia y España". *Revista de historia de la psicología*, 30–2/3, 145–52.

Iglesias, Graciela. 2017. "José Joaquín de Mora in Chile: From Neo-Europe to the *Beocia Americana*". *Bulletin of Latin America Research* 36–2, 326–39.

Irwin, Douglas A. 1996. *Against the Tide. An Intellectual History of Free Trade*. Princeton: PUP.

Kliesser, R. Grant. 2021. "An Empire of Free Ports. British Commerce Imperialism in the 1776 Free Port Act". *The Journal of British Studies* 60–2, 334–61.

Larriba, Elisabel. 2020. "La prensa". In *El Triernio Liberal (1820–1823). Una mirada política*, edited by Pedro Rújula and Ivana Frasquet, 187–211. Granada: Comares.

Levan-Lemesle, Lucette. 1985. "Guillaumin, éditeur d'économie politique, 1801–1864". *Revue d'économie politique* XCV–2, 134–49.

Llorens, Vicente. 1968. *Liberales y románticos. Una emigración española en Inglaterra, 1823–1834*. Madrid: Castalia.

Lluch, Ernest. 1973. *El pensament econòmic a Catalunya (1760–1840)*. Barcelona: Edicions 62.

Lluch, Ernest. 1980. "Sobre la historia nacional del pensamiento económico". In *Curso de economía política,* by Antonio Flórez Estrada, edited by Salvador Almenar, vol. I, VII–XXXIII. Madrid: IEF.

Lluch, Ernest. 1988. "La 'gira trionfal' de Cobden per Espanya (1846)". *Recerques* XXI, 71–90.

Lluch, Ernest and Salvador Almenar. 2000. "Difusión e influencia de los economistas clásicos en España (1776–1870)". In *Economía y economistas españoles. Vol. IV. La economía clásica*, edited by Enrique Fuentes, 93–170. Barcelona: Galaxia Gütenberg and Círculo de Lectores.

López-Ocón, Leoncio. 1982. "*La América. Crónica hispano-americana.* Génesis y significación de una empresa americanista del liberalismo democrático español". *Quinto Centenario* 4, 137–74.

Loromer, David G. 1987. *Merchants and Reform in Livorno, 1814–1868.* Berkeley: University of California Press.

Macintyre, Iona. 2010. *Woman and Print Culture in Post-Independence Buenos Aires.* London: Tamesis.

Macintyre, Iona. 2018. "An Exponent of Scottish Common Sense Philosophy in Revolutionary South America". *Journal of Scottish Historical Studies* 38–2, 219–37.

Marichal, Carlos. 1999. *La bancarrota del Virreinato. Nueva España y las finanzas del imperio español, 1760–1810.* México: FCE.

Marichal, Carlos and Marcello Carmagnani. 2006. "Mexico: From colonial regime to liberal financial order, 1750–1912". In *Transferring Wealth and Power from the Old to the New World: Monetary and Fiscal Institutions in the 17th Century through the 19th Centuries*, edited by Michael D. Bordo and Roberto Cortes-Conde, 284–326. New York: CUP.

Martín Rodríguez, Manuel. 1989. "La institucionalización de los estudios de Economía Política en la universidad española (1784–1857)". In *Elementos de economía política con aplicación particular a España*, by Marqués de Valle Santoro, XI–CCXXXIV. Madrid: IEF.

Martín Rodríguez, Manuel. 2009. *Análisis económico y revolución liberal en España. Economistas académicos en las Cortes liberales, 1834–1874*, Madrid, Civitas and Thomson Reuters.

Martínez Marín, Jesús A. 2009. *Vivir de la pluma. La profesionalización del escritor, 1836–1936.* Madrid: Marcial Pons.

Martínez Marín, Jesús A. 2018. *Los negocios y las letras. El editor Francisco de Paula Mellado (1807–1876).* Zaragoza: Prensas universitarias.

Medina, Sara. 2022. *José Joaquín de Mora and Britain: Cultural Transfers and Transformations.* Berlin: Peter Lang.

Menudo, José Manuel. 2015. "Correspondencia y economía política en España (1809–1831). La relación epistolar con Jeremy Bentham y Jean-Baptiste Say". *Cuadernos de Ilustración y Romanticismo* 21, 109–20.

Menudo, José Manuel and José María O'Kean. 2019. "Ediciones, reimpresiones y traducciones en español del *Tratado de economía política* de Jean-Baptiste Say". *Revista de historia económica* 37–1, 169–92.

Mesa, José de and Teresa Gisbert. 1965. *José Joaquín de Mora secretario del Mariscal Andrés de Santa Cruz.* La Paz: Academia Nacional de Ciencias de Bolivia.

Monguió, Luis. 1965. "José Joaquín de Mora en Buenos Aires en 1827". *Revista hispánica moderna* 31, 303–28.

Monguió, Luis. 1967. *Don José Joaquín de Mora y el Perú del ochocientos*. Madrid: Castalia.

Moral Ruiz, Joaquín del. 1975. *Hacienda y sociedad en el Trienio Constitucional (1820–1823)*. Madrid: IEF.

Morán Ortí, Manuel. 1996. *La "Miscelánea" de Javier de Burgos: la prensa en el debate ideológico del Trienio Liberal*. Madrid: Universidad Europea and CEES Ediciones.

Muñoz Sempere, Daniel y Alonso García, Alonso, eds. 2011. *Londres y el liberalismo hispánico*. Madrid and Frankfurt am Main: Iberoamericana and Verbuet.

Myers, Jorge. 2003. "La paradoja de la opinión. El discurso político *rivadaviano* y sus dos polos: el 'gobierno de las luces' y la 'opinión pública'". In *La vida política en la Argentina del siglo XIX: amas, votos y voces*, edited by Hilda Sábato and Alberto Lettieri, 75–96. Buenos Aires: FCE.

Núñez, Estuardo. 1961. *D. José Joaquín Mora en el Perú. Cartas al Mariscal Santa Cruz*. Lima: Editorial San Marcos.

O'Brien, Denis Patrick. 1970. *J. R. McCulloch, A Study in Classical Economics*. New York: Routledge.

O'Brien, Denis Patrick. 1989. *Los economistas clásicos*. Madrid: Alianza.

O'Brien, Denis Patrick. 1992. *J. R. McCulloch. A Study in Classical Economics*, London and Aldershot: Gregg Revivals and Routledge.

O'Brien, Denis Patrick. 1995. "Introduction". In *The Collected Works of J. R. McCulloch. Vol. VIII. Articles in the Edinburgh Review*. London: Routledge and Thoemmes Press.

O'Brien, Denis Patrick. 2004, The Classical Economists Revisited. Princeton: PUP.

Paganelli, Maria Pia. 2022. "Adam Smith and Economic Development in Theory and Practice: A Rejection of the Stadial Model?". *Journal of the History of Economic Thought* 44–1, 95–104.

Peralta, Víctor. 2020. "Parlamentos y soberanías durante la *Confederación* del General Andrés de Santa Cruz. Chile, Perú y Bolivia". *Historia* 53–1, 155–81.

Pérez, Rodrigo Andrés. 2011. "Los inicios de la enseñanza del Derecho Constitucional en el Chile decimonónico: El Liceo de Chile y el Colegio de Santiago (1828–1831)." *Anuario de Estudios Americanos* 68, 141–62.

Pérez Godoy, Fernando. 2017. "Johannes Heineccius y la historia trasatlántica del *Ius Gentium*". *Revista chilena de Derecho* 44–2, 539–72.

Pérez Sánchez, Aránzazu. 2005. *El Liceo artístico y literario de Madrid (1837–1851)*. Madrid: Fundación Universitaria Española.

Perrot, Jean-Claude. 1992. *Une histoire intellectuelle de l'économie politique (XVIIe–XVIIIe siècles)*. Paris: EHESS.

Piccirilli, Ricardo. 1960. *Rivadavia y su tiempo*, 3 vols. Buenos Aires: Editorial Peuser.

Pinto, José Joaquín. 2012. "Los orígenes del impuesto directo y progresivo en América Latina". *Historia y Sociedad* 23, 53–77.

Pitollet, Camille. 1909. *La querelle caldéronienne de Johann Nikolas Böhl von Faber et José Joaquín de Mora, réconstituée d'après les documents originaux*. Paris: Félix Alcan.

Portillo, José María. 2006. *Crisis atlántica. Autonomía e independencia en la crisis de la monarquía hispánica*. Madrid: Marcial Pons.

Prados de la Escosura, Leandro. 2000. *El progreso económico de España (1850–2000)*. Bilbao: Fundación BBVA.

Quinziano, Francisco. 2013. "Prensa periódica y campo cultural en el Río de la Plata: Pedro de Angelis, 'escritor oficial'". *Anales* 25, 253–81.

Ramos, Carlos. 2000. "La cultura jurídica en la época de la Confederación Peruano-Boliviana". *Revista de estudios históricos-jurídicos* 22, 267–97.

Reeder, John. 2003. "Nota bibliográfica sobre un economista español decimonónico". In *Estudios de historia y de pensamiento económico. Homenaje a Francisco Bustelo García del Real*, 295–99. Madrid: Universidad Complutense.

Riveros, Luis and Rodrigo Ferraro. 1985. "La historia económica del siglo XIX a la luz de la evolución de los precios". *Estudios de economía* 12–1, 50–78.

Robledo, Ricardo. 1993. *Economistas y reformadores españoles: la cuestión agraria (1760–1935)*. Madrid: Ministerio de agricultura, pesca y alimentación.

Robledo, Ricardo. 2014. *La universidad española, de Ramón de Salas a la guerra civil*. Salamanca: Junta de Castilla y León.

Rodríguez, Gregorio. 1924. "Cartas autógrafas de Don José Joaquín de Mora a Don Florencia Varela". *Revista chilena de historia y geografía* 54, 35–66.

Roldán, Eugenia. 2003. *The British Book Trade and Spanish American Independence. Education and Knowledge Transmission in Transcontinental Perspective*. Aldershot: Ashgate.

Rubio Cremades, Enrique. 2013. "Hispanoamérica y España a mediados del siglo XIX: el editor Francisco de Paula Mellado y la *Revista española de ambos mundos*". *Anales de literatura española* 25, 317–39.

Ruiz Acosta, María José, ed. 2016. *La prensa hispánica en el exilio de Londres (1810–1850)*. Salamanca: Comunicación social.

Ruiz Salvador, Antonio. 1971. *El Ateneo científico, literario y artístico de Madrid*. Londres: Tamesis Books.

Rújula, Pedro and Manuel Chust. 2020. *El Trienio Liberal en la monarquía hispánica*. Madrid: Catarata.

Rújula, Pedro and Ivana Frasquet, eds. 2020. *El Trienio Liberal (1820–1823). Una mirada política*. Granada: Comares.

Sagredo, Rafael. 1989. "Pragmatismo proteccionista en los orígenes de la República". *Historia* 24, 267–86.

Sagredo, Rafael. 1997. "Chile 1823–1831. El desafío de la administración y organización de la Hacienda Pública". *Historia* 30, 287–312.

Salazar, Gabriel. 2009. *Mercaderes, empresarios y capitalistas. Chile, Siglo XIX*. Santiago: Editorial sudamericana.

Salvadori, Neri and Rodolfo Signorino. 2013 "The Classical Notion of Competition Revisited". *History of Political Economy* 45–1, 149–75.

Sánchez Albornoz, Nicolás. 1968. *España hace un siglo: una economía dual.* Madrid: Península.

Schumpeter, Josep A. 1955. *History of Economic Analysis.* New York: OUP. Spanish translation, *Historia del análisis económico*, Barcelona, Caracas and Mexico, Ariel, 1971.

Schwartz, Pedro. 1970. "*De la libertad del comercio*, por Joaquín de Mora: una defensa del libre-cambio a mediados del siglo XIX". *Anales de economía* 5–8, 189–224.

Schwartz, Pedro. 1976. "La influencia de Jeremías Bentham en España". *Información Comercial Española* 517, 37–57.

Schwartz, Pedro. 1999. "Estudio Preliminar". In *De la libertad del comercio*, by José Joaquín de Mora, VIII–XLIX. Madrid: IEF.

Schwartz, Pedro and Carlos Rodríguez. 1983. "Cartas españolas de Jeremías Bentham". *Moneda y Crédito* 165, 59–88.

Siegrist de Gentile, Nora. 1992. *José Joaquín de Mora y su manuscrito sobre la industria y el comercio de España hacia 1850.* Cádiz: Universidad de Cádiz.

Simal, Juan Luis. 2012. *Emigrados. España y el exilio internacional, 1814–1843.* Madrid: CEPC.

Smith, Robert Sidney. 1957. "La *Riqueza de las Naciones* en España e Hispanoamérica, 1780–1830". *Revista de economía política* VIII–3, 1215–53.

Smith, Robert Sidney. 1967. "Aspectos del libre comercio y proteccionismo en la economía española. 1800–1850". *Humanitas* VIII, 635–50.

Smith, Robert Sidney. 1968. "El pensamiento económico de José Joaquín de Mora", *Humanitas* IX, 595–607.

Smith, Robert Sidney. 2000. "El pensamiento económico inglés en España (1776–1848)". In *Economía y economistas españoles. Vol. IV. La economía clásica*, edited by Enrique Fuentes, 305–38. Barcelona: Galaxia Gütenberg and Círculo de Lectores.

Sobrevilla, Natalia. 2011. *The Caudillo of the Andes, Andrés Santa Cruz.* Cambridge: CUP.

Sobrevilla, Natalia. 2021. "Disputando el poder de la fuerza con la ley: los liberales en la temprana república peruana y la guerra civil de 1834". *Jahrbuch für Geschichte Lateinamerikas/Anuario de Historia de América Latina* 58, 45–76.

Sockwell, William D. 1994. *Popularizing Classical Economics. Henry Brougham and William Ellis.* New York: St. Martin's Press.

Sowell, Thomas. 1977. *Classical Economics Reconsidered.* Princeton: PUP.

Stuardo, Carlos. 1950. *El Liceo de Chile. Antecedentes para su historia, 1828–1831.* Santiago de Chile: Imprenta universitaria.

Stuven, Ana María. 2012. "De la autonomía a la república: el debate constitucional en Chile, 1808–1833". In *El laboratorio constitucional iberoamericano:*

1807/1808–1830, edited by Antonio Annino y Marcela Ternavasio, 179–202. Madrid and Frankfurt am Main: Iberoamericana and Verbuet, 179–202.

Stuven, Ana María. 2000. *La seducción de un orden: las elites y la construcción de Chile en las polémicas culturales y políticas del siglo XIX*. Santiago: Universidad Católica.

Subercaseaux, Bernardo. 1981. *Cultura y sociedad liberal en el Siglo XIX. Lastarria, ideología y literature*. Santiago: Aconcagua.

Tazzara, Corey. 2017, *The Free Port of Livorno and the Tranformation of the Mediterranean World*. Oxford: OUP.

Tena-Junguito, Antonio, Markus Lampe and Felipe Tàmega. 2012. "How Much Trade Liberalization Was there in the World Before and after Cobden-Chevalier?". *The Journal of Economic History* 72, 708–40.

Ternavasio, Marcela. 1998. "Las reformas *rivadavianas* en Buenos Aires y el Congreso General Constituyente". In *Revolución, república, confederación (1806–1852)*, edited by Noemí Goldman, 161–97. Buenos Aires: Sudamericana.

Ternavasio, Marcela. 2002. *La revolución del voto. Política y elecciones en Buenos Aires, 1810–1852*. Buenos Aires: Siglo XXI.

Todd, David. 2008. "John Bowring and the Global Dissemination of Free Trade". *The Historical Journal* 51–2, 373–97.

Trease, B. David. 1953. *José Joaquín de Mora: A Spaniard Abroad*. PhD. Michigan, University of Michigan.

Tsoulfidis, Lefteris. 2007. "Classical Economists and Public Debt". *International Review of Economics* 54, 1–12.

Tully, Carol. 2011. "Ackermann, Mora and the Transnational Context: Cultural Transfer in the Old World and the New World". In *Londres y el liberalismo hispánico*, edited by Daniel Muñoz and Alonso García, 153–64. Madrid and Frankfurt am Main: Iberoamericana and Verbuet.

Usoz, Javier. 2022. "Adam Smith and the *Cortes de Cádiz* (1810–1813): More than Enlightened Liberalism". In *Adam Smith and 'The Wealth of Nations' in Spain*, edited by Jesús Astigarraga and Juan Zabalza, 186–204. New York and London: Routldege.

Vallejo, Rafael. 2018, "La política comercial liberal desde 1820 a 1869. Entre la apertura exterior y las resistencias prohibicionistas". *Áreas. Revista Internacional de Ciencias Sociales* 37, 61–77.

Varela, Joaquín. 1983–1984. "La Constitución española de 1837: una Constitución transaccional". *Revista de derecho político* 20, 95–106.

Varela, Joaquín. 1996. "La Monarquía imposible: la Constitución de Cádiz durante el Trienio". *Anuario de Historia del Derecho Español* 66, 653–88.

Varela, Joaquín. 2016. "La prensa liberal española en Londres y París ante la Constitución de Cádiz, 1824–1830". *Cuadernos de Ilustración y romanticismo* 22, 329–38.

Velasco, Rogelio. 1989. "El debate de la ley de reforma de aranceles de 1841: librecambistas frente a proteccionistas". *Revista de historia económica*, 7, extra 2, 95–98.

Velasco, Rogelio. 1990. *Pensamiento económico en Andalucía (1800–1850). Economía política, librecambio y proteccionismo*. Málaga: Ágora.

Velázquez, Marcel and Gustavo Morales. 2021. "El mercado de esclavos en la ciudad de Lima desde el *Mercurio Peruano*". *Desde el sur* 13–3, 1–25.

Verdo, Geneviève. 2006. *L'independece argentine entre cités et nation (1808–1821)*. Paris: Publications de la Sorbonne.

Villacorta, Francisco. 1980. *Burguesía y cultura. Los intelectuales españoles en la sociedad liberal, 1808–1931*. Madrid: Siglo XXI.

Villalobos, Sergio and Rafael *Sagredo*. 1987. *El proteccionismo económico en Chile. Siglo XIX*. Santiago de Chile: Instituto Blas Cañas.

Viner, Jacob. 1937. *Studies in the Theory of International Trade*. London: Allen and Unwin.

Wasserman, Fabio. 2012. "Entre la moral y la política. Las transformaciones conceptuales de 'liberal' en el Río de la Plata, 1750–1850". In *La aurora de la libertad. Los primeros liberalismos en el mundo iberoamericano*, edited by Javier Fernández, 37–73. Madrid: Marcial Pons.

Will, Robert M. 1960. "La política económica de Chile, 1810–64". *El trimestre económico* 106–2, 238–57.

Will, Robert M. 1964. "The Introduction of Classical Economics into Chile". *Hispanic American Historical Review* 44–1, 1–21.

Zabalza, Juan. 2001, "The Spread of Italian Economic Thought in Spain 1850–1950: from Historicism to Corporatism". In *From Economists to Economists. The International Spread of Italian Economic Thought, 1750–1950*, edited by Piero F. Asso, 227–53. Firenze: Polistampa.

Zabalza, Juan. 2022. "Adam Smith in the Economic Debates during the Liberal Triennium (1820–1823): the Second Liberal Exile and Hispanic America". In *Adam Smith and 'The Wealth of Nations' in Spain*, edited by Jesús Astigarraga and Juan Zabalza, 205–21. New York and London: Routledge.

Zabalza, Juan and Jesús Astigarraga. 2020. "Entre España y Chile. José Joaquín Mora y los proyectos de un diccionario de economía política (1825–1855)". In *El pensamiento económico del reformismo criollo*, edited by José Antonio Piqueras and Johanna von Grafenstein, 435–75. Santa Marta: Editorial Unimagdalena and Instituto Mora.

Zavala, Iris M. 1971. *Masones, comuneros y carbonarios*. Madrid: Siglo XXI.

Index[1]

[1] Note: Page numbers followed by 'n' refer to notes.

J. Astigarraga et al., *The Economic Legacy of José Joaquín de Mora*, Palgrave Studies in the History of Economic Thought,
https://doi.org/10.1007/978-3-031-49446-8

SPRINGER NATURE

GPSR Compliance

The European Union's (EU) General Product Safety Regulation (GPSR) is a set of rules that requires consumer products to be safe and our obligations to ensure this.

If you have any concerns about our products, you can contact us on ProductSafety@springernature.com

In case Publisher is established outside the EU, the EU authorized representative is:

Springer Nature Customer Service Center GmbH
Europaplatz 3
69115 Heidelberg, Germany